MARRIAGE

MARRIAGE

AN EXAMINATION
OF THE MAN-WOMAN RELATIONSHIP

Herman R. Lantz

and

Eloise C. Snyder

Department of Sociology
Southern Illinois University

New York • London John Wiley & Sons, Inc.

Photographs appearing at the beginning of Chapters 1, 7, 9, 11, 12, 13, 16, 17,
18, 19 by Esther Bubley; Chapter 2 by Culver Service; Chapter 10 by Charles P.
Cushing; Chapter 15 by Arthur Leipzig; Chapters 3, 4, 5, 6, 14 by Marc Slade.

The authors dedicate this book to
SARAH COBURN LANTZ
daughter, friend, and shrewd observer
of the social scene.

Preface

There are many ways in which marriage and the family may be described; the many published works with different frames of reference clearly point this out. We have chosen as our task a behavioral analysis of the middle-class, man-woman relationship as it is found in dating, courtship, and marriage in the United States today.

In pursuing this task we have tried to identify the kinds of relationships which middle-class persons increasingly seek, the nature of their involvements with one another, and the types of problems which come about. In such an analysis it becomes clear that the social controls which formerly governed and dictated the goals of the man-woman relationship are no longer as effective as they were in the past. Indeed these goals, both in and out of marriage, are increasingly the results of a search for personal considerations, involving companionship, love, and self-realization. Such goals are largely the result of changes from a rural, sacred society to an urbanized, secular society. Although social change inevitably brings with it dislocation, the current difficulties in marriage and the family are deeply rooted in the fact that many of the goals which men and women seek in such relationships are not easily realized. Thus, while many seek the personally fulfilling goals of love, companionship, and self-realization, they are lacking in the intellectual and emotional maturity which is demanded in order to realize these goals. While marriage and the family derived their stability in the past from social, economic, and religious expectations, the willingness of persons to remain married today depends to a great extent on whether or not they do, in effect, find marriage and the family meaningful and personally satisfying. There is, to be sure, no single path to the search for love, companionship, and self-realization, but there are patterns which are fraught with difficulty and which prove in the end to be self-defeating. We have tried, in this book, to identify these negative patterns, in so far as possible, as well as other more positive patterns which may facilitate the search for the personally fulfilling goals. We have tried to relate both types of patterns to what is currently accepted in behavioral science.

In the pursuit of our analysis of the man-woman relationship we repeatedly refer to such terms as "constructive" and "meaningful." In order to avoid confusion about the use of these terms we should like to point out that constructive and meaningful relationships are relationships in which the individuals are intrinsically interested in each other as people, and not as commodities. In constructive and meaningful relationships each person has the opportunity to grow intellectually and emotionally.

The analysis found here represents the cumulative efforts of the writers who have been concerned for a number of years with the issues discussed. Although major responsibility for the different chapters was divided between the authors, the book is in every sense a collaboration. Each of us read and criticized the work of the other before a synthesis of any chapter emerged. A book, however, is inevitably the result of the contributions of many persons. We wish to mention the names of those persons who have had a significant influence on the thinking and orientation of the authors.

Herman Lantz wishes to mention John F. Cuber, Robert A. Harper, Leonard Broom, Brewton Berry, Ray Sletto, and James T. Laing. Professional interaction and communication with these persons over a period of time has influenced him in his thinking regarding family sociology. John Cuber was particularly significant in introducing this author to the sociology of the family, and for patience and encouragement offered, the author is deeply grateful. A special word of thanks must be extended to Robert A. Harper for his stimulating insights and discussions of the current issues of contemporary American family life. To Michael Hakeem, Gerald Leslie, Atlee Stroup, Al Clarke, Marvin Koller, J. S. McCrary, and Donald Longworth, the author owes a great deal for the valuable discussions he has had with each regarding the major problems in family sociology. Michael Hakeem, Gerald Leslie, and Al Clarke have been especially important for their insightful analysis of particular problems in the man-woman relationship.

To Ralph N. Harris, M.D., the author is also deeply grateful. Dr. Harris contributed to the development of many of the ideas in this book. His sensitive and keen observation on the nature of the man-woman relationship in America today has influenced this author greatly in his thinking and writing. Furthermore, as a friend his consistent encouragement during the formidable period of writing is deeply appreciated.

Eloise Snyder wishes to express her deep and everlasting gratitude to Jessie Bernard. Jessie Bernard played a significant role in the author's orientation to sociology, and as a teacher and friend she has been a constant source of inspiration and encouragement.

To Seth Russell, this author expresses her deep gratitude for his faith in her, and for his consistent help as adviser and teacher.

Both of us wish to express our very sincere appreciation to Al Clarke and Mark Flappan for their constructively critical analysis of this manuscript prior to publication. Their insights helped to call attention to shortcomings which we took seriously and tried to correct.

To Professor John Anderson, and members of the Graduate Research Committee of Southern Illinois University, and to Dean T. W. Abbott, Professors J. K. Johnson, Max W. Turner, Raymond Dey, and Paul J. Campisi of Southern Illinois University we are deeply grateful for the aid provided to finish this project.

To Charles R. Snyder we express our thanks for his helpful comments on the overall orientation of this book.

We would also like to express our appreciation to Sid Aronson for his evaluation and helpful comments on the section dealing with the history of the family.

We owe a great debt to Mrs. Judith Lantz, who was responsible for typing the several drafts of this manuscript and for a considerable part of the editorial work. She gave unselfishly of her time and energies. Her helpful and critical comments added greatly both to the content and the communication of ideas.

We would like to add a note of thanks to Page Frank for her assistance with revisions made in this manuscript.

Carbondale, Illinois　　　　　　　　　　　　HERMAN R. LANTZ
April, 1962　　　　　　　　　　　　　　　　ELOISE C. SNYDER

Contents

Introduction

1

This book deals with the man-woman relationship as it is found in dating, courtship, marriage, and family life among the middle class in contemporary America. We have oriented our treatment toward the middle-class family for several reasons. To begin with, the middle-class family is becoming almost a model type; many of its values and orientations are rapidly permeating all groups in our society. Secondly, the majority of readers of this book either come from the middle class or aspire to membership in it. Thus, a discussion of the behavior patterns and attitudes which characterize people in the middle class would be pertinent.

The magnitude of our task and the pursuit of our analysis are complicated, for there are many directions from which the problems introduced in this book may be approached. We have, therefore, tried to bring to bear on each problem the materials which, in our opinion, will allow the reader the greatest amount of enlightenment. In our analysis we make use of the combined knowledges of the several human behavior sciences, and we relate these knowledges to the specific problems raised in this book. Thus, at times we approach a problem sociologically, or psychologically, or psychiatrically; at other times we have a balance of each.

The employment of knowledge from the different behavioral sciences does not, of course, mean that the authors intend to deal with all problems in the man-woman relationship. Neither do the authors be-

lieve that it is possible to give the reader ready-made solutions for the
issues raised in this book. We do intend to single out what appear
to be the more significant problems in the man-woman relationship
and suggest ways in which these may be examined and more clearly
understood.

As part of the orientation of this book, the authors would like to
clarify for the reader what he may expect as he pursues the topics
presented. Therefore, in this chapter we will present the main objectives of the book and attempt to outline certain of its basic themes in
order that the reader may develop some appreciation for their importance.

THE SIGNIFICANCE OF THE MAN-WOMAN RELATIONSHIP.
At the outset we wish to stress that the main objective of this book
is an attempt to understand the man-woman relationship as it emerges,
matures, and, under certain circumstances, deteriorates. No aspect
of human interaction is more demanding of either the social scientist
or the layman than the man-woman relationship, and yet an understanding of this relationship is a must if we are to increase the number of marriages based on purposeful, meaningful associations. Having
said this we likewise recognize that we are only beginning to scratch
the surface with respect to our understanding of these aspects of
human interaction. Thus, humility is indeed in order. Nevertheless,
there are areas of knowledge for which there is substantial agreement
and it is these materials that we plan to present in this book.

When we point out that the man-woman relationship will be the
focus of our attention, we suggest that the basis of much marital incompatibility lies in the quality of the interpersonal relationship which
husband and wife have established with each other. The variety of
ways in which husbands and wives treat one another, both in the interpersonal sense as well as in sexual relations, are expressions of all
that is felt between the two marital partners. Thus, the basic attitudes
which husband and wife feel toward one another find their expression
in all phases of marital life. It follows, then, that a breakdown in the
interpersonal relationship between husband and wife sets the stage
for their subsequent marital difficulties. It may be that the marital
relationship has become meaningless to both; or it may be that one
has become tired of the relationship, while the other has not; or it
may be that one has emotional difficulties which make cooperative
living difficult. For example, a breakdown in the interpersonal relationship between husband and wife may become manifest in extramarital sexual relations. Such a development is well brought out in

the case of Mr. and Mrs. T., both of whom appeared for assistance with their marital difficulties. Mrs. T. had been involved in an extramarital affair with a friend of the family. The affair had been going on for several months before Mr. T. discovered what was happening. His first impulse was to obtain a divorce but on the chance that the marriage might be salvaged, he asked for outside assistance. Mr. T.'s definition of the difficulty was that his wife had become involved with another man because he was unable to support her adequately and that the unhappiness from this situation drove her to another relationship.

In talking with Mrs. T. about the marital difficulty an entirely different story emerged. Mrs. T. described her husband as one who had let the marriage deteriorate. He was aloof from her and their two children. He constantly found excuses to be away from home and never included her or the children in any of his plans. In addition, although his income was limited, he was unnecessarily frugal to the point where Mrs. T. and the children went without certain necessities. Mrs. T. went on to add that while their income was not substantial, the reasons for her infidelity were rooted in her husband's consistent indifference to her and to the children. This made her feel that he was no longer interested in her or the family, which precipitated her feeling of being unwanted and unloved.

In further discussions with Mr. T., he revealed that his preoccupations outside the home were largely concerned with business contacts which might lead to better economic opportunities. Over a period of time he came to accept his part in the difficulty and he was willing to assume his share of the responsibility for creating the unfavorable attitudes in his wife and children. Needless to say, this case of Mr. and Mrs. T. was an involved one with both partners sharing in the responsibility for the poor marital relationship. For our purposes, however, we can point out that the case of Mr. and Mrs. T. demonstrates that Mrs. T.'s extramarital involvement did not stem from a problem of sexual incompatibility as such. Nor was the difficulty the result of economic stress. Mrs. T.'s extramarital affair was symptomatic of a basic misunderstanding and a breakdown in the interpersonal relationship between herself and her husband. She saw herself as unloved, then, desperate, she became involved with another person. In order to rehabilitate this marital relationship, an understanding of all these factors in the interpersonal relationship which produced the breakdown between Mr. and Mrs. T. was, of course, indicated. Any attempt to treat the difficulty in terms of a sexual problem, as such, would not have produced change.

Having pointed this out, we wish to remind the reader that although this particular illustration has a sexual component, much marital incompatibility is not rooted in sex. Indeed, there are many experts who take the position that most sexual problems in marriage are manifestations of difficulty in the interpersonal relationship. It might also be well to point out that in this book the treatment of the role of sex in marriage is perhaps different from the treatment which the reader has encountered elsewhere. We do not concern ourselves directly with either the anatomy or physiology of reproduction; but we include in the appendix descriptive materials which will answer the most common questions that students have about these areas of information. The same principle applies to the area of consumer problems. We do, however, discuss problems of sexual adjustment and economic difficulties as they relate to the type and quality of the interpersonal relationship which husband and wife have established. For example, we will be concerned with the way certain attitudes held by husband and wife toward one another affect their economic habits and their sexual habits. The point is simple enough to conceive, since all of us have known people who tend to control their mates through the purse string or through sexual relations. We have approached the subject in this fashion because it is our conviction that as behavorial scientists, we are in a unique position to make a contribution to the study of the man-woman relationship by focusing on the frame of reference of behavioral science, namely the study of the human relationship.

THE COMPLEXITY OF MARITAL PROBLEMS. One major theme which runs throughout this book has to do with the way in which the authors view marital relationships. They see the relationships between men and women as being generally more involved, indeed more complex, than do persons who are not confronted with these problems daily. For the writers, as well as for other behavioral scientists, there is the immediate recognition that in these relationships we are dealing with the most involved types of human interactions. Here we are confronted with a variety of different types of people; each of whom brings into the marriage a psychological organization which was in process of formation since infancy and nurtured in a complex social environment.

It is not uncommon for the untrained observer, however, to view the dynamics of the man-woman relationship in simple terms, very much as Mr. T. did in the case presented. The student often tends to see premarital and marital problems in relatively uncomplicated terms.

A problem to the student is an economic problem or an in-law problem. The most common error is one of failing to see all of the ramifications to the problem. For indeed, a problem is seldom one thing; it is many. That is, a problem is invariably the result of numerous factors, often interrelated in ways which are complex.

When the student sees the problem in relatively simple terms he fails to appreciate the very real complexities that are present in the man-woman relationship and the insights which must be accomplished if marital problems are to be understood and worked through. Furthermore, the tendency to see these problems in the simplest terms obscures the possibility of an early diagnosis. This is a case in point:

Mr. S. sought assistance for a problem with his daughter. Mr. S. complained that his daughter was quite rebellious and she insisted on dating "the wrong kinds of boys." Mr. S. claimed that he could not understand his daughter's behavior, since he and his wife had always tried, in his own words, to "rear her properly to be a good girl." He saw the problem as simply one of lack of self-discipline in the girl. He sought a counselor's assistance to try to convince the girl that she was in error and that she should date only the boys the parents might approve.

As the reader already suspects, Mr. S. had little understanding of the problem with his daughter. Although he saw the difficulty as simply a lack of self-discipline, the counselor saw more basic difficulties, involving the basic relationship which the daughter had with her parents; the attempt of the parents to rigidly control the daughter's behavior; and the need of the daughter to live her own life. These were all possibilities which Mr. S. was unprepared to examine since he insisted on clinging to his one-sided, oversimplified definition of the difficulty. Yet we realize that until Mr. S. was prepared to examine these broader possibilities, he was likely to achieve little understanding.

As we proceed in our analysis, we plan to deal in a detailed fashion with the involved dynamics of the man-woman relationship. We will not be satisfied with an analysis of superficial symptoms, but will search for the more basic elements.

THE IMPORTANCE OF UNDERSTANDING THE MOTIVATIONS FOR ACTIONS. A second theme, which appears throughout this book, has to do with understanding the motives for your own actions, as well as those of the person with whom you are involved. Such understanding is, of course, never completely possible, but the authors do feel that raising questions with oneself about why you wish to follow a particular course of action can open up several possibilities which can be of value in avoiding future difficulties. You are invariably in a better position to cope with certain attitudes in yourselves when you know what they are; herein lies the therapeutic value of self-examination. Let us apply the understanding of motivations to enrolling in a course in marriage.

Much of what you derive from a marriage course will depend on your reasons for being there in the first place. A small number of students invariably enroll because they are seeking easy credit. This is the important motivation for them. They assume that since the subject deals with such commonplace topics as dating, courtship, and marriage, the subject matter cannot really be very difficult. In the words of a student, "This will be pleasant chit-chat about love and marriage." Such students enter the course with a lack of serious purpose, perhaps with an unwillingness to really put out the effort necessary to come to grips with the issues raised. When they are confronted with the need for work, they frequently become annoyed and resentful. Thus, they learn little. On the other hand it is entirely possible for a student who discovers such attitudes in himself to decide that this outlook is not consistent with a desire to grow and learn. For him the possibility of change can become a reality.

The vast majority of students who enroll in a marriage course do so because they hope that in some way they may benefit from the experience. For such well-meaning people there are other obstacles. Much of what they derive will depend on their ability to successfully uproot attitudes and ways of behaving which restrict personal growth and the ability to build a sound human relationship with the opposite sex.

The example of Miss A. illustrates our point. Miss A. had been dating a boy for a period of two years. Although Miss A. had never taken the relationship seriously, the boy had. He had lavished a great deal of attention on Miss A. and had spent a considerable amount of money on gifts, more than he could really afford. He proposed matrimony several times, but this was rejected by Miss A. Since she was now being pressed by her boy friend for a yes or no answer regarding marriage, Miss A. felt it necessary to act, and sought counseling assistance. Miss A. was seen for several weeks, during which time the following facts were established. Miss A. considered herself to be physically unattractive and lacking in poise, and her deep inferiority feelings were obvious. She had no consistent feeling or interest in the boy except that he might give her some security. She in turn was willing to give nothing to him. She soon realized that with the attitudes she possessed that a commitment of marriage was out of the question. On the other hand she was unwilling to give up the boy and preferred "to string him along" because he served certain needs for her.

What is most interesting, and related to our discussion here, is that Miss A. was enrolled in a course in marriage and had recently completed the section dealing with immature-exploitative relationships, including the necessity for working them through. Miss A. knew what ought to be done, but she was unable to integrate the material because her immature patterns still served important functions. Thus, although she knew better intellectually, she still committed herself emotionally to an immature relationship; knowing that it would eventually be disastrous for her and for the boy involved.

In this particular instance the motives of Miss A. were brought out into the open and made clear to her. At the time she was unable to act, but the issues were obvious and there was always the hope that over a period of time she would act in her own best interest, as well as in the best interests of her boy friend.

As you read this book many of your attitudes may be challenged. Some of you have immature relationships with your boy friends or girl friends; others have immature relationships with your parents. Some of you have difficulty in thinking about sex. All of these difficulties are in the nature of mental blocks which retard your ability to fully appreciate the data. Furthermore, as you probe your own feelings you may discover attitudes which are unpleasant, and deeply rooted in your personality. The realization that some of these ways of behaving may have to be changed before better relationships can emerge may be frustrating and disturbing. It is at these times that you may become hostile toward the text, its authors, or your teacher. You may subconsciously block out some new information as though it did not exist. Moreover, the fact that many people feel quite hopeless about understanding themselves and about their ability to change does not help matters. All of these developments are frequent occurrences for people attempting self-examination and change. The experience can be therapeutic, however, if you perceive your reactions as stemming from the fact that you are attempting self-examination and change.

Having pointed out certain unpleasant aspects of self-examination, let us quickly add that the authors' motives are not to create turmoil for the sake of making the reader uncomfortable. Instead, these motives stem from our very deep desire to give the reader the very best we can. For we believe that change can come about only through coming to grips with inner motivations, and removing the obstacles to growth.

A PROBLEM-ORIENTED ANALYSIS. A third major theme has to do with the problem orientation of our data. By problem orientation we simply mean an approach which focuses on those areas of the man-woman relationship which are sources of disturbance. Thus, as we analyze our material we constantly raise questions and probe the man-woman relationship. We employ this method for several reasons. To begin with, there is certainly no need to extol the virtues of marriage, nor to describe the basic satisfactions which emerge out of constructive family living. The cultural milieu constantly blasts everyone with the joyful bliss of marriage and family life.

On the other hand, although many people undoubtedly possess some understanding of what a constructive man-woman relationship can mean, probably only a few appreciate the very real work involved in building and maintaining such a relationship. It is one thing to speak in terms of clichés, such as "marriage is a partnership," and it is quite another thing to attempt to live a partnership and be willing to examine attitudes and feelings when the relationship fails to function properly.

With an orientation such as we have outlined, it is common to find persons who feel that they are only learning about the problems of marriage, not about the happiness of marriage. To these people we can only reply that happiness in marriage does not emerge from thinking happy thoughts, but rather from active efforts to detect and work through problem areas; in reality, no human relationships are ever immune from these problems. Probably no human relationship can ever reach a mature level without the active efforts of the persons involved. This may seem to the reader to be an essentially negative view of the man-woman relationship; it is not. For, indeed, the authors are both realistic and optimistic. For if man can destroy his relationships, he also possesses the power to construct and improve his relationships.

A FINAL WORD FOR THE STUDENT. The course of study which you are about to undertake will undoubtedly offer tremendous possibilities for your personal growth. In many ways this course may be different from any you have ever had. It deals with subject matters with which you are all concerned, and yet areas which you most frequently treat with some neglect and a lack of appreciation. There can be no greater challenge to any man or woman than that of attempting to build a successful marital relationship; and yet we recognize that it is perhaps more difficult to build sound, creative, marital relationships than to succeed in other endeavors. All of us have known persons in the various artistic, professional, and business fields who are successful in their own occupational endeavors, but whose marriages are poor and neglected. Is it a matter of intelligence? Indeed not. These are all people who might have had successful marital relationships were it simply a matter of intelligence. It is not simply a matter of intelligence; rather, it is a combination of certain knowledges of what it takes to build a good marital relationship plus the ability to emotionally integrate these knowledges so that they become part of one's life. How this can be accomplished will be a major preoccupation of the text.

As teachers, we recognize that it is sometimes difficult to tell which student has achieved the greatest amount of integration from his exposure to these materials. Although the student will undoubtedly be preoccupied with his grade, the teacher recognizes that grades are not the only criterion upon which to make a judgment about what the student has integrated.

All of us know some students, with excellent grades, who have made gross errors in judgment with respect to their marriages; and poor students who chose wisely. Moreover, it is not uncommon for the student to integrate an insight which enables him to drop a poor relationship or find his way into a good one. How may such a result be graded? Is the grade A, B, C, or D equivalent to such an experience, or to the growth of the personality? Can the grade really convey what the person derived?

Grades are part of the university system and it is unrealistic to expect that we can eliminate formal grading in the near future. Nevertheless, in this instance, as teachers, we wish to appeal to the better judgment of the student with the hope that, in addition to his concern with grades, he can become sensitive to the ever-present possibility of integrating material which will be significant for personal growth.

SUMMARY

The main objective of this book is to understand the man-woman relationship as it emerges, matures, and, under certain circumstances, deteriorates. In pursuing this objective, we will deal with several themes throughout the text. To begin with, marriage and family problems are viewed as being more involved and complex than they might appear to the untrained observer. Frequently, for example, problems which are superficially regarded as financial or sexual are in reality the expressions of a breakdown of the interpersonal relationship. Thus we believe that to treat such problems as financial or sexual is to treat the symptoms and not the causes of the basic difficulties involved.

Secondly, an emphasis is placed on understanding the motivations for behavior. Although this is a difficult task, it is only through such an understanding that people can learn to cope with basic attitudes, thus minimizing difficulties in the man-woman relationship in the future.

Thirdly, a problem-oriented analysis is employed. Thus, the focus is on selected areas in the man-woman relationship which appear to be the greatest sources of difficulty. The problem-oriented analysis is employed because the authors believe that meaningful man-woman relationships arise only when problem areas have been constructively resolved. Needless to say, the resolution of problem areas in the man-woman relationship is ultimately reflected in the personal growth and development of the individual marital partners.

QUESTIONS

1. What is the main objective of this text?
2. Discuss the problems involved in the case of Mr. and Mrs. T.
3. Discuss the following statement: "A marital problem is seldom one thing; it is many."
4. Why is it important to understand the motivations for actions?
5. Why have you enrolled in this course?
6. Explain the following statement: "Much of what you derive from this book will depend upon your ability to uproot successfully attitudes and ways of behaving which restrict your personal growth and your ability to build a sound relationship with the opposite sex."
7. What did Miss A. derive from her marriage course? Why was she unable to derive more?
8. Explain what is meant by a problem-oriented analysis in the area of the man-woman relationship.
9. Agree or disagree with the following statement and explain your answer: "Marriage failure is usually caused by a lack of intelligence on the part of one or both of the marriage partners."

SUGGESTIONS FOR RESEARCH AND RELATED ACTIVITIES

1. Construct a questionnaire to discover what reasons the members of your class give for taking this course. In the same questionnaire find out the kinds of information the members of your class expect to acquire from this course. On the basis of comparing the results you receive with the contents of this book, do you feel that your fellow class members have a realistic view of this course and its offerings? Explain your answer. If the members of your class acquire the kinds of information that they think they will, do you feel that they will have learned enough to participate in a meaningful marriage relationship; or do you feel that they still have a lot more to learn? Explain your answer.
2. Conduct a survey to determine what, in the opinion of your fellow students, are the important problems confronted in marriage. Do the men

and women agree on what these problems are? If not, how do you account for their differences? Have several students submit your results to their parents and find out whether or not the parents agree that the problems pointed out by your fellow students are the important ones which have to be met in marriage. If the parents do not agree, find out why they do not agree.

3. Make a check list of certain attitudes which in your opinion would lead to difficulty in marriage. Submit this list to both single and married men and women, and have them rank the attitudes according to their importance as potential sources of difficulty in marriage. On the basis of your results, what attitudes are considered to be potential sources of difficulty? Do you agree with your findings? Why? Do both married and single people rank these attitudes in the same, or very similar, manner? Do both men and women rank these attitudes in the same, or very similar, manner? If not, how do you account for whatever differences you find?

SUGGESTED READINGS

Cavan, Ruth Shonle, Ed., *Marriage and Family in the Modern World: A Book of Readings,* Thomas Y. Crowell Co., New York, 1960, reading 49, Henry Bowman, "Healthy Adult Personality," pp. 283–289, reading 50, Abraham Stone and Lena Levine, "The Dynamics of the Marital Relationship," pp. 289–296.

Goode, William J., *After Divorce,* Free Press, Glencoe, Ill., 1956, Ch. 10, "The Conflict Process: Themes of Complaint Made by the Wife."

Horney, Karen, *Self-Analysis,* W. W. Norton and Co., Inc., New York, 1942, Ch. 2, "The Driving Forces in Neuroses."

Landis, Paul H., *Making the Most of Marriage,* Appleton-Century-Crofts Inc., New York, 2nd ed., 1960, Ch. 1, "Values and Goals of Modern Marriage," and Ch. 2, "Shortcomings of Modern Marriage."

Magoun, F. Alexander, *Love and Marriage,* Harper and Brothers, New York, 1956, Ch. 2, "The Nature of Marriage," and Ch. 11, "Emotional Adjustments."

Simpson, George, *People in Families,* Thomas Y. Crowell Co., New York, 1960, Ch. 2, "Biological and Psychological Orientations to Marriage and the Family."

Vincent, Clark E., *Readings in Marriage Counseling,* Thomas Y. Crowell Co., New York, 1957, reading 39, Gordon W. Allport, "The Trend in Motivational Theory," pp. 357–369, reading 41, Nathan W. Acherman, "The Diagnosis of Neurotic Marital Interaction," pp. 378–391.

Historical and contemporary aspects of American family life

2

The main objective of this book, as we pointed out in the previous chapter, is an attempt to analyze the man-woman relationship as it emerges, matures, and, under certain circumstances, deteriorates. We now begin to pursue this objective by examining the important social unit in which the man-woman relationship is found, namely the American family.

We will conduct this examination of the American family by focusing our attention upon certain historical and contemporary aspects of American family life as follows: first, we will attempt to analyze the typical early American family and the social milieu in which it was nurtured; [1] second, we will point out certain major social changes and their impact upon family relationships; third, we will attempt to point out the direction of family change and comment on emergent family values; fourth and last, we will comment on the contemporary American middle-class family and the problems it faces.

THE TYPICAL EARLY AMERICAN FAMILY. The typical early American family was a rural family with a predominately agricultural

[1] Although we recognize that there was no single early American family type, but rather several types in which certain cultural and regional differences were apparent, our reference here to the typical early American family will include those aspects of family life which tended to be common to most early American family types, during the eighteenth and greater part of the nineteenth centuries.

economic base. This family was mostly a self-sufficient and extremely cooperative unit which operated within a materialistic and practical setting.

A Self-Sufficient and Extremely Cooperative Unit. The self-sufficiency of the early American family is shown by the fact that such basic needs as food and clothing, provision for shelter, recreation, education, religious and medical needs, socialization and protection of family members were fulfilled largely within the home. The family could not depend upon agencies outside the home to satisfy its needs because, in many areas, there were no agencies. For example, there were no bakeries, laundries, construction companies, theaters, medical specialists, furniture factories, unemployment agencies and very few, if any, clothing stores, food stores, churches, and schools. Therefore, if the family was to survive it had to fulfill its own needs, and the adequate fulfillment of these needs required the active participation and full cooperation of all family members.

A Materialistic and Practical Setting. The dependence of the early American family upon itself for survival, in addition to requiring the extensive cooperation of its members, also required a setting in which materialism and practicality were highly valued. The great importance placed upon material and practical concerns by the early American family is shown in the view that marriage itself, more frequently than not, was an economic arrangement. In fact, mate selection was primarily centered about such practical concerns as having a sturdy constitution, good working habits, and the ability to perform household duties. These were frequently the basic ingredients which men and women sought in each other.[2] Marriage for love and regard for the affectional quality of the marriage relationship were given subordinate positions in the hierarchy of family values.

In such a self-sufficient, cooperative, and extremely practical social unit as the early American family, there developed a unity based upon economic ties and personal loyalties from which the purpose and meaning of family life emerged.[3] We will now consider how this early family was internally organized.

[2] See: Arthur W. Calhoun, *A Social History of the American Family from Colonial Times to the Present*, Barnes and Noble, New York, 1945, Vol. 1, Ch. 3.

[3] James Truslow Adams, *Provincial Society, 1690–1763*, The Macmillan Co., New York, 1927, pp. 10–11. Also see: Arthur W. Calhoun, "The Early American Family," *The Annals of the American Academy of Political and Social Science*, 160 (March, 1932), pp. 7–12.

INTERNAL ORGANIZATION OF FAMILY RELATIONSHIPS.

The internal organization of the early American rural family was based upon two important principles: familism and authoritarianism.

Familism. Familism, as used here, refers to the subordination of the individual's interests to the interests of the family as a whole. This means that the goals which the members of the early American family pursued most vigorously were expected to be the goals of the family as a whole and not goals which the individual set for himself. Thus, if a son wanted to become a musician but the family desired his services as a farmer, the son was expected to give up his musical aspirations and give his service to his family as a farmer. If he did not become a farmer but persisted in becoming a musician, his ignoring of the goal set for him by his family was viewed as a disobedient and selfish act, and he was considered to be a most ungrateful and inconsiderate son.

To fit into the general goals of the family was the primary obligation of the individual, and in order to avoid misunderstanding it was necessary for the family to assign well-defined goals to each member, and to make certain that these goals fitted into the general pattern of family goals. In such a family, the desire of one daughter to become a particularly good dressmaker may have had to go unsatisfied because another person, probably her mother or an older sister, was already assigned to doing most of the family sewing; thus, the younger girl had little choice but to forget her interest and concentrate on other useful duties which were not exclusively claimed by other family members.

It follows, then, that the training which the early American family gave its members, in addition to providing knowledge about oneself, also had to provide knowledge about the likes and dislikes, talents, and abilities of other family members as well; because the behavior of one member was certainly important in determining what another might or might not be permitted to do.[4] This clearly indicates what we said previously: under the principle of familism, the individual's interests are secondary to the interests of the family as a whole.

Authoritarianism. Authoritarianism is the second principle upon which the internal organization of the early American family was based.

---

[4] Arthur W. Calhoun, *A Social History of the American Family from Colonial Times to the Present, op. cit.*, Vol. I, Chs. 5–6. Also see: Katharine DuPré Lumpkin, *The Family: A Study of Member Roles*, University of North Carolina Press, Chapel Hill, N.C., 1933, pp. xii–xvii.

Authoritarianism, as used here, is considered to have occurred when the power to make decisions and pass judgments, in effect, when the power to rule was in the hands of a person who demanded immediate obedience and allowed little individual freedom. The power to rule in this early family is traditionally viewed as having been given to the eldest male of the family who was then looked upon as head of the household. This may be identified as patriarchal authoritarianism.[5]

Thus, this patriarchal authoritarian family is portrayed as one in which the power to rule emanated from the patriarch to the lower echelons of the family.[6] The effectiveness of this power in regard to the wife during the colonial period is shown in the following passage.

Do you say, the slave is held to involuntary servitude? So is the wife. Her relation to her husband, in the immense majority of cases, is made for her, and not by her. And when she makes it for herself, how often, and how soon, does it become involuntary! How often, and how soon, would she throw off the yoke if she could! O ye wives, I know how superior you are to your husbands in many respects—not only in personal attraction . . . in grace, in refined thought, in passive fortitude, in enduring love, and in a heart to be filled with the spirit of heaven. . . . Nay, I know you may surpass him in his own sphere of boasted prudence and worldly wisdom about dollars and cents. Nevertheless he has authority from God to rule over you. . . . You are bound to obey him in all things. Your service is very, very, very often involuntary from the first, and, if voluntary at first, becomes hopeless necessity afterwards. I know God has laid upon the husband to love you as Christ loved the church. . . . But the husband may not so love you. He may rule you with the rod of iron. What can you do? Be divorced? God forbid it, save for crime. Will you say that you are free, that you will go where you please, do as you please? Why ye dear wives, your husbands may forbid. And listen, you cannot leave New York, nor your palaces, any more than your shanties. No; you cannot leave your parlor, nor your bed-chamber, nor your couch, if your husband commands you to stay there. What can you do? Will you run away with your stick and your bundle? He can advertise you! What can you do? You can, and I fear some of you do, wish him, from the bottom of your hearts at the bottom of the Hudson.[7]

Although the above quote illustrates the power of the husband, the influence of the wife is not to be underestimated. Some behavioral scientists believe that the common assertion that the patriarch alone de-

[5] When the power to rule is given to the eldest female, it is termed "matriarchal authoritarianism."

[6] Lumpkin, *loc. cit.* Also see: Robert Bierstedt, "The Problem of Authority," in Morroe Berger, et al., Eds., *Freedom and Control in Modern Society,* D. Van Nostrand Co., Inc., New York, 1954, pp. 67–81 for an excellent analysis of the concept of authority.

[7] Calhoun, *A Social History of the American Family from Colonial Times to the Present, op. cit.,* Vol. II, p. 96.

termined the family's course of action may be an oversimplification and may warrant critical re-examination.[8] One author, for example, states that the common acceptance of this belief is based upon what may turn out to be insufficient evidence.[9] Thus, it would seem advisable at least to qualify our statements concerning the extent to which the patriarch ruled the early American family. To this end, it is noted that the wife-mother was frequently influential in determining the family's course of action and this influence was effected in at least two ways. First, the wife-mother was frequently able to influence the decisions of the patriarch by the use of certain persuasive tactics which she employed in her personal interaction with him. It should be noted however that by persuasive tactics we do not suggest that the wife-mother argued with her husband nor do we imply that she actually told him what he should do. Rather, we do suggest that many early American wives were frequently able to influence their husbands by making use of subtle suggestions. And in addition to this ability to weave subtle patterns of suggestion, there was yet a second and perhaps more important method through which the wife-mother not only influenced, but actually determined, the family's course of action; this was done by means of what we identify as a mother-centered pattern.

A mother-centered, or mother-dominated home, is believed to have developed out of situations in which the continuation of the father's role was in danger. This would include situations where the cultural and occupational hazards of the early American society served as constant sources of possible injury or even death for the father. When the husband was no longer able to perform his role adequately, many women assumed the husband's role and power.

Thus we see that although the early American family was formally organized about patriarchal authoritarianism, there is reason to believe that a more critical examination of the personal interactions of this family would uncover certain important influences of the wife-mother and even certain pronounced mother-centered patterns. The authoritarian nature of the family, however, was pronounced, irrespective of whether the father or mother was in control. There was no place for overt disagreement in this family because its successful operation de-

[8] Among others, see: Michael Young and Peter Willmott, *Family and Kinship in East London,* Routledge and Kegan Paul, London, 1957; Raymond Firth and Judith Djamour, *Two Studies of Kinship in London, Kinships in Southborough,* Athlone Press, London, 1956. Also, some anthropologists are of the opinion that the prevalence of the father-centered family in American society has been overstated.

[9] Herman R. Lantz, *People of Coal Town,* Columbia University Press, New York, 1958, Ch. 8.

pended upon the ability of each member to follow the goals set by the authoritarian; and goals that the individual may have had were secondary. Let us now point out certain consequences of this type of family organization.

Consequences of Authoritarian Familistic Organization. The authoritarian familistic organization of the early American family which has already been described tended to bring about four important consequences. First, the authoritarian tended to feel a strong psychological need to be right. Second, family control tended to be based on irrational authority. Third, the family tended to be an association of unequals. And fourth, the individual family members tended to be treated as commodities.

The Authoritarian's Need to Be Right. As we have already noted, the successful operation of authoritarian family control required that the person designated as authoritarian be able to command immediate, complete, and unquestioning obedience. In order to command this obedience it was necessary for the decisions and the commands of the authoritarian to be viewed by the family as always being right. Indeed, any question raised about a decision of the authoritarian tended to threaten his position, and any hesitation in obeying his commands made it necessary for the authoritarian to wage a vigorous battle if he were to maintain his control over the family.

The weapons generally used by the authoritarian in fighting this battle were tradition and custom. By using these weapons, the authoritarian was almost always able to maintain his power because customs and traditions were highly valued and not subject to any critical examination or change.[10]

Furthermore the authoritarian had an emotional vested interest in seeing that his decisions and commands were viewed as being right. His personal security was intimately tied to his being right and any implication to the contrary tended to be shattering to him psychologically.[11] Some appreciation of what it would be like to interact with an authoritarian who has to be right may be seen by recalling our own associations with such people. Here we note that such individuals attempt to win their point by resorting to whatever means may be necessary, by telling people what to think, at times by berating, humiliating, or using destructive humor. Should they lose, they become hostile; they may pout and retreat from the situation. The clue to their

[10] Erich Fromm, *Man for Himself*, Rinehart and Co., Inc., New York, 1947, pp. 12–13.

[11] Richard Christie and Marie Jahoda, Eds., *Studies in the Scope and Method of The Authoritarian Personality*, The Free Press, Glencoe, Ill., 1954.

behavior may be found in their personal worth being tied to their being right and the insecurity and self-doubt which result when they feel they could be wrong.

Family Control Based on Irrational Authority. As we have pointed out, the maintenance of authoritarian family control was based on the authoritarian's ability to maintain order in his family. While order is always a prerequisite for the adequate functioning of group life, the order brought about through authoritarianism is based on irrational authority. Persons who rule or govern by irrational authority (as exemplified by such authoritarians as patriarchs, matriarchs, monarchs, and dictators) derive their power from the privileges which are traditionally associated with their position. This means that the authoritarian is given the power to rule, not necessarily because he is the most competent, but because he occupies a certain position in the group. As we have already noted, in the early American family the power to rule is usually viewed as having been given to the person occupying the particular position of eldest male, or father. No one was expected to question whether he was the most competent family member to rule; indeed, no one was to ask whether he was competent to rule at all! He was the father and therefore he, by custom, became the authoritarian. This, then, was irrational authority; noticeably absent was the right to govern based on the demonstrated ability to govern which we call rational authority. The concept of rational authority will be discussed in a later section of this chapter.

The Family: an Association of Unequals. In an authoritarian setting the family is viewed as an association of human beings who are inferior or superior, but never equal. By saying that the early American family members were not equals we do not have reference to such characteristics as intelligence, capabilities, experiences, and the like, for the family members may or may not have been equal in these respects; however we do have reference to the fact that the family members were not looked upon as equals, nor were they treated as equals. In the first place, all were treated as inferior to the authoritarian and even beyond this, among family members themselves the physically frail and the overtly fearful were treated as inferior. On the other hand, persons who were physically strong and those who knew no fear, save fear for the authoritarian and God, were greatly admired.[12] In this family, differential treatment was also given to members on the basis of age and sex. In this respect, males and adults possessed a favorable position, while women and children fared less favorably. Such cate-

[12] A. H. Maslow, "The Authoritarian Character Structure," *J. soc. Psychol.*, SPSSI Bulletin, **18** (1943), 401–411.

gorical treatment of family members presented a formidable barrier against any equal or democratic treatment.[13]

Family Members Treated as Commodities. When family members are treated as commodities, their worth is based on how much they can produce, they are not viewed as ends in themselves.[14] For example, members of the early American family were not primarily valued for what they themselves were, namely their intrinsic worth as human beings, but rather for their abilities to contribute to the family's economic well being. Thus, in the most materialistic and practical sense, family members were viewed as things to be used. Indeed, in many instances those who were considered to be the inferior were often unfairly used to the benefit of those considered to be superior. This type of exploitation was a common ingredient in the early American family, as well as in other authoritarian systems. Such an attitude was largely an outgrowth of the harsh physical environment which demanded the complete efforts of all family members if material needs were to be fulfilled.

In this connection, the high birth rate of the early American family is interesting. The high birth rate resulted from: the need to offset the high death rate, the disinterest and lack of knowledge about birth control, and the tradition of large families. Mainly, however, a high birth rate meant an adequate labor supply, a necessity for survival in an economy where there was little or no mechanization. One author quotes Adam Smith on the matter of American fecundity:

> The value of children is the greatest of all encouragement to marriage. We cannot, therefore, wonder that the young people in North America should generally marry very young. Notwithstanding the great increase occasioned by such early marriages, there is a continual complaint of the scarcity of hands in North America.[15]

STABILITY OF THE EARLY AMERICAN FAMILY. It should be apparent that the early American family was an extremely stable unit with little divorce. Such stability arose in part out of the loyalties that emerged from the economic interdependence of family members. However, we must not overlook the fact that in addition to the forces within the family, the community as a whole shared certain attitudes which were highly effective in bringing about family stability. For

[13] Harry Emerson Fosdick, *Twelve Tests of Character,* George H. Doran Co., New York, 1923, p. 117.

[14] Maslow, *loc. cit.* Also see: Lumpkin, *op. cit.,* pp. xii–xviii.

[15] Calhoun, *A Social History of the American Family from Colonial Times to the Present, op. cit.,* Vol. II, p. 17.

example, in connection with family relationships, it was implicitly understood that wives, formally, should obey their husbands, and children their parents. Therefore, when family conflict did arise, despite the circumstances involved, it was viewed by the community as being caused by an ungrateful wife or a disobedient child. This simple interpretation of family conflict, which was made by the community, tended to have a stabilizing effect on the family because few persons wanted to be wrong in the eyes of the community. Marriage itself was viewed as a permanent association, and separation or divorce were both socially and religiously unacceptable as adjustments to marital conflict.[16] Thus, in any family, when the internal forces failed to maintain family stability, community and religious attitudes and values served to retain it.

It is interesting to note here, however, that in describing the early American family as a permanent and stable social unit, we do not imply that it was necessarily a happy configuration or one conducive to healthy emotional development. How happy one might have been as a member of this authoritarian familistic group, or how healthy one's emotional development, may well be open to question. But available evidence indicates that in spite of its permanence and stability, personal adjustment in the early American family was not unlike that found in the dictatorial society, where the individual is subordinate to the demands of the strong leader.[17] This strongly suggests that authoritarian familism was not conducive to the realization of the individual's fullest potential, a goal with which many people are concerned today.

Let us now turn to the second major consideration of this chapter, the social factors which tended to influence and change these traditional patterns of family relationships.

MAJOR SOCIAL CHANGES AND THEIR IMPACT ON FAMILY RELATIONSHIPS. There were several social changes which influenced the early American family and brought about changes in its patterns of family relationships. We will deal with these social changes under two major headings, namely, the shift from a rural to an urban society; and, secondly, the socio-historic factors which influenced the family.

[16] Ray E. Baber, *Marriage and the Family*, McGraw-Hill Book Co., Inc., New York, 1953, pp. 443–444.

[17] Calhoun, *A Social History of the American Family from Colonial Times to the Present, op. cit.*, Vol. I, Chs. 5–6.

The Shift from a Rural to an Urban Society. Within the past one hundred and fifty years, America has changed from an agricultural to a predominately industrial economy. This change, which involved a shift from a rural to an urban society, required the migration of large numbers of people from the country to the city. Let us look at certain factors which encouraged this migration.

Incentives for Migration. The industrialization of America offered many economic and social opportunities to those who were willing to move to the city.[18] This appeal, which gave promise of greater economic security through higher wages and more attractive working conditions, was aided by the periodic declines in agricultural prices and a reduction in the employment needs of the rural area due to the increased mechanization of agriculture.[19] In addition to these economic incentives, certain social opportunities such as more adequate educational, cultural, and medical facilities aided in encouraging urban migration.[20]

Effects of the Rural to Urban Shift. The shift from a rural to an urban society brought about many social changes which had an impact on the pattern of family relationships. There were three such important effects: first, the family became less self-sufficient; second, the authoritarian lost some of his power; and third, the individual tended to undergo attitudinal changes toward his family.

Decline in Self-Sufficiency. The family in the industrial society was no longer forced to depend upon its own resources for survival. The fulfillment of such basic needs as food, clothing, shelter, provision for medicine, recreation, education, and protection was largely taken over by specialized agencies outside the home. And many of the duties which were still performed in the home such as cooking and cleaning were greatly simplified through technology and mechanization. Thus the family was freed from performing many chores which previously were necessary for its survival.[21] It is evident, therefore, that much of the time and energy which the family originally had to spend on the basic problem of physical survival could now be applied to other areas of family living; these energies were applied, for example, to-

[18] Calhoun, *A Social History of the American Family from Colonial Times to the Present, op. cit.,* Vol. II, pp. 171–175. See also: R. D. McKenzie, *The Metropolitan Community,* McGraw-Hill Book Co., Inc., New York, 1933, p. 53.

[19] Arthur Charles Cole, *The Irrepressible Conflict, 1850–1865,* The Macmillan Co., New York, 1934, p. 106.

[20] Noel P. Gist and L. A. Halbert, *Urban Society,* Thomas Y. Crowell Co., New York, 1956, pp. 90–92.

[21] William F. Ogburn, *Recent Social Trends in the United States,* McGraw-Hill Book Co., New York, 1931, Vol. II, Ch. 13.

ward the development of an interest in the needs of the individual. This concern for the individual is something quite different from the previously described familism of the earlier period and will be elaborated more fully in later sections.

Decline in Authoritarian Power. The family in the industrial society no longer composed the work unit; instead, with the rise of factories and mills, individuals sought employment outside the home. Thus the power which the authoritarian had previously held in connection with the work lives of family members was now transferred to persons other than the authoritarian, such as foremen, managers, and plant owners. This pointedly indicates a decrease in authoritarian power.

It is interesting to note further that, in addition to losing control of the work lives of family members, the authoritarian, unless he was able to establish his own business, frequently lost control of his own work situation because employment in the factory for him meant taking rather than giving orders. Thus by decreasing the power of the authoritarian, industrialization tended to strike at the very core of authoritarian familism, which, in effect, was the power of the authoritarian to command.

Attitudinal Changes Toward Family. In the urban society, individuals tended to undergo fundamental changes in their attitudes toward their families. In part, this attitudinal change resulted from the decline of the self-sufficiency of the family and the decline of the authoritarian's power. But this attitudinal change also stemmed from the exposure of family members to new and different social patterns. As the individual moved within the urban area and interacted with persons of different backgrounds, he was constantly being confronted by different rules of conduct and new value systems. Such factors as working daily with non-family members and receiving formal education outside the home tended to increase the individual's awareness of these new and different patterns. Moreover, religious and community control were no longer as binding as they were in the past. Thus the individual in the urban setting came to view the particular social patterns of his family as only one of many existing patterns; consequently, the patterns of his family lost their exclusive position in his framework of values. It follows, then, that the individual underwent certain attitudinal changes toward his family as his loyalty to his family's particular standards began to be challenged by these new and different standards.

The Family in Its Urban Setting. The growing dependence on agencies outside the home, the decentralization of authority, and the increasing awareness of new and different value systems all tended to weaken the economic ties and the personal loyalties upon which the very purpose and meaning of early American family life were founded. Urbanism, therefore, produced a milieu which made certain changes in the family inevitable.[22]

SOCIO-HISTORIC FACTORS WHICH INFLUENCED THE FAMILY. Although urbanism represented the cultural medium which nurtured change in the American family, certain important socio-historic forces, which tended to weaken the very foundations of authoritarian familism, were also present. These forces, which we will discuss presently, are as follows:

1. Secularism
2. Humanism
3. The influence of democracy at the political level
4. The emancipation of the female and associated competence
5. The American frontier

Secularism. The doctrine of secularism, as used here, views customs, traditions, and values as being the result of man's efforts, and not the direct result of divine intervention. This doctrine is important in two respects. First, it implied that man was becoming aware of his ability to create and modify customs, traditions, and values. Second, and more important, it implied that if one found it necessary to question the standards presented to him, he was questioning man's edicts and not God's! Indeed, under secularism the individual was not only free to examine standards, he could even change them without fear of divine reprisal.

It follows, then, that the way of life under secularism was under constant examination. If the prevailing patterns were found wanting, they became subject to change; continued adherence to tradition, a cardinal principle of authoritarianism, became an unacceptable alternative. This doctrine, therefore, which gave man the responsibility for determining his way of life challenged the very principle of authoritarianism.[23]

Humanism. Humanism, which became manifest in literary, philosophical, and political movements, put forth a doctrine of faith in the

[22] Ernest W. Burgess, "The Family in a Changing Society," *Am. J. Sociol.*, **53** (May, 1948), 417–422. Also see: William F. Ogburn, "The Changing Family," *The Family*, **19** (July, 1938), 139–143.

[23] Howard Becker, "Sacred and Secular Societies," *Social Forces*, **28** (May, 1950) 361–376.

human personality and in the significance of human values. We note here that man was now not only aware of his ability to determine social standards, as already exemplified by secularism, but he developed a trust and a faith in his ability to do so. Thus, humanism tended further to weaken authoritarian familism which had placed trust only in custom and the patriarch.[24]

Influence of Democracy at the Political Level. The spread of democratic values through the rise of democracies both here and abroad contributed a great deal to an undermining of authoritarian familism. Although democracy at the political level does not insure its existence at the family level, there is a strong tendency for political thinking to ultimately become a part of the individual's personal reasoning. Thus, if a person believes in his ability to govern himself politically, he might well rebel against any situation in which he is considered to be incapable of self-direction. And, in effect, this is what he did. Thus, democratic principles at the political level made their contribution to the undermining of authoritarian familism because they created rebellion against the authoritarian familistic principle which denied the individual any right of self-direction.[25]

The Emancipation of the Female and Associated Competence. The dissatisfaction of women both here and abroad tended to center about the subservience demanded of them in a man's world. Women, as we have previously noted, were a part of that category which was looked upon as inferior, and were thus frequently exploited. However, under the impact of urbanization the position of the woman changed considerably. The economic opportunities which were opening to her in industrial and professional fields tended to give her a bargaining power that she could use in relationships which were unsatisfactory to her. Thus urbanization and its associated doctrines not only gave women reason to expect more equal treatment but also gave them the opportunity to obtain more equal treatment. Bernhard J. Stern pointedly illustrated this and other effects which the emancipation of women had upon the family:

As the technological changes of the industrial revolution transformed the processes of production, the women of the urban proletariat and many of the artisan class were drawn into the factories, mills and mines as unskilled wage-workers. The majority of women found it necessary to work outside

[24] George R. Geiger, *Philosophy and the Social Order,* Houghton Mifflin Co., New York, 1947, pp. 384–397.
[25] Willystine Goodsell, "The American Family in the Nineteenth Century," *The Annals of the Academy of Political and Social Science,* Vol. 160 (March, 1932), pp. 13–22.

of the household in order to augment the family income. The leisure which the industrial revolution brought to a relatively small number of women of the upper classes was made possible in part by the labor of the women of the proletariat. The latter acquired a certain element of power within family councils by virtue of their contributions to the support of their families; and their employment away from home increased their personal contacts and released them to some extent from domestic controls and thus modified male dominance within the family. The growing urbanization and secularization of life likewise changed the status of women within the family. As the factory took over the industrial functions of the family, the state encroached upon its educational functions and this detracted from the cohesion of the patriarchal family group, which had perpetuated women's inferiority.[26]

The American Frontier. The frontier, which was that section of our country at the very edge of organized group life, should be distinguished from the more heavily populated rural settlements. The American frontier tended to be an important factor in changing patterns of family relationships, particularly for those who accepted its challenge. We note, for example, that young married people frequently migrated to frontier territories which offered them greater economic opportunities; such migration, in removing the newlyweds from the traditional parental imposition of values, served to create opportunities which allowed the more experimentally inclined to explore new patterns of conduct.

Furthermore, for young and old alike, life on the frontier was so difficult that it frequently called forth behavioral responses which differed markedly from the traditional patterns. For example, in the process of migration itself, as well as in the process of establishing homesteads, women and children were frequently required to perform tasks which previously would have been performed primarily by men.

The emergencies and hardships of the frontier were so severe that they tended to create situations in which the physical well-being of the father was under constant threat. For example, the frequent encounters with bandits, wild beasts, and Indians were ever-present threats to the frontier family as a whole, and particularly to the father as he attempted to defend his family against these attacks. And, as we noted previously in this chapter, situations which threaten the role of the father may tend to produce mother-centered patterns in the family. It follows, then, that the effects of the frontier, such as the removal of newlyweds from direct parental control, the difficulties which called

---

[26] Bernhard J. Stern, "Woman: Position in Society," *Encyclopaedia of the Social Sciences*, The Macmillan Co., New York, 1935, Vol. XV, pp. 444–445.

for behavioral responses that differed from the traditional responses, and the hardships which threatened injury or even death to the father, all tended to create a milieu in which certain changes in the traditional patterns of relationships in the frontier family were inevitable. To the extent that the old patterns were tested and found wanting, new patterns developed and became the foundations of family organization on the American frontier.

FAMILY CHANGES. The shift from a rural to an urban society and the existence of such socio-historic factors as secularism, scientific humanism, democracy at the political level, the emancipation of women, and the American frontier over an extended period of time contributed markedly to the creation of a new social and psychological setting. In this new setting, the survival of the early American family with its authoritarian familistic organization became very difficult if not, indeed, impossible. Family members were no longer willing to obey, and in many cases no longer able to obey, the traditional rules of conduct imposed by authoritarian familism. After a long period of intensive conflict, the old finally gave way to the new. Thus, we witness here the beginning of the reorganization of family relationships, in effect, the rise of new family types on the American scene.

One such major type which is of interest to us is the contemporary American middle-class family. This particular family is in a state of transition between two kinds of values: the values derived from the early American family encompassed in authoritarianism and familism; and democracy and individualism, the values which emerged out of urbanism and the socio-historic factors previously mentioned. If authoritarianism and familism represent one extreme with respect to the unimportance of the individual in the family, democracy and individualism represent the other extreme—the supreme importance of the individual in the family. Since we have already dealt with authoritarianism and familism, let us examine their opposites, individualism and democracy. Such an analysis, which is the third major consideration of this chapter, will facilitate an understanding of where the contemporary American middle-class family is moving and why it is torn with so many conflicts.

Individualism. Individualism here refers to the right of a person to be the active agent in selecting his own interests out of the array of interests which are available. This means that the goals which an individual pursues are goals which he himself selected; and the individual is no longer forced to accept goals which were set for him by his family. We must note here, however, that individualism is not to be confused with indiscriminate rebelliousness, since rebelliousness usually operates within a framework of self-concern alone and usually does not consider the dignity and rights of others. Individualism, however, is designed to create in the person an awareness of and respect for the rights and dignity of others and as such it differs markedly from rebelliousness.

Democracy. In a democratic family the power to make decisions and pass judgments—in effect, the power to rule—is given to that person, who, in the opinion of a majority of the family members, is most competent to do so. This means that authority in the democratic family is delegated on the basis of consensus and competence; and with respect to the latter, it is interesting to note that because one family member may be the most competent to pass judgments and make decisions about certain matters, it does not necessarily follow that he is capable of doing so in all matters. Therefore, authority, in the democratic family, tends to be delegated to more than one person at a time; each person is responsible for decisions regarding specific matters. It is entirely possible, of course, for one person in the democratic family to be given all of the authority, since this person may be considered by the family members to be the most capable decision maker in all matters. Democratic family control, therefore, is not based upon the number of family members who are given authority, but rather upon how this authority is given.

If we pursue our analysis further we note certain consequences of the democratic-individualistic organization for the family.

Consequences of Democratic Individualistic Organization. The democratic individualistic family organization, which has already been described, tends to bring about the following four important consequences.

Family Control Based on Rational Authority. Authority in the traditional family, as the reader will recall, was based on one's position in the family irrespective of competence. As such, it was considered irrational authority. Under democratic individualism authority is rational because it is given to that person who, in the opinion of family members, is most capable of governing.

Authority Associated with the Desire to be Right. The authoritarian of the early American family, as previously indicated, tended to experience a strong psychological need to be right. In the democratic family, however, since the person selected to pass judgment is not led to believe that he possesses an inherent superiority, although he may certainly possess a desire to be right, he nevertheless can accept a proneness toward error.

The Family: an Association of Equals. In the democratic individualistic system the family does not tend to categorize its members into superior and inferior groupings as was the case in the early American family. The tendency to abolish categorical treatment of family members is due to a number of factors. First, since the person who makes the necessary decisions in the democratic individualistic family receives his authority from the family members themselves, he is viewed more as one who leads than as one who commands immediate obedience.

A second factor regarding the family as an association of equals had to do with the changing status of women and children. In the early American family, women and children were often treated as inferiors. Increasingly, however, women are now able to attain more equal treatment because they have a bargaining power which early American women didn't have. Today, women have pursuits other than marriage which are available to them, and consequently, if a woman finds herself in a situation not to her liking she can use the opportunities open to her in business and industry to remove herself from it. Thus, unlike the early American woman, the woman of today has a power which she can use to her benefit in seeking more equal treatment in her family relationships.

We can also recognize significant changes in regard to the position of children in the family. There is increasing recognition of their needs as children, as well as the necessity to give them every available opportunity to develop their potentialities to the fullest extent.

Family Members Treated as "Ends." With the emergence of a concern for the intrinsic worth of each family member, the individual is no longer measured only in terms of what he produces. In this connection it is interesting to note that the declining birth rate probably does not stem from a lack of interest in children, but from an intense desire on the part of the family to give each member every available opportunity to utilize his fullest potentiality of development. Such a goal, many believe, is more adequately fulfilled when the family is able to concentrate its resources on a few, rather than many, children.

Now that we have examined authoritarianism, familism, individualism, and democracy it might be helpful to the reader to see Table 1, which is a summary of our remarks on these points.

TABLE 1

Changing Values of the American Family

Traditional Values	Emergent Values
I. Family control predominately based on authoritarian familism	I. Family control predominately based on democratic individualism
a. Authority associated with strong *need* to be right	a. Authority associated with *desire* to be right
b. Authority irrational	b. Authority rational
c. Family an association of unequals	c. Family an association of equals
d. Family members treated as commodities	d. Family members treated as human beings with inherent dignity
II. Values focused on tradition, allowing little change	II. Values focused on examination, allowing much change

THE CONTEMPORARY AMERICAN MIDDLE-CLASS FAMILY. The fourth major consideration of this chapter concerns the contemporary middle-class family and the problems it faces. In this regard it is noted that this family, as suggested previously, is in transition from authoritarian familism to democratic individualism. Since the middle-class family is in the process of change, it contains a mixture of traditional and emergent values. The existence of such diverse values is, however, not without its consequences; for it means that many people who grow up in a period of transition may be thrown into confusion.[27]

Such confusion is manifest in different ways. It appears in relation to the role of sex in dating behavior. In a period where social norms are changing and no longer clearly defined, the question of how involved one should become is no longer easily determined. With regard to marriage, we note that since the basis for marriage has shifted from an economic arrangement to an emphasis on a relationship centering around satisfaction of personal needs, the characteristics which people seek in a mate have undergone change.[28] Young people today must decide for themselves such important issues as: What are the meaningful traits worth seeking in a mate? How may these traits be found? What assurance is there that these traits will not change? What is love? Will it last? Can I base a marriage on love?

[27] Robert F. Winch and Robert McGinnis, Eds., *Selected Studies in Marriage and the Family*, Henry Holt and Co., New York, 1953, pp. 18–23.

[28] Margaret Mead, "The Contemporary American Family as an Anthropologist Sees It," *Am. J. Sociol.*, **53** (May, 1948), 453–459.

At the level of family life, issues tend to center about the conflict between authoritarian familistic values and democratic individualistic values, not only between husband and wife but between parents and children as well. Important questions arise, such as: What are the responsibilities and obligations of the father, mother, son, or daughter? Should a wife pursue a career? And if she decides to pursue a career, what then are her responsibilities in the home and in the community? What are the family values and goals and how shall these be determined and accomplished? [29]

The following conversations pointedly illustrate certain of these controversies:

A short time ago I heard a worthy lawyer remark that he disapproved of women in business and the professions. "If a woman is capable and ambitious," he said, "let her marry a good man, stick to him, and push him to success. Let her rear fine, upstanding children. A woman in business is not a woman at all. She's a half-baked man in petticoats."

This vehement statement did not go unchallenged. A mild social gathering was abruptly converted into a forum on feminism versus the home, or the nature of woman, and finally on the function of marriage. Discussion rapidly became animated to the point of violent argument. A young anthropologist maintained that he would have neither love nor respect for a woman who subordinated herself to him. He wanted a strong partner who could stand on her own feet. He wanted his wife to have her own career. Only through economic independence could she preserve her independence of spirit and avoid clinging about his neck like a millstone.

"Millstone indeed!" protested another man indignantly. "Young fellow, you don't know the first thing about marriage. You ought to be glad to look after your wife. That's the trouble with marriage these days. We blame the girls for kicking over the traces, but we ought to blame the men. Young men won't take responsibility for a family. They want to keep all their independence and they think a good wife is a millstone. Well, I say, call her an anchor instead of a millstone. Stop drifting and take care of a woman and children. You'll get more solid satisfaction out of the devotion of a fine little woman than from all the equality in the world. And you'll pay for it by bringing home the bacon yourself and being the kind of man she can trust and admire. You'll both be happy. A woman wants to be shielded and cared for, and a man who is a man wants to do the protecting."

"But we don't want to be taken care of," said a young woman. "We have brains of our own and education. I want to go on with my own life and be something myself. The masterful male was all very well so long as women didn't know how to do anything but housework. I want a love life and children as much as anyone, but I'm no hothouse flower. I know the kind

[29] Clifford Kirkpatrick, "Inconsistency in Marriage Roles and Marriage Conflict," *The International Journal of Ethics,* XLVI (1936), 444–460. Also see: Mirra Kamarovsky, "Cultural Contradictions and Sex Roles," *Am. J. of Sociol.,* **52** (1946), 184–189.

of life my mother led, and I don't want one like it. My husband and I will be friends. We'll work out a life together, and it'll be *our* life, not his." [30]

These and many problems and anxieties which are currently found in contemporary man-woman relationships in general are probably best summarized by Ruth Cavan who suggests that some of the "issues in the American family at mid-century" are as follows:

1. What is the basic meaning of marriage?
2. Should marriage be a permanent or a temporary relationship?
3. Should young people have a free hand in selecting a mate?
4. Should sex relations be limited to marriage?
5. Is it necessary for husband and wife to have complementary roles?
6. What constitutes an adequate number of children?
7. What is the family's function in personality development in children? [31]

Although the man-woman relationship in contemporary American society is undergoing a crisis, many people believe that there is promise of an integration at a new and more significant level than ever before was possible in American society. The reason for such hope tends to be based upon increasing evidence that marriages will remain together, not only because of external social pressures but because people will discover in marriages the satisfaction of their most basic wishes.[32]

The problems involved in achieving such voluntary and personally meaningful relationships are indeed complex and this book has been written as an attempt to clarify and assess certain of these important problems, in the hope that its readers might come to understand more fully the man-woman relationship as it emerges, matures, and, under certain circumstances, deteriorates.

SUMMARY

In our discussion of the historical aspects of American family life, it was noted that the early American family was a self-sufficient, extremely cooperative, rural, agricultural unit which operated within a materialistic and practical setting. Its internal organization was largely based on two principles, familism and patriarchal authoritarianism. The consequences of authoritarian familism were: (1) the authori-

[30] John Levy and Ruth Monroe, *The Happy Family*, Alfred A. Knopf, New York, 1943, pp. 145–146.
[31] Ruth S. Cavan, *The American Family*, Thomas Y. Crowell Co., New York, 1953, pp. 7–29.
[32] Ernest Burgess, *loc. cit.* Also see: Paul H. Landis, "The Changing Family," *Current History*, 19 (Sept., 1950), 151–153.

tarian had a strong psychological need to be right; (2) family control was based on irrational authority; (3) the family was an association of unequals; and (4) individual family members were treated as commodities.

Under the impact of urbanization and the socio-historic factors of secularism, humanism, and the emancipation of the female and associated competence, the influence of democracy at the political level and the American frontier family values underwent change in the direction of more individualism and democracy. Individualism refers to the right of a person to be the active agent in selecting his own interests out of the array of interests which are available. Democracy is conceived as the power to rule given to that person (or persons) who, in the opinion of a majority of family members, is most competent to do so. The consequences of democratic individualism are: (1) family control is based on rational authority; (2) authority is associated with the desire to be right; (3) the family is an association of equals; and (4) family members are treated as ends in themselves and not merely as means to ends.

The contemporary American middle-class family is one in transition between the traditional and emergent values. Such transition has resulted in conflicting values regarding dating, courtship, and the goals of marriage.

QUESTIONS

1. Explain the following statement: The typical early American family was a self-sufficient and extremely cooperative unit which operated within a materialistic and practical setting. Compare the contemporary American family with the early family on each of the above items.
2. Describe the internal organization of family relationships in the early family. List and describe the consequences of this type of organization.
3. How did the change from a rural to an urban society affect family life?
4. List and define each of the socio-historic factors which influenced the family. Show how each was responsible for bringing about changes in family life.
5. Describe the consequences of democratic individualistic family organization.
6. What are some of the issues facing the contemporary family? How, in your opinion, could some or all of these issues most effectively be resolved?

SUGGESTIONS FOR RESEARCH AND RELATED ACTIVITIES

1. Write and enact a script which portrays a scene in an authoritarian-familistic type family, and also one which portrays the same scene in a

democratic-individualistic type family. Have the class members list the behavioral differences portrayed by each family type, and discuss the advantages and disadvantages of each family type.

2. Make case studies of several families that you know quite well. In what ways do you find these families to be authoritarian-familistic and in what ways do you find these families to be democratic-individualistic? Do you find any instances in which the family members think that they are democratic-individualistic when actually, in your opinion, they are not? If so, explain why you think they are not.

3. Make a list consisting of the expectations which one might make of an authoritarian-familistic type of marriage and of the expectations which one might make of a democratic-individualistic type of marriage. Submit this list to married men and women of different age groupings and have them check those expectations which they made of marriage. What expectations were most frequently made? Are those expectations authoritarian-familistic or democratic-individualistic? Are men more inclined than women to have made expectations which tend to be authoritarian-familistic or not? Are older people more inclined than younger people to have made expectations which tend to be authoritarian-familistic or not? Explain each of your answers.

4. Hold a debate or a panel discussion on the merits and demerits of family living in the urban setting.

SUGGESTED READINGS

Cavan, Ruth Shonle, *American Marriage: A Way of Life,* Thomas Y. Crowell Co., New York, 1959, Ch. 2, "Fitting Your Marriage to the Times."

Calhoun, Arthur W., *A Social History of the American Family from Colonial Times to the Present,* Barnes and Noble, New York, 1945.

Jaco, E. G., and Ivan Belknap, "Is a New Family Form Emerging in the Urban Fringe?" *Am. Soc. Rev.,* 18 (Oct., 1953), 551–557.

Landis, Paul H., *Making the Most of Marriage,* Appleton-Century-Crofts Inc., New York, 2nd ed., 1960, Ch. 6, "Female Roles in Transition," Ch. 7, "Male Roles in Transition," and Ch. 8, "Unsolved Problems in Role Behavior."

Ogburn, W. F., and M. F. Nimkoff, *Technology and the Changing Family,* Houghton Mifflin Co., Boston, 1955.

Peterson, James A., *Education for Marriage,* Charles Scribner's Sons, New York, 1956, Ch. 1, "Marriage in Transition."

Simpson, George, *People in Families,* Thomas Y. Crowell Co., New York, 1960, Ch. 1, "Toward Analysis of Marriage and the Family in the United States."

Contemporary family functions

3

In the previous chapter we discussed the loss of several traditional family activities and the social changes that followed. When summarized, however, the net effect of these changes resulted in the breakdown of familism and authoritarianism and in the development of a person-centered family. Thus, in this chapter we plan to undertake an analysis of the family functions which have remained, and point out how the socio-historic factors which produced the social changes of the past have also contributed directly to the person-centered orientation which characterizes middle-class family life.

The contemporary American middle-class family is primarily organized around three sets of functions.[1]

Briefly they may be described as:

[1] In addition to these three sets of functions, some writers in the field also include the protective function with the above listed functions. The protective function has undergone marked change and will be mentioned only briefly. The protective function has had numerous facets, but it refers at this time to the provision for economic and physical security for family members. These provisions include an adequate standard of living and protection against the ravages of illness. Historically, the protective function was basic to the maintenance of the traditional household, and it consumed much time and energy. Changes in the role of government and its relation to the family have removed many of the protective functions from the home. Note particularly the development of programs of social security and pensions, programs for the blind and handicapped, programs of aid to dependent children, as well as police and fire protection. The economic problems which stem from deficits and value differences will be discussed later.

1. Procreative function
2. Socialization function
3. Affectional function

Although the family has always been concerned with these functions, fulfillment in them in the past was related less to the needs of the individual than to the needs of the group. In a rural society in which the active efforts of all family members for survival was a necessity, individual needs assumed less importance. Today, however, it is clearly evident that among large sections of the middle class, the family functions that remain are primarily oriented toward the needs and values of the individual.[2] This person-centered orientation will become increasingly self-evident as we proceed with our analysis. At this point, however, let us examine those factors which have been responsible for this new orientation.

THE SIGNIFICANCE OF MECHANICAL AND TECHNOLOGICAL PROGRESS. Initially we must note that the mechanical and technological progress which has been made in our country has helped reorient our thinking with respect to the needs of the individual in the fulfillment of family functions. Such progress had made it possible for people to turn their attention to matters other than those that relate to problems of physical existence. It is difficult to realize that for the greater part of our history, the most formidable problem was that of staying alive. With primitive techniques and limited knowledge of agriculture, what energies the family had went into the maintenance of physical existence. The fact that there were threats of destruction from animals and bandits helped matters little. Under such a system, concern for the individual did not and could not assume much importance.

Thus the preoccupation with individual values emerged when our society had evolved to a point where the energies of its people did not need to be completely consumed by physical labor or protection from destructive influences on the outside. Only then did it become possible to deal with problems of the individual, especially with the psychological and social conditions out of which he develops.[3]

[2] Some writers have made serious efforts to statistically assess the extent to which Americans are adequately fulfilling the contemporary family functions. See: Jessie Bernard, *American Family Behavior*, Harper and Brothers, New York, 1942.

[3] Ray F. Hendrickson, "Technology: Its Advance and Implications," in *Technological Trends and National Policy*, National Resources Committee, Government Printing Office, 1937, p. 99.

THE SIGNIFICANCE OF SECULARISM, DEMOCRACY, AND HUMANISM. A second significant factor which has enabled us to re-orient our thinking with respect to the place of the individual in the fulfillment of family functions has to do with the introduction of new values responsible for a change in man's social climate. In the previous chapter we stressed the meaning and importance of secularism, democracy and humanism as influences which were gradually incorpo-rated into the thinking and actions of people. The significance of these values cannot be overestimated, since they provided the social climate within which new varieties of attitudes and human relationships could emerge. These values were widespread in their impact; and they were significant in reorienting the place of the individual in his relationships to external forces, whether they were the pressures of social groups or traditions. Thus the values which emanated from secularism, democ-racy and humanism had much to do with creating a new conception of the role of man in his universe. Whereas, prior to the introduction of these values man was passive in his cultural world (that is, he felt impotent to change his status), the advent of the social forces of secularism, democracy, and humanism ushered in the realization that man could become the active agent in his life. Thus man actively turned to an improvement of his position. Once man decides that he is not so bound by matters of tradition or the pressures from social groups, it becomes possible to reorient his values and behavior in ways which were not possible under the older order. Such a realization ex-tended itself into patterns of family living and fulfillment of family functions.

PROCREATIVE FUNCTION. In turning our attention to the pro-creative function (sometimes referred to as the reproductive function), we note several indices which suggest the concern with individual needs and values of parents, as well as children. For example, we recognize that formerly the size of the family was determined by ex-ternal factors, such as economic, social, and religious pressures, while today this situation is less prevalent. Indeed, today the number of chil-dren that middle-class parents have tends to result primarily from the personal values they hold. These values include a family with fewer children than was traditionally found in American families. It has been recognized, for example, that at the end of the eighteenth century the average American wife bore more than eight children during her lifetime. In the decade of the 1930's the average was less than two children per family. In less than one hundred and fifty years, then, reproduction in the United States decreased by more than 75 percent.[4, 5] Table 2 also shows the general decline in the birth rate.

TABLE 2

Birth Rate . . . United States *
(Based on Estimated Total of Live Births per 1,000 Population)

Year	Birth Rate †
1820	55.2
1840	51.8
1860	44.3
1880	39.8
1900	32.3
1920	27.7
1940	19.4
1950	24.1
1956	25.2
1958	24.6

* Rates for 1820 to 1956 were abstracted from U.S. Bureau of the Census, *Historical Statistics of the United States—Colonial Times to 1957*, Washington, D.C., 1960, p. 23. Rate for 1958 was abstracted from *Vital Statistics of the United States, 1958*, Vol. 1, Washington, D.C., U.S. Government Printing Office, 1960, pp. 3–14, Table 3-A.

† Lowest birth rate was 18.4 which occurred in 1933 and 1936.

With respect to the middle class, the decrease in the number of their children is due to several factors. First, it has become fashionable in many quarters to associate large families with a lower socio-economic status. Many middle-class families consciously refrain from having too many children in order to avoid any unfavorable stigma. A second factor, however, has to do with the personal values of middle-class parents regarding how they will spend their time. Rather than devoting what seem to them to be their best years to rearing, let us say, six children, they consciously decide to rear a smaller number in order that they may have time to pursue their own values or interests. Such an assertion of individual values would have been unheard of in the traditional, rural society.

[4] Robert McGinnis, "Patterns of Fertility in the United States," in Robert F. Winch and Robert McGinnis, Eds., *Selected Studies in Marriage and the Family*, Henry Holt & Co., New York, 1953, pp. 145–146.

[5] Inter-Agency Committee for the National Conference on Family Life, *The American Family: A Factual Background*, Washington, D.C., U.S. Government Printing Office, 1949, p. 39.

A third significant factor has to do with the class consciousness and the concern for social mobility which characterizes the American middle class. Middle-class people are conscious of a need to maintain their class position and feel impelled to improve such position whenever possible. In order to be upwardly mobile, however, it is necessary to accumulate economic assets. One of the ways in which economic security may be achieved is through a restriction of family size.[6]

Not only is family size largely determined by the personal values of the middle class, but familial innovations regarding the handling of pregnancies, as well as the prenatal and postnatal care, suggest concern for the welfare of mother and child. From the first sign of pregnancy until sometime following the birth, both mother and child are under constant medical care and supervision. All of this is facilitated by the excellent advances in medicine, but the fact that prospective middle-class mothers and fathers insist on such care is indicative of the change which has occurred.

SOCIALIZATION FUNCTION. The person-centered orientation is once more in evidence in the socialization function. For the very concept itself refers to the learning process which enables the child to acquire the knowledges, values, and rules of conduct which his society expects of him. The well-socialized child is familiar with the expectations of the group and patterns his behavior accordingly. Thus, behavior which is markedly deviant represents a failure in socialization at some point in the individual's life history. Although parents have always been concerned with the socialization function, middle-class parents are especially sensitive to the need to fulfill this function effectively. They are, as a class, conscious of a need to do things well; thus they are greatly concerned that their children become well socialized. This concern has resulted in marked emphasis on such problems as nursing, weaning, toilet training, teaching of sex, social values, and discipline; and it has been an important factor in the amount of reading material now available dealing with socialization problems.[7, 8] Such interest in problems of socialization appears not only in literature for parents but also in the research interests and professional journals of human behavior scientists; this stems from at

[6] Raymond J. Murphy, "Psychodynamic Factors Affecting Fertility in the United States," in Robert F. Winch and Robert McGinnis, Eds., *Selected Studies in Marriage and the Family, op. cit.,* pp. 156–170.

[7] W. A. Davis and R. J. Havighurst, *Father of the Man,* Houghton Mifflin Co., Boston, 1947.

[8] James C. Maloney, "The Cornelian Corner and its Rationale," in M. J. E. Senn, Ed., *Problems of Early Infancy,* Josiah May Jr. Foundation, New York, 1947.

least two important sources: a pure interest in the theory and nature of social learning which has always been present, plus a more recent development—a necessity for finding practical answers to the consequences of different socialization practices. The latter development is an outgrowth of pressures originating with the public.[9, 10] For example, research has been designed and implemented within the last few years to test empirically the consequences of certain child rearing practices.[11]

If we proceed with our analysis, we note that interest in the problem of socialization has also become manifest in formal as well as informal discussion groups. For example, all of us have probably been in planned or spontaneous discussions concerned with the pros and cons of discipline or the teaching of sex. Often many of these discussions provoke lively, heated exchanges, suggesting how interested people have become in these issues.

In turning our attention to planned discussions of socialization practices, we note the importance of Parent-Teacher Associations. These organizations give parents and teachers the opportunity to conduct informative, challenging discussions centering on the methods that are most conducive to the achievement of socialization. Similarly, the rise of organized groups designed to improve the mental health of our citizens, to reduce juvenile delinquency, crime, and emotional instability has also been marked.[12]

THE AFFECTIONAL FUNCTION. At the outset we should note that the affectional function may be regarded as one aspect of the total socialization process which was discussed previously; and, as such, it has been to some extent traditionally a part of the family's functions.[13] The emphasis which the affectional function receives from the contemporary American middle-class family, however, is of such

[9] Martha Ericson Dale, "Child-Rearing and Social Status," *Am. J. Sociol.*, **52** (1946), 191–192.

[10] Robert R. Sears, "Ordinal Position in the Family as a Psychological Variable," *Am. Soc. Rev.*, **15** (June, 1950), 397–401.

[11] Robert O. Blood, Jr., "A Situational Approach to the Study of Permissiveness in Child-Rearing," *Am. Soc. Rev.*, **18** (Feb. 1953), 84–87.

[12] For example, the Judge Baker Foundation, Boston, Mass., and the Leo Potishman Foundation associated with Texas Christian University, Fort Worth, Texas are devoted to the problems of juvenile delinquency and crime. The Auxiliary Council to the Association for the Advancement of Psychoanalysis, located in New York, was a lay group interested in educating the public about problems of emotional instability.

[13] William F. Ogburn, "What Is Happening to the Family?," *J. Home Econ.*, **25** (Oct. 1933), pp. 660–664.

importance and is such a departure from that which characterized the traditional rural family that we have chosen to single it out for special attention by treating it as a specific function.

Although we plan to deal with the affectional function in a theoretical way in a later chapter, we will introduce at this time its general understanding as held by the middle class. The affectional function is the process whereby the parental concern for the development of the child is oriented toward the emergence of a personality characterized by positive feelings which include, love, emotional acceptance, and respect for oneself as well as for others. With these personal attributes the individual becomes capable of relating to others in a meaningful way, for he possesses the capacity to accept others and to have feeling and appreciation for them as human beings. Although this capacity is a significant attribute in all human relationships, it is especially important in regard to mate selection. For it means that individuals, who have come from homes where the affectional function has been adequately fulfilled, are perhaps more capable than most of establishing meaningful relationships in marriage. They are free to express love, to receive love, and to treat each other with dignity and respect.

In this regard it is important to note that the affectional function is not only of importance to individual human beings, but it is also of importance to the society as a whole—in that the affectional function, once achieved, becomes a significant integrating force in producing greater family stability. Likewise it can be noted that in marital and familial deterioration the quality of the feelings characterized by the affectional function may be regarded as having broken down, and the case of Mr. and Mrs. W. brings this out clearly.

Mr. W. was referred for marital assistance by his pastor, with whom he had been discussing his marital difficulties. At the time he appeared for help, his wife had already initiated divorce proceedings and was awaiting the final decree. Mr. W. stated that his marriage had deteriorated; he admitted to numerous arguments over an eight-month period and to slapping his wife on two occasions. The slapping occurred, according to Mr. W., whenever his wife had been "nagging him." Mr. W. recognized that there was little possibility that his marriage could be rehabilitated but he pleaded with the counselor to arrange to see his wife in order that some attempt at reconciliation be made.

Mrs. W. appeared within a few days and stated at the outset that she had come only because her husband had begged her to keep the appointment. She stated that she was going through with the divorce and that her mind had been made up for some time. When asked about what considerations had gone into her decision, she stated that she no longer had any deep feeling for Mr. W. She pointed out that she found the relationship with Mr. W. to be unsatisfactory. Specifically she stated that Mr. W. had little to do with her, he would not consult her or convey his concerns or feelings; instead he kept to himself and had a marked tendency to brood. Mrs. W. stated that she had attempted to get close to Mr. W. but was never successful. Mrs. W. pointed out that due to Mr. W.'s behavior she felt repeatedly rejected and left out of his life. She was hurt and no longer wished to try to rebuild the relationship. She reported that the slappings were, in themselves, not important; instead they symbolized rejection for her. Although we will not deal with all the complications in this relationship, nevertheless, this case indicates clearly the deterioration of the affectional component of their marriage. Mrs. W.'s reaction is typical of reactions frequently encountered by the marriage counselor. Here especially the reader will note that Mrs. W.'s complaints are not with money or sex; instead, the kinds of personal feelings, warmth, and satisfactions which she had come to expect were not present. In our terms, the affectional function had broken down.

Impersonality and the Affectional Function. If we pursue our analysis we will discover that the great emphasis placed on the affectional function is intimately related to the impersonal nature of modern life. Although impersonality was undoubtedly present in rural America, the large scale urban community now symbolizes the epitome of impersonality.[14] Many of the traditional family ties have been broken. Moreover, contemporary urban life is characterized by secondary relationships, with interest in the human relationship centered on what one can market or purchase; perhaps a skill, a talent, or even a favor. Out of such relationships the individual has come to view himself and others in terms of what they have to offer. Interest in the person as a human being, his feelings, his likes, or his tastes, becomes relatively unimportant.[15, 16]

Out of these impersonal associations a sense of isolation emerges. Such a feeling of isolation becomes manifest in a search for human relationships that promise personal acceptance and concern, and many

---

[14] Paul H. Landis, "The Changing Family," *Current History,* **19** (Sept., 1950), pp. 151–153.

[15] Erich Fromm, *Man for Himself,* Rinehart and Co., Inc., New York, 1947, Ch. 2.

[16] Louis Wirth, "Urbanism as a Way of Life," *Am. J. Sociol.* **44** (July 1938), pp. 10–18.

people throughout our society recognize this need. People have come to recognize that the family may be the most effective social unit in dealing with the problem of impersonality. At the level of child rearing we have already suggested how the adequate fulfillment of the affectional function may enable the individual to deal with the impersonal world. Moreover, many enter the marital relationship with the hope that compensations for the feeling of impersonality will emerge in the form of love and acceptance at home. Thus the husband and wife who greet each other in the evening may look forward to a more meaningful relationship than the impersonality experienced outside the home. When such compensations are not present, men and women become dissatisfied with their marriages. Such feelings of dissatisfaction become especially pronounced when husband and wife discover that within their marital relationship there are the very impersonal qualities they had hoped to avoid. One of our major tasks in subsequent chapters will be to examine impersonal qualities in the man-woman relationship, to indicate how they may disturb the marital relationship, and to suggest how these might be dealt with.

SUMMARY

Many of the functions originally fulfilled by the family are now largely cared for by agencies outside the home. Three important sets of functions still remain, however; they are: (1) procreation, which refers to the bearing of children; (2) socialization, which is the process whereby the child is taught acceptable modes of behavior, thereby enabling him to become integrated into his society; and (3) the affectional function, which is the process which facilitates socialization by teaching the child to interact with others within a framework of love, warmth, and acceptance. The affectional function becomes manifest with feelings of dignity and respect toward self and others.

Although these functions were, in part, present in the family of the past, the manner in which they are now fulfilled has undergone considerable change. For example, the family of the past had little time to devote to the individual needs of its members. Thus, although large families may have been rooted partly in religious values, the existence of a large number of children made it easier to fulfill the family's economic function. The socialization and affectional functions, too, were primarily directed toward fulfilling the needs of the family as a whole with little regard for the individual's interests.

Today, however, under the influences of mechanical and technological innovations, and the new values engendered by such ideologies as secularism, democracy, and humanism, it has become possible for parents to concern themselves more directly with the needs of the individual in fulfilling the three traditional functions. The restriction of the birth rate, which is reflected in the increasing value placed on the small family, is believed by many to be more conductive to the personal and social development of the individual than was the large family of yesterday. Both the socialization and affectional functions, in addition to training the individual to interact meaningfully with others, now largely center about a concern for the growth of the individual.

QUESTIONS

1. In what ways did secularism, democracy, and humanism affect the fulfillment of family functions?
2. In what ways did mechanical and technological progress further change the fulfillment of family functions?
3. What is the procreation function? List and discuss the factors which are largely responsible for the decreasing size of the contemporary family.
4. What is the socialization function? In what way does the manner in which this function is fulfilled today differ from the manner in which it was fulfilled in the past?
5. What is the affectional function? Illustrate how the example of Mr. and Mrs. W. represents a breakdown in the affectional function.
6. In what way is the impersonality of modern society related to the importance ascribed to the affectional function?
7. Explain what is meant by the following statement: "In the past the family consisted of family-centered persons, while today it is largely a person-centered family."
8. Agree or disagree with the following statement and explain your choice. "The person-centered characteristic of the contemporary family is indicative of a lack of concern for family stability."

SUGGESTIONS FOR RESEARCH AND RELATED PROJECTS

1. Ask several men and women of various age groupings the following questions and in each case have them explain their answers:
    a. In what ways is the small family superior to the large family?
    b. In what ways is the large family superior to the small family?
    c. Does the family today rely too much on outside agencies in the socialization of the child?
    d. Should the family rely more on outside agencies in socializing the child? If so, upon what agencies should the family rely?
    e. In what areas are children today given too much freedom in making their own decisions?

f. In what areas should children today be given more freedom in making their own decisions?

Tabulate your results and find out how people feel with regard to these topics. Do you find any differences between the opinions of men and women, or between the opinions of persons of different age groupings? If so, how do you explain these differences?

2. Make a list of the changing trends in the functions of the American family. Interview several members of your class to determine which of these trends they regard as being beneficial to marriage and family living, and which they regard as detrimental and why. What are your results? Have several of the students submit your results to their parents in order to determine whether or not they agree with the results and what basis they offer for doing so.

3. It is generally agreed that through modern homemaking devices and reliance on outside agencies the contemporary homemaker is freed from much time previously spent in performing homemaking duties. Interview several married women to find out: first, whether or not they are aware of having more free time than their mothers and grandmothers; and second, how they spend their free time. Describe your results, showing whether or not women are aware of having more free time, how they spend their free time, and explain whether or not, in your opinion, the time could be spent more effectively than it is.

SUGGESTED READINGS

Anshen, Ruth Nanda, Ed., *The Family: Its Function and Destiny,* Revised Ed., Harper and Brothers, New York, 1959.

Burgess, Ernest W., and Harvey J. Locke, *The Family,* 2nd ed., American Book Co., New York, 1960, Ch. 16, "The Family in Transition," especially pp. 462–470.

Kenkel, William F., *The Family in Perspective,* Appleton-Century-Crofts, Inc., New York, 1960, Ch. 9, "The Family as an Institution," Ch. 10, "The Childbearing Function of the Family," and Ch. 11, "The Function of Socialization."

Ogburn, William F., "What Is Happening to the Family?" *J. Home Econ.,* 1933, **25**, 660–664.

Parsons, Talcott and Robert F. Bales, et al., *Family, Socialization and Interaction Process,* The Free Press, Glencoe, Ill., 1955, Ch. 1, "The American Family: Its Relations to Personality and to the Social Structure," especially pp. 16–22.

Winch, Robert F., *The Modern Family,* Henry Holt and Co., New York, 1952, Part 2—"The Family and Its Functions."

Motivations
for marriage

4

In the previous chapter we were concerned with the kind of marital relationship middle-class Americans desire; at this point let us shift our attention to some of those factors which inhibit its realization. The fact that middle-class Americans search for a meaningful interpersonal relationship in marriage should not obscure the fact that these people often possess personality patterns and motivations which impose obstacles to the achievement of their marital goals.

To begin with, we are torn by contradictions and often seek contradictory behavior in ourselves and in others. For example, we espouse ethical beliefs regarding the treatment of our fellow men, but we value material success so highly that we don't mind manipulating others in order to achieve what we desire. Or we purport to believe in democratic values, but tend toward authoritarian and dictatorial values in our relations with others. The existence of expectations which are diametrically opposed to each other is certainly not new; it has been recognized and given wide attention in the human behavior sciences for some time. Nevertheless, the fact that we seek values opposed to each other creates confusion about what we want in ourselves and in others.[1, 2]

[1] Read Bain, "Our Schizoid Culture," *Sociology and Social Research*, **19** (Jan–Feb. 1935), 266–276.
[2] Karen Horney, *The Neurotic Personality of Our Time*, W. W. Norton and Co., Inc., New York, 1937.

When we turn our attention to specific values which dominate our thinking, we discover that these are often the very things which make a meaningful relationship difficult to achieve. Indeed, it should be clear that the impersonality of life in our society, pointed out in the previous chapter, imposes serious limitations on the person's ability to appreciate warm, meaningful, human associations. Such a way of life inculcates the value of using others as commodities, and helps create a pattern of casual and superficial concern for others which is poor preparation for the heavy emotional commitments modern marriage makes on the person. To be sure, many people enter the marital relationship with the hope that in this relationship they may discover compensations for the empty, impersonal associations of their daily lives. Unfortunately, however, people frequently discover within their marriage the very same qualities of impersonality they wished to avoid. Although frustrating to the person, such a development is understandable to the human behavior scientist. For although persons seek in marriage an escape from an impersonal world, the marital partners have been nurtured in a society with impersonal values. Thus, in spite of a desire to find a meaningful relationship, a husband and wife reared in an impersonal milieu tend to carry into their home the values which govern their lives on the outside.

Our difficulties are compounded when we recognize that our society is also conducive to the development of personal immaturities, so much so that it is certainly no easy task to grow up in our social order without acquiring many of these immaturities. We do not wish to deal with the very complex subject of the conditions which produce immaturity. Nevertheless, we can point out that any situation which fosters in the person a lack of confidence in himself, and thus a fear of dealing with others or of assuming life's responsibilities, fosters personal immaturity. In our society there are many such situations. Few people come from homes where the parents have sufficient integration to afford the child a clear, realistic set of values by which to live his life. Instead, it is much more common to find parents who are confused not only about what they might expect from their children, but also about what to expect from each other in their roles as husbands or wives. This is not the kind of familial situation which engenders in the person a sense of confidence about self. Instead, it is out of these situations of conflict and confusion that patterns of overprotection or rejection develop; these serve only to entrench immaturities and the rejection of life's responsibilities.

Immaturities are seldom confined to one segment of personality, however; instead they find expression in the entire system of motivations for behavior. With respect to marriage, it is important to recognize that immature people possess motivations which are not only faulty in terms of fulfilling the affectional function, but which also lead to additional difficulties and impose unnecessary burdens on the stability of the marital relationship. If one marries to escape responsibilities in the parental home, the realization of even greater responsibilities in marriage becomes very frustrating. The motivations which we have for marriage are important determinants of what we expect from marriage and the kind of relationship that follows. Moreover, an understanding of why people marry enables us to understand why some relationships are better than others, and why some people are happier in their marriages than are others. The value of such an understanding is brought out in the conversation one of the writers had with Miss B. In discussing Miss B.'s interest in marriage, she was asked, "Why do you wish to marry?"

Miss B.: "Well, why does anyone want to marry?"
Teacher: "Let's forget about others, why do you want to marry?"
Miss B.: "I want to marry—because I want to marry. Why do you think I should want to marry?"
Teacher: "I don't know, that's why I raised the question."

Miss B. gave very little evidence to indicate that she possessed much insight into why she wanted to marry. Although such an understanding is exceedingly helpful in any instance, it was crucial in this case, since the young lady's motivations for marriage were directly related to some of her courtship difficulties.

Miss B. grew up in a home where little had been expected of her. She was markedly indifferent to making decisions or assuming her own responsibilities. Although the idea of marriage appealed to Miss B. she was searching for a man with whom she might continue a dependent relationship. Her conception of a husband was a man who would take over her life and solve her problems so that she would not have to worry about them. The boy with whom Miss B. had become involved grew up with an entirely different concept of a wife and of a wife's responsibilities. He expected his wife to be more reliant and assertive than Miss B.'s actions indicated. When Miss B. discovered her boy friend would not assume her responsibilities and in fact expected her to change, she became hostile and would torment him.

One of the important motivations for marriage which Miss B. had should be apparent; she was looking for a man to assume responsibility for her life. She had outgrown her parents and needed a husband to carry on as her parents had. In this particular situation a pattern for future marital difficulty was already present in courtship. Whether Miss B.'s immaturities could be resolved depended to a great extent on whether she was willing to examine them, their relationship to her motivation for marriage, and her resultant interpersonal problems with others.

MOTIVATIONS WHICH DISTURB THE MARITAL UNION. Since we have outlined briefly some of the problems which interfere with the efforts of the middle-class person to build a meaningful relationship, let us turn to the main section of this chapter and pursue some of these problems systematically. In the material that follows we have selected, out of many possible cases, those which illustrate personal immaturities and motivations for marriage commonly found in our society. In each instance we attempt to point out how the combination of personal immaturity and the specific motivation for marriage leads to successive involvements which impose burdens on the marital union. In some examples the problems deal with marked egocentricity; at other times they deal with a lack of basic interest in the marriage partner; in other cases they are associated with being unable to relate to or to share with another person. As the reader examines this material, he will probably recall persons who resemble the kinds of people we are describing.

Escape from an Unhappy Home. Let us consider the type of individual who complains about being unhappy at home. He does not get along well with his parents or siblings; he may feel unfairly treated, perhaps misunderstood. Sometimes there is some basis for the complaints, but more often than not these difficulties in dealing with people are expressions of an inability (of which the person is unaware) to get along with others. This type of person looks for a relationship which may remove him from his unhappiness. His predominant motivation for marriage is to escape.

The example of F.A., female, age nineteen, is a case in point. The girl in question came to the attention of a counseling center through her mother, who was concerned with the daughter's tendency to become seriously involved with boys after a short period of acquaintance. Usually these involvements were accompanied by expressions of serious intentions, love letters, and marriage commitments. The pattern of involvement appeared to be with boys who were emotionally immature. At the time she was seen at the counseling center, F.A. was two months pregnant out of wedlock. Although the boy involved had previously stated he would marry the girl, he had recently changed his mind. The mother was quite distraught and anxious. The girl's reaction was difficult to assess, although she appeared uncomfortable.

In analyzing the family background of the case, the following important features emerged. F.A. grew up in a home with a possessive mother. The father had died when F.A. was a child. Relationships with the mother were never satisfactory and the girl had followed a pattern of rebelling against the mother's constant interference in her life. Whenever the girl developed an interest in a boy, the mother exerted all her influence to break up the relationship. In some instances the mother would demand that the boy stop seeing her daughter; in others, the mother would move F.A. to another community in order to avoid the involvement. Over the years this tug of war continued with the daughter developing more resentment and hostility. After several sessions with the counselor, it became apparent that F.A. had no healthy interest in the father of her child-to-be. She had allowed herself to become pregnant thinking that the boy involved would marry her. Thus she viewed the boy as one who might enable her to escape from a parental relationship which she did not like.

In analyzing the case of F.A., we recognize that the pregnancy is incidental to the case. Most persons who marry to escape a family background are less drastic in their actions. Nevertheless, there are many factors in the personality of F.A. which would have to be worked through before she could become an adequate partner in marriage. To begin with, although we can sympathize with F.A.'s need to get away from her mother, her methods are reckless to herself and to others. There is no real interest in the boy since he is merely the means for getting F.A. out of something unpleasant. F.A. is essentially self-centered, concerned with her own needs regardless of the consequences which these may have for others. She is therefore not given to sharing with others, or to understanding their wishes or needs. Furthermore, there is no assurance that the pattern of rebellion which characterizes F.A. would diminish in marriage. Instead, it is likely that rebellion might emerge in relation to familial responsibilities and thus threaten the stability of the marital relationship. All of these factors would appear to suggest that F.A. would have considerable difficulty becoming part of a meaningful and stable marital union.

Escape from Feelings of Loneliness. A second type that frequently encounters difficulty in marriage is the person who marries to escape from intense feelings of loneliness. Frequently these are people with involved personality difficulties, who hope that in some way life will become more comfortable if they marry. They believe that a change in the environment will make life more enjoyable and meaningful. Unfortunately such people usually discover that marriage is not a solution for inner problems. In the following case we learn of a male who marries primarily out of a sense of desperation to avoid loneliness.

Mr. J., one of three brothers, had been supporting and caring for his mother for fifteen years. Since he was moderately successful in business, he was able to build an attractive home in which he and his mother lived. The brothers informed both the mother and Mr. J. that the relationship was not a good one for either, but especially for their brother, who they felt should marry and raise a family. Mr. J., however, expressed no dissatisfaction with the relationship, claiming that it was his duty as a son to care for his mother. Within a six month period the mother became ill and died. During the early months after the mother's death, Mr. J. went through periods of marked anxiety and intense feelings of loneliness. He was quite hostile, as though fate had robbed him of his relationship with his mother. Soon he reached a point of desperation and it was then that he frantically began his search for female companionship. Within a year after his mother's death, Mr. J. was married.

The case of Mr. J. raises several interesting problems. He had been a dependent type of individual, and it is common for people of this type to become dependent on their friends and cling desperately. Frequently they try to be of great service to others. From such service they derive a sense of meaning and purpose to their lives. Although such dedication to others appears, on the surface, to be a fine attribute, there are negative aspects; for these people make claims on their relationships. That is, they come to believe that since they are of service to others, that others must not leave them, or lead lives of their own. When such a relationship is terminated the dependent individual often becomes quite disturbed. Thus, the adjustment is tenuous. For Mr. J., if anything happens to his wife or if she becomes separated from him, he is thrown back on his own minimal resources. Thus he is always on the verge of insecurity and loneliness. Also, we must recognize that Mrs. J. would certainly have problems in such a marriage. Her husband might expect her to include him in all her plans. Thus he might become possessive to the point where his wife would discover that her life had little freedom, and this she might well resent.

Marriage for the Purpose of Living Through Others. A third category of persons who may encounter difficulty in marriage are those who feel hopeless about finding meaning to life through their own potentialities and abilities. Marriage for these people means the opportunity to live through the accomplishments of the marital partner. Often these people settle for less in a marital partner than they could obtain. It is not uncommon to find people who are objectively gifted, talented, and attractive, but who possess inferiority feelings to the point where they are fearful of any form of self-assertion. Such a pattern is perhaps more common with women than with men, since many women have grown up in environments which looked down on the efforts of women to realize themselves. Such women come to regard themselves as being less worthy than they really are, and frequently they are torn by inner conflicts as a result.

The involvements as well as the dangers which are found in relationships containing the need to live through others are brought out in the case of S.A., female, age twenty-one. S.A. was considered attractive and possessed a very pleasant personality. At the time she was seen in the counseling center she was quite disturbed, having been jilted recently in what she thought was a serious love affair. Although one might expect some disturbance after such an experience, the general quality of S.A.'s reaction was quite intense. It was then that the counselor began to suspect some hidden involvements.

The family background of S.A. revealed that she had grown up in a home with aloof parents. The father was described as domineering and opinionated, with a marked preference for male children. The mother appeared to be an ineffectual person, quite subservient to the father. S.A. had learned to relate to her father by giving in to all his wishes, by behaving in a subservient manner, by repressing her own interests and identifying with his. This was the pattern she employed in her attempt to establish a relationship with males outside her home. The boy with whom she had been involved was uninterested in a compliant woman who appeared never to be able to handle her affairs properly. Consequently he dissolved the relationship. After several counseling sessions, S.A. realized that her personal disturbance about the broken love affair resulted less from having been jilted than from the realization that her lifelong pattern of relating to men in a subservient way, including various forms of self-berating about her physical appearance and intelligence, had failed. A pattern which had formerly brought her a sense of security no longer functioned and she was utterly confused and panic-ridden as a result. Although traumatic for the moment, the disturbing events of her broken relationship became a motivating factor for change; she reorganized her thinking and feeling, and over an extended period of time she began to examine the possibility of establishing a relationship with a man on a new and more healthy, as well as realistic, basis. Needless to say, such a change involved the acceptance of herself as a person with her own set of interests, feelings, wishes, and hopes. Thus, instead of perpetually trying to relate to men by hiding her identity, she began to realize that her identity, when brought out into the open, would become a basis for the relationship she hoped to build.

This is an interesting case since it points out not only the involvements which would have prevented the girl from becoming an adequate marital partner, but also how through guidance she was able to reorient her behavior in order that she might work toward a healthy relationship with a man. A further aspect of this case which bears note has to do with the conditions which produced change. It was only after being jilted that she began to realize her plight. We do not recommend a traumatic shock as a requirement for change, but nevertheless we recognize that a sense of discomfort is often a requirement for change.

Marriage for Material Possessions and Wealth. A fourth category of persons who marry for reasons that will lead to difficulty are those who marry in order to obtain possessions and wealth. The layman tends to see the motivations of these people in relatively simple terms. That is, they are "money mad" or they are ruthlessly ambitious, willing to do anything to get ahead. In reality the motivations of these people are frequently quite complex. Indeed, many of these people who marry for material wealth and possessions have really given up the possibility of finding a good love relationship. Some are cynical and do not believe that good relationships really exist. Others possess such self-doubt that they question whether it is really possible for anybody to love them. Regardless of cause, once they decide that love is not really to be found, they compensate by settling for material things. As one person put it, "I can't have love, but I may find wealth."

There is the case of Mr. S.S., age twenty-five, which illustrates many of the points we have just discussed. Mr. S.S. grew up in an emotionally impoverished family where warmth among family members appeared infrequently and where his parents had to struggle desperately in order to care for the family. Mr. S.S. had decided early in life that meaningful human relations were not to be had; and his goal in life was to accumulate as much money as rapidly as possible through whatever means were necessary. Included in these plans was a marriage that would be financially profitable. Mr. S.S. implemented his marital plans by circulating in all of the best places in his community where eligible girls from wealthy families would be present. Before becoming seriously involved Mr. S.S. would check informally into the prospective father-in-law's financial background, in order that he might calculate the possible wedding gift, as well as the future inheritance.

One day Mr. S.S. met a young lady who seemed to meet all of his financial requirements. He went through the usual procedure of checking the background. What he failed to realize at the time was that the girl's father, who had been disbarred as a lawyer for illegal practice, was aware of what was taking place. Thus, the father saw to it that the young man would receive favorable financial reports. Mr. S.S. worked according to plan and when he was satisfied with what he had heard, he made a proposal of marriage. The wedding date was set and plans were made when he discovered that he had been duped by his prospective father-in-law. He had finally discovered there was no wealth in the girl's family. After receiving such information he promptly wired the girl that he would not marry her and asked that the diamond ring which he had given her be returned.

Although this experience undoubtedly was very traumatic to the young woman involved, it was probably quite fortunate for her that this marriage did not take place, because it is doubtful that Mr. S.S. would be equipped to, or interested in, building a meaningful marital relationship. With his ruthless ambition he would hardly have been concerned with the needs of others. He had demonstrated that he was self-centered, concerned with his own needs, and not able to relate in a way involving mutuality. Such people with a need to deny that love is possible often find it necessary to avoid committing themselves emotionally to a relationship; and in fact they have to actively discourage a potentially meaningful relationship from developing.

Although many might not be so calculating as Mr. S.S., it would be foolish to assume that his case is unique. For indeed, marriage for wealth, both disguised or undisguised, is common in our culture.

Marriage on the Rebound. A fifth category of persons who may encounter difficulty in marriage are those people who marry "on the rebound." These are people who have had an unsatisfactory love relationship, perhaps one where they were jilted. They are frequently subject to feelings of unworthiness. After losing a relationship, self-attacks of unworthiness become quite intense and these attacks become a motivating factor in the person's need to prove himself. Frequently such people proceed hastily to find a marital partner.

As an illustration of such haste, let us consider G.T., female, age twenty-three, who had been engaged to a serviceman for about a year. Shortly thereafter, letters from her fiancé became less frequent and less personal. One day Miss G.T. received a letter from her fiancé informing her that he had met another girl and thought it best that his engagement be terminated. Miss G.T. was very upset and quite anxious for several weeks. She consciously looked for another male and felt desperately driven to prove to her friends that she could get married. Finally, she met Mr. K.B., an individual with serious personal difficulties who had never emancipated himself from his mother. He was, at the time of marriage, still dependent on his mother even for simple decisions. He had never been allowed to mature or to assume adult responsibilities. It was also quite apparent that Mr. K.B.'s mother actively planned to take a role in managing the affairs of any marriage which her son would undertake. Miss G.T. thought none of these problems to be serious, believing that they could be overcome easily. Two months after her initial meeting with K.B. she received a proposal of marriage from him. She accepted and they were married shortly thereafter.

In this case, we see how the sense of urgency about saving face drives G.T. into a marriage fraught with difficulty. Being so desperate, she fails to examine her relationship. Thus, she marries a person who has pronounced personal difficulties and who does not possess, at the time of marriage, the basic qualities necessary to become a partner in a relationship with emotional commitments. We also note that, with her personality organization which included a considerable amount of self-hate, Miss G.T.'s need is for a warm, accepting male who could help her establish some sense of security in herself. In the relationship which she chose it would be difficult to receive such assistance from her husband. Instead she can only look forward to an immature relationship with him and conflicts with her mother-in-law due to interference.

Let us turn now to an assessment of the cases which have been outlined and emphasize what may be learned from them.

CASE ASSESSMENT. If we retrace our steps and synthesize the insights which our cases have afforded us, we recognize that the motivations for marriage which result from personal immaturities tend to share three elements in common which clearly pose limitations to the building of a meaningful marriage relationship.

In the first place, in almost all of our cases the motivations for marriage involved an escape from some personal problem. As such, these reasons are essentially negative reasons for marrying. To the extent that this is true, the person seeking a marital partner lacks intrinsic interest in the partner as a human being; instead, the person he is married to becomes a tool used to help in the escape from the undesirable condition.

A second element found in almost all of our cases is the compulsive nature that characterizes the search for the marital partner. If one seeks to escape from a problem there is often a sense of urgency about finding a marital partner; for one then feels that "time is running out." Under a strain of this sort, rational judgment or evaluation of the marital partner is overlooked.

"I appreciate this surprise party folks . . . NOW can I take off the blindfold and see where I am?"

Figure. 1. "Grin and Bear It" cartoon (April 16, 1961), courtesy George Lichty and the Sun-Times–Daily News Syndicate.

Thirdly, in the cases which have been presented, the problems were primarily inner difficulties in which a change on the outside—that is, marriage—was likely to bring little abatement of the difficulty. It follows, then, that for people who marry for the motivations we have described, a period of disillusionment is almost inevitable. Such disillusionment occurs when there is the realization that marriage failed to solve the difficulties and they are still left to cope with their difficulties. Often such realization brings with it bitterness and resentment not only toward oneself but also toward the marital partner upon whom may fall gross blame for the unhappy relationship.

Having analyzed our cases, we recognize that up to this point we have been dealing only with motivations for marriage which result from personal immaturities. We have selected to do this because we feel that the subtle and complex nature of these negative motivations warrants close attention. This is not to say that all motivations for marriage are negative, for indeed many people are motivated to marry for reasons which are quite positive. Such people do not regard marriage as a means of escaping from something, but rather as an end or a goal in itself. In other words, where there is positive motivation for marriage, the motivation to marry does not arise from the desire to avoid unpleasant conditions but rather from the attractiveness of what these individuals are moving toward, namely the marriage itself. The next chapter presents many of the specific points of positive motivations toward marriage, and the specific ends that are involved in this kind of relationship are discussed in some detail. These specific ends are companionship, emotional reassurance, emotional interdependence, freedom of communication and activity, and physical sexual strivings. For our present purposes it will be sufficient to simply point out that for those whose motivations toward marriage are more positive than negative, the marriage will not be treated as a means of escape, but rather the marriage and the marital partner himself will be viewed for what is intrinsically represented emotionally, intellectually, and physically. The marriage relationship as such is neither used nor exploited but instead becomes the framework within which mutual understanding, empathy, and personal acceptance emerge. At this point we would like to introduce the idea of a personal assessment of the motivations for marriage.

PERSONAL ASSESSMENT. Needless to say, it becomes exceedingly necessary to understand one's motivations for marriage and the extent to which one is capable of entering into a mature and meaningful relationship. Those who have worked with marital problems have come to recognize that these areas of understanding are frequently at the very heart of much marital unhappiness. It would seem highly profitable, therefore, for persons contemplating marriage to undergo some self-assessment. By so doing it becomes possible to detect facets of the personality which may not be conducive to the building of a meaningful relationship. It is, to be sure, somewhat difficult for one to tell when his motivations or personal organization are or are not conducive to taking part in a meaningful relationship. This is not an area of human experience which lends itself easily to critical inspection. This is especially so since most of us have difficulty facing attitudes in ourselves which are unpleasant. In spite of these formidable problems, however, we do find people who, upon examining both their motivations and those of the prospective mates, frequently discover some new glimpse or additional insight which was previously hidden. When this is accomplished there is at least the possibility of an improvement in the quality of the relationship. Although some relationships may fall apart under the impact of examination, more often than not the elimination of a factor which constituted a hindrance brings with it an improved quality and a relationship which is stronger and more lasting.

SUMMARY

An understanding of the motivations for our actions is important in building meaningful man-woman relationships. Specifically, the motivations which we have for marrying are important determinants of what we expect from marriage and the quality of the relationship that follows. When motivations to marry are the result of immature personality patterns they invariably lead to marital difficulties. Since immaturities are so prevalent in our society today, it becomes important for each person to understand more fully his reasons for marrying.

Some motivations for marriage which reflect personal immaturity and lead to poor marital relationships are as follows: (1) marrying to escape from an unhappy home; (2) marrying to escape from feelings of loneliness; (3) marrying for the purpose of living through others; (4) marrying for material possessions and wealth; and (5) marrying on the rebound.

These motivations for marriage may lead to difficulty because in each case the individual is escaping from some personal problem; thus, the marriage partner is not regarded as an end in himself, but rather as a means to an end. When one marries primarily to escape there is a sense of urgency about marrying; and when marriage is entered into with the feeling that "time is running out," rational judgment and careful evaluation of the marriage are minimized, if not completely absent. Finally, when people use marriage as a means of solving their personal difficulties, they often become bitter and disillusioned. Bitterness and disillusionment occur when it is discovered that neither marriage nor the marital partner can solve the difficulties, instead, the resolution of these personal difficulties is dependent on how adequately the individual himself comes to grips with the problems involved.

QUESTIONS

1. How does the impersonality of life in our society hinder us in appreciating meaningful human relationships? In what manner does impersonality affect our motivations for marriage?

2. How are personal immaturities nurtured in the home? In what manner do these personal immaturities affect our motivations for marriage?
3. Analyze the case of Miss B. and show the relationship between her home life and her motivations for marriage. How could her difficulty have been avoided? How might her difficulties be resolved?
4. Analyze the case of Miss F.A. and show the relationship between her home life and her involvements with boys. Which of Miss F.A.'s personality traits would have to be altered before she might be able to participate in a meaningful relationship? Why?
5. List and describe the five motivations for marriage which tend to lead to difficulty in marriage. Why are these motivations considered to be immature approaches to marriage?
6. Describe the problems which might arise in marriages entered into on the basis of these five immature motivations.
7. On the basis of what you learned in this chapter, list and describe several motivations which in your opinion would constitute a mature basis for marriage.
8. Do you think it is necessary for people contemplating marriage to consider their reasons for doing so? Why? Is it always possible for one to know what his motivations for marriage are? If not, what should one do in order to determine his motivations?
9. If, after consideration, one discovers that his motivations for marriage are immature, what should he do?
10. If the realization that one's motivations for marriage are immature causes personal discomfort, would it not have been better to ignore them to begin with? Why or why not? Explain.

SUGGESTIONS FOR RESEARCH AND RELATED PROJECTS

1. Make a list of all the motivations you can think of that one might have for marrying. Submit this list to several married men and women of various age groups. Have the respondent rate each motivation in terms of its applicability to his own motivations for marriage. Have the respondent give ten points to those motivations which most directly apply to his case, five points to those which have less application to his case, and no points to those which do not apply at all. Do you find any differences between the answers of men and women or between the answers given by the different age groups? If so, how do you explain these differences? Do you feel that these answers represent a realistic picture of what motivated these men and women to marry? Why or why not?

2. Write a short skit depicting a scene in which an engaged couple discuss their future marriage. In the skit have one person represent mature motivations for marrying, and the other, immature motivations. After presenting the skit to the class, have a discussion concerning what problems might arise in this marriage and how these problems might

have been avoided, or how they might now be resolved. It might also be possible to write five short skits as described above, one for each of the five immature motivations discussed in this chapter.

3. Hold a panel discussion on the following topic: "What might be done to help people acquire mature motivations for marriage."

SUGGESTED READINGS

Blood, Robert O., Jr., *Anticipating Your Marriage*, The Free Press, Glencoe, Ill., 1957, Ch. 6, "Deciding When to Get Married."

Cavan, Ruth Shonle, *American Marriage*, Thomas Y. Crowell Co., New York, 1959, Ch. 3, "Personal Readiness for Marriage," and Ch. 7, "Choosing a Compatible Mate."

Horney, Karen, *Self-Analysis*, W. W. Norton and Co., Inc., New York, 1942, Ch. 2, "The Driving Forces in Neuroses," especially pp. 54–72.

Magoun, F. Alexander, *Love and Marriage*, Harper and Brothers, New York, 1948, Ch. 2, "The Nature of Marriage."

Waller, Willard, revised by Reuben Hill, *The Family*, Dryden Press, New York, 1951, Ch. 11, "Selective Mating," especially pp. 194–200 and pp. 206–215.

Love in the man-woman relationship part I

5

In the previous chapter our concern was with immature motivations for marriage and the difficulties which these impose on building a meaningful relationship. Another obstacle which interferes with the development of a meaningful man-woman relationship is the confusion which arises out of the misunderstandings that prevail concerning the nature of love. As we proceed with our material, we will discuss: (1) the significance of love in the human relationship; (2) confusions regarding the nature of love; and (3) the nature of the love experience itself. Also, we will attempt to point out how misunderstandings concerning love may result in problems within the man-woman relationship.

THE SIGNIFICANCE OF LOVE IN THE HUMAN RELATION-SHIP. Although we indicated in an earlier chapter that the American family has not always been concerned with love as a basis for its existence, marked changes have occurred within the last fifty years. These shifts have been manifest not only in the changing basis for family life but in writings which reflect the spirit of the period.[1] Thus some writers have advanced the idea of the fulfillment of love as a human necessity. Other writers have been critical of love's impact on human affairs, but few have denied that it is a reality that all people have to come to terms with. Why the present concern with love? In part, the

[1] Erich Fromm, *The Art of Loving*, Harper and Brothers, New York, 1956.

preoccupation arises out of the place in the marital relationship which love has come to assume. In a more fundamental way, however, it is clear that many people now realize the significance and necessity of love for personal welfare and happiness. The need to express and receive love is recognized not simply because our culture stresses its importance but also because we have come to a greater understanding of the role of love in the life of the individual. As Smiley Blanton suggests:

Love's greatest glory lies in the fact that it alone provides the strength, protection and encouragement without which full growth is impossible. We are all aware of this truth when it comes to the life of a helpless infant. Unfortunately, too many of us ignore its equal applicability to humanity as a whole. Since men and women rarely die before our eyes for lack of love, we assume that they can live well enough without it. We do not stop to think that it is a form of death, when we crawl through our days in the constant shadow of talent needlessly thwarted, of all those fears, illnesses and psychological self-mutilations to which we resort when hate chokes off our normal outlets of development.[2]

Although love is so essential, relatively few people find mature, stable love relationships. As suggested in an earlier chapter, a good many people, markedly cynical, have already abandoned the possibility of finding a mature love relationship even though they marry. Marriage for these persons frequently involves an implicit contractual business relationship in which husband or wife promises certain benefits in return for other benefits. To illustrate this point, let us look at Mr. C., a very aggressive, domineering young man, known around college as a "big man on campus." Mr. C. was a fraternity member and maintained membership in several important campus organizations. He was also actively engaged in campus politics. Mr. C. was contemplating marriage to a young lady who was markedly different from him. She could be described as quiet, sensitive to the needs of others, unassuming, and modest. At the time she appeared for assistance, she spoke of her anxieties regarding her involvement with Mr. C. She complained that he was indifferent to her, would fail to show up for dates, and would explain his behavior only after several days had passed. Most often, his explanations appeared somewhat farfetched and inappropriate. He reported that he either forgot the date or was too engrossed in what he was doing to appear for the date. When Mr. C. did appear on time he seemed preoccupied with other matters, usually his campus involvements. In the actual dating relationship, Mr. C.

[2] From *Love or Perish*, © 1956 by Dr. Smiley Blanton, reprinted by permission of Simon and Schuster, Inc. p. 21.

was emotionally aloof from his girl friend. Necking and petting occurred so infrequently that the young lady found it necessary to complain. Mr. C. appeared for help at the insistence of his girl friend. It was obvious from the first that Mr. C. was uninterested in any real help. His aloofness from the counseling relationship was apparent. When questioned about problems in the relationship, he became defensive and spoke of "those silly ideas of my girl friend." He was certain that with time this girl would come to appreciate his basic qualities. Mr. C. went on to point out that he had his sights set on becoming president of a large business firm. What he needed from marriage, he suggested, was somebody to add the flourishes and extras to his life. By this he meant a neat, attractive wife, not too attractive to men, just attractive enough; one who could entertain socially in a way that would help advance him in his work. Mr. C. cared little for the needs of his future wife. Further, he was unconcerned with love, thought it silly, and felt it would only get in the way of the goals he wished to achieve. The young lady finally married Mr. C. in spite of his almost total unwillingness to examine himself, let alone change. We might add that the young lady has lived unhappily ever after.

Thus, there are those who have abandoned the possibility of a mature love relationship, but even for those who seek mature love, there are many problems to be resolved. To begin with, we are a terribly confused people regarding the nature of love and what it means. Much of this confusion stems from the particular views which men and women hold in regard to love. We refer here to the belief that love is fundamentally unknown, unknowable, and is therefore rooted in magic. Thus, persons who commit themselves to these beliefs view the nature of love as being beyond human comprehension,[3] and feel any attempt to understand the phenomenon is bound to lead to disappointment and frustration.

The fact that love is viewed as belonging to the realm of magic and the unknowable points up interesting contradictions regarding our society. Specifically, it suggests that in spite of all our emphasis on science, our thinking with respect to the nature of love is more characteristic of the primitive than it is of the civilized mind. For, although we are willing to accept the teachings of science when they relate to particular areas of the physical universe, we reject the possibility of similar inquiries into such significant personal phenomena as love. Such anti-scientific attitudes hinder the ultimate contribution which scientific studies may offer with respect to the nature of love.

[3] Andrew G. Truxal and Francis E. Merrill, *The Family in American Culture*, Prentice-Hall, Inc., New York, 1947, pp. 121–130.

The authors are obviously not in sympathy with the point of view which places the understanding of love in the realm of the unknown and unknowable. Indeed, it seems reasonable to state that the belief that love is unknown or unknowable is not only an expression of ignorance, but also an expression of hopelessness, and a fear of facing human experiences realistically. We are reminded of the young man who reported that he wished to be in love and marry but wanted to avoid the process of falling in love. Instead, he hoped that somehow he could fall asleep, awake, and discover that he was already in love and married. Thus, he might somehow magically be spared the problems of doing his own selecting, or actively entering into a relationship and resolving the problems that might exist. We sense in the reaction of this young man a desire to avoid the reality of experiencing the love relationship. Instead, his wish is to assume a passive role, letting the love experience sweep him along without any emotional involvement on his part.

This young man is not unique. There are many people committed to the notion that love is unknowable, who possess similar attitudes of passivity and hopelessness about understanding or facing the dilemmas of the love relationship. Unfortunately, however, there are negative consequences to the possession of these attitudes toward love. For people who are so inclined, an understanding or examination of their love involvements is made unnecessarily difficult and at times impossible.

CONFUSIONS REGARDING THE NATURE OF LOVE.

Falling in Love and Remaining in Love. In turning our attention to specific confusions, we note that a first confusion regarding the nature of love stems from the failure of large numbers of people to appreciate the differences between falling in love and remaining in love. Many assume that if one can fall in love, one is also capable of remaining in love. Nothing could be further from the truth. To fall in love may be relatively easy, since so often it may be based primarily on sexual considerations; to remain in love involves the ability to build and maintain a relationship out of which stability can be realized. In order to accomplish this task it is necessary for one to know what one wants, to understand one's wishes, to be able to maintain consistent feelings, and to respond to the changes and growth of the partner in the relationship. None of this is easily accomplished; and the reader's personal experiences are probably replete with people who were emotionally unable to remain in love. There is the case of the married woman who felt she was in love with her husband only when she was actually with him. Whenever her husband went away, even for only a little while, she would have serious doubts regarding whether or not she was in love with him. During one period in her marriage when her husband entered military service, she was separated from him for a considerable period of time. During this time she had the gravest doubts about her feelings and was considering divorce when her husband came home for a furlough. Once he came home, her confidence in her love for him was temporarily restored. Nevertheless, it is clear that this woman had no real basis for a mature love commitment and regardless of her feelings at the moment, it was exceedingly difficult for her emotionally to remain in love.

A final important consideration with regard to falling in love and remaining in love has to do with the basis of the love relationship, a problem to be discussed more fully later in this chapter. When the basis of one's love rests on an unreal image of the partner, that is, when one sees the other in a way which makes the other appear much better and superior than in fact he is, then the relationship may indeed be fragile. For as contact with the loved one continues, the realities begin to break through and imperfections appear. Under these circumstances the unreal image is shattered; a gradual disillusionment with the love partner occurs and results in a diminution of love feelings.[4] Such disillusionment with the love partner is a common experience for many people. It is indeed unfortunate that many are unaware of how they construct unreal images of others; inevitably these unreal images crumble.

Some writers, in their attempt to emphasize the active participation demanded of people in the maintenance of consistent feelings toward the love relationship, have made marriage appear like a tremendous chore. It is doubtful whether such attitudes were really intended. Nevertheless, in order for the love relationship to be successful, a sensitivity to the dynamics of the relationship is required. This requirement is no different from the requirements of other human relationships.

Self-Love and Love for Others. A second basic confusion regarding the nature of love has to do with the notion that love for self negates the possibility of love for others. Here the confusion is one which comes from a failure to differentiate self-love from narcissism. To be sure, the narcissist (with whom we will deal later) is in love with an

[4] Theodor Reik, *Of Love and Lust,* Farrar, Straus and Cudahy, New York, 1957, p. 82.

idealized image of himself and is therefore not capable of loving others. The prevalence of the confusion between self-love and narcissism is understandable since certain ethical and religious values have been interpreted as requiring sacrifice without regard for self. Thus, signs of personal concern have frequently been interpreted as an inability to have deep feelings for others. Although such a view is prevalent, its logic breaks down on examination. If it is expected that you are to love your neighbor, and in fact, humanity, but not yourself, does this not constitute an inherent contradiction? If you are expected to love others, why exclude yourself, since all of us are members of the human race? The argument here is not for narcissistic absorption with self, but for love of self which is reflected in such attitudes of self-acceptance as: (1) I like what I am; (2) I am a decent person; and (3) I possess dignity and deserve respect. The significance of the capacity for self-love is seen in the now widely held professional view that genuine love for others springs from the ability to care for and love yourself.[5] When you have developed a deep appreciation, respect, and love for what you are, you do not feel the scarcity of love which characterizes the insecure person. Thus, when you feel that love is plentiful rather than in short supply, the energies and feelings formerly bound up with yourself in an egocentric fashion may be turned outward and expressed toward other people.[6]

A consideration of the nature of the love experience is now in order, since such an understanding will enable us to pursue our subsequent discussions with greater clarity.

THE NATURE OF THE LOVE EXPERIENCE. Frequently when behavioral scientists attempt to explain love, they present us with an extensive amount of information about love but very little concerning what love is. And, although such statements as "love is blind," "love is both giving and receiving," or "love is a complex emotional feeling," do tell us something about love, they do very little toward explaining the essential nature of love. We will offer a more specific explanation here, since a fuller understanding is crucial to our present discussion.

Although we are primarily concerned with analyzing the types of love which emerge in the man-woman relationship, we believe that the importance of such an analysis is dependent on a basic understanding of love as it becomes manifest in the broader sense. One method

[5] Fromm, *op. cit.*, pp. 57–63. Harry Stack Sullivan, *Conceptions of Modern Psychiatry*, Second Ed., W. W. Norton and Co., Inc., New York, 1953, pp. 14–27.
[6] *Ibid.*

of arriving at a basic understanding of love is to search for those factors which are found to exist in all types of love. Such an investigation leads to the discovery that different kinds of love have one basic element in common. We refer here to the presence of a conscious or unconscious set of need satisfactions which one derives from a specific object or person, be it home, country, wife, mother, brother, or whatever. By this we simply mean that an individual comes to feel love for a particular object or person because certain conscious or unconscious needs which have come to be important to him are fulfilled. Thus the essential experience of love appears to be rooted in the needs that individuals have, and in a general sense therefore, love may be thought of as an emotional feeling which arises out of a complex composite of need satisfactions.

One way of looking at the relationship between need fulfillment and love is represented in the formulation offered by Theodor Reik.[7] Reik believes that all love arises out of a basic dissatisfaction with oneself.[8] Such dissatisfaction results in the creation of an ego ideal; that is, an image of what one would like to aspire to. The ego ideal's basic characteristic is perfectionism in all qualities deemed important, such as knowledge, manners, or power over people. The ego ideal is always in the process of making demands on the individual to measure up to these perfections. Since the individual always falls short of the fulfillment of the ego ideal there is a pervasive sense of guilt about not measuring up to the standards. Thus, the individual seeks for one in whom the traits of his ego ideal may be experienced. At first there is unconscious envy of those traits which one may see in the other person, since there is a desire for these traits in oneself. When the envy of the person with the traits in the ego ideal is turned into an identification with this person, love emerges. Reik states: "Love is in its essential nature an emotional reaction-formation to envy, possessiveness, and hostility." [9]

In regard to Reik's formulation, we would say that all love does not, in our view, stem from dissatisfaction with self, for such a view negates the possibility of other needs operating, such as healthy needs involved in growth, creativity, and respect. Nevertheless, Reik does present one scheme of need fulfillment and love, and such a scheme

---

[7] Reik, op. cit., p. 32.

[8] Although the authors do not completely agree with Reik's point of view (see p. 108 for our discussion of the relationship between self-acceptance and genuine love for another), it is nevertheless a point of view which warrants mention.

[9] Ibid., p. 66.

does enable us to understand the basis of love for some people; as such it deserves careful consideration. Reik's analysis does, of course, raise an important question that has to do with the kinds of needs people have and the quality of the relationship which emerges. Some may, for example, have needs which result in mature relationships; and others may have needs which result in immature relationships.

Needs and the Man-Woman Relationship. Needs are deemed mature when (1) they contribute to both the intellectual and emotional growth of the members, and (2) when they are rooted in reality. With respect to the first requirement we can assert that when the needs are rooted in marked egocentricity and revolve around an excessive need for flattery, the need to use and exploit others, the need to dominate and control, the need always to be right, and the need to escape from self when the needs are not conducive to the development of a mature relationship. These are not the kinds of needs which allow for sensitivity to others, and for the development of the persons in a relationship. On the other hand, when a relationship is based on needs to be appreciated, respected, to be close emotionally, to be creative and explore, and to be understood, then the relationship is based on needs which contribute to the growth and development of the members and as such the relationship is mature. There is an important lesson to be learned from all this; for most people are quite unaware of their needs. They simply search for someone with whom they feel comfortable, and this is fine as far as it goes. A basic question, however, relates to why we feel comfortable with the other person. What needs are being satisfied? Are these needs conducive to our own growth, or to the growth of the relationship? If not, might they be understood and changed? Let us be specific. There are many instances in which two people with needs that are not conducive to their growth meet and experience love. The case of a man with a need to dominate and a woman who has a need to be dominated is illustrative. These are needs that are complementary and it may be that a marriage based on such needs would have little overt conflict. This is certainly one measure of success. Nevertheless, we can afford to aspire to something more than an absence of overt conflict and ask ourselves whether such a relationship can contribute to the growth of the individual partners. Obviously it cannot. For the dominant partner, there is a need to be right and to control. Thus, he is afraid to learn and profit through experience. Instead, he must impose his will on others. In turning our attention to the woman with a need to be dominated, we see a person who looks for someone to take over her life.

Thus, the center of gravity, so to speak, is not in her but entirely in her love object. For such people the love object is expected to fulfill all desires and to take all of the responsibility for the relationship itself. The presence of this type of need in a love relationship hinders the capacity to grow, to make judgments and decisions, to participate as an adult in the responsibilities of family living.

With respect to our second requirement for mature needs, namely that needs be rooted in reality, we can point out that it is essential to determine whether the needs we have are realistic, in order to ascertain the degree of maturity involved. For example, it is obvious that people who have needs to see love as a mystical force which solves all problems have unreal conceptions; thus, their love involvements tend to be immature and childlike. People who have needs to achieve without making efforts, have needs not rooted in reality. The same would apply to people who feel entitled to be waited on hand and foot and who always seek special privileges.

We can say, therefore, that when a relationship is based either on needs rooted in unreality, or on needs which themselves are of such a limited character that they are not oriented toward the intellectual and emotional development of the couple, the relationship tends to be immature.

We can illustrate our point further by presenting a grouping of representative needs found among many middle-class people which are consistent with our requirements for reality as well as their intrinsic contribution to personality growth.[10]

1. Companionship. In a mature relationship, the individuals have needs to share in common interests, to explore and stimulate each other's personalities, and to have sympathetic understanding for each other.

2. Freedom of Communication and Activity. In a mature relationship the individuals have needs to be accepted for what they are. There is a minimum of pretense, thus communication and activity become spontaneous and free.

3. Emotional Interdependence. In a mature relationship the individuals have needs to be related to one another in manifest affection, tenderness, and trust. Thus, need fulfillment is reciprocated in that each party to the relationship is giving need fulfillment to the other and receiving need fulfillment from the other.

4. Sexual Strivings. In a mature relationship the individuals have

[10] Ernest W. Burgess, Harvey J. Locke, *The Family*, American Book Co., New York, 2nd ed., 1960, pp. 322–326.

needs not only for physical demonstrativeness, but to integrate sexual strivings with the total relationship in order that it not become over-balanced or egocentric.

The foregoing list of needs fulfills our requirements for mature satisfactions, since each need is rooted in realistic expectations and gives promise of contributing to the growth of both individuals and their subsequent relationship. Many love relationships, however, fall short of meeting these requirements. The adolescent love relationship is a case in point. Frequently adolescent relationships are fraught with confusions and misunderstandings—with parents insisting that their adolescent son or daughter cannot be in love, since he or she does not know what love is. These assertions invariably bring forth bewilderment and resentment from the person whose feelings are being diagnosed. The young person who feels an intense attraction for a member of the opposite sex has a strange reaction indeed when he is informed that he is not really in love. The point is that such experiences as puppy love, infatuation, romantic love, platonic love, are forms of love, in that each consists of a pattern of need satisfaction which one derives from another. However, in each of these cases the love is an immature love, in the respect that the needs being fulfilled have an unreal quality and, furthermore, are limited in character so that intellectual and emotional development are not enhanced. For example, the need satisfactions found in puppy love or infatuation, instead of being based on several of the needs discussed, are limited to physical attraction or the need to escape from the problems of adolescence. Further there is considerable idealization and distortion of the reality of the persons involved, with a tendency for each to make the other better and more glamorous than he is. Such needs are hardly conducive to the overall emotional and intellectual development of the persons involved.[11]

We would like to point out that an understanding of the personal needs involved will enable one to understand relationships which otherwise make little sense. For example, there is the case of an attractive young lady, intelligent and well informed, who fell in love with a young man who mistreated her repeatedly. He stood her up on dates and when he did appear, he was late. More often than not he became intoxicated on the date and was unable to get home on his own. He borrowed money from the young lady without any real interest in returning it. All signs pointed to an irresponsible individual

[11] Erik H. Erikson, *Childhood and Society*, W. W. Norton and Co., Inc., New York, 1950, p. 228.

with a very uncertain future. One would normally expect the young lady to abandon the relationship. Instead she became more desperate and continued to pursue the relationship. Why? Obviously there were certain personal needs which the relationship fulfilled, although it is clear that the relationship was not a good one. In this instance the needs were deeply repressed. When they were understood, however, the young lady discovered that she had a need to belittle herself. Thus without being consciously aware of what she was doing, she set out to find a boy who would embarrass and belittle her. This situation is illustrative of many that might be presented, and serves to illustrate our point with respect to the significance of understanding the needs which produce particular kinds of love relationships.

Mature and Immature Love—a Continuum. The differences between mature and immature love are, of course, a matter of degree rather than kind. Thus, it may be possible to think of mature and immature love as representing opposite extremes of a continuum, with the various degrees of maturity in the man-woman relationships falling somewhere in between. Put another way, if we knew enough about the pattern of need satisfaction in a specific relationship we could plot the degree to which the relationship approximates the characteristics of mature love, or the degree to which it does not, and place it on a continuum as indicated below.

Extremely Immature	Very Immature	Moderately Immature	Moderately Mature	Very Mature	Extremely Mature

From all that we have said it should be clear that whether or not one is capable of experiencing mature love is not necessarily a matter of chronological age, but rather of emotional development. There are many people well on in years who are incapable of experiencing anything other than immature love feelings. There is, for example, the extreme illustration of a couple engaged for thirty years. They were going steady, to be sure, and reported that theirs was a serious relationship. Honorable intentions on both sides were reported. Marriage had not taken place since the man in the relationship felt it necessary to support his parents and did not believe he could support a wife and his parents. Needless to say this man, who was fifty-five at the time, and the woman, who was fifty-three, had an exceedingly immature relationship. The man was known to have been tied emotionally to his parents and to be fearful, basically, of marriage. The woman was an exceedingly dependent and insecure person, afraid to give up even this relationship lest she not find another.

Further, marital status is not indicative of the degree of maturity. Many single persons are capable of mature unions. On the other hand, there are persons, married for many years, who are totally incapable of having a mature love relationship. There is the case of a couple, married for fifteen years, who have worked out a pattern of life in which there is a minimum of interaction between them. The man, a successful business executive, spends as much time as he can away from home. Whenever it is possible for him to remain at home, he consistently thinks of diversions in the form of club activities and meetings to keep him from having any interaction with his wife. So impersonal is his relationship with his wife and home that he prefers to eat in restaurants rather than at home. Left to his own devices he would eat all three meals in a restaurant. The wife, who is likewise a success in her chosen profession, prefers more of a home life but has given up the possibility of a meaningful relationship with her husband and has come to follow a similar pattern of non-involvement.

SUMMARY

Although love is regarded as an extremely important aspect of the man-woman relationship, some people abandon the hope of ever finding it. To them marriage becomes a contractual business relationship in which certain benefits are exchanged.

Even for those who seek love, however, confusions regarding the nature of love arise. These are due to the belief that love is mystical, magical, and therefore unknowable. Such an anti-scientific view suggests not only ignorance but hopelessness about understanding an important aspect of human involvement.

A first confusion concerning the nature of love is found in the failure to understand the difference between falling in love and remaining in love; it is frequently assumed that attaining the former automatically insures the latter. This is an erroneous idea, since remaining in love requires the ability to build and maintain a stable relationship. Thus stability, predictability, and maturity are necessary for the individuals involved.

A second confusion concerning love is found in the notion that love for self negates the possibility of love for others. This confusion arises out of the failure to differentiate self-love from narcissism. In narcissism one is in love with a glorified image of self, and one is unable to love others. But self-love, per se, need not involve this complete absorption in oneself. Instead, self-love is founded in such basic attitudes as liking what you are, and feeling that you are a person who possesses dignity and deserves respect. Believing these things about oneself brings about a security which enables one to feel that he is not merely a receiver in the love relationship but that he has something to offer in return.

In turning to the nature of love, we noted that love is an emotional feeling which arises out of a complex composite of need satisfactions. Thus, the essential experience of love is rooted in the needs that individuals have. It was suggested that love relationships differ with respect to degree of maturity involved. The degree to which a love relationship may be regarded as mature or immature is determined by the degree to which the needs involved are conducive to the intellectual and emotional development of the couple; and the degree to which the needs present are rooted in reality. A grouping of such needs as: (1) companionship, (2) freedom of communication and activity, (3) emotional interdependence, and (4) sexual strivings is illustrative of a mature need pattern, since the needs contained therein are realistic and sufficiently broad to provide for the overall emotional and intellectual development of the persons involved.

QUESTIONS

1. How has the place of love in the man-woman relationship changed in the past fifty years?
2. Why do some people abandon the hope of ever finding love in their man-woman relationships?
3. Is it true that those who seek a mature love relationship may confront problems in so doing? If so, what problems do they confront?
4. What is the difference between "falling in love" and "remaining in love"?
5. How do you account for the lack of systematic study concerning love as a human experience?
6. What is the difference between narcissism and self-love? Give illustrations.
7. In its broadest sense, explain what love is.
8. What are the two basic qualities of needs which are conducive to mature love? Give examples.
9. List and fully describe the four needs found among middle-class people which are illustrative of a mature relationship. Why are these needs considered to be significant for a mature relationship?
10. What are the consequences of accepting the following point of view: "Love is an unknown and unknowable force"?

SUGGESTIONS FOR RESEARCH AND RELATED PROJECTS

1. Analyze the marital relationship of a few couples whom you know well. To the best of your knowledge and without identifying the people involved, attempt to determine the degree to which each relationship may be considered to be mature. Illustrate this by means of the kinds of

needs being satisfied. For those relationships which you regard as immature (if any) show what changes would have to occur if, in your opinion, they were to be regarded as mature relationships.

2. Write two brief skits: one portraying a scene depicting a couple with an immature love relationship; the other for a couple with a mature love relationship. After having presented both skits to the class, have the class members point out why each was considered to be immature and mature respectively.

3. Hold a panel discussion on the following topic: "The study of love as a human experience is nonsense."

4. Analyze a man-woman relationship in which you have participated. Attempt to objectively determine the needs which were being fulfilled in this relationship and the degree to which you now regard it as having been a mature relationship.

SUGGESTED READINGS

Bee, Lawrence S., *Marriage and Family Relations,* Harper and Brothers, New York, 1959, Ch. 6, "The Meaning of Love."

Ellis, Albert, "A Study of Human Love Relationships," *J. genet. Psychol.,* **75** (1949), pp. 61–71.

Magoun, F. Alexander, *Love and Marriage,* Harper and Brothers, New York, 1948, Ch. 1, "The Nature of Love."

Reik, Theodor, *A Psychologist Looks at Love,* Farrar and Rinehart, Inc., New York, 1944.

Waller, Willard, revised by Reuben Hill, *The Family,* Dryden Press, New York, 1951, Ch. 7, "The Sentiment of Love."

Love in the man-woman relationship part II

6

In the present chapter we plan to continue our analysis of love by presenting a discussion of the attitudes which engender immature love relationships, how one develops the capacity to love maturely, and finally a discussion of persons who are unable to love maturely.

ATTITUDES WHICH ENGENDER IMMATURE LOVE. The reader is undoubtedly familiar with many of the beliefs associated with immature love, for example: (1) the idea of the one and only; (2) the idea of love at first sight; and (3) the idea that love solves all problems. An examination of all three of these ideas points up a connection between the ideas themselves and a logic which underlies them. The idea of the one and only suggests that destiny has ordained someone for you. If you wonder how you will recognize the person when you meet him or her, you are confronted by the second component, namely love at first sight. Here you learn that you can tell in a moment when the proper person has been met. You are told to look for inner signs, a feeling of excitement, an increase in pulse and heart rate. Finally, if you are concerned about incompatibilities, wide differences in background, and personal tastes, you learn that these are not important since love will solve all problems. Thus do all of these ideas constitute a point of view which some people hold regarding the nature of love. Furthermore, once you accept the premise expressed in point one, you inevitably are lulled into accepting the remaining ideas.

As an example of such immature involvement, one of the authors recalls a young lady, a college graduate, reared in an upper middle-class family who met and claimed she was in love with a lower-class semi-literate truck driver. After a short period of acquaintance, the young lady made plans to marry. Her family was quite upset since the relationship was not what they had hoped for and appeared to be fraught with dangers. It took no family expert to predict problems for this couple. The young lady, at the insistence of her parents, appeared for counseling. In discussing the obvious social and personal incompatibilities she was asked how she hoped to overcome these differences.

Her answer: "Oh, they will work out."

Counselor's question: "Why will they work out—because you want them to?"

Her answer: "I just know they will, if you knew how much we loved each other, you would see that it will all work out."

The young lady was insistent that the marriage take place, and so after a short period of time the couple married. Within three months the marriage was terminated by divorce.

Even more common than the belief that love will overcome marked social incompatibilities are cases in which people assume that love will overcome serious emotional difficulties. It is, of course, possible for mature love relationships sometimes to aid in the alleviation of problems imposed by diverse social backgrounds or emotional conflicts, but it is unrealistic to assume that even a good love relationship will eliminate problems of this type.

Origin of Immature Attitudes toward Love. Understanding the origin of immature attitudes toward love is in itself an interesting pursuit. Needless to say, our society in general plays an important role in their development, but in a more specific way the movies, popular ballads, and certain aspects of literature are significant. With respect to the movies, we note that love at first sight is portrayed as being a valid index of love. Hero and heroine meet and in a flash it is clear that they were meant for each other. The idea that there is a one and only is frequently brought home by the introduction of discord between hero and heroine. Each attempts to find happiness with another only to return to the original love with the realization that happiness can only be found with one. This general theme is likewise apparent in many television programs. There is little that corresponds to reality in any of these media when it comes to dealing with love. Not only are the ideas of love unreal, even the actors and actresses are atypical and unusual. Invariably they represent persons unusually handsome or attractive. Make-believe has a field day.

Popular ballads, with their reference to the unreal, offer us another excellent source of immature attitudes toward love. During the depression years, and continuing until World War II, the phenomenon of the song sheet was in vogue. The song sheet was, as the name implies, a rather large sheet which contained printed lyrics for the popular ballads of the day. In the large urban centers large numbers of these sheets were sold. This suggests that there was some personal satisfaction derived in singing the lyrics to the tune of an orchestra on the radio. It has been claimed that the sale of the song sheet was related to the need to lose oneself in fantasy and find happiness in love in the midst of a grim social and economic environment. There would certainly appear to be some truth in such an assertion.

With respect to literary forms, novels, short stories, and magazine articles, there is also a marked tendency toward propagating immature attitudes regarding love. It is frequently assumed that immature love themes are portrayed only in cheap pulp magazines. Nothing could be further from the truth. As a matter of fact in some ways the pulp magazines may carry even fewer tales involving immature love attitudes of the type we have described than other publications, since so often they carry sordid tales which end in disaster for all parties concerned. Thus the so-called better ladies' magazines may be the more serious offenders. Not only are immature attitudes toward love carried in adult literature but these are equally apparent in the books of children, particularly fairy tales in which the prince marries the maid of inferior social status and both live happily ever after.

The fact that millions of dollars each year are poured into products which promote immature attitudes toward love suggests that these attitudes still have considerable appeal for the populace. Regardless of what is known intellectually, large numbers of people still find satisfaction in these immature attitudes toward love and have incorporated much of what is implied by these attitudes into both their thinking and behavior. The likelihood of this is especially apparent when we realize that from the time we were children, we have been bombarded from all sides by immature attitudes toward love. Few people indeed are completely emancipated from any of these attitudes which inevitably lead to turmoil in the man-woman relationship. Having pointed this out, we recognize immediately that some people cling to immature attitudes toward love more than others do. There are those, of course, who are so cynical that they view with disdain any concept of love. There are others who are simply lacking in knowledge. Nevertheless, aside from these kinds of people, it is likely that the person who rejects these essentially immature attitudes toward love is more secure and capable of self-acceptance than is the person who must cling to them. Why this is so should not be difficult to understand. Since these immature attitudes tend to be replete with magic and unreality, they offer something special to the individual who feels insecure and unworthy. For, in essence, the philosophy which underlies these attitudes informs you that no matter how you may feel, be it homely, stupid or awkward, there is someone destined for you—the one and only. When you meet him (or her) you will know, since the meeting will be associated with certain kinds of feelings and experiences—love at first sight. If there are difficulties, they will be resolved since love solves all things. Thus for the person who feels lonely, homely, insecure or in general out of tune with things, there is the promise of love, marriage, and happiness through a faith and belief in these attitudes, and a very real identification with these attitudes therefore emerges.[1]

There is the case of a very attractive young lady, age eighteen, who was forced to lead a very sheltered life due to the fears of her parents who wanted to protect her from "unscrupulous men." Unfortunately the young lady came to look upon herself as a misfit. She came to believe that there must be something very wrong with her since her parents were so insistent on keeping men away from her presence. With such needs to compensate for her own feelings of inferiority, she soon became committed to an immature view of love in which she conceived of a one and only who would rescue her from her turmoil.

The reassurance which immature attitudes provide is terribly important for these insecure, lonely people, since at heart they feel despised, unlovable, and unwanted. Furthermore, such attitudes of self-effacement are indeed unfortunate since they so often involve considerable personal misery, imply a fundamental rejection of self, in fact an active need to cover up what the individual is, both from himself and from others. Even when these people marry, their inability to accept themselves, as well as their fundamental lack of being in touch with reality, is bound to cause many problems and limit the personal happiness which might be achieved in the marital relationship.

[1] Robert F. Winch, *The Modern Family*, Henry Holt and Co., New York, 1952, p. 367.

Attitudes Which Engender Mature Love. Attitudes which are conducive to mature love, we notice, differ markedly from those associated with immature love. To begin with, the process of falling in love is stripped of its unreality and magic. It has little to do with love at first sight, or the view that love solves all problems. Instead, love develops out of the attractions which people feel, and attractions emerge out of human interaction. Attractions, as previously noted, are rooted in particular kinds of need satisfactions. Finally, the entire process of falling in love and remaining in love is seen as a dynamic one which involves adjustment and readjustment to one another. These latter views, just expressed, are most characteristic of persons who have developed a capacity to fall in love maturely.

THE DEVELOPMENT OF THE CAPACITY TO LOVE MATURELY. The capacity to love another maturely is rooted in a wide variety of personal and social influences which begin at birth. The process of developing the capacity to love maturely is therefore not a mysterious process for it develops out of specific types of human values and relationships which are recognized and understood as operating within the context of society. These include the family social climate and familial interpersonal involvements.

At the outset we can assert that whenever the society in which one lives espouses values which lead to superficial and shallow living, the likelihood of mature love relationships developing will be reduced. An inspection of our society reveals that it emphasizes several values which impose obstacles to the development of mature love relationships. For example, our society is one which is impressed by externals and appearances. Our culture places more emphasis on glamour and sophistication than it does on integrity, or responsibility, or the capacity to love. Thus we are much less concerned with the inner nature of people. Such attitudes are facilitated by the fact that modern man views himself and others as commodities, a view in which one person gives something in order to receive something in return; here a deep emotional commitment to a human relationship is avoided.[2] Moreover, the materialistic and competitive values which characterize life in our society are hardly conducive to the development of the capacity to love maturely. Materialism, when overemphasized in the man-women relationship, may give the erroneous impression that material possessions insure love. This point is illustrated by the man who built his wife a beautiful home, bought her a new automobile, employed a

[2] Erich Fromm, *The Art of Loving,* Harper and Brothers, New York, 1956, Ch. 1.

maid, and gave her an unlimited expense account. In spite of all these material advantages, however, he discovered that she was taking large amounts of tranquillizers and was quite unhappy in the marriage. He was at a loss to understand his wife's unhappiness since "he had given her all the possessions a woman could desire." In terms of his materialistic values this man had provided for his wife. Nevertheless, in the process of accumulating such wealth, he was seldom home and had an exceedingly poor interpersonal relationship with his wife.

With respect to competitiveness as a value we must note that frequently competitiveness may be so ingrained that it results in certain destructive patterns bringing about marked egocentricity; here people step on others in order to achieve certain ends. Such patterns when brought into the home are incompatible with demands of a mature love relationship.

The social values which we have described are not restricted to specific areas of living, but are pervasive in all the things in which we engage. If one lives superficially without a deep commitment to life in general, it becomes difficult to love fully and deeply. Thus, at some level the values in the social order become a significant factor in the development of the individual's capacity to love.

In turning our attention to the family, we can point out that these relationships are recognized as being the most significant ones in the development of the individual's capacity to love maturely. We may ask what are the minimal family essentials necessary for the development of the individual's capacity to love? In general, the familial climate must be one in which love as a human experience is valued, with an environment in which the actions of persons within the family reflect such positive attitudes. The positive attitudes toward love are contagious and are easily incorporated into the personality. Therefore, the emphasis which the family gives to the importance of love as a human experience is significant in determining the individual's receptivity for expressing or receiving love. For example, when one is reared in a home where the "cult of manliness" prevails—that is, where love is looked upon as a sign of femininity and weakness, and is therefore undesirable—certain consequences tend to occur. In such a home the individual woman or man internalizes negative attitudes toward the desirability of love. This may lead to a rejection of love as a human experience; or what happens more often—results in an ambivalent reaction, that is, where one both wishes for and rejects love. Such ambivalence invariably causes inner turmoil and produces immature love involvements.

Negative attitudes toward becoming involved in love relationships may come not only from direct indoctrination, but also from the witnessing of the disappointments which others have endured because they have been in love. The child who witnesses the lifelong frustrations of his mother, who loves an alcoholic father, may come to feel that the price one pays for love may not be worth the satisfactions derived. Neither are familial situations characterized by lifelong tensions and anxieties conducive to positive attitudes toward love. Needless to say, family experiences may also be positive in that they contribute to a healthy acceptance and a desire for love.

Perhaps more important than the familial situations previously described are the personal interactions between the child and adults in the family environment which are so significant for the development of the capacity to love.

We note in these specific familial relationships that the development of the capacity to love maturely is initially nurtured by the relationships with one's parents, and adult siblings. When these have been favorable, and of a particular order, the essential foundation for the capacity to love maturely has been aided greatly. Let us consider three important periods involved in the development of one's capacity to love.

Period I: Infancy. During the first period in the development of the capacity to love maturely it is essential for the child to have a set of consistent, dependable relationships with its mother. The mother is the first adult to initiate the child into a human emotional relationship. When these initial experiences are satisfactory, devoid of inconsistency, rejection, or separation through death or divorce, the child begins to sense a feeling of trust in human relationships. The relationship between mother and child is an involved one calling forth a high degree of maturity on the part of the mother. It involves care for the physical needs as well as the emotional needs for warmth and security; and a successful relationship at this level involves the mother's ability to care for all of these things. Although it is difficult to separate physical needs from emotional needs in early life, it seems reasonable to assert that at the outset of the child's life the physical needs, that is, food and protection from all those elements that create fear to the physical organism, are as important as the emotional needs. It is difficult for an adult to gain a clear picture of how the child perceives the world, but the fact that the world would be formidable and somewhat frightening to an infant is well recognized. Thus it has been asserted that the earliest fears which the child has are fears about the destruction of its physical being; [3] these fears are easily engendered when physical needs are not met. When both the physical and emotional needs are satisfied, then the earliest relationship for the infant has been one associated with social trust that is trust in the environment.

When the infant demonstrates an ease at feeding and a depth of sleep, we have the first evidence of social trust in the environment. The fear of physical and emotional abandonment is beginning to disappear and such reduction of fear becomes associated with a willingness to let the mother out of sight, without anxiety or rage. Social trust occurs most readily when the infant can count on what will happen when it is in need. In addition it should be noted that the development of social trust is not simply a matter of pouring large amounts of food and love into the infant; social trust depends also on the manner in which these are accomplished. An essentially insensitive mother, for example, may force large amounts of food into a child and produce added discomfort and tension. A sensitive mother, on the other hand, will be aware of the infant's individual needs and behave accordingly.[4] The same principle of sensitivity applies to the demonstration of the mother's love for the infant since it involves a delicate balance of giving enough love to avoid the problems of overprotection and/or rejection. Such sensitivity to individual infant needs is believed by some to be associated with the infant's developing a sense of identity. This is to say that the mother's sensitivity to the infant's needs begins to create in the infant an awareness of himself.[5]

Finally, it should be noted that once social trust has emerged in the infant, then the infant develops the necessary courage to explore interactions with persons other than the mother, since he feels safe and secure in his surroundings.

Blanton summarizes several important points regarding the overall reaction of the infant to the environment.

Adults have in the past been misled into assuming that the child, because it lacks the power of speech, also lacks power of perception. The truth is that the human infant, like any primitive animal, is marvelously aware of everything that affects its welfare. It has the capacity to read what one may call our "muscle tensions"—those silent, but eloquent, betrayers of our true emotional attitudes.

It is through these muscle tensions that the mother transmits her true

[3] Melanie Klein, *The Psycho-Analysis of Children*, The Hogarth Press Ltd., London, 1954.

[4] Erik H. Erikson, *Childhood and Society*, W. W. Norton, New York, 1950, p. 219.

[5] Erikson, *op. cit.*, pp. 221–229.

feelings to her child. And it is through her manner and attitude while caring for it that the child learns to develop security or fear. To the adult, feeding and dressing a baby may appear as routine duties without significance. But to the infant, these apparently innocuous events are momentous adventures which enable it to discover the nature and meaning of the outside world. They represent the impact of environment, affording the child its first experiences of pleasure and pain, of gratification and frustration, of love and hate, security and fear.

The newborn infant is by itself unprepared to evaluate these terrifying experiences. It is torn between its own selfish instinctual impulses and the outward demands that are suddenly imposed without warning. The mother is the only one who can guide the harassed little creature through the seething emotional whirlpool. Her love is the child's only possible reward for the painful sacrifices and adjustments it is called upon to make. The infant registers her approval or disapproval as a seismograph catches the faintest tremor of the earth. The mother's confidence becomes the child's confidence; her antagonism, a shattering catastrophe.

Psychiatric research has shown that the child's success or failure in negotiating these hazardous first steps depends largely on the parent's emotional attitudes. An anxious young mother, for example, may try her best to conceal her agitated feelings, but through her muscle tensions the infant will perceive the true state of affairs infallibly. It may react by nursing badly, and indigestion will follow. If the mother's disturbed condition persists, the child may form symptoms of serious illness. I have seen infants who, at the age of only two months, had already developed real neuroses because of the way they had been handled by their mothers and fathers. The infants had absorbed the parents' anxieties like a blotter.[6]

Period II: Childhood. A second important period in the child's development of the capacity to love maturely occurs at the time when his concept of self develops. During this period it becomes possible for the individual to differentiate himself from others and to engage in active role taking, which involves taking over attitudes from others. It is difficult to ascertain precisely at what age role taking starts and a concept of the self originates, but it has been variously estimated as beginning somewhere between the second and third years of life. Although role taking is a continuous process throughout life, and one which is essential to much social learning, it is of special significance for our discussion since it explains how the child takes over feelings of love which parents and adults in the environment express toward it. The feelings from others are internalized when the child can imagine itself in place of the mother or father and take over what it feels these adults feel in relation to itself.[7]

[6] Smiley Blanton, *op. cit.*, pp. 92–94.

[7] Charles H. Cooley, *Human Nature and the Social Order*, Charles Scribner's Sons, New York, 1902, pp. 152–153. George Herbert Mead, *Mind, Self, and Society*, University of Chicago Press, Chicago, 1934, pp. 135–226.

Child places himself in position of parent

Child takes over parental attitudes toward himself

Figure 2

In Figure 2, note the process whereby the child places himself in the position of the parent and then reacts toward itself as it assumes the parent to feel. The child may come to take over positive or negative attitudes, that is, I am lovable, or I am unlovable. It is generally assumed that these early experiences with the mother and other adults with whom this can occur are fairly basic in establishing the child's capacity for love. When the child feels that it is loved and lovable, the social trust previously mentioned becomes more firmly implanted. Moreover, the child comes to view the world in a light of acceptance and warmth rather than hostility and rejection. When the child has love for himself and feels that he is loved by others, he does not constantly have to search for affirmation from others. He may turn his energies outward, utilizing them for the acceptance and love of others. Thus, when the child knows emotionally how it feels to be loved, this feeling may be expressed toward others.

Period III. Preadolescence and adolescence. A third significant period which prepares the child for his capacity to love maturely has been described as occurring during preadolescence, between the ages of eight to twelve and extending on into adolescence.[8] It is during this period that some of the egocentricity which was so completely bound up with infancy and childhood is reduced. Thus, if one's life has been characterized by love and social trust it becomes possible to express love toward another and to derive personal pleasure from

[8] Harry Stack Sullivan, *Conceptions of Modern Psychiatry*, The William Alanson White Psychiatric Foundation, Washington, 1947, p. 20.

the fact that someone else feels secure and loved. As greater personal security evolves and egocentricity is reduced, such love grows. The expression of such love has been described as initially felt in relation to persons who are similar, such as members of the same sex.[9] This love for members of one's own sex may result from the fact that a person is more able to identify with his own sex grouping than with the opposite sex grouping. Consequently, he initially may feel safer sharing love with those of his own sex (the known); later, however, his love is expanded to include members of the opposite sex.

In the final analysis the capacity to love another person maturely is also expressed in a capacity to have love for people in general. The process of the transfer of love from self to others is accomplished easily if love is not arrested or fixated, that is, when it does not become too tied to oneself as in narcissism or to one's parents as in parental fixation, or one's own sex as in homosexuality.

TABLE 3

Periods in Developing a Capacity to Love Maturely *

Period	Development	Love Object
Infancy	Initial development of security or insecurity, social trust, or social distrust.	Mother
Childhood	Initial development of social self.	Family members
Preadolescence and Adolescence	Love objects broaden to include those outside family.	Peers Phase 1—homosexual Phase 2—heterosexual

* The stages described above are not intended to include all details. They are merely designed to present the broad outline within which the processes described occur.

Thus, infancy, childhood, and preadolescence-adolescence are three essential periods in the development of the individual's capacity to love maturely, and we hasten to add that much can occur during these periods to retard this development. When the early relationships between mother and infant break down, that is, when there is too little attention or too much attention, then patterns not conducive to the development of the capacity to love maturely may appear. If the infant is neglected or rejected then the emotional relationship with the mother is associated with insecurity or withdrawal from love involve-

[9] *Ibid.,* pp. 14–27.

ments with human beings. If there is overprotection there is the difficulty of prolonging egocentricity, making it difficult to share mature love with others.

Likewise, during the period of childhood it is necessary for the family members to extend a "balanced" love toward the child. This point is summarized by Blanton, who states:

> This is the crux of the problem that faces all conscientious parents. At what point of the child's scale will they find the "adequate" mark on which to balance their love? If they are too harsh in their demands upon the child and do not give him enough love, he will be crippled in his ability to cope with his environment. He may become sullen and backward, or rebellious and overaggressive. In either case he will feel rejected and robbed of his due, thus creating a permanent distortion of his personality and his faith in love.
>
> Equally harmful effects will follow if the parents lavish too much love upon the child. He may become too strongly dependent in his emotional life, requiring a constant support and protection that will weaken his capacity to face stern realities alone. He may grow to feel dominated by his parents' love, and to resent the price he is compelled to pay in return. In that case he will learn to fear love as a burden and to hate all those who make its claims upon him.[10]

Further, when role taking starts and self-attitudes begin to emerge, there is always the danger that negative self-attitudes will become internalized. When this development occurs then the individual sees himself as being essentially unloved and unlovable. With such a view of his self it is difficult for the person to feel that others are in love with him, thus what love he does feel is always shaky and insecure. Finally, it is difficult for such people to love others since they operate in a world in which they feel love to be in short supply. Thus they are, so to speak, "stingy with love" and keep it to themselves. When the initial stages we have described have not been passed through successfully, it is difficult to lose one's self-centeredness in order to relate to the needs of others.

The patterns of parental acceptance or rejection have still further implications for the capacity to love maturely, since they may be associated with the way in which one relates to the opposite sex. The girl who finds her father harsh and demanding, finds it difficult to relate at a later age to a man without being fearful or intimidated. The boy who discovers that he can never please his mother, frequently finds women a source of frustration. Thus, the early concepts about men and women which emerge in part from parent-child relationships are important in the individual's development of the capacity to love.

[10] Smiley Blanton, op. cit., p. 97.

Furthermore, the kinds of attitudes derived from one's siblings and peers may also be significant in one's capacity to love the opposite sex. Attitudes of depreciation about members of the opposite sex are not conducive to the expression of love.

We cannot conclude this section without emphasizing that in a rather fundamental way the development of the capacity to love maturely extends itself into many other aspects of life. For, as we have pointed out, the individual who is prepared to love others is first and foremost one who possesses a healthy self-image and is therefore one who is not readily afraid of people. Such a person does not fear human involvement or the new experiences which emerge out of such involvement. He has the capacity to grow, to expand his horizons, and in a sense to pursue the quest for continued discovery of what he is. As such, to be prepared for mature love means also to be prepared for full participation in the experiences of life.[11]

Our discussion in this chapter has centered around the essential differences between mature and immature love as well as the development of the capacity to love maturely. It might be well at this time to summarize for the reader some of the essential differences between the two types of love. Such a summary will not only synthesize many of the things we have said, but may also assist the reader who is interested in self-examination or evaluation. Thus, as the reader moves through this material, he will note many opportunities to evaluate the nature of his own involvements. It should be clear that immature love relationships lead to instability and successive difficulties. The mature love relationships afford the greatest opportunities for stability and growth in the marital union.

TABLE 4

A Comparison of Significant Characteristics which Engender Immature and Mature Love

Immature	Mature
1. Love arises through the ideas of the one and only, love at first sight, and love wins out over all.	1. Love is an emergent experience which grows out of interaction, with a realistic understanding of the relationship.
2. The love relationship is characterized by considerable ambivalence, with alternate feelings of attraction, indifference, or repulsion. Such feelings of ambivalence are	2. The love relationship is characterized by relatively consistent feelings once the relationship has been established. Although the mature love relationship may be char-

[11] Erikson, *op. cit.*, pp. 228–231.

TABLE 4 (*Continued*)

Immature	Mature
frustrating for the person who feels ambivalent; and perhaps even more frustrating to the person who experiences ambivalence in the partner. The person who is on the receiving end of the ambivalence frequently develops considerable hostility and resentment.	acterized by some ambivalence, it is seldom a pattern in the relationship, and when it is present it is usually related to some objective change in the relationship rather than inner doubts without foundation.
3. The love relationship is rooted primarily in sexual attraction. The concern is with personal, sexual satisfaction. A pronounced tendency for sexual involvement to remain static is present since the quality of the involvement is egocentric. The tendency here is for people to avoid evaluating their capability of loving another in the complete sense. Thus there tends to be little recognition that love involves a capacity to love and to be loved, both of which have to be developed like other human attributes. To be able to love another human being consistently with completeness involves an emotional commitment and a high degree of personal integration devoid of the immaturities and personal difficulties discussed in the present chapter.	3. The love relationship is concerned with sexual satisfaction which is one aspect of the total relationship. Sexual involvement is not static but takes on more meaning as the relationship evolves, since there is a pronounced tendency to be concerned with the sexual and non-sexual needs of one another. The sexual involvement is much more relationship centered then egocentric.
4. The love relationship is characterized by considerable jealousy and insecurity with considerable fears regarding the continuance of the relationship.	4. The love relationship is characterized by mutual trust, feelings of confidence, and security in each other.
5. The love relationship tends to be exploitative with considerable using of each other for own ends.	5. The love relationship is oriented toward acceptance of each other as persons deserving dignity and respect. There is an absence of using each other as commodities.
6. The love relationship is characterized by considerable idealiza-	6. The love relationship is characterized by an identification, and

Immature	Mature

tion based on fantasy, with marked tendency to distort the reality of one another and to fall in love with the distorted image.

7. The love relationship is characterized by marked tendency to change the partner and to impose one's values on the partner without regard to the other's wishes.

8. The love feeling is characterized by sensing that one may be in love with more than one member of the opposite sex at one time. There is the case of a young lady who was engaged to a man who was employed in a community about 100 miles from her home. The fiancé visited every week end and the young lady reported that she always had a wonderful time with him. Nevertheless she was confused since she discovered that as soon as her boy friend left, she began hoping that the phone would ring, in order that she be asked out by another boy.

9. The love relationship is characterized by overt competitiveness toward the other partner, as well as feelings of repressed envy, and the feeling that the achievement of one partner detracts from the desirability of the other. There is the case of the woman married to a public health officer. As a result of the husband's occupation he was called upon to speak to P.T.A. groups frequently on the role of the family in maintaining proper health. His wife accompanied him on his talks and almost always whenever the man had completed his talk, his wife felt compelled to get up and add to her husband's comments. When she was

---

pride based on the favorable qualities which have been developed and realized.

7. The love relationship is characterized by the tendency to accept differences as potentially enriching the union.

8. The love feeling is oriented toward a single member of the opposite sex.

9. The love relationship is characterized by pride and identification with the achievements of each other. Thus as each member achieves something new, the other member has the feeling of sharing in the new achievement.

TABLE 4 (*Continued*)

Immature	Mature
through the husband felt it necessary to clear up some point his wife had made; and so they went on until the audience became bored. This kind of competitiveness characterized their marriage for several years. Finally, the husband wrote a book only to discover that shortly after his book appeared his wife discovered a need to write articles for ladies' magazines.	

TYPES OF PEOPLE NOT CAPABLE OF MATURE LOVE RE-LATIONSHIPS. From all that has been said, both in this chapter as well as in the previous ones, it is apparent that there are many persons who are not capable of experiencing mature love; they would, therefore, encounter great difficulty in building a meaningful man-woman relationship. There are those who are lacking in the essential experiences which are conducive to the development of the capacity to love. It is probably safe to assert that few people have been fortunate enough to come from a home in which the kinds of familial relationships necessary for the development of the capacity to love have been sufficiently plentiful and consistent. When the capacity to love maturely has not been properly developed, there are, almost always, certain kinds of emotional difficulties—immaturities, egocentricity, dependency, the wish to exploit, or narcissism. All of these complicate one's love relationships. Such persons, for example, may only feel secure when they can control or dominate the partner. Or they may give themselves up, including their wishes, and their beliefs, so long as someone will promise to love them. Neither of these patterns can lead to mature love relationships, since in mature love relationships each partner preserves his integrity. There are still other kinds of people who have not developed beyond the stage of receptive hoarding; they want only to receive, not to give. Such a person views love only as a sacrifice, of having to give up things; this person is, therefore, not prepared for relationships involving mutuality.[12]

To some extent, each person with personal immaturities and difficulties is cynical with respect to finding love. Thus, he tends to be

[12] Erich Fromm, *op. cit.*, Ch. 2.

somewhat on guard and suspicious about deep emotional commitments. He tends to be exploitative, in that he uses the partner to satisfy
his own personal needs with no regard for reciprocity. The predominant characteristics of emotionally immature persons is their
marked self-centeredness which makes them incapable of experiencing
mature love. They are generally too busy relieving their own anxieties
or fears to be able to become concerned with the needs of other
people. The term narcissism is employed when self-centeredness becomes pronounced. Although we have referred to the narcissist earlier
in the chapter, we will now deal with this individual in detail. Initially
we may introduce our discussion with a description:

> The term narcissism comes from the Greek legend about Narcissus, a
> boy who happened one day to see his image in a pool. He fell in love with
> his beautiful image, couldn't leave it, pined away and died. The boy was
> infatuated with an image of himself, but certainly he was not in love with
> his true self, for he neglected his real interests and welfare. Similarly, the
> narcissist is not in love with his true self, but with an image of himself,
> shimmering in all its glory and magnificence, not in a pool of water but
> in his imagination.[13]

The above description points out clearly the extent to which the
narcissist is concerned with an imagined concept of himself. The
fantastic creations which the narcissist may construct about himself
are brought out in the following case history of a woman undergoing
psychoanalysis.

> "My pulchritude exceeds my mental endowment. I am respectable, cul-
> tured, well-behaved. I am poised, proud, quiet and refined, clean-minded
> and meek. I am immaculate, delicate, tender, big-hearted, lovable, unselfish,
> unspoiled, generous, and ambitious. I don't gossip. I'm not vengeful. I don't
> gamble or drink. I have rare dexterity, am supermundane, possess savoir-
> faire. I'm perspicacious, perceptive, euphemistic, strong, healthy, and ideal-
> istic, and I make my own clothes."
>
> This woman seems at first glance to have a world of self-confidence; in
> fact, she seems to have genuine self-love. A moment's reflection makes it
> clear, however, that she does not have genuine affection for herself, but
> rather is infatuated with her imaginative concept of herself. In fact at a
> deeper level this woman hates herself for what she really is. Her regard for
> herself is excessive, and inflated out of proportion with the reality of her-
> self. Who has ever known a woman or man with all the virtues (including
> such contradictory ones as "proud" and "meek") which this lady ascribes to
> herself? This psychological condition, self-infatuation, is known clinically
> as narcissism.[14]

[13] Ralph Slater, "Narcissism Versus Self-Love," paper prepared for *Auxiliary
Council to the Association for the Advancement of Psychoanalysis*, 1953.
[14] *Ibid.*

An analysis of this case immediately reveals some common characteristics of the narcissistic individual, including the colossal egocentricity and the disregard for the needs of others. These stem essentially from the need to realize the image of oneself which has been constructed. Thus, it is relatively easy for the narcissist to become exploitative and use people in a most casual and reckless manner with little remorse or feeling of guilt. Moreover, since such people feel entitled to attention from others, they use others without any emotional commitment or interest in them as people.

Although many of the essential features of the narcissist are clearly brought out in the above case it is important to remind the reader that this individual reveals the picture of herself in therapy. It is not likely that one will openly reveal himself as our patient has. Nevertheless, it is important to recognize that a great deal of narcissism is present in our society and is found among large numbers of persons in love involvements. Needless to say, narcissistic patterns create great difficulty in the man-woman relationship and make a meaningful association difficult.

In the present analysis we have concentrated our attention on people with personal problems and immaturities; and the ways in which these affect their relationships with others. Perhaps we can conclude this discussion with an excellent quotation which summarizes much of what we have stated.

The emotionally unstable person cannot help being self-centered. He is constantly preoccupied with his personal problems: how to keep his balance, how to adjust reality to his needs, how to impress people, how to steer clear of his inner turmoil. There is little incentive left for becoming acquainted with another person. The basic foundation of a good relationship and the development of mutuality—the real knowing of one another—is quite impossible. Emotionally unstable people do not, cannot, know each other. In the person with emotional problems there is not only unawareness of oneself and resistance to knowing oneself, but also unawareness of the love partner and an aversion to knowing her.[15]

SUMMARY

Such beliefs as the existence of "a one and only," "love at first sight," and "love solves all problems" are conductive to the development of immature love, since the acceptance of such ideas leads to the formation of attitudes toward love which are rooted in unreality and magic. In this regard it is important to note that our society in general plays an important role in fostering these attitudes in the minds of people.

[15] *Ibid.*

Movies, television, popular ballads, novels, and magazine articles are replete with immature notions concerning love. The fact that millions of dollars are poured each year into products which promote these immature attitudes toward love suggests that they have considerable appeal for the populace.

Mature love, on the other hand, has little to do with the ideas of love at first sight or destiny. Mature attitudes imply that love is rooted in needs that contribute to the intellectual and emotional growth of the partners; and they are rooted in reality. As such, mature love is viewed as an integration of personalities, which arises out of adjustment and readjustment of the personalities involved.

The capacity to love maturely develops out of a wide variety of personal and social experiences. When, for example, one is reared in a home where love is viewed as a sign of femininity and weakness, he is likely to acquire negative attitudes toward the desirability of love. Whereas, when one is reared in a family which values love as a human experience, he is likely to acquire positive attitudes toward the desirability of love.

There are at least three important periods of interaction which greatly influence the development of one's capacity to love maturely. The first is the period of infancy. During this period the individual experiences his initial interaction with adults (particularly the mother) in the environment. If this interaction evokes positive responses from others, the infant feels secure and tends to explore further interactions with others without fearfulness.

During the childhood period one learns to take over the feelings which he believes others express toward him. Thus, the child on the basis of his interpretations of how others feel about him comes to view himself as being lovable or unlovable. When the child regards himself as lovable he is capable of receiving and expressing love quite easily, whereas feelings of being unlovable markedly hinder his ability both to receive as well as to express love.

The third period in the development of the capacity to love maturely occurs during preadolescence and adolescence. It is during this period that the individual increases the number of his love objects. The process of broadening one's love objects begins very early in life with love for self, which then grows to include love for parents and family members, and finally, during preadolescence and adolescence includes love for people in general, starting with the members of one's own sex and ultimately including members of the opposite sex. When one's life is characterized by love and security it becomes possible for him to widen his array of love objects quite easily. However, when one's life is devoid of love and security, he may fear expressing love toward others and retain all his love for himself, or express it toward his parents with whom he feels more secure. In cases such as these, where one becomes fixated with respect to love objects, the expressing of love toward people in general becomes markedly difficult and consequently one's capacity to love maturely is greatly impaired. Indeed, there are those who, because of their interaction with others and the resulting attitudes they acquire, are incapable of participating in a mature and healthy love relationship. The emotionally immature and unstable are illustrative of this point. In such cases the preoccupation with self and with one's own problems presents too great an obstacle; consequently one's ability to relate to others in a love relationship is made markedly difficult, if not impossible.

QUESTIONS

1. List several beliefs concerning love and show how each is associated with either mature or immature notions of love.
2. In what ways does society contribute to the growth of immature love? What, if anything, can be done to correct this?
3. In what way does the "cult of manliness" hinder the development of the capacity to love maturely?
4. How do interactions during infancy affect one's capacity to love maturely?
5. Describe fully the process of role taking and show how it affects the development of one's capacity to love maturely.
6. Explain what is meant by a fixation with respect to love objects. In what way does this impair one's ability to love maturely?
7. What is narcissism? How do narcissistic patterns make meaningful love relationships difficult?
8. List several types of emotionally immature and unstable people and show how each encounters difficulty in sharing a mature love relationship.

SUGGESTIONS FOR RESEARCH AND RELATED ACTIVITIES

1. Write down the words of at least three currently popular love songs and analyze the ideas contained in each showing how they contribute to mature and/or immature love.
2. Select several magazine advertisements which you feel promote products associated with immature love. Explain why you regard these products as contributing to the development of immature love.
3. Analyze two love stories selected from any popular magazine. Using the list of characteristics of mature and immature love presented in this chapter, show how each story represents a mature and/or immature love relationship.
4. Hold a panel discussion on the following topic: "Teen-Agers' Exposure to Mature and Immature Attitudes Concerning Love."

SUGGESTED READINGS

Burgess, Ernest W., and Harvey J. Locke, *The Family*, American Book Co., New York, 1960, 2nd ed., Ch. 7, "Culture and Personality," Ch. 8, "Psychogenic Conditioning," and Ch. 9, "Expectations and Roles."

Ellis, Albert, "Some Significant Correlates of Love and Family Attitudes and Behavior," *J. soc. Psychol.*, **30** (Aug. 1949), pp. 3–16.

Murphy, Gardner, *Personality: A Biosocial Approach to Origins and Structure*, Harper and Brothers, New York, 1947, Ch. 20, "The Origin of the Self," Ch. 21, "The Evolution of the Self," and Ch. 22, "Enhancement and Defense of the Self."

Piaget, Jean, *The Child's Conception of the World*, Harcourt, Brace and Co., Inc., New York, 1929.

Simpson, George, *People in Families*, Thomas Y. Crowell Co., New York, 1960, Ch. 13, "Problems of Infancy," Ch. 14, "Problems of Infancy (continued)," and Ch. 15, "Self-Realization in the Family: Childhood and Adolescence."

The role of dating in man-woman relationship

7

The development of a meaningful man-woman relationship is intimately related to the patterns of dating which people pursue. Dating, of course, was not always important, since in the past young people began the man-woman relationship by "courting" rather than dating. Courting, which was expected to result in marriage, was under the rigorous control of the family, neighborhood, and church. The influence of each was combined in such a way as to demand that every step in the premarital man-woman involvement follow a well-defined pattern. The strictness of formal courtship is apparent in that such behaviors as a kiss, a declaration of love, or the attendance of a young man with the same young woman at the "Thursday night prayer-meeting for two consecutive weeks" were viewed by all as definite commitments toward marriage. And, if any doubt existed in the young people's minds, they were quickly reminded that this was the case and their intentions were immediately asked for in no uncertain terms.[1]

Today, however, this formal courtship pattern has largely given way to a more informal pattern known as dating. Just as courtship is considered to be the prelude to marriage, dating has come to be viewed as the prelude to courtship.

Under the informal dating pattern the behaviors of the unmarried

[1] Niles Carpenter, "Courtship Practices and Contemporary Social Change in America," *Annals of the American Academy of Political and Social Sciences,* **160** (1932), pp. 38–44.

are no longer under the binding controls of the family, neighborhood, and church. Instead young people have demanded and have largely received the right to set their own limitations on dating behavior. In addition to setting their own limitations on dating behavior, young people today also work out their own definitions of behaviors which in their opinion may or may not constitute commitments to marry. This informal dating pattern (which, incidentally, is predominantly American) is largely due to certain social changes which have taken place.[2]

THE EMERGENCE OF DATING. The replacement of the formal courtship pattern by the informal dating pattern as a means of initiating man-woman relationships was made necessary first, by the urbanization of American society, and second, by the increasing demands which young people began to make on marriage.

The urbanization of society, with its many different kinds of people and point of view, tended to reduce the homogeneity which existed in a rural setting. Thus, similarity of background or interests could not be taken for granted, and the extent of a couple's differences or similarities could only be discovered through an informal pattern which came to be termed dating.

Moreover, as suggested in an earlier chapter, the urban environment and the person-centered orientation that it ushered in brought about greater individuality with respect to mate selection. Young people, for example, no longer wished to have their choices dictated or controlled by the church, the family, or the neighborhood. Under these conditions dating patterns were developed which provided a means of initiating the man-woman relationship without the conventional constraints of the church or family.[3]

A second and perhaps more important reason for the emergence of the informal dating pattern is that young people began to seek more personally fulfilling marriage relationships than did their predecessors. Indeed, marriage, which was once viewed predominantly as an economic arrangement, increasingly came to be viewed as a means of fulfilling such personal needs as being loved, being appreciated and respected, as well as a means of expressing interpersonal compatibility, which involved the sharing of interests and values. So long as the basis of marriage centered around economic and practical concerns there was little need for determining compatibilities or interests. It is only

[2] John F. Cuber, "Changing Courtship Customs," *Annals of the American Academy of Political and Social Sciences*, **229** (1943), pp. 31–34.

[3] Marvin R. Koller, "Some Changes in Courtship Behavior in Three Generations of Ohio Women," *Am. Soc. Rev.*, **16** (June, 1951), pp. 366–370.

when the very basis of what was sought in marriage underwent change that it became necessary to establish new ways of discovering whether or not these more personal values were present in the relationship.[4]

THE SIGNIFICANCE OF DATING IN BUILDING A MEAN-INGFUL MAN-WOMAN RELATIONSHIP. There can be little doubt that when conducted with maturity and realism dating may become an essential stage in the development of a meaningful man-woman relationship, since every date offers a potential opportunity to acquire knowledge of a particular member of the opposite sex, and about the nature of man-woman involvement in general. There is indeed much to be learned about the sexes, and although many of us pride ourselves on our assumed knowledge of the opposite sex, our knowledge is generally limited and faulty.[5] Why is this so?

To begin with, it is questionable whether our society prepares us adequately to understand or to get along with persons of the opposite sex. All of us by virtue of our sex are reared for many years in "closed societies." Until adolescence, interactions with the opposite sex are few indeed. Thus, during this formative period of our development, our associations and experiences have been restricted largely to members of our own sex. The tendency for each sex to interact with its own grouping helps to orient us in terms of how we are to behave and think as boys or girls. Thus, we normally acquire an ideology, point of view, or set of attitudes which members of the sex to which we belong possess.

Nevertheless, the very same process which teaches us to become like those of our own sex is often the source from which distortions and erroneous notions about the opposite sex are acquired. Such distortions immediately impose obstacles to free and spontaneous interaction between the sexes, since men and women do not see each other as they are, but instead view one another through distorted perceptions. Although in some instances we may come to idealize the opposite sex and view them as being better than they are, there is also a contradictory pattern of viewing the opposite sex as being worse than they are. Some distortions are conscious, such as "women are impractical, overemotional, scatter brains"; or "men are motivated only by sexual pleasures"; or "men are really big boys who haven't grown up." At a deeper, unconscious level women may feel that men are

[4] James A. Peterson, *Education for Marriage*, Charles Scribner's Sons, New York, 1956, pp. 120–125.

[5] Samuel Harman Lowrie, "Dating Theories and Student Responses," *Am. Soc. Rev.*, **16** (June, 1951), pp. 334–339.

gross and insensitive; men may feel that women are exploitative. Such deep-seated attitudes frequently arise out of particular personal experiences in the life history of the individual. For example, a boy who grew up with a mother who exploited his father came to feel that all women were exploitative. He stated that his mother had been seriously ill during her adolescence. Although she recovered quite well, she insisted on presenting herself to others as sickly and ill. Whenever permissible she took advantage of her presumed state of ill health in order to shift her responsibilities to her husband. Thus, very frequently the husband had to rise early, dress and feed his children, and go to work. On his return for lunch he would feed his children, do the dishes, and return to work. Often he prepared the evening meal and did the laundry when this was indicated. This young man, who observed the exploitation of his father by his mother, categorizes all women as exploitative and fears involvement with them.

While it may be true that some men are crude or insensitive, and some women exploitative, it is obviously inaccurate to categorize men or women simply as being specifically one thing or another. Each man, just as each woman, is essentially different and each has to be evaluated separately. A failure to evaluate properly results in prejudice and distortion. In this instance, however, it is a prejudice based on one's sex rather than on a religious or racial affiliation. There is little doubt that all of us have acquired distortions about the opposite sex which serve to hinder our ultimate adjustment and understanding of them. Since such distortions have developed over long periods of time and out of experiences which have been forgotten and repressed, they are not easily removed. Thus, as with other habit systems, they tend to resist change. Furthermore, when such stereotypes about women or men develop, they become well-entrenched ways of thinking and feeling about the opposite sex. Some people, for example, may even prefer to avoid interaction with the opposite sex in order to avoid exposing their attitudes to reality. There is the case of a young lady who at the age of eighteen had a traumatic involvement with a man ten years older. Although sexual relations had not occurred, the man had apparently initiated the girl into heavy necking and petting. All of this occurred so suddenly during a date that the girl became hysterical and felt that she was fortunate to have escaped sexual involvement. Ever since this experience the young lady insists on seeing men as essentially crude and insensitive. She refrains from dating since to her all men are the same and she prefers to cling to her views rather than to expose them to reality.

We would like to emphasize that the most significant benefits that come from extensive dating are those which promote a breakdown of the prejudices and distortions about the opposite sex, and facilitate the understanding of the nature of men and women. The dating relationship may afford an opportunity to change preconceived notions about men or women. With a breakdown of acquired distortions, it becomes possible to develop a clearer picture of the opposite sex and to develop a concept of what one wants in a husband or wife out of interaction rather than distorted fantasy. In this way, dating may, under the most favorable conditions, lead to meaningful relationships; that is, relationships which involve deep emotional commitments, based on mature needs, interests, and feelings for one another.

You may wonder, at this point, why the sexes pursue one another if each has certain negative views toward the other. In spite of all that has been said, there are very real erotic and emotional needs which most persons can only satisfy in a relationship with the opposite sex. Unfortunately, however, the distortions we have described create ambivalence toward the opposite sex; they result in tendencies to limit one's commitment to a relationship and therefore thwart the fulfillment of expectations.[6]

Although we have devoted several pages to a discussion of the potential fruitfulness of dating, we immediately recognize that frequently the values of dating are thwarted. If dating nurtures maturities, it can lead to meaningful man-woman relationships. On the other hand, if dating nurtures immaturities, it may lead to meaningless relationships. Ruth Cavan best summarizes the latter of these two alternatives with respect to marriage by stating that:

. . . dating develops some attitudes that are opposed to those needed in marriage. The grasping after individual ego-satisfaction, the exploitation, the noncommittal attitude that takes little or no responsibility for the welfare of the partner, and the constant playing with sex on a superficial basis are all contrary to the relationship that underlies a harmonious marriage.[7]

DATING PROBLEMS WHICH INTERFERE WITH THE BUILDING OF A MEANINGFUL MAN-WOMAN RELATIONSHIP.

Motivations. The motivations for dating can constitute serious obstacles to the development of a meaningful man-woman relationship. If the predominant motivation is simply "to put in time" or "to have

[6] For a discussion of other positive functions of dating see: Evelyn M. Duvall and Reuben Hill, *Being Married*, D. C. Heath and Co., Boston, 1960, pp. 4–5.

[7] Ruth Shonle Cavan, *The American Family*, Thomas Y. Crowell Co., New York, 1953, p. 307.

fun," then little which is of potential value can be realized. When students in a marriage and parenthood class were asked why they dated, the immediate response was, "I date because . . . well, I don't know, I never really tried to figure it out. I date because everybody dates. I don't ask myself why, I just date." On pressing for more concrete reasons, however, the writers found that young people apparently date for several reasons.

The first, and most frequently given reason, is that "dating is fun, nothing more. It's just fun and I enjoy it. It's relaxing." Secondly, young people sometimes date because they feel they have to. "Where can a guy go on a Saturday night without a date? To a dance, to the movies, for a walk in the park, yeah, then everybody says what's wrong with him that he doesn't date? If you want to attend the important social events you must date. They're set up for couples not for stags." Or as a coed pointedly asked, "Did you ever sit in the dorm on a date night?" Thirdly, young people sometimes date in order to retain or achieve popularity. "It's simple, if you want to be popular you have to date. Otherwise, you're nobody. It's through dating certain fellows that I came to be accepted by this crowd. They're the popular set here, and without dating fellows from their group, I don't know how I could have become one of them."

Admittedly, these are probably but a few of many motives which young people have for dating. And each person may have different reasons for dating different people. As we have seen, some people are dated because they're fun to be with, some because the individual was "stuck for a date," some because they maintain or even add to popularity and yet others, we might add, are dated for purposes of financial or sexual exploitation. The important point here is that dating for the purpose of developing an understanding of the opposite sex and in order that meaningful relationships may arise is only one of many reasons; it is frequently overlooked by young people as a motive for dating, and it is apparently regarded as not too important a reason at that! Thus many young people fail to receive the full benefits which the dating experience can afford them. Further, there are those who look on dating and marriage as unrelated activities. A young lady reported:

> It's common sense that when I marry it will be to someone whom I've dated casually at first. But here I think I have a problem because although each of the fellas I date is my idea of a good dating partner, he is not my idea of a good marriage partner. Let me tell you what I mean. I date fellas who are considered to be the top daters, that is, those who are acknowledged as the men about campus—good looking, smooth dancers, popular as

athletic heroes, adventurous, and the life of the party. However, I know that none of these fellas is the one that I would want to marry because for marriage I want someone who is very ambitious, serious, and offers security, most of the things which my dates are not.

This young lady recognizes her dilemma and readily appreciates the fact that her dating practices are inconsistent with her marital goals. Moreover, since she has presumably not dated serious and ambitious men she assumes that they may not also possess many of the qualities she enjoys in a dating partner. Many people rebel when they are told that their motivations for dating are not designed to contribute to the development of a meaningful man-woman relationship. They insist, instead, that dating does prepare them for meaningful relationships.

Let us stop for a moment to clarify some of the points we have made. It should be clear that although we stress the more purposeful aspects of dating we are not suggesting that dating couples become preoccupied immediately with marriage; indeed, quite the opposite. If dating is to be fully utilized as preparation for marriage, people should share dating experiences with many persons of the opposite sex. Our point is that one's dating should not be motivated only by such short-range considerations as getting out of the dorm on a date night or having lots of dates merely for the sake of being considered popular; more important, dating should include the long-range considerations we have indicated. When young people regard dating merely as a means of "killing time" until marriage becomes more feasible, they are ignoring the very real opportunities for understanding one another which dating holds for them. The following statement by a young man pointedly illustrates the complete exclusion of long-range consideration:

I've dated quite a few girls and will probably date a lot more before I am ready to think about marriage. I enjoy dating, of course, but the thing that troubles me is the interest which many of my dates have in marriage. It seems that just when we're having a good time my date starts to ask me things like—what do I think about a wife working after marriage; or whether I think the husband and wife should share decision making in marriage? When I hear this I know it's time to get out because maybe my dates are ready to talk about these things, but I'm not. I've got a lot to do before I even start to think about that little gal who will look good in an apron.

The above illustration points out that the young man obviously views dating merely as a means of killing time until marriage becomes more feasible and that he obviously regards any mention of marriage as an attempt to commit him to marriage. Both of these show his exclusive concern with short-range motivations in his dating. Also, his attitudes do not permit him to learn about women since he grows impatient so readily.

It is clear from all that we have said that a radical change in the motivations of people with respect to dating will have to occur if preparation for meaningful man-woman relationships is to result. When it becomes possible for people to approach the dating involvement with greater seriousness of purpose than is currently manifest, then the basic understandings about the sexes which produce successful marriages may develop more readily.

Premature "Going Steady." A second pattern which thwarts the development of a meaningful man-woman relationship is premature "going steady."[8] Within recent years, many lay groups representing the different religious orientations have become alarmed at the prevalence of the going-steady pattern among the youth. Although their apprehension is related to fears about becoming involved in premarital sexual relations, our concern is primarily with other problems.

Premature steady dating removes the individual from gaining meaningful knowledge about members of the opposite sex since it restricts one's interactions. Furthermore, since this premature steady pattern so frequently arises without careful consideration, relationships fall apart and terminate often with considerable misunderstanding for one or both persons. The reasons for becoming involved in going together prematurely are several; there are the social pressures of the group, as well as the need to be popular. The factor which interests us most, however, is the personal insecurity which characterizes so many of the persons who become involved in this pattern. For these people the premature going steady relationship is frequently a compensation for the insecurity they feel, and it becomes personally important since it signifies that they are capable of attracting another. The anxiety centered around the carrying on of a conversation, getting acquainted, and the fear of rejection all appear quite painful to these insecure people.[9]

Such concern may best be illustrated by the hypothetical case of an insecure individual wishing to date. Such a person, let us assume it

---

[8] We are concerned at this point only with the implications of this particular pattern for those who have had relatively little dating experience. Also see: Robert D. Herman, "The Going Steady Complex: A Re-Examination," *Marriage and Family Living*, 17 (Feb., 1955), pp. 36–40.

[9] For a discussion of arguments for and arguments against going steady see: Francis E. Merrill, *Courtship and Marriage*, rev. ed., Henry Holt and Co., New York, 1959, pp. 104–106.

is a male, must first muster up the courage to ask for a date. He may get turned down once or several times before he finds a date. If he does find a date, he often worries about how he looks, whether or not his conversation will interest the girl, and whether the girl will have an enjoyable time. Finally, it is entirely possible that after all his worrying, the girl will in fact not wish to date him again. The experience we have described is for many people a recurrent one, and one fraught with a good deal of personal stress.

Under such circumstances many people prefer not to experience the discomfort involved in dating different people. Going together as early as possible appears to them to be a solution for their problem. Such insecurity may at times become so intense that it relentlessly drives a person to repeat the same mistakes. There is the case of a male college student who was intelligent, handsome, well mannered, but very insecure. Usually after a second or third date with a girl he would ask her to date only him. Once the girl agreed, the student began to monopolize her time. He would walk her to class in the morning, meet her after class whenever possible, walk her back to the dormitory, study with her in the evening, and call her on the telephone in his spare time. This pattern was personally so repulsive to the girl that within a week the student found himself jilted and without a girl friend. This accentuated his insecurity and he would be driven to seek another girl, repeating the pattern and making the same error. Only when this student was able to understand his fundamental insecurity, and the way in which this disturbed his dating relationships with women, was he able to change his behavior.

Thus for those who discover tendencies to become involved with the premature going-together pattern, an understanding of the reasons for their involvement might prove exceedingly fruitful since it may provide them with leads for changing their behavior.

Meaningful and Meaningless Interaction in the Dating Relationship. Perhaps the most serious dating problem which hinders the development of a sound man-woman relationship arises out of meaningless interaction. By meaningless interaction we refer to patterns of behavior which are designed to hide the identity of the dating partners and restrict their understanding of each other. Meaningless interaction in the dating relationship serves little purpose either in educating the dating partners about themselves or in enabling them to build a relationship with some stability. Thus, by meaningful interaction we refer to interaction which allows the personalities to reveal themselves as people, including their basic feelings, interests, opinions, attitudes, fears, and life goals.[10]

In analyzing patterns of meaningless interaction we note that these are so widespread that we cannot dismiss them as chance occurrences without plan or purpose. Instead, we must assert that meaningless interaction is purposeful (conscious or unconscious) and is designed to keep relationships superficial by limiting the involvement between the sexes and by hiding identity and reality. Patterns of meaningless interaction are intimately tied to broader social values which characterize life in America today. For example, our society is one which places much value on attending social events. To receive invitations and attend social gatherings is valued highly among large sections of American society. Nevertheless, there is much less concern with the quality of the interaction which ensues between people. Rather, the conventional gathering may be one in which several people "mill around," engaging in superficial conversation and interaction.[11] In many ways we value superficiality and run away from depth in human relationships. So marked is the pattern of superficial involvement that Europeans have been known to remark that "Americans are friendly, but they are very difficult to get to know." Any dating pattern which hides the reality of what one is, contributes to meaningless interaction, since meaningful interaction can only take place when persons have the capacity and desire to reveal themselves. Thus, let us turn our attention to specific dating practices which contribute to the hiding of one's identity.

Stereotyped Dating and Hiding One's Identity. Stereotyped dating, which refers to the practice of engaging in the same activity, at the same time, in the same way, serves to hide one's identity since it limits what people can learn about each other. As a result only limited aspects of the personalities may be observed. Thus, depending on the patterns of the couple, they may gather a glimpse of the personality on the movie date, or the concert date, but seldom the total personality.[12] Stereotyped dating is not only limiting in that selected segments of the personalities are revealed, but it may also tend to lend itself to circumstances in which interaction, the prerequisite for mean-

---

[10] For an interesting study on the emergence of empathy in the man-woman relationship see: Glenn M. Vernon and Robert L. Stewart, "Empathy as a Process in the Dating Situation," *Am. Soc. Rev.*, **22** (Feb., 1957), pp. 48–52.

[11] Erich Fromm, *The Art of Loving*, Harper and Brothers, New York, 1956, pp. 83–106.

[12] William M. Smith, Jr., "Rating and Dating: A Re-Study," *Marriage and Family Living*, **14** (Nov., 1952), p. 313.

ingful associations, is greatly limited. For example, the typical movie date, in addition to what has already been said, is deficient since it places many restrictions on verbal interaction between the dating partners. It is interesting in this regard to note that when people are asked about why the movie date is so often a pattern in our society, they state "what else can one do?" Although many communities are limited in regard to dating activities, one wonders whether the movie date is not in reality designed to avoid meaningful interaction and to remove the burdens of interaction from the dating partners. The movie date is not, of course, the only type of date which may be designed to minimize interaction. There are those persons who have a pattern of dating in groups, sometimes referred to as double dating. Although there are undoubtedly several reasons for such dating, when it is a preferred pattern of an individual or a couple one may well wonder whether the constant need for others is not based on a need to shift the burden of interaction to others in the group.

Conformity and Hiding One's Identity. The fact that dating behavior may be characterized by a high degree of expected conformity makes it difficult for many people to reveal themselves as they are. There is usually a pronounced effort to impress. For example, both persons invariably dress better than they usually do, and both persons, eager to please, have their "best foot forward." Thus, each person learns very little that may be real about the other and to the extent that such dates occur, there is in fact little opportunity for much knowledge of one another to emerge.

Furthermore, the fear of being different or expressing opinions and beliefs which may be at variance with others is often so pronounced that the very impulses of people to express themselves are dampened. Such behavior leads to a minimization of the individual's basic interests and ideas, aspects of personality which are basic to the development of a meaningful man-woman relationship. Often verbal interaction is limited by the dating partners, since one may feel it is better to say nothing than to say the wrong thing. Finally, interests may be feigned in order to please, to give the appearance of harmony and agreement. A blotting out of one's identity may apply not only to interests but often includes a distortion of one's familial and cultural background. Conversation about one's family may be eliminated, or they may be made to appear to be better than they are. Likewise, religious or cultural minority status may be hidden, particularly when one fears rejection on such a basis.

Thus, from what has been discussed, it can readily be seen that dating relationships characterized by hiding one's identity, which include stereotyped dating, needs to impress, and conformity all contribute to meaningless interaction. Interaction of this type is based on minimizing the basic attitudes and feelings of the dating partners; when the personalities are oriented toward hiding their real feelings, the interaction frequently becomes non-controversial and mundane. Unfortunately many daters discover that "simply talking" without regard to content is the road to popularity. Here is a case in point:

> One characteristic which holds an important place in dating among my friends is bantering. This involves engaging in a rapid exchange of light remarks. Bantering was very difficult for me, particularly since it usually occurred in a group where everybody was rapidly talking back and forth. I just seemed to be dumb struck and when a remark was addressed to me, I could only manage to laugh nervously and finally, when it was too late, I'd manage to think of a clever reply. Even when I would think of something to answer right away, I was always afraid it wouldn't be witty enough. I really worried about my inability to "banter" and finally discussed it with one of the girls who is very popular in our set. Her advice to me was, when at a party I should start talking about anything at all and in a continual flow. Then eventually people would begin to direct their talk to me and they would leave with the impression that we all had carried on a terrific conversation. I tried this and it works, because under circumstances such as these, it's not what you say that counts, it's having the ability to keep talking that's important.

Relationships which rest on the quality of interaction described in the previous quote may capture the temporary interest of some, but when interaction is meaningless, one or both often become bored with the interaction as well as with the relationship. The boredom in such a relationship is due to the fact that the persons involved are not fundamentally interested in what they are saying or doing. Many people abandon a relationship because of such premature boredom when the relationship might potentially be worth continuing. For example, a relationship may be uninteresting or dull not because the personalities are intrinsically dull; but because each individual is afraid to be himself, each is afraid to express himself, or each is afraid to show his real interests. Thus, depth is never reached, and the identity of each person is hidden. There are those who become acclimated to meaningless interaction and in fact cannot cope with more serious involvements. Many marry on the basis of such superficial understandings, only to discover in marriage vast incompatibilities which plague them. One often hears, "If I'd known he was like that, I would never have married him." Although understandable, much of this could be avoided if the man-woman relationship had been characterized by more meaningful interaction than is currently evident.

Although we recognize the significance of meaningful interaction in the dating relationship, its establishment may not be simple since there appear to be many factors in the social setting, and in our individual personalities, which work against it. Frequently the person who engages in meaningful interaction is defined as too serious—"a square," and therefore undesirable. Such views tend to discourage purposeful interaction. Indeed, much personal integrity is required for one to take a stand against such views.

Aside from these social pressures there are personal pressures of even greater significance. If the essential purpose of meaningless interaction is to hide one's identity, then we can only assume that many of us feel that what we are is unacceptable and should be made obscure. When we use the term "what we are" we suggest the total concept of ourselves, attitudes, beliefs, interests, and opinions. If one feels unacceptable and wishes to hide what he or she may be, certain consequences emerge. For example, one may feel that he basically knows very little and therefore has no right to express an opinion. Possibly, one may feel that his interests are of such little importance that they are not worth introducing into a conversation, and so it goes. Many people feel that if they reveal themselves, they will be humiliated; with such low self-esteem they can only anticipate the disapproval of others. The negative self-concept curbs one's spontaneity and expressions. One may come to prefer a pattern of meaningless interaction after many years of social conditioning and personal experiences which make hiding the identity the most rewarding procedure. Nevertheless, in spite of these obstacles it is essential that active efforts be exerted in order that these barriers to meaningful relationships be removed.

As a final note to this discussion we would like to point out that one must have some sensitivity about individuals with whom (and under what circumstances) meaningful interaction is possible. For example, to reveal oneself to some persons could well result in their using such information in a harmful manner. The girl who reveals some of her insecurities to a boy, without knowing much about him, might discover that such information is used to embarrass or injure her. Also, some people simply might not have the capacity to engage in meaningful interaction. Such people might find it so painful and difficult that to force such interaction would destroy whatever is positive in the relationship. Nevertheless, the main point to our discussion is that meaningful interaction is an important objective in the dating relationship and it is certainly essential if the full potentialities of the relationship are to emerge.

Exploitation. The pattern of exploitation is another dating problem which hinders the development of a meaningful man-woman relationship. Although this topic was introduced briefly in a previous portion of the chapter, we wish to expand our treatment at this time. By "exploitation" we mean the using of others to satisfy our needs without regard to their needs or wishes. It follows that when relationships are exploitative there is a lack of intrinsic interest in the other person. Thus the possibility of developing a meaningful relationship is hindered since exploitation is always associated with marked indifference and callousness toward others; it is hardly conducive to the development of deep, emotional commitments. Although we tend to deny the existence of exploitativeness in human relationships (since it runs counter to some of our espoused virtues), its existence is marked and is in fact fostered by the cultural milieu, the social groups in which we interact; and it becomes entrenched in the personalities which arise out of these socio-cultural influences.

Exploitation Engendered by Our Culture. Our culture plays a significant role in the development of exploitativeness by fostering particular values and beliefs. An example of this can be found in the saying, "a sucker is born every minute," and "only a fool fails to take advantage of a sucker." Another belief suggests that our world is a predatory one where each man must take care of himself lest others take advantage of him. The value which our culture places on competitiveness for material possessions, social prestige, and wealth, often results in exploitation, since competition may become so intense that people use one another to gain advantage. Our culture permits certain practices which foster exploitativeness: for example, the businessman who uses others for his own benefit is simply using good business sense. The employee who takes advantage of his employer by restricting his productivity and "taking it easy" is not really cheating his employer but simply taking advantage of a good opportunity.

Exploitation Engendered by Social Groups. Although we have discussed in a general way the cultural influences which foster exploitativeness, let us examine how these beliefs are expressed in the values and behavior of social groups.

The Role of the Family in the Development of Exploitation. The family is a crucial agency in the development of exploitative patterns. An inspection of the family backgrounds of exploitative people suggests that they are characterized by a great deal of emotional impoverishment, and they are the ones in which the positive counter influences have been lacking. Such conditions of impoverishment cut across social class lines; we must not assume that these are characteristic of any single segment of our society.

A family in which parents and siblings espouse exploitative values as norms on which to pattern one's life fosters such values. Thus, conditions where one parent exploits another, where one parent exploits a child, or where one sibling exploits another, create an environment which fosters exploitation. There is the instance of a young girl who was given adult responsibilities of caring for a home at the age of twelve. Such responsibilities included washing of breakfast and lunch dishes, preparation of the evening meal, including cleaning up the kitchen after the dinner. The mother was usually visiting friends and following her personal pleasures while the girl assumed these familial responsibilities. The girl experienced great hostility and resentment toward her mother and felt that she was a fool for letting her mother take such advantage of her. She vowed that when she could, she would use others just as she had been used. This person, who is now married, has a fully developed set of exploitative patterns which permeate her human relationships. They interfere with her marriage and cause her considerable difficulty.

Not all familial patterns of exploitation are as overt as those we have described. More common, and perhaps more subtle, are those instances in which a parent exploits a child for the personal prestige and benefit the parent may derive. We are thinking here particularly of situations in which parents coerce a child to excel at school or in artistic activity, not because they are interested in the child's achievement but because they wish to brag to others about the child's accomplishments. Such exploitation on the part of parents often develops resentment in the child, which can be expressed by the child's own development of exploitative patterns.

The One Sex Group. Most young men have experienced situations, particularly during the very popular bull session, where it becomes fashionable to brag about one's latest sexual conquest, or to give a detailed account of how one was able to hand out a line to some girl so skillfully that she immediately fell for it. Indeed, to have no stories to tell frequently means that one is somewhat of a "square" and certainly behind the times because much importance is given to these testimonies of skillful exploitation.

Undoubtedly many of the stories told are exaggerated to a great extent, or even completely untrue, but especially significant is the apparent need which people have to pass themselves off as being able to exploit others even if it means that they must make up stories and lie about their ability to do so.

Girls, we might add, are frequently no less involved in these exploitative strategies, for often a girl is regarded as knowing her way around when she is able to exploit, or at least lead her girl friends to believe that she is able to use her boy friends and thus control her dating situations. Many girls are aware of the personal deficiency which will be ascribed to them if they are unable to control the dating situation; or worse yet, if they themselves are exploited by their dating partners.

It is not too difficult therefore to understand how a group of girls came to form a club exclusively devoted to exploiting their boy friends. In this club each girl, unknown to her boy friend, was required to get her boy friend to buy her a certain item or take her to a certain place, agreed to in the club meeting. Thus, her rating as a club member was based on her ability to achieve these goals. Indeed, one Christmas it was decided that each club member was to manipulate her boy friend into buying her a cashmere sweater. Thus, those who got cashmere sweaters from their boy friends for Christmas were regarded as successful and those who did not as failures.

Certainly this club is not to be regarded as a typical case of female exploitation, but it is nonetheless important for us to recognize its existence because, although exploitation here is formalized and concentrated, it does not differ in kind from what we as individuals frequently attempt in our interactions with others.

Exploitative values of the type we have just described become group norms and are passed on to new members as they become part of the group. People come to internalize exploitative values which become manifest in the very basis for dating. The leading spokesman of this point of view was the late Willard Waller, who regarded dating as a competitive game of premarital dalliance in which the primary objective of young people was not to build meaningful relationships but rather to exploit or use the dating partner for personal benefit. This exploitative element, which makes dating a competitive game of strategies, was found to be extremely prevalent among the dating pairs Waller studied. All of this is well illustrated in his insightful analysis "The Rating and Dating Complex." [13]

Waller discovered that young people tend to rate one another according to such criteria as physical appearance, dancing ability, access to an automobile, popularity with the opposite sex, clique membership, and having a "good line." On the basis of these ratings, some persons were considered to be class A daters, while others, not faring so well, were considered to be class B, C, or D daters. Nevertheless, in spite of one's rating, Waller found that almost all young persons tended to acquire some knowledge about where he and each of his

---

[13] Willard Waller, "The Rating and Dating Complex," *Am. Soc. Rev.*, **2** (Oct., 1937), pp. 727–734.

potential dating partners fell on the rating scale. Dating invitations were then extended or withheld, accepted or rejected, with the clear notion of whether or not the particular date would raise or lower one's own prestige. This type of exploitation is exemplified when one's dating of a class A person is not primarily motivated by the desire to be with that particular person, but rather by the desire to use that person's class A prestige to enhance one's own reputation.

The awareness of such exploitation makes it necessary for the young person to guard himself against becoming seriously involved, at least, until he is fairly certain that the dating partner is sincerely interested in him and not merely using him as a means to some other end, or what young people today call merely "stringing him along." The following excerpt from a young lady points out such a fear.

I date several fellows even though I really only want to date Harry. But a girl can't afford to let her preference be known. She must wait for the boy to make the bid. You see, if I let Harry know how I feel, or if I just stop dating other guys and wait for his dates, he'd be sure to know how I feel and then he'd either lose interest or more likely he'd take advantage of his hold on me. I know this can happen because it happened to me before and I don't want it to happen again. We all know that the female gets taken advantage of by the male. So I guess I'll just have to wait and see what Harry does because if he makes the first move, I know I'm O.K., but if I do—I know he'll get smart.

Waller states that assessing the dating partner's motivations is extremely difficult because young people further tend to exploit one another by pretending serious emotional involvement in their dating relationships. This pretense was referred to as having a "good line" and its effectiveness is based on the principle that the relationship tends to be controlled by the person who is least interested in its continuance. Thus, in attempting to exploit the dating partner and control the relationship one makes believe that he has fallen seriously in love with the dating partner. He does this with the hope of convincing the partner, thus causing the partner to relax his guard and become seriously involved in the relationship. When this happens and one is able to use the partner's emotional involvement as a means of controlling the relationship, one regards himself as having been successful and in turn is viewed as "knowing his way around" in this complex dating strategy.

Thus, Waller's analysis of the dating pattern presents a picture of man-woman involvements as a game of the unmarried in which exploitation is paramount. Neither party is ever quite certain of the motives of the other, thus relationships are created in which exploitation is feared as well as promoted.

THE GIRLS   By Franklin Folger

"I've been sitting here all night trying to think of some
way I can show Ted his dating other girls couldn't
affect me less."

Figure 3. Courtesy Franklin Folger and the Sun-Times–Daily News Syndicate
(June 7, 1961).

Waller claims, however, that in spite of all the forces which oppose
it, true courtship sometimes emerges from this complex process. That
is, in spite of their attempts to withstand serious involvement, young
people may eventually become emotionally involved and marry. However, emotional involvements under these conditions tend to be entered into with unwillingness and this would not seem to be a satisfactory way of initiating meaningful relationships.

Waller's critical opinion of dating is shared by Burgess and Wallin who, after studying the contemporary dating pattern, found many of its standards to be adolescent, immature, superficial, and undemocratic.[14]

Personality Organization and Exploitation. The prevalence of exploitation in society, including the family and the one sex group, clearly suggests that such patterns are an integral aspect of personality. The socio-cultural influences we have described are all conducive to the development of exploitative patterns within the personality. An examination of the prevalence of exploitative patterns suggests that many of us are not fundamentally disturbed by the pattern; instead we feel a certain amount of pride and cleverness in the ability to manipulate and use people for our personal benefit. By such means people derive a feeling of strength and power out of their ability to exploit. When a pattern of this sort is anchored in the personality, and indeed serves a need, it is not readily changed.

Nevertheless, though it may have a purpose, exploitation destroys the very basis of meaningful man-woman relationships. It defeats the possibility of spontaneity and freedom to be ones self in the relationship; it fosters suspicion, ambivalence, and distrust on the part of the exploiter and the exploited. To understand the extent to which one uses others becomes, therefore, essential; and to exert active efforts to remove such behavior becomes mandatory if one wishes to build a constructive marital relationship.

SUMMARY

In the past man-woman relationships were begun by "courting." This meant that each relationship was under the rigorous controls of family, neighborhood, and church and it was expected to result in marriage. Today, however, this formal courtship pattern has largely given way to dating. Under the informal pattern of dating, the behavior of the unmarried is no longer completely in the hands of family, church, and neighborhood, but rather has largely been taken over by the dating pairs who themselves determine what behavior is acceptable and what is not. Furthermore, each relationship is viewed as an end in itself and is not necessarily expected to result in marriage.

[14] Ernest W. Burgess and Paul Wallin, *Engagement and Marriage*, J. B. Lippincott Co., Philadelphia, 1953, p. 109. Samuel Harman Lowrie, "Dating Theories and Student Responses," *Am. Soc. Rev.*, 16 (June, 1951), pp. 334–339. Others, however, disagree with this critical viewpoint of dating and believe that people look on dating as a means of seeking partners with whom to build sound relationships. For the reader interested in pursuing this particular aspect of the problem see: Robert O. Blood, Jr., *Anticipating Your Marriage*, The Free Press, Glencoe, Ill., 1955, p. 24.

The emergence of dating was largely the result of urbanization and changes which came about in the qualities desired in a marriage partner. The complexity of the urban community made it difficult for young people to learn about each other without first undergoing a period of interaction. Marriage in the urban area was rooted in such facets as companionship, mutual interests, and values, and the determination of compatibility was intimately tied to the development of dating.

There can be little doubt that dating, when conducted with maturity and realism, is an essential stage in the development of meaningful man-woman relationships. Dating enables young people to learn more about each other by helping to break down the distortions that each sex holds about the other.

The benefits of dating, however, can be greatly reduced through certain conditions which all too often arise in the contemporary pattern, for example, such conditions as: (1) dating merely to "kill time" without giving any serious attention to the dating involvements, (2) going steady too soon, (3) meaningless interaction in dating which involves conforming to a set pattern of behavior in order to hide one's real identity, and (4) exploiting the dating partner in order to gain one's own end; all reduce the benefits which dating offers young people. Not only do the above conditions limit the amount of knowledge that each sex may acquire about the other, but since the circumstances under which dating is conducted are so superficial, realistic attempts to adjust to each other are limited.

Although several authorities clearly see the dangers of the contemporary dating pattern, the leading spokesman in this area was the late Willard Waller who pointedly noted that dating is becoming a competitive game of premarital dalliance in which the primary objective of young people is not to build a meaningful relationship but rather to exploit or use the dating partner for personal benefit. As such, the more skilled one becomes at exploiting others, the more chance he has of becoming regarded as a "sharp dater." Not only does the competitive aspect of dating limit premarital training which would undoubtedly be useful in building a meaningful marriage relationship, but it also creates a situation which leads to a fear of being exploited. Thus, persons often enter courtship and marriage with feelings of ambivalence and doubt. It follows, then, that if dating experiences are to be used in building meaningful man-woman relationships, it is necessary for young people to analyze their dating behavior in order that they may remove the superficiality and exploitativeness which is often so pronounced.

QUESTIONS

1. What is dating? What is courtship? In what ways do they differ and in what ways are they similar?
2. How do you account for the emergence of dating in the American society?
3. What is meant by being reared in "closed societies"? How does this affect the concepts we acquire of the opposite sex?
4. List and explain the benefits offered to unmarried men and women through dating.
5. In what manner do one's motivations for dating affect what one learns through dating?
6. What is meant by premature going steady and how does it affect the benefits one can derive from dating? List and explain the types of reasons for premature going steady.
7. What is meant by meaningless interaction in dating? What purpose does such interaction serve? List and explain specific dating practices which contribute to meaningless interaction in dating.
8. What is exploitation? What is the role of society in fostering exploitation? Is exploitation ever a part of the contemporary dating pattern? If so, give several examples.
9. Who was Willard Waller? Describe fully his views concerning the contemporary dating pattern.

SUGGESTIONS FOR RESEARCH AND RELATED ACTIVITIES

1. Take a poll to determine the reasons young people give for dating. Classify the answers you receive and analyze them in terms of how you think they will affect what is learned from dating. Do you find any differences in the responses? If so, how do you account for such differences?
2. Write and have your fellow students enact two brief skits: one portraying a scene from a man-woman relationship operating under the formal code of courtship, and the other portraying the same scene operating under the informal code of dating. Have your fellow students point out and discuss the differences in the behaviors between the two skits showing the advantages and/or disadvantages of each in terms of building a mean ingful relationship.
3. List several stereotypes which young people hold toward the opposite sex and submit this list to both married and unmarried men and women in order to determine the degree to which these stereotypes are believed to be true. Do you find that these stereotypes are accepted? Do any differences exist between the answers given by men and women, or between those given by the married and unmarried? If so, how do you explain these differences? You might also want to check the dating frequency of your unmarried respondents and determine whether or not dating tends to reduce these distortions.

4. Hold a debate on the following topic: "Men and Women Today Expect Too Much of Each Other in Marriage."

5. Hold a panel discussion concerning the prevalence of "rating-dating" at your school.

SUGGESTED READINGS

Breed, Warren, "Sex, Class and Socialization in Dating," *Marriage and Family Living*, **18** (May, 1956), pp. 137–144.

Cavan, Ruth Shonle, *American Marriage*, Thomas Y. Crowell Co., New York, 1959, Ch. 5, "Dating While in College."

Ehrmann, Winston, *Premarital Dating Behavior*, Henry Holt and Co., New York, 1959.

Kirkpatrick, Clifford, and Theodore Caplow, "Courtship in a Group of Minnesota Students, *Am. J. Sociol.*, **51** (Sept., 1945), pp. 114–125.

LeMasters, E. E., *Modern Courtship and Marriage*, Macmillan Co., New York, 1957, Ch. 5, "Random Dating."

Lowrie, Samuel H., "Factors Involved in the Frequency of Dating," *Marriage and Family Living*, **18** (Feb., 1956), pp. 46–51.

Merrill, Francis E., *Courtship and Marriage*, Henry Holt and Co., New York, 1959, Ch. 6, "Dating Theory," and Ch. 7, "Dating Practice."

Waller, Willard, revised by Reuben Hill, *The Family*, The Dryden Press, New York, 1951, Ch. 8, "The Social Contexts of Courtship," Ch. 9, "Bargaining and Exploitative Attitudes," and Ch. 10, "Courtship As An Interactive Process."

Waller, Willard, "The Rating and Dating Complex," *Am. Soc. Rev.*, **2** (Oct., 1937), pp. 727–734.

Necking, petting, and premarital sexual intercourse [1]

8

An understanding of the nature and function of necking, petting, and premarital sexual relations is essential if one wishes to develop a meaningful man-woman relationship. To be able to develop such an understanding, and to appreciate its bearing on the man-woman relationship, is no simple task since our society fails to provide an orderly way for understanding the role and meaning of sexual involvements in general. For the most part, people who work out definitions about necking, petting, and premarital sexual behavior do so with half truths, confusions, and distortions.[2] Further, an understanding of this aspect of the man-woman involvement is made exceedingly difficult by the fact that our society is going through considerable social change.[3] Thus, the rules governing acceptable and unacceptable behavior are no longer well defined. In a rural homogeneous society the codes of behavior were presumably much less ambiguous; rules for proper or improper behavior were well formulated and understood. Under such circumstances, kissing or necking may have been discouraged by the respectable young lady and not expected by the respectable young

[1] The difference between necking and petting is one of the degree of physical involvement, the latter refers to the fondling of the breasts and genitalia.

[2] Maureen Daly, *Profile of Youth*, J. B. Lippincott Co., Philadelphia, 1951, pp. 64–74.

[3] Lewis M. Terman, et al., *Psychological Factors in Marital Happiness*, Mc-Graw-Hill Book Co., Inc., New York, 1938, p. 323.

n. Today, however, the norms regarding such personal behavior are
t so clearly defined.[4] There is much less certainty about what one
should or should not do in dating and courtship activities. How far
should one go in the necking and petting involvement? What kinds of
factors should one take into account in deciding how far to go? Are
couples who engage in the premarital sex act immoral or is it only
a matter of another kind of morality? These are not simple questions
for which simple rules are available. The fact that large numbers of
people are concerned with these kinds of problems suggests their complexity, and highlights the need for a point of view which will enable
these people to think intelligently about the issues.

The authors do not believe that it is their task to advocate a particular code of conduct with respect to necking, petting, and premarital sexual relations.[5] Nevertheless, we plan to suggest some ideas,
based in part on research findings and in part on clinical observations,
which are worthy of consideration and evaluation in attempting to arrive at a mature attitude regarding these areas of human experience.

SOME ESSENTIAL IDEAS REGARDING THE NATURE OF SEXUAL INVOLVEMENT

Sexual Involvement As Relatedness. At the outset it is important to
state that sexual involvements of any type represent one way in which
men and women establish relationships with each other.[6] Thus sexual
involvement is primarily a type of social relationship, and like all such
relationships it tells us something about the kinds of people involved
and their motivations for the involvement. It is important to be aware
of the role of sexual involvement in the man-woman relationship for at
least two reasons. First, as a sensitive and subtle indicator of behavior,
the sexual relationship may reveal needs which could create difficulty
in the overall relationship. A second and somewhat related reason has

[4] John McPartland, "Footnote on Sex," *Harper's Magazine*, **192** (March, 1946),
p. 212. Our clearly two-valued attitude toward sex is stated by McPartland,
who says, "At one level of our social existence we are the most sensual and
profligate of peoples, worshippers of breast and thigh, separating the fun and
frolic of sex from any bindings of family and child. At the other level of our
social existence we are the prissiest of prudes, a monogamous and chaste people
to whom virginity is so sacred that it cannot be mentioned on our radios."

[5] For a listing of reasons for and against premarital sexual intercourse, see:
Alfred C. Kinsey, et al., *Sexual Behavior in the Human Female*, W. B. Saunders
Co., Philadelphia, 1953, pp. 307–309.

[6] Lester Kirkendall, "A Viewpoint on the Premarital Sex Problem," in: *Readings
in Marriage Counseling* by Clark E. Vincent, Thomas Y. Crowell Co., New York,
1957, pp. 117–126.

to do with the possibility of differentiating an essentially immature expression of sex from one which may involve a mature and healthy sex interest. Let us turn to several illustrations.

The Commodity Orientation. For those who manifest the commodity orientation, the worth of a person is measured in terms of what he has to offer.[7] Within this orientation, human relationships tend to be evaluated on the basis of what can be derived from them. Indeed, persons embracing such views may regard a date as an investment. The male invests his money and time and may expect repayment from the female in terms of physical pleasures. The female may make herself sexually available and believe that this is necessary in order to repay the male. Although understandable and perhaps even necessary in the commercial world, this commodity orientation when applied to the man-woman relationship becomes responsible for many problems. For to the extent that the commodity orientation operates, a deep concern for the person as a person is not present. Interaction based on such an orientation is not conducive to a meaningful union.

The Exploitative Orientation. In the commodity orientation just presented there is usually an element of reciprocity, narrow though it may be; that is, value is given for value received. For those who believe in the exploitative orientation, however, there is a need to manipulate others without any regard for their wishes. This is to say, there is no value given but a value is sought.

An examination of some man-woman relationships reveals a pervasive need to use another person sexually. The reader has undoubtedly encountered the man or woman who enjoyed involving others in amorous adventures without regard for their feelings. One often finds that such a person derives considerable pride from his ability to manipulate others so that necking or sexual relations will take place.

Consider the example of a young man whose history of involvements with women appeared to be patterned. When first meeting a young lady he would be polite and charming in every conceivable way. His motives were based on a desire that the girl become sexually involved with him. This necessitated a considerable amount of planning and effort on his part. His friends noticed that whenever the young lady resisted his advances, he would become even more interested. When asked about this he replied, "It's not the sexual pleasure that I enjoy as much as the thrill of the chase." For this man it was the thrill involved in manipulating and using another which found expression in the sexual relationship.

[7] Erich Fromm, *Man for Himself*, Rinehart and Co., Inc., New York, 1947.

Insecurity. For the insecure person erotic relationships may be employed as compensation for insecurity. Insecurity may be a motivating factor for both sexes. With respect to the male, we must note that there is evidence to show that the desire for necking and petting is as much a desire for acceptance and security as it is for erotic satisfaction.[8] In a research project conducted by a student of one of the authors, it was reported that the majority of men felt that personal acceptance as exemplified by necking or petting was even more important to them than the sexual pleasures derived from these activities.

With respect to women, erotic involvements may also serve their needs for personal acceptance and security. This is especially so when we realize that a woman, perhaps to a greater extent than a man, finds her personal security intimately tied to her physical attractiveness. Although the man who is physically unattractive has other compensations in the form of physical or athletic prowess, prestige in clubs or fraternal orders, and occupational success, these are not readily available to women. For some women the need for security may be so great that they are driven into a series of indiscriminate necking and petting involvements with many men, suggesting promiscuity.[9] But simply calling it promiscuity tells us little; in terms of psychological needs we can say that there are those women whose needs for security are so excessive that they must have the demonstrativeness of every man with whom they are involved. Thus, in some instances, women who are sufficiently insecure may become indiscriminate in their necking and petting habits.

Lust. Finally, the physical involvement may take the form of a quest for biological satisfaction, sometimes referred to as lust. Relationships in which the desire for lustful satisfaction is present may possess an egocentric quality. A misunderstanding of the nature of lust frequently creates difficulty. This is especially applicable in those cases where individuals cannot accept their basic biological impulses as natural and healthy. Under these circumstances people often attempt to repress the significance of lust in their relationships by unconsciously overemphasizing the importance of other non-sexual qualities and then tend to see these as the real bases for their relationships. Indeed, in the majority of such relationships these other non-sexual qualities are probably not even present. Consequently, by imagining that they are

[8] For a discussion of sexual intercourse motivated by reasons other than physical satisfaction see: F. Alexander Magoun, *Love and Marriage*, Harper and Brothers, New York, 1948, pp. 94–95.

[9] Norman E. Himes and Donald L. Taylor, *Your Marriage*, rev. ed., Rinehart & Co., Inc., New York, 1955, p. 35.

present or by overemphasizing their importance (if they are present), one is distorting the relationship and may make commitments to become engaged or married when in reality there is no stable basis for such commitments. Needless to say, many relationships of this type could be based on a more realistic foundation if it were possible to assess the significance of the lust component. With a realistic view these relationships could be accepted for what they are, and unwise commitments might be avoided.

The lust component in the man-woman relationship is so powerful that it becomes formidable and difficult to deal with. The difficulty in even recognizing its existence in a relationship, as has just been discussed, illustrates this point. Without a doubt, the inability to recognize the importance of lust in a man-woman relationship has resulted in marriages where each partner is quite sure that a mature love was present only to discover within a few months following marriage that such was not the case.

Healthy Relatedness. Although we have suggested certain negative components in the erotic relationship, this need not necessarily be so. For the involvement of which we speak may be an expression of a mature and healthy love relationship. In a previous chapter we pointed out that mature relationships are rooted in needs based on reality, and needs that contribute to the intellectual and emotional growth of the members. Unfortunately relationships in which the necking, petting, and premarital involvement are an expression of a mature love relationship are not particularly prevalent in our culture today.

In dealing with the necking and petting relationship it is important to recognize that since people vary with regard to stages of maturity, the nature of the erotic involvement has to be carefully appraised. Necking and petting for the uninitiated or inexperienced could mean curiosity; but for a mature and integrated individual it means something else again. Finally, it is apparent that one ought to be alert to the immature personality pattern which may appear in the erotic relationship.[10] For these may reveal tendencies which will cause difficulties not only in subsequent erotic unions but may become equally manifest in the overall relationship. Moreover, such an awareness is important since it may enable one to avoid premature commitments and involvements in relationships that have no stable basis. We recognize, however, that it is terribly difficult to deal with oneself in such objective terms. Few of us like to recognize the several facets of per-

---

[10] Lawrence S. Bee, *Marriage and Family Relations,* Harper and Brothers, New York, 1959, pp. 80–81.

sonality which may be expressed in the erotic involvement, but there is no more sober experience than the realization of what a particular relationship really means without illusions and without distortions.

Now that we have examined certain general considerations concerning the nature of sexual involvement, let us move to another phase of inquiry; the degree of sexual involvement and its meaning for the man-woman relationship.

A CONTINUUM OF NECKING, PETTING, AND PREMARITAL SEXUAL INTERCOURSE. At the outset it might be helpful if we deal with the degree of sexual involvement by looking at necking, petting, and premarital sexual intercourse in terms of a continuum. This continuum is simply a convenient way of describing the degrees of sexual involvement, with necking blending into petting, and petting blending into premarital sexual intercourse. The sequence in such a continuum is indicated below.

Absence of	Involvement Increases——→	Indiscriminate
Necking	(----/----/----/----/----/----/----)	Premarital
	←——Involvement Decreases	Sexual Intercourse

The basic question for most persons centers around how far on the continuum one ought to go and what factors one should take into account in reaching this decision. However, let us deal first with the two extremes of the continuum. These include those who refuse to engage in any form of necking at the one end and those who pursue sexual relations with anyone at the other end. For both these extreme groups the question of how involved they should become would appear to be already answered. However, we cannot infer that the question has been satisfactorily answered; indeed, in the authors' experience many of the individuals in these categories have considerable inner turmoil and anxiety due to unresolved conflicts about physical involvements. Those who refuse to engage in any necking often possess a rigidity and fear of physical involvement, which suggests emotional conflicts.[11] One of the predominant characteristics of these people is their emotional distance from others; since they have some basic fears about intimate human contact, sex becomes very frightening, and any emotional closeness is disturbing. Many of these people rationalize such aloofness as stemming from superior moral standards. Upon closer inspection, however, one frequently learns that such people use a moral code to justify a fear of becoming involved with others.

[11] Walter R. Stokes and David R. Mace, "Premarital Sexual Behavior," *Marriage and Family Living*, **15** (Aug., 1953), pp. 234–249.

For those who can engage in sexual relations indiscriminantly there may be an equally serious problem: these people may never have developed a sense of discrimination and appropriateness. As with all things—art, food, or sex—the mark of a mature, integrated person is the presence of discrimination. It is out of discrimination that things come to have a special meaning and significance. If anyone can be your friend, then the meaning of a friendship is obscure, since this implies that you may establish a friendship with any type of individual, even a destructive person. Likewise, if an individual can have sexual relations with any member of the opposite sex, then sex loses much of its meaning. Persons in this category rather than being driven, in a sense, to run from the opposite sex, are indiscriminate in sex and engage in what we term compulsive sexual behavior. This does not necessarily mean that they are driven by sexual needs, but rather by some need to prove themselves; for example, perhaps to prove their manliness they become Don Juan types. Or a narcissistic woman may have a goddess-like image of herself and thus be driven to prove that no man that she desires can resist her. That such people are beset by inner problems should be clear, and it is also obvious that those who engage in compulsive sex behavior use sex as a means of trying to resolve their problems.

For perhaps a majority of people, however, the basic question is neither one of completely refraining from physical involvements nor one of becoming indiscriminately involved in sexual relations. Instead, it is a question of deciding how involved they wish to become in the erotic relationship. At this point, therefore, we would like to introduce to the reader a frame of reference from which necking and petting may be viewed. We suggest that a meaningful point of view can be found in the examination of three crucial ideas:

1. The personality organization of the individuals involved
2. The meaning of the erotic involvement for the partners
3. The nature of the relationship

We believe that these ideas are significant for two reasons. First, they offer a frame of reference from which one can examine his attitudes and develop a point of view. Secondly, these ideas permit a maximum of respect and consideration for the needs and values of the partners of the relationship.

The Personality Organization of the Individuals Involved. An understanding of what each person is capable of experiencing in the physical relationship without creation of anxiety and guilt is essential. The range of variability among persons is considerable [12] and in mature relationships the people involved develop an understanding about what each is capable of experiencing before anxieties are aroused. If one or both partners are dissatisfied with the extent of the erotic involvement, whether it is too little or too much, they possibly can understand one another better through discussion; or they may even consult a counselor with whom they can explore the difference. As a rule it is poor practice to manipulate a partner into more physical intimacies than he is capable of accepting. This is especially true in cases where personal taboos are well entrenched. To the extent that each person knows what the other can handle and accepts these facts, the air is cleared so that each is acting in his own best interests as well as in the best interests of the other person.

TABLE 5

Relationship Involvement and Erotic Intimacy Level at Which Offensiveness Occurs, by Episodes *

	Necking and Petting Above the Waist		Petting Below the Waist		Attempted Intercourse and Attempted Intercourse with Violence		Total
	N	Per-cent	N	Per-cent	N	Per-cent	
Ride home, first date, or occasional date	411	55.0	60	31.4	25	30.1	496 (48.5%)
Regular or steady date	295	39.4	104	54.5	43	51.8	442 (43.3%)
Pinned or engaged	42	5.6	27	14.1	15	18.1	84 (8.2%)
Totals	748	100.0	191	100.0	83	100.0	1022 (100.0%)

* From: Clifford Kirkpatrick and Eugene Kanin, "Male Sex Aggression on a University Campus," *Am. Soc. Rev.*, **22** (Feb., 1957), p. 55.

That an understanding in regard to erotic intimacies is reached is noted in the above table. This table illustrates, for example, confusion regarding appropriateness of necking and petting on the first date, as well as for the regular or steady date. It also points out, however,

[12] Paul H. Landis, *Making the Most of Marriage*, Appleton-Century-Crofts, Inc., New York, 2nd ed., 1960, pp. 336–341.

that when pinning or engagement have occurred, little offensive behavior is reported. It is reasonable to assume that in these latter relationships there has been an attempt to understand the erotic needs of
the partners, and an assessment of how far each can move toward
erotic need fulfillment.

The Meaning of the Erotic Involvement for the Partners. An understanding of what the physical involvement means is also worthy
of consideration for those who wish to develop a frame of reference
for necking and petting. The basic question here is one of whether
the erotic relationship has been defined so that each person recognizes its meaning in the particular relationship. Heavy petting, for
example, may mean that the relationship is serious to one person,
but for the other there may be no such definition. Such definitions appear to be important since unwarranted assumptions about the meaning of heavy petting can create misunderstanding and resentment. The
total relationship will be on a more realistic, honest foundation when
the erotic involvement has been defined. The manner in which the
meaning of necking and petting is made clear obviously involves tact,
discrimination, and judgment; nevertheless, this usually can be accomplished to the very real satisfaction of both persons. We recognize, of course, that such a recommendation constitutes a very real
challenge from several points of view. There are those who refuse to
define the meaning of necking and petting in order to avoid the risks
of losing the pleasures of the necking and petting relationship. Further,
there are those who purposely mislead others into assuming that the
erotic involvement is indicative of a more serious relationship than in
fact it is. Often, of course, it is impossible to define the meaning of
necking and petting since the people involved are confused. Even in
these cases, however, it is of value to the couple to know that confusion exists as to the meaning of erotic involvement.

The Nature of the Relationship. The third significant variable to be
considered in deciding how far to continue the erotic involvement has
been partly suggested in our second point, and has to do with the nature of the relationship. Here we are talking about the degree of meaningfulness, which includes the relative absence or presence of mature
love. We are not primarily concerned with whether a particular relationship will result in marriage, but instead with its overall quality.
With this in mind we would like to suggest the possibility of viewing
the extent of erotic involvement as a function of the kind of relationship present. The more meaningful and mature the relationship, the
greater the physical involvement—although the exact degree of in-

volvement must, in the final analysis, be an individual matter. For those who are interested in developing meaning for the erotic involvement beyond the stage of pure lust, our point may be of some significance.

In contrast, it is interesting to note that for many people in our society, love and sexual involvements are separate entities with no real connection between the two.[13] These people often look at sexual involvements in the most derogatory terms, as unclean and indicative of man's most depraved nature.[14] In the grossest form this attitude may be seen in the man who holds up his wife as the epitome of virtue and therefore is unable to have sexual relations with her. Thus, he may be able to enjoy sexual relations with women for whom he has little regard, sometimes only prostitutes. The result of such attitudes, both before and after marriage, is that many people become more intimately involved with those they care least about and remain aloof

TABLE 6

Need Fulfillment and Degree of Sexual Involvement *

Need Areas	Degree of Need Fulfillment	
	(minimum)	(maximum)
Companionship		
Freedom of communication—activity		
Emotional interdependence		
Sexual strivings		

* The solid line profile signifies little need involvement in three areas but a heavy sexual involvement, as in the case of lust; the profile consisting of a broken line signifies a heavy need involvement in three areas but only a slight sexual involvement as in the cases of the young man and young woman mentioned below.

from those for whom they have great feeling. There is the case of the boy who was asked how far he "was able to go" with his girl. His reply was "That's the girl I'm going to marry, I wouldn't try anything like that." Or the case of a girl who wanted to point out how much her boy friend thought of her. She stated, "He has the highest regard for me. He won't even touch me."

[13] Allan Fromme, *The Psychologist Looks at Sex and Marriage,* Barnes and Noble, Inc., New York, 1955.

[14] Sigmund Freud, "Contributions of the Psychology of Love: The Most Prevalent Form of Degradation in Erotic Life," *Collected Papers,* Vol. 16, Hogarth Press, 1934.

In each of these cases there are distorted notions regarding place of physical involvement in the man-woman relationship. In e~ instance, the greater the love, the less the physical involvement; a..u by implication, the less the love, the greater the physical involvement. Table 6 shows one way of portraying the point; it does so by using as a frame of reference the need areas discussed previously in Chapter 5.

To be sure, there are situations in which a boy's refusal to become involved physically may be indicative of respect. This is especially so in cases where the girl may have been sexually exploited earlier and where the male in question wishes to respect her wishes for limited physical involvement. But to the extent that this results in the notion that physical involvement and love are two separate things it may well prove to be damaging to the relationship as a whole.

PREMARITAL SEXUAL RELATIONS AND THE MAN-WOMAN RELATIONSHIP. Many people who can accept the viewpoint that the degree of physical involvement ought to be a function of the kind of relationship a couple have, frequently wonder if such a philosophy does not invariably lead to premarital sexual relations? This is indeed a realistic and important question. This philosophy need not necessarily lead to premarital sexual relations but it certainly may.[15] Thus, no mature couple can afford to become erotically involved without a clear understanding of the implications of their behavior. Here they would certainly have to assess, in addition to the pleasurable and what they may consider to be positive aspects, the very real problems associated with the premarital sex act. What, for example, are the responsibilities that each has to the other? Is the sexual involvement likely to result in harm to one or both persons? [16]

Obviously there are couples who have considered the consequences; a great number perhaps have convinced themselves that they have evaluated the problems realistically. There are those couples who believe that the premarital sex act brings them closer to one another and makes the relationship more meaningful than it was before, since now there has been both an intellectual as well as a sexual union. Many of these couples also believe that participation in premarital

[15] For a discussion of the petting complex see: Alfred C. Kinsey, et. al., *op. cit.,* Ch. 16. For a discussion of the petting complex as an ingenious compromise between moral demands and sexual needs see: E. E. LeMasters, *Modern Courtship and Marriage,* The Macmillan Co., New York, 1957, pp. 199–206.

[16] One study involving the question of what premarital intercourse does to the quality of the interrelationship of those involved is reported in: Lester Kirkendall, *op. cit.,* pp. 119–123.

sexual relations will facilitate their sexual adjustment in marriage. There is no doubt that many of these people are sincere in what they believe and their views represent one approach to this question. It is difficult, however, to tell how valid these views are. With respect to research concerning whether the premarital sex act brings couples closer to one another, we can say that in at least one study the majority of couples who admitted having premarital intercourse did claim it strengthened their relationship.[17] With respect to the question of whether premarital intercourse facilitates marital success, Kanin and Howard report that sexual intercourse between engaged couples was associated with a higher degree of sexual adjustment (measured by orgastic capacity of the female) on the honeymoon than was found for a control group who had no previous sexual relations.[18] Both of these studies are interesting and perhaps significant; certainly they indicate the very real need for additional studies in this area since they run counter to what many would have anticipated.

These findings, however, would have to be weighed against other research which deals with premarital sexual relations and overall marital success; this is more inclusive than sexual adjustment.[19] For the most part, the studies which do deal with the effect of premarital sexual relations on overall marital adjustment show that couples who have not had premarital intercourse have a slightly better chance to attain overall marital success than do those couples who have had premarital relations with their mates and with others.[20] As to whether the chances

[17] Ernest W. Burgess and Paul Wallin, *Engagement and Marriage*, J. B. Lippincott Co., Philadelphia, 1953, pp. 361, 371–376. However, couples who refrained from having premarital intercourse were not asked whether abstinence strengthened or weakened their relationship. They might have reported unanimously that their relationship had been strengthened by their restraint. This study also found (p. 361) that those couples who shared premarital intercourse had only slightly lower engagement success scores than those who did not.

[18] Eugene J. Kanin and David H. Howard, "Postmarital Consequences of Premarital Sex Adjustments," *Am. Soc. Rev.*, 23 (Oct., 1958), p. 562. Other studies which also show a relationship between premarital sexual orgasm and orgasm in marriage are: Alfred C. Kinsey, et. al., *op. cit.*, pp. 385–390. Lewis M. Terman, et. al., *op. cit.*, p. 383. Ernest W. Burgess and Paul Wallin, *op. cit.*, pp. 362–363. However, it is also noted that those who had premarital intercourse are also more likely than others to engage in extramarital intercourse. See: Alfred C. Kinsey, et. al., *op. cit.*, p. 427.

[19] Harriet R. Mowrer, "Sex and Marital Adjustment: A Critique of Kinsey's Approach," *Social Problems*, 1 (April, 1954), pp. 147–152.

[20] Burgess and Wallin, *op. cit.*, pp. 368–371. Lewis M. Terman, et. al., *op. cit.*, p. 329. Harvey J. Locke, *Predicting Adjustment in Marriage: A Comparison of a Divorced and a Happily Married Group*, Henry Holt and Co., New York, 1951, p. 133.

of marital success are better for persons who had intercourse only with their future mate, as opposed to those who had sexual relations with additional individuals, the evidence is quite unclear.[21]

In evaluating the research with respect to the effect which premarital sexual intercourse has on the man-woman relationship, we must conclude that the findings are based on a small number of studies, employing different methods, with restricted samples of people. They are extremely limited in their scope. As such, the research findings are regarded as suggestive and not as conclusive.[22]

Finally, to understand more fully the impact of premarital sex on one's relationship, there are at least two other important considerations which must be taken into account. These are: (1) the conditions under which premarital sexual relations occur, and (2) the possibility of pregnancy.

Conditions under which Premarital Sexual Relations Occur. The conditions under which the premarital sex act occurs are such that they may lead to difficulty between the persons.[23] For example, there is the need for a place where the couple can feel relatively safe and secure. This frequently involves leaving the community and going to another where the roles of husband and wife are assumed for registry at hotels or motels. Even under these conditions the anxiety about discovery continues to be a problem. Further, the need to hide, to disguise one's identity, and the duplicity involved, many couples find personally repugnant. All of this, which is a by-product of the premarital sexual involvement, may become associated with sexual relations with a particular person. Thus, these negative reactions may destroy a good relationship because one or both partners were not really emotionally prepared for all that the premarital sexual involvement entails. Under these circumstances, couples perfectly capable of good adjustments, sexual and otherwise, may abandon the relationship since it has become identified with things unpleasant.[24]

---

[21] Burgess and Wallin, *op. cit.*, p. 371.

[22] Ehrmann states that whether one enters marriage as a virgin or non-virgin may not be a sufficiently discriminating measure of the effect which premarital intercourse has on marital success. He suggests, for example, that more attention be given to the meaning which the premarital sex act has for the person. Winston Ehrmann, "Premarital Sexual Behavior and Sex Codes of Conduct with Acquaintances, Friends, and Lovers," *Social Forces*, 38 (Dec., 1959), pp. 158–164.

[23] James A. Peterson, *Education for Marriage,* Charles Scribner's Sons, New York, 1956, pp. 101–102.

[24] For a discussion of how premarital sex may hinder or aid personal adjustment see: Allan Fromme, *op. cit.*, pp. 80–82.

Premarital Sexual Relations and Pregnancy. Of all the difficulties associated with premarital sexual relations, pregnancy is the most serious, in the opinion of the authors. To be sure, it is difficult to ascertain the likelihood that pregnancy will occur in any particular case.[25] Furthermore, with modern contraceptive devices which are readily available today, one might assume that the chances for pregnancy are limited. All of this is offset, however, by the fact that the conditions under which the premarital sex act occurs are such that frequently proper precautions are not taken. Furthermore, the age range of the unmarried often coincides with the years of high fertility. Thus, whenever sexual relations occur the persons involved have to be emotionally ready to accept the possibility that a pregnancy may take place. There are those persons who feel that their relationship has progressed to the point where they would go ahead with marriage plans were a pregnancy to occur. Although both persons in the relationship may have good intentions at the time such declarations are made, we recognize that feelings do change. The boy friend who was eager and willing to become married, may suddenly resent the coercion which he feels impinging when the premarital pregnancy is discovered. Even when such couples go ahead with the marriage, the likelihood of successful marriages seems to be less than in non-pregnancy related marriages.[26]

In turning our attention to the actual plight of the woman, we must note that the woman bears the biological consequences of pregnancy and carries the burden and stigma in our culture.[27] For the middle-class woman in this situation it often means moving from the com-

[25] Harold T. Christensen, "Studies in Child Spacing: I—Premarital Pregnancy as Measured by the Spacing of the First Birth from Marriage," *Am. Soc. Rev.*, 18 (Feb., 1953), pp. 53–59. By checking marriage and birth records in an Indiana county, Christensen conservatively estimated that about one-fifth of all first births within marriage were conceived before marriage. He presents conditions (age, occupation, etc.) which may cause this rate to vary.

[26] Harold T. Christensen and Hanna H. Meissner, "Studies in Child Spacing: III—Premarital Pregnancy as a Factor in Divorce," *Am. Soc. Rev.*, 18 (Dec., 1953), pp. 641–644. These authors found that chances of unsuccessful marriage are related (from most to least) to the following: (1) delayed marriage following pregnancy; (2) early marriage following pregnancy; (3) early pregnancy following marriage; (4) delayed pregnancy following marriage. Harold T. Christensen, "Cultural Relativism and Premarital Sex Norms," *Am. Soc. Rev.*, 25 (Feb., 1960), pp. 31–39. However, when comparing samples from Utah, Indiana, and Denmark Christensen found that sexual permissiveness (in Denmark) was associated with higher incidences of premarital pregnancy but lower negative effects of premarital pregnancy. The study is significant in indicating the importance of the overall cultural milieu as a variable.

[27] Ruth Shonle Cavan, *American Marriage*, Thomas Y. Crowell Co., New York, 1959, pp. 210–212.

munity and having her baby in another environment.[28] Frequently this occurs without the essential emotional support of those close to her. This is followed by decisions concerning what to do with the infant and the problem of re-establishment of the mother in the community. The psychic scars produced by the fears and anxieties often remain as unpleasant reminders of memories which might best be forgotten. The reader need not be reminded that our culture has not yet resolved its inconsistencies with respect to the handling of the unwed mother. On the one hand we inadvertently encourage intimacies by glorifying sex through ads, movies, and popular ballads; at the same time we have a mixture of both pity and contempt for the unwed mother. The young lady who may have been the pride of a community is treated like a pariah when it is learned that she has become pregnant out of wedlock.

CONCLUSION. In conclusion, we may say that we have certainly not exhausted all of the ways in which the premarital sex act may be viewed. It is well recognized, for example, that large numbers of premarital sexual relationships occur in our society. And certainly there are those who would argue that no real harm comes to these people as a result. Further, people with an essentially individualistic philosophy believe that mature love, or meaningfulness, need not be an important criterion for premarital sexual involvement. Instead, such persons would simply assert that if the sexual act is not harmful to the partners involved, then its indulgence becomes a personal prerogative. These are all points of view to which many people subscribe; they are therefore determinants of action and conduct.

The authors have tried to assess some of the basic considerations which might be examined in relation to the erotic involvement. Perhaps out of this the reader may be able to formulate and crystallize an approach to premarital sexual relations which makes sense to him. Ultimately, of course, questions of this type are found to be deeply woven in the morality and system of ethics in which one has been nurtured. But ethics and morality need not stand apart from knowledge. In some instances knowledge may fortify one's moral and ethical position, yet in another it can cause a reassessment. The reader has the opportunity inherent in this challenge.

[28] Clark E. Vincent, "The Unwed Mother and Sampling Bias," *Am. Soc. Rev.*, **19** (Oct., 1954), pp. 562–567. This study reports that unwed motherhood is more general than we know and claims that a distorted concept of unwed motherhood (as lower class, poor, uneducated) exists because our information has been largely derived from social agencies.

SUMMARY

An objective understanding of the role of necking, petting, and pre-marital sexual intercourse in the man-woman relationship is frequently impaired by two factors; first by the difficulty of individuals realistically to come to grips with the meaning which sex holds for them, and second, by the presence of half truths and distortions concerning sexual involvement in the American society. Although sexual involvement may be regarded as one means whereby a man and woman relate to each other, it is important to note that the meaning which this relatedness has, may not only be different for each person involved in the relationship but also may be oriented very narrowly. Some people, for example, may be sexually motivated by commodity, exploitative, insecurity, or lust orientations; while sexual motivation for other people may be an expression of healthy and meaningful relatedness.

Without attempting to establish a code of sexual conduct to be indiscriminately followed by all, it was suggested that couples give serious attention to the role which sexual involvement plays in their specific relationships; as an aid in doing so, the following areas of consideration were offered: (1) the personality organization of the individuals involved, (2) the meaning of the erotic involvement for the partners, (3) the nature of the relationship.

Viewing sexual involvement as something apart from love can impair the development of a meaningful relationship. Indeed, sexual involvement is a part of the total love relationship and may serve as a reflection of the general quality of the total love relationship. Unfortunately, love relationships of unmarried couples which have developed meaning and depth sufficient enough to warrant a deep sexual involvement are not prevalent. In cases where couples are attempting to determine the extent to which they should become sexually involved, it is important to consider the effects on the relationship of the conditions under which the premarital sexual act occurs, and the possibility of pregnancy.

QUESTIONS

1. What is meant by "sexual involvement as relatedness?" Define the following and give one example of each:
   a. commodity orientation
   b. exploitative orientation
   c. insecurity and sexual relatedness
   d. lust and sexual relatedness
2. In what way are those people who refuse to engage in any necking or

petting activities similar to those who engage in indiscriminate necking and petting?

3. List and describe the three crucial ideas involved in establishing one's own sexual code in a man-woman relationship. Why are these ideas significant?

4. What is the danger in the following statement: "I wouldn't try anything sexual with her, because she's the girl I'm going to marry." For what reasons might such thinking become prevalent in the American society?

5. What is the difference between sexual adjustment in marriage and overall marital success? What do research findings tend to show: concerning the relationships between premarital sexual intercourse and sexual adjustment; and concerning premarital sexual intercourse and overall marital success? Are these findings to be regarded as being conclusive? Why?

6. What effect might the conditions under which premarital sexual involvement takes place have upon the total man-woman relationship?

7. Is the American society prepared to deal with premarital pregnancy? If so, explain how. If not, explain why not.

PROJECTS

1. Have a panel discussion concerning the pros and cons of granting social approval to premarital sexual intercourse in the United States today.

2. Read one of the current books concerning premarital sexual behavior and compare the advice it offers with what has been discussed in this chapter.

SUGGESTED READINGS

Burgess, Ernest W., and Paul Wallin, *Engagement and Marriage,* J. B. Lippincott Co., Philadelphia, 1953, Ch. 12, "Assessing Premarital Intercourse."

Clothier, Florence, "The Unmarried Mother of School Age as Seen by a Psychiatrist," *Mental Hygiene,* 39 (Oct., 1955), pp. 631–646.

Drucker, A. J., Harold T. Christensen, and H. H. Remmers, "Some Background Factors in Socio-Sexual Modernism," *Marriage and Family Living,* 14 (Nov., 1952), pp. 334–337.

Kanin, Eugene J., and David H. Howard, "Postmarital Consequences of Premarital Sex Adjustments," *Am. Soc. Rev.,* 23 (Oct., 1958), pp. 556–562.

Levy, Dorothy, "A Follow-up Study of Unmarried Mothers," *Social Casework,* 36 (Jan., 1955), pp. 27–33.

Magoun, F. Alexander, *Love and Marriage,* Harper and Brothers, New York, 1948, Ch. 4, "The Pre-marital Sex Problem."

"Sexual Behavior: How Shall We Define and Motivate What Is Acceptable?" A Symposium, *J. Soc. Hyg.,* 36 (April, 1950), pp. 129–161.

Stokes, Walter R., David R. Mace, et. al., "Premarital Sexual Behavior," *Marriage and Family Living,* 15 (Aug., 1953), pp. 234–249.

preconceived notions about such characteristics as race, religion, nationality, education, and socio-economic status often serve to eliminate large numbers of people from one's marital choices. But these characteristics, although important, frequently operate without the person's awareness of their importance in his concept of an ideal mate. Thus, one tends to think about his "dream" partner in terms of personality and physical characteristics. In this respect one investigator, Anselm Strauss, found that the majority of men and women report that their ideal mates and their real mates are "identical," "very close," or "close" both in physical and in personality characteristics.[1] In regard to these physical and personality characteristics, this study indicates the greater similarity between real and ideal mates tends to be reflected by personality characteristics. Moreover, when subjects compared the mate finally selected with the one they liked next best, there was practically no difference between them in approximation to the ideal on physical traits, but marked differences between them in regard to personality characteristics, with the mate finally selected more closely approximating the ideal. All of this would seem to show that a person's first concern in mate selection is to seek out those persons who meet his general physical standards, once this has been accomplished his selection of a mate is made from this group on the basis of the specific personality characteristics which he desires in a mate. Thus, physical characteristics may be the initial selective factors within which personality discrimination takes place.

Although most people in this study claim to have married their ideal mates, we cannot assume that these assertions are correct. Much more has to be known about how the concept of the ideal mate may have been revised by the presence of particular types of individuals who were available as marriage partners. Until all of this is known the results of ideal mate studies should be regarded as suggestive rather than conclusive.

Implications of Ideal Mate Studies for Selecting a Marriage Partner. There appears to be little doubt that many of us possess a concept of the ideal mate. Such a concept need not necessarily cause problems in mate selection. Nevertheless, there are several potential difficulties which one has to recognize. For example, to the extent that the concept of the ideal mate may be a denial of the relative worth of oneself and an exaggerated superiority of others, it represents an un-

[1] Anselm Strauss, "The Ideal and the Chosen Mate," *Am. J. Sociol.,* **52** (Oct., 1946), pp. 204–208. For another study concerning the influences which the ideal mate has on one's selection of a mate see: Ernest W. Burgess and Paul Wallin, *Engagement and Marriage,* J. B. Lippincott Co., Philadelphia, 1953, p. 175.

healthy approach to mate selection and is often associated with the need to live through others; a problem with which we are already familiar since it has been discussed in an earlier chapter dealing with motivations for marriage. A further problem which is concerned with the concept of the ideal mate is its divorcement from reality. There are those, for example, who in dating and courtship grossly distort the other person and see in him all of the qualities of their ideal. In these cases the dating partner is frequently seen in perfectionistic terms and is viewed as all knowing, all wise, all good, and so it goes. The difficulty increases for those who may have come to expect contradictory characteristics from their ideal mate. There are people, for example, who expect the ideal mate to be all knowing but at the same time to be dependent upon them for advice. In light of all the demands exercised on us by our concept of the ideal mate certain reactions often follow. If our concept of the ideal mate is sufficiently rigid, the actual persons we are dating may come to be viewed as possessing only imperfections and they may be regarded as being undesirable or contemptible. Many potentially good mates have been lost this way and some people fail to marry precisely because they cannot adjust their concept to reality. If, on the other hand, we expect contradictory things of the partner, we are perpetually ambivalent and uncertain in our feelings and reactions toward him. Finally, many marry what they believe to be the ideal mate only to experience the real person in marriage. These people frequently come to believe that the mate misrepresented himself, presenting himself as superior to what he actually was. Much hostility may develop out of such a realization.

There is the case of a woman who had been married for fifteen years. At the time she married she believed herself to be fortunate to have found herself a husband. She saw herself as homely, unlovable, and inferior; to her the husband possessed all of the qualities of an ideal mate. He was strong, handsome, and had a mind of his own. Over the years this woman discovered that her husband did not quite fit her image, instead he was, in her terms, weak, could not make up his mind, and was easily dominated. She developed tremendous hostility and resentment toward him, felt that he had misrepresented himself, and became very vindictive toward him as a result. Her vindictiveness took the form of "brow beating" her husband, refusing any type of erotic involvement, and humiliating him in front of their children. It took a considerable amount of time with much difficulty involved for her to understand that her concept of the ideal mate, which she had imposed on her husband, was responsible for her marital problems.

Parental Image Studies. A second type of mate selection study in which a limited amount of work has been done concerns the degree to which one's image of his parents influences his selection of a marriage partner. Originally it was assumed that one tended to marry a person who was similar to his, or her, parent of the opposite sex. Thus, men presumably tended to select mates who resembled their mothers, and women mates who resembled their fathers. Research did not uphold this hypothesis, since little relationship was found to exist between one's mate and parent of the opposite sex, per se. It has been demonstrated, however, that a person's selection of a mate does tend to be influenced by the kind of relationship he shared with his parents. Strauss reports a number of such kinds of parental influences on mate selection.[2] For example, it appears that when one has shared a rather meaningful relationship with one parent, he tends to seek a mate who is very similar to that parent. Or, in cases where one has shared an extremely hostile relationship with a parent, the tendency is to select a marriage partner who differs markedly from that parent. Thus, if a young man shared his most meaningful family relationship with his mother, he tends to select a marriage partner with characteristics similar to hers. If his relationships with both his mother and father were equally meaningful to him, his selection of a marriage partner seems to reflect both parents. On the other hand, if the young man's relationship with his mother was ridden with hostility, his tendency seems to be to select a marriage partner who possesses characteristics which differ markedly from those of his mother.

It should be noted, however, that the relationship between mate selection and parental image exists with respect to temperamental and ideational characteristics, but is apparent to a much lesser degree with respect to physical characteristics.[3] In effect this means that the kind of relationship one shares with either one or both parents tends to influence his selection of a marriage partner, but this influence is most apparent with respect to the dispositions and sets of values and less apparent with respect to physical appearances.

When we shift our attention to what is observed in counseling, however, in addition to the type of parental influence just described we find cases in which people sharing a poor relationship with their parents look for a marital partner who resembles their parents, instead of looking for marital partners who differ from their parents. They do this with the hope of finding acceptance in a symbolic way.

[2] Anselm Strauss, "The Influence of Parent-Images upon Marital Choice," *Am. Soc. Rev.*, **11** (Oct., 1946), pp. 554–559.
[3] *Ibid.*

Finally, it should be noted that the research findings of parental image studies, as was also true of ideal mate studies, should be regarded as suggestive rather than conclusive.

Implications of Parental Image Studies for Selecting a Marriage Partner. The concept of the parental image presents difficulties which are in certain respects similar to those encountered in the ideal mate. For example, there are those persons who idealize their parents to such an extent that much distortion of the parents occurs. Under such circumstances the dating partner may be compared with an exaggerated view of a parent which is completely divorced from reality. Thus, the dating partner may be judged and evaluated quite unfairly.

There was a young lady who was the daughter of a successful physician. She saw her father in the most ideal terms; to her he was a brilliant, self-sacrificing person who had surmounted serious economic and personal problems in order to become a physician. Although there was some basis in fact for the view she held of her father, much of what she believed was grossly distorted. She nevertheless insisted on comparing any boy she dated with this distorted view of her father. Needless to say, none of her boy friends could measure up to her parental image. Her problem became apparent to her father and it became necessary for him to aid his daughter in acquiring a more realistic view. Once she was able to do this, she became more accepting of her dates.

In addition, one's parental image may include personality traits which are likely to lead to difficulties. For example, one may come to admire a parent's power to manipulate and coerce others into a decision. One may come to feel that such a trait is indicative of power and strength in the marital relationship. To internalize such a parental image and further to seek such traits in a mate frequently leads to difficulty in the marriage relationship.

Assortative Mating Studies. In the studies dealing with the ideal mate and parental image we were primarily concerned with the factors that determined the traits which individuals sought in a marital relationship. The third approach to the study of mate selection deals with another question, namely, the extent to which people select marriage partners who are similar to them and the extent to which they select partners who are dissimilar to them. This approach is known as assortative mating and involves two major hypotheses: the first is called homogamy and postulates that like marries like; the second is called heterogamy and postulates that opposites marry each other. In an attempt to shed light on these hypotheses a number of physical, psychological, and social factors have been investigated.

For the most part research findings tend to support the homogamous hypothesis in that it appears that like tends to marry like. This is particularly true of such items as race, religion, I.Q., ethnic origin, place of residence before marriage, marital status before marriage, socio-economic status, social class, occupation, height, age, attitudes, and interests.[4] With respect to the last two items, namely attitudes and interests, the evidence does not seem to be conclusive.[5] With respect to height and age, homogamy tends to occur far more frequently than heterogamy. Although the tendency is for women to marry older and taller men, the differences between men and women who marry are not great with respect to height and age. We are confronted with data on personality characteristics which suggests that both homogamy[6] and heterogamy[7] are involved. Homogamy is particularly apparent when we deal with certain broad categories of personality. For example, we find that there is a tendency for neurotics to marry

[4] For reviews of the many assortative mating studies see: Helen M. Richardson, "Studies of Mental Resemblance Between Husbands and Wives and Between Friends," *Psychological Bulletin*, 36 (Feb., 1939), pp. 104–120. Robert F. Winch in Joseph B. Gittler's *Review of Sociology*, John Wiley and Sons, Inc., New York, 1957, Ch. 11, pp. 349–352.

[5] Most assortative mating studies are conducted by testing people who are already engaged or married and who, therefore, have had a great deal of interaction with each other which might be responsible for producing a similarity in their attitudes and interests that was not present prior to this interaction. In other words, it is possible that the similarity found among engaged and married partners with respect to attitudes and interests may be the result of their interaction in engagement and marriage and not necessarily present at the outset. One of the authors conducted a study of assortative mating which tested couples, not after they had become engaged or married, but rather, just prior to their having met. The results of this study suggest that attitudes and interests of married people are not as similar prior to engagement or marriage as we have been led to believe, but rather that they may tend to become similar after intensive interaction in engagement and marriage. For a detailed account of this research see: Eloise C. Snyder, "Marital Selectivity with Respect to Five Variables: A Study of Assortative Mating," University Park, Pennsylvania State University Libraries, M.A. Thesis, 1953.

[6] In reviewing studies on psychological characteristics Stagner points out that although homogamy is found it is more apparent in intellectual interest and attitude scores than it is in temperament scores. Ross Stagner, *Psychology of Personality*, McGraw-Hill Book Co., New York, 1948, p. 387.

[7] Horace Gray, "Psychological Types in Married People," *J. soc. Psychol.*, 29, Second Half (May, 1949), pp. 189–200. Using Jung's psychological types this study found heterogamy predominant.

neurotics.[8] We also discover, however, that there are other studies which report that although neurotics tend to marry other neurotics, the kinds of neuroses involved tend to be different.[9] An overly aggressive male, for example, instead of marrying an overly aggressive female tends to marry an overly submissive female. Thus, the seemingly contradictory findings (e.g., personality is homogamous and personality is heterogamous) at least in part tend to result from the fact that in most cases the various studies are concerned not with the same personality characteristics but with different characteristics. It is also evident that in those cases where the same characteristic is being considered, the methods of getting at similarity or dissimilarity (in other words the methodologies of the studies) differ, and this too may account for certain differences in results.

Before concluding this discussion of the findings of assortative mating studies, it should be noted that another area of study, namely complementary needs, might be subsumed under assortative mating. These studies of complementary needs, which indicate that married pairs tend to be heterogamous with respect to need fulfillment, will be discussed separately in a following section of this chapter.

Implications of Assortative Mating for Selecting a Marriage Partner. Persons with similar backgrounds tend to get along well together since they possess a common basis of experiences. Such experiences enable them to share sentiments and values and to communicate in ways which have meaning to them. On the other hand, we must recognize that similarity of background alone is no assurance against difficulties in the man-woman relationship. Indeed, the fact that two people come from similar backgrounds frequently obscures the existence of some very serious problems. Two people who come from unstable families are indeed poor risks in marriage. Although each might believe that the difficulties which are common to their backgrounds will enable him to understand and deal with family problems, his image of the nature of family life may be extremely negative. Indeed, the very personalities which these people have developed as a result of such families may make them very poor marital risks. In essence, one may compound his difficulties in many instances by marrying a person from a similar background.

[8] Raymond R. Willoughby, "Neuroticism in Marriage, IV. Homogamy, V. Summary and Conclusions," *J. soc. Psychol.,* 7 (Feb., 1936), pp. 19–48.

[9] Bela Mittelmann, "Complementary Neurotic Reactions in Intimate Relationships," *Psychoanalytic Quarterly,* 13 (1944), pp. 479–491. In one study, however, homogamy was not only found in neurotic tendency but also in the items comprising it. See: Ernest W. Burgess and Paul Wallin, "Homogamy in Personality Characteristics," *J. abnorm. soc. Psychol.,* 39 (Oct., 1944), pp. 475–481.

This can be illustrated by citing this situation: a couple who were contemplating marriage had both come from homes in which the parents had been unhappily married and subsequently divorced. The couple also reported that they both had an unhappy childhood and unhappy family relations. They believed that since they knew what an unhappy family life was like, they were in a position to avoid repetition of the same errors. For them, having a happy family was simply a matter of effort. After they were married they began to fight and argue, and the immaturities of each began to appear. Soon they became very discouraged, and began to think in terms of divorce. Since they had no concept of a happy family it was difficult for them to have much faith that their problems could be resolved.

Complementary Needs. One aspect of heterogamy, which might be regarded as a fourth approach to the analysis of mate selection, is that of complementary needs. In this area the major hypothesis is that the selection of a mate tends to be made on the basis of each person's ability to satisfy "opposite kinds of needs" in the other.

Robert F. Winch, for example, who has spent a considerable amount of time studying this question, sees mate selection as occurring on the basis of complementary needs.[10] He does not disregard the importance of the previously noted findings on homogamy studies, but claims that although homogamy operates in such a way as to cause an individual to sort out from an entire population of potential mates those who are similar to him with respect to social background, cultural interests and values, the process of falling in love tends to occur through complementary need fulfillment. For example, this could mean that a male who has a need to express hostility would be attracted to a woman with a need to have hostility expressed toward her.

Implications of Complementary Needs for Selecting a Marriage Partner. The findings regarding complementary needs suggest the following implications for mate selection. The fact that we apparently are attracted to people who complement our needs and traits should alert us to certain difficulties. It suggests, as indicated in an earlier chapter on love, that we should concern ourselves not only with the fact that we are attracted to certain types of people, but why we are attracted to them. It becomes apparent that complementariness may not necessarily be conducive to the development of a mature relationship. Such difficulties become especially apparent in relationships

[10] Robert F. Winch, *Mate Selection,* Harper and Brothers, New York, 1958. See also: Gray, *loc. cit.,* Thomas and Virginia Ktsanes, "The Theory of Complementary Needs in Mate-Selection," in R. F. Winch and R. McGinnis: *Marriage and the Family,* Henry Holt, New York, 1953, pp. 435–453.

where one person may have a need to dominate and the other a need to be dominated, or where one person has a need to be aggressive and the other a need to be submissive.

Finally, we should point out that the reader might well make some effort to assess the extent to which the variables in the concept of ideal mate, parental image, complementary needs, and assortative mating operate to influence his or her mate selection. From such an analysis there may be the opportunity to appreciate the factors in mate selection which can operate against finding and developing the best possible relationship.

PREDICTION OF SUCCESS IN MARRIAGE. Having examined some of the factors involved in the selection of a mate and some of the dangers which these factors may lead to, a discussion of the factors which research has shown to be related to marital success and the factors which are related to marital failure is in order. Much of the information here is based on what researchers in the area of marriage prediction have found in their numerous studies.

To begin with, it should be pointed out that in the area of marriage prediction there is an attempt to determine the probability of marital success for those who are contemplating marriage and/or for those who are already married. The assumption which underlies marriage prediction, as was noted previously in regard to mate selection studies, is rooted in the relationship between one's past experiences and future behavior. This is to say that marriage prediction is predicated on the assumption that the experiences which one has had prior to marriage will affect his behavior in marriage.

In order to analyze the relationship between past experience and marital success and failure, it first becomes necessary to clarify what is meant by marital success and what is meant by marital failure. To be sure, divorce and separation are indicative of marital failure, but it is incorrect to assume that these are the only criteria of marital failure. Indeed, many marriages which are not broken by divorce or separation are constantly ridden by conflict and unhappiness and as such are regarded as being unsuccessful. Let us look therefore at the criteria which have been used (either in entirety or in part) in defining successful marriage.

A successful marriage is one in which:

1. Both husband and wife are happy and satisfied with their marriage.
2. There is a quality of permanence to the relationship.
3. There is good adjustment (including sexual adjustment).

ity, ethnicity, race, and socio-economic status, are related to success in marriage and dissimilarity with respect to these areas, particularly if it is sufficiently great, is associated with failure in marriage.

Furthermore, the following characteristics tend to be associated with successful marriage:

1. Couples who have been reared in the country rather than in the city.

2. Couples possessing similar levels of education, with the higher the educational level the greater the tendency for successful marriage.

3. Couples who are similar in age with the best adjustment occurring in cases where the husband is a little older than the wife and is at least twenty-two years old at marriage and the wife is at least twenty.[14]

4. Couples who had no previous marriages.

5. Couples who display a pattern of church attendance, particularly if they both attend the same church.[15]

6. Couples who regard their childhood and the marriage of their parents as having been happy.

7. Couples who have had a strong positive feeling for their parents.

8. Couples who received firm but moderate discipline as children.

9. Couples who have had parental approval of their marriage.

10. Couples without a pattern of divorce among their relatives.

Social Participation. With respect to social participation and successful marriage the following factors appear to be important.

1. Both marriage partners are members of several organized social groups.

2. Both partners engage in outside activities together and share common interests.

[14] In one study, however, absolute and relative ages of spouses were not found to be consistently and significantly related to reported marital adjustment. Clifford Kirkpatrick and John Cotton, "Physical Attractiveness, Age, and Marital Adjustment," *Am. Soc. Rev.*, 16 (Feb., 1951), pp. 81–86.

[15] On this last point, however, Locke found that the degree of actual agreement or disagreement between spouses on religion was a minor factor in marital success. See: Harvey J. Locke, *op. cit.*, pp. 79, 338. Further, in a study using Swedish data Karlsson found religious participation to be either uncorrelated or slightly negatively correlated with marital success. See: G. Karlsson, *Adaptability and Communication in Marriage: A Swedish Predictive Study of Marital Satisfaction,* Uppsala, Almqvist, and Wiksells, Boktryckeri Aktiebolag, 1951. This latter finding leads some authorities to wonder whether this difference between Karlsson's findings and the American findings, which generally report religious participation as being related to good marriage adjustment, might not corroborate the charge that American studies for the most part tend to select conservative and conforming subjects.

3. Both partners are in agreement on the persons who are to be regarded as friends, each having several friends of his own, and also sharing several friends with his partner.

Economic Status. It was previously noted that similarity with respect to socio-economic status is related to successful marriage. When differences between the partners do exist, cases in which the husband is from the higher socio-economic background have a greater chance for success than cases in which the wife's socio-economic background is higher.

Other economic factors which have been found to be related to successful marriage are:

1. Occupations characterized by a high degree of social control.
2. A moderate rather than high or low income at marriage.
3. Gainful employment for husband and wife prior to marriage. This factor appears to be especially significant for the women who were employed in certain occupations, such as professional or skilled office positions.
4. A steady work record.
5. Savings before marriage.
6. Agreement on and efficiency in spending income.

Response Patterns. In this category we are concerned with how the couple has responded to the love relationship. The findings are:

1. Couples who "fall in love at first sight" are less likely to be as successful in marriage than those whose love develops out of companionship and friendship.
2. Couples who knew each other for approximately a year or two before becoming engaged are more likely to be successful in marriage than are couples who knew each other for a shorter period.
3. Couples who have an engagement of at least a year or more are more likely to be successful in marriage than are couples whose engagement was for a shorter period.
4. Couples who utilize their engagement period to work out interpersonal adjustments are more likely to succeed in marriage than those who view the engagement period as a series of social events and those who "meet and marry."

Sexual Factors. The findings which deal with the relationship between sexual factors and successful marriage are:

1. Those who received sex information from parents in a straight forward but tactful and non-embarrassed manner.

2. Those who are not shy about sex matters.

3. Wives who do not fear pregnancy.

4. Couples who desire children.

5. Couples where each of the partners has about the same degree of interest in sex; rarely, or infrequently, refusing or demanding, sexual intercourse with the spouse.

6. Marriage in which there is an absence of extramarital sexual relations.

Sexual factors conducive to failure in marriage include:

1. The wife's desire to be of the opposite sex.

2. Wife's having a traumatic sexual experience during adolescence.

3. Wife's sexual intercourse before marriage.[16]

4. Marrying because of pregnancy.

Significance of Marriage Prediction Findings for Selecting a Marriage Partner. We have presented some of the major research findings with respect to the personal and social characteristics which are involved in marital success or failure. It is important at this point to ask ourselves: what do these results tell us about what to look for in a mate? Although much is known about the factors which are associated with successful marriage, less is known about why they are so associated. For example, church attendance and success in marriage appear together, but it is difficult to say whether church attendance causes success in marriage or whether success is due to another variable—conservatism (since conservative people go to church and are likely to be successful in marriage). These are the kinds of dilemmas that arise in trying to make some sense out of the information which is available. In the analysis to follow we have attempted to present our interpretation in light of what appears most reasonable in view of the knowledge available at this time.

Favorable Family Background. In regard to the family, we should note that emotional climate in the home is a significant factor. Furthermore, the parental relationship and the view of family life which parents present to their children are also significant. These factors result in models about the nature of family life, as well as images of what a father or mother, husband or wife, ought to be. When one internalizes a positive concept of family living, and has a concept of a parental model or image associated with consistency and happiness, he can take these into his own marriage. Another im-

---

[16] In one study it was found that when restricted to future spouse, results were negligible. See Lewis M. Terman, *op. cit.*

portant dimension has to do with the quality of the interpersonal relationships at home. When these relationships are characterized by warmth and acceptance the basis for a mature and emotionally stable personality has been established, and this in turn lends itself to good interpersonal relationships in marriage.

It is likewise obvious that unhappy family relationships and inadequate models result in disturbances in personality and role confusion about the expectations of marriage. Thus, there is a chain of events in which poor family relationships tend to create emotionally unstable personalities. Persons having such personalities may be motivated to marry for reasons which are not conducive to building a successful marriage. Mate selection suffers since, as suggested in an earlier chapter, these people may feel desperate about the need to marry. This may result once more in poor marital relationships, unhappy families, and emotionally unstable children.

Emotional Stability. On the basis of what we have just pointed out it follows that mature and emotionally stable personalities with healthy sexual attitudes, who are sociable, are good risks in marriage; and immature, unstable personalities, who are isolates, are poor risks in marriage. We have indicated throughout this book that the man-woman relationship is a type of social involvement with all of the complexities found in any kind of human relationship plus the additional burdens imposed on the relationship by the demands of marriage. Persons who are successful in developing healthy human relationships in general also tend to be successful in marriage.

The research on marriage prediction suggests further that conservative and conventional people do well in marriage. This is probably to be expected since marriage and the family are by nature conservative institutions.[17] Conservatism becomes manifest in relation to the reported absence of premarital sexual activity and in relation to economic factors, including steady work habits, savings in the bank, and occupations over which society exerts social control; all of which are related to marriage success. The latter is especially interesting since we recognize that in certain occupational roles—those in which society has a stake—a high degree of social control becomes manifest. In these occupational roles, such as minister or teacher, society sees to it that conventional behavior is followed and deviations are discouraged. Other occupations with a low degree of social control, such as traveling salesman or unskilled laborer, are occupations about

[17] On the other hand the authors in their own experience have known of numerous marriages which were not conventional but which would have to be considered as successful by most any criteria.

which society is either less concerned or unable to control behavior. We are, of course, unable to tell whether it is the occupation that produces the conformity or the deviation; or whether certain personality types are inclined to seek certain occupational areas.

Limitations of the Research Findings. Let us now discuss certain limitations to the research findings derived from marriage prediction. In the first place, the findings were obtained for the most part from a sample of people who were largely urban, white, middle-class Protestants. The extent to which these findings would hold for other groups remains questionable. Even for those persons who fall within the scope of the sample there are further questions which lead us to the second major limitation of research findings in marriage prediction. This limitation has to do with the fact that while the findings tell us much about conventional marriages, they give us little information about marriages which are nonconventional. Indeed the implication is that nonconventional marriages are unsuccessful. And, although this may be valid in a broad sense, it fails to take into account the many exceptions to the rule. It conveys the erroneous impression that if one is not conventional, he is doomed to marital failure.

In this connection it should be pointed out that virtually all counselors have encountered marriages which were in difficulty precisely because one or both partners were conventional to the point where they did only what was expected of them, personally and socially. They never permitted themselves deviations and thus found themselves either in conflict, or generally unhappy and bored.

From the foregoing discussion, it becomes apparent that the entire notion of conventionality and nonconventionality in marriage is one which is still to be studied if understanding is to be acquired. How nonconventional can one be, and in what areas, before a marriage is threatened? Such an inquiry would appear to be a "must" before we can draw very many conclusions about the relationship between conventionality and marital success.

If one recognizes the limitations to the research findings derived from marriage prediction studies, these results can be an aid in understanding in a broad sense some of the important factors in success or failure in marriage.

Finally, in concluding this chapter, we would like to comment on its underlying theme; in pointing out that our behavior in the future is determined by what has come before, we do not wish to present the reader with a hopeless view about the future. Those who may be motivated to choose a mate unwisely as a result of, let us say, a concept of an ideal mate, or those who are concerned that their backgrounds do not lend themselves to success in marriage, will discover that a knowledge of these facts may enable them to examine critically and perhaps to gain an understanding of those facets of their backgrounds which are involved in the potential difficulty. When one understands the potential areas of difficulty and is prepared to deal with them, the possibility for success in marriage increases.

SUMMARY

One's previous experiences result in his ability or inability to accept certain personal and social characteristics in other people, and, as such, they play an important and influential role in the specific choice made in selecting a marital partner. In this regard it was noted that several types of studies have been undertaken in the attempt to shed light on specific factors which seem to be most influential in mate selection. These marital selection studies are in the areas of: (1) the ideal mate, (2) the parental image, (3) assortative mating, and (4) complementary needs. The findings of these studies and the implications which these findings have for mate selection were discussed in this chapter.

Also discussed was the area of marriage prediction. It is important to note that, while mate selection studies are primarily concerned with determining the existence of a pattern in who marries whom, marriage prediction studies concentrate on what types of persons tend to be most successful and what types tend to be least successful in marriage. The findings of marriage prediction studies and the implications which these findings have for mate selection were discussed under the following six categories: (1) personality characteristics, (2) cultural backgrounds, (3) social participation, (4) economic status, (5) response patterns, and (6) sexual factors.

It was suggested that an understanding of these findings concerning mate selection and marriage prediction when assessed in terms of their impact upon individual behavior might provide the reader with a basis from which to begin to explore his own involvements in selecting a mate and in attempting to build a sound marriage relationship.

QUESTIONS

1. How exactly does one's previous experience affect his choice of a marital partner?
2. State the major purpose of each of the following areas of scientific inquiry and discuss the major findings of each area:
   a. Ideal mate studies.
   b. Parental image studies.

    c. Assortative mating studies.

    d. Complementary needs studies.

3. In what ways might the knowledge which one acquires through the findings of each of the four areas of marital selection studies help him in selecting a marriage partner?

4. What is the difference between the purpose of mate selection studies and the purpose of marriage prediction studies?

5. Exactly how are the findings from marriage prediction derived? Explain in full.

6. List the six areas of human experience into which the results of marriage prediction studies can be classified. Discuss the major findings of each of these six areas.

7. List and discuss the major limitations of marriage prediction findings.

8. How might marriage prediction findings be useful to individuals contemplating marriage? Give examples.

PROJECTS

1. Interview a grouping of young married couples and a grouping of older married couples in the attempt to determine whether these two groupings differed and, if so, in what ways they differed, in regard to the criteria they used in selecting their marriage partners.

2. Invite a marriage counselor to class to talk about counseling young people in regard to marriage. If there is no marriage counselor at your school, invite a clergyman to speak on this same topic.

SUGGESTED READINGS

Burgess, Ernest W., and Leonard S. Cottrell, Jr., *Predicting Success or Failure in Marriage*, Prentice-Hall, Inc., New York, 1939.

Kennedy, Ruby Jo Reeves, "Premarital Residential Propinquity and Ethnic Endogamy," *Am. J. Social.*, **48** (Mar., 1943), pp. 580–584.

Kirkpatrick, Clifford, "A Statistical Investigation of the Psychoanalytic Theory of Mate Selection," *J. abnorm. soc. Psychol.*, **32** (Oct.–Dec., 1937), pp. 427–430.

Locke, Harvey J., *Predicting Adjustment in Marriage: A Comparison of a Divorced and a Happily Married Group*, Henry Holt and Co., New York, 1951.

Mangus, Arthur Raymond, "Relationships between the Young Woman's Conceptions of Her Intimate Male Associates and of Her Ideal Husband," *J. soc. Psychol.*, **7** (Nov., 1936), pp. 403–420.

Strauss, Anselm, "The Influence of Parent-Images Upon Marital Choice," *Am. Soc. Rev.*, **11** (Oct., 1946), pp. 554–559.

Strauss, Anselm, "The Ideal and Chosen Mate," *Am. J. Sociol.*, **52** (Nov., 1946), pp. 204–208.

Terman, Lewis M., et al., *Psychological Factors in Marital Happiness*, McGraw-Hill Book Co., New York, 1938.

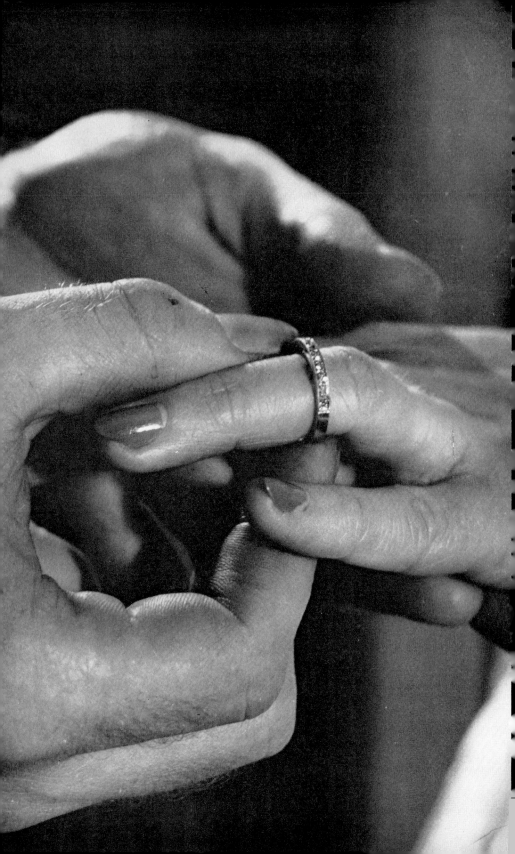

The mixed religious marriage: a cultural and psychological dilemma

10

In the preceding chapter it was noted that people who come from similar backgrounds confront fewer obstacles in attaining successful marital relationships than do those with divergent backgrounds. This favorable combination of similarity is particularly true when applied to such background traits as race, nationality, ethnic group, and religion. Marriages in which the partners are dissimilar with respect to the aforementioned traits are frequently referred to as mixed marriages. Nevertheless, while there may be a wide variety of mixed marriages based on differences in race, nationality, or religion, we will limit our discussion in this chapter to the mixed religious marriage. We have limited our discussion for several reasons. To begin with, in comparison with racial intermarriage mixed religious marriages are by far more numerous in our society.[1] Thus, it is of the greatest immediate concern to the majority of readers.[2] Furthermore, the prob-

---

[1] See: Ruth Shonle Cavan, who says, "The most frowned upon mixed marriage and one rarely occurring in the U.S. is that between whites and nonwhites." Cavan, *American Marriage*, Thomas Y. Crowell Co., New York, 1959, p. 162. See also: August B. Hollingshead, who states "Although inter-racial marriages are legal in Connecticut, they are extremely rare." Hollinghead, "Cultural Factors in the Selection of Marriage Mates," *Am. Soc. Rev.*, 15 (Oct., 1950), pp. 619–627.

[2] It is interesting to note that many college students claim that if other aspects of the relationship were satisfactory they would be willing to marry persons of another faith. However, not all would be willing to change their faith. One study, for example, found that although 72 percent of Catholics and 51 percent of

lems encountered in a mixed religious marriage are in many ways similar to problems encountered in mixed racial and mixed ethnic marriages.[3] There are, for example, the problems of ethnic or racial incompatibilities between husband and wife, and the question of racial or ethnic affiliation for the children. Thus, it would seem that by dealing with the mixed religious marriage we will in effect deal with problems which could apply to other types of mixed marriages.

SOCIAL CONCERN FOR THE MIXED RELIGIOUS MARRIAGE. The concern about the number of mixed religious marriages as well as the instability which seems to be present in them is not new.[4] As is noted in Table 7, the divorce rate is approximately three times as high for mixed religious marriages as it is for those marriages in which the partners are of the same religious background.[5] Throughout history the different religious groups, Jewish, Protestant, and Catholic, have been concerned with and have applied sanctions and threats against those who married out of their faith, especially those who gave up their own religion in this process.[6] The mixed religious marriage historically has been an ideological dilemma as well as a threat to the different religious groups. It has been a dilemma because each religion espouses the doctrine of brotherly love and acceptance of others. Nevertheless, such beliefs when carried to their logical conclusion often result in marriages outside the faith with the ever present danger that many will lose their original religious affiliations. The abandonment of one's religious faith in order to accept another in marriage constitutes a threat to the organized religious

Protestants would marry outside of the faith, only 11 percent and 37 percent respectively would be willing to change their religious affiliation in so doing. Judson T. and Mary G. Landis, *Building a Successful Marriage*, 3rd ed., Prentice-Hall, Inc., Englewood Cliffs, New Jersey, 1958, pp. 241–242.

[3] For a study which dealt with interracial marriages between whites and non-whites, see: Ray E. Baber, "A Study of 325 Mixed Marriages," *Am. Soc. Rev.*, 2 (Oct., 1937), pp. 705–716.

[4] Ray E. Baber, *Marriage and the Family*, 2nd ed., McGraw-Hill Book Co., Inc., New York, 1953, p. 119. Judson T. and Mary G. Landis, *Building a Successful Marriage*, 3rd ed., Prentice-Hall, Inc., Englewood Cliffs, New Jersey, 1958, pp. 237–258.

[5] For the table and discussion of the divorce rate in mixed and non-mixed religious marriages, see: Judson T. Landis, "Marriages of Mixed and Non-mixed Religious Faith," *Am. Soc. Rev.*, 14 (June, 1949), pp. 401–407. Although one study found no significant differences between the happiness of couples in mixed and non-mixed religious marriages, the couples studied were in the early years of marriage. Ernest W. Burgess and Leonard S. Cottrell, Jr., *Predicting Success or Failure in Marriage*, Prentice-Hall, Inc., Englewood Cliffs, New Jersey, 1939, pp. 87–88.

[6] See: John L. Thomas, S.J., *The American Catholic Family*, Prentice-Hall, Inc., Englewood Cliffs, New Jersey, 1956, pp. 148–153.

bodies since it means an eventual loss of followers.[7] With respect to the U.S. today, we note that despite their teachings none of the major religions advocates an involvement with a member of another faith, especially if such marriage necessitates adopting a different religion.

TABLE 7
Percentage of Marriages of Mixed and Non-Mixed Religious Faiths ending in Divorce or Separation as Revealed by Studies of Marriages in Michigan, Maryland, and Washington

Religious Categories	Number	Landis Study in Michigan ($N = 4,108$) Percent	Bell Study in Maryland ($N = 13,528$) Percent	Weeks Study in Washington ($N = 6,548$) Percent
Both Catholic	583	4.4	6.4	3.8
Both Jewish	96	5.2	4.6	—
Both Protestant	2,794	6.0	6.8	10.0
Mixed, Catholic-Protestant	192	14.1	15.2	17.4
Both none	39	17.9	16.7	23.9
Protestant changed to Catholic	56	10.7		
Catholic changed to Protestant	57	10.6		
Protestant father—Catholic mother	90	6.7		
Catholic father—Protestant mother	102	20.6		
Father none—Mother Catholic	41	9.8		
Father none—Mother Protestant	84	19.0		

INDOCTRINATION AGAINST MARITAL INVOLVEMENT WITH OUTSIDERS. One of the ways in which religious bodies have dealt and do deal with the potential loss of followers and the dissolu-

---

[7] "The number of interfaith marriages is large, and it is increasing. . . . It is unfair to argue, however, that the concern of the church is purely one of self-interest, growing out of fear of losing members. It is true that persons contracting mixed marriages tend to drop away from their respective churches and are somewhat less concerned than usual with the religious rearing of their children. But there are other reasons for the attitude of the various churches. Their leaders, for example, have long known what recent sociological studies verify concerning the high divorce and separation rates found among such marriages." See: James H. S. Bossard, "Eight Reasons Why Marriages Go Wrong," in *New York Times Magazine* (June 24, 1956), pp. 5, 20–23.

tion of their religious traditions is to foster attitudes and beliefs which enable their members to differentiate themselves from members of other religious groups.[8] Such attitudes often involve an element of ethnocentrism—that is, the belief that one's ways are superior to the ways of others.[9] Although many people may be consciously indoctrinated with the superiority of their own religious beliefs, unconscious, informal methods are also evident. One learns a great deal through informal means, gestures, jokes, reactions of parents and peers. Furthermore, one comes to perceive the attitudes and definitions which those around him have about people who are different, be they Jews, Catholics, or Protestants. Thus, over a period of time we come to believe, not necessarily knowing how or why, that some religious views and groups, especially our own, are superior to others. It is apparent that the development of attitudes regarding the superiority of one's religious views and of the people with whom these are identified is not without its logic and usefulness. Indeed, these are very functional and necessary from the point of view of a religious group. They are a means of perpetuating the religious values of a particular group and constitute an aid in the survival of said group. This is clearly pointed out by David Kirshenbaum who claims that the lack of teaching Jewish children to be Jews, or the lack of maintaining group consciousness, is largely responsible for the increasing rate of Jewish-Gentile marriage, a factor which, according to Kirshenbaum, may well prove detrimental to the future of Judaism itself.[10] Catholicism and Protestantism likewise are not unaware of the need to guard against the potential threat of the mixed marriage. Catholicism requires all non-Catholics in the marriages of Catholics to non-Catholics to sign prenuptial contracts guaranteeing that the faith of the Catholic partner will not be "perverted" and that all children born

[8] A priest allegedly is distressed by the signs which he sees as indications of the possibility that many Catholics may gradually abandon the teachings of their church and accept the customs of the secular society in which they live. His solution: an "open ghetto," in which Catholics should avoid intimate contact as far as possible with non-Catholic culture. Mixed marriages are out of the question. "I don't think a Protestant should seriously date a Catholic, and vice versa. Of course we want to get to know and do business with persons of other faiths, but I wonder if a devout person should bring someone of another faith into his home, into his family surroundings. Catholics should not have close associates who are in a different religious situation. You soon compromise with a cultural pattern." Quoted by *Time Magazine* (July 4, 1960), p. 38.

[9] For a discussion of this point see: John L. Thomas, *op. cit.,* p. 148.

[10] David Kirshenbaum, *Mixed Marriage and the Jewish Future,* Bloch Publishing Co., New York, 1958.

to the union will be baptized and brought up in the Catholic faith.[11] Various Protestant denominations for perhaps similar reasons strongly advise their members against committing themselves to these agreements.

My advice to young Christian people is never date a Roman Catholic and you will never marry a Roman Catholic. If you will want to marry a Roman Catholic because you love him or her above all else, you can prevent a mixed marriage by helping the Catholic person find the true Saviour through studying and accepting the Scriptural truths in the Holy Bible before marriage. If, however you have already married a Roman Catholic, and have signed the Pre-Nuptial document, it then becomes your sacred duty to amend by helping your Roman Catholic partner, and your children, if any, to find and accept the true way of salvation.[12]

The Episcopal Church issued a pamphlet warning its young members that in signing the antenuptial agreement they will deny the validity of their own faith in the upbringing of their children. Similarly, the West German Conference of Lutheran Bishops, aware of the growing number of interfaith marriages in that area, objected sharply to what it called Catholic "pressure" on Protestant partners to solve the problem. The bishops' statement concluded with a plea to Lutherans to "remain loyal" to their own church and to "insist" that their children be brought up as Protestants.[13]

Although there are these attempts to keep members of a particular faith loyal to that faith, other factors enter. For the individual in the course of growing up, religious values become identified with parents, siblings, and other loved ones. Thus, the interfaith involvement may be experienced not only as turning away from one faith but as an abandonment of one's group affiliation. Under these circumstances the need to identify with the group may be a more powerful pressure than the religious ideas as such and this causes considerable conflict. It is always a moot point whether the problems in the interfaith marriage pertain to differences in religion, or whether these difficulties stem from differences in cultural background.[14] This it would seem is a

---

[11] A copy of the antenuptial agreement of the Catholic church which must be signed by the non-Catholic party, the Catholic party, the witnesses, and pastor, appears in: James A. Peterson, *Education for Marriage*, Charles Scribner's Sons, New York, 1956, pp. 402–404.

[12] Dr. Joseph Zacchello, "A Priest on Mixed Marriage," (A Tract), *The Convert*, P.O. Box 90, Clairton, Pa.

[13] United Press International, "Mixed Marriages a Problem for Catholics, Protestants," *The Daily Register* (newspaper), Harrisburg, Ill., Nov. 19, 1958.

[14] One author, for example, states that some of the problems in Protestant-Catholic marriages may result from social class differences rather than religious differences as such. He also discusses and cites a case history concerning the fact

question which must be raised repeatedly in the interfaith involvement.

If these socializing experiences which tend to perpetuate the strength of the several religious groups were completely effective, people would never marry out of their religious faith. In a society such as our own, however, with a wide diversity of influences, people are exposed to values and points of view which are often at variance with the pressures which their own background may bring to bear. On the one hand there are the beliefs regarding the inherent superiority of one's own religious background and people, on the other hand these ideas may conflict with democratic values and the equality of people, plus the right of the individual to make personal choices even when these conflict with group pressures. Thus, people do become involved with members of other religious groups. The question, of course, is what happens to many of these relationships.

INTELLECTUAL AND INTELLECTUAL-EMOTIONAL COMMITMENTS. Adequate resolutions of the dilemmas raised by religious ethnocentrism vis-à-vis democratic values are difficult to make and this results in a good deal of ambivalence, contradictory attitudes toward spouse, or spouse to be, repression of negative feelings, and potential conflict. The most common expression of these conflicts is seen in the ever present tendency for people to verbally commit themselves to a mixed religious marriage, without really being aware of all that is involved.[15] We term commitments of this type intellectual, as distinguished from the intellectual-emotional commitment. The difference between the intellectual and intellectual-emotional commitment may first be illustrated by certain common experiences. For example, how many times have we all promised ourselves that we would do something which we knew we should do, and had every intention of doing, only to discover that when the appointed time arrived we were unable to fulfill our good intentions. College students promise themselves that they will spend the major part of the holiday vacation studying

---

that religion is only one of the several cultural factors which determine marital adjustment in interfaith marriage: E. E. LeMasters, *Modern Courtship and Marriage*, The Macmillan Co., New York, 1957, pp. 331, 346–350. "A marriage between members of different religious groups is not merely a union between two persons who happen to 'go to different churches' . . . . It is, instead, a supposedly permanent relationship between people who have been reared with fundamental differences in ways of living and thinking." James H. S. Bossard and Eleanor Stoker Boll, *The Sociology of Child Development*, 3rd ed., Harper and Brothers, New York, 1960, p. 415.

[15] Lawrence S. Bee, *Marriage and Family Relations*, Harper and Brothers, New York, 1959, pp. 234–235.

for finals, only to discover that when the vacation arrives they are unable to forego its attendant events and frequently do very little, if any, serious studying. The difference here is one between wishing to follow a course of action, and having the ability to follow a course of action. With respect to intellectual as compared with intellectual-emotional commitments, we can say that commitments are intellectual when they contain only an intent, with a minimum of awareness about the underlying feelings and attitudes which may or may not be consistent with the intent; a commitment becomes intellectual-emotional when it includes not only the intent to follow a course of action but the integration of intent with underlying attitudes and feelings. When both thinking and feeling are in agreement about a course of action, then a commitment that has consistency and predictability has been reached.

When applied to mixed religious marriages, understanding the difference between a commitment which is primarily intellectual and one which is intellectual-emotional is significant, since it is precisely this confusion which results in the failure of people to fulfill the promises and agreements about the issues in the mixed religious marriage, be they questions of religious faith for parents, or religious faith for children.[16] The pertinence of this can be appreciated in the following illustration.

A very devout Catholic girl was dating a Protestant from a religiously liberal background. As the relationship became serious, the question of religious differences was raised by the girl. She pointed out the importance of her religion, and the difficulty which she might have were she asked to abandon her religious views. The boy reported that he was not really concerned about the question of religion. Thus he offered to become Catholic himself and to sign the required contract with respect to the rearing of his children. Since he had come to such a decision with a minimum of contemplation or difficulty, suspicions arose in the minds of the girl's parents and the boy's parents. They asked him over and over again whether he was certain about his decision. He gave every indication of having made up his mind. One evening prior to undertaking instruction in Catholicism, the boy casually asked how long a process this entailed. The girl could give no definite answer and asked why he raised the question. At that point the boy simply stated, "I hope it doesn't take too long because I get

---

[16] There are many people who intellectually commit themselves in agreeing to have their children reared in the religious faith of the partner, who find that when the time arrives they are unable to do so. For a discussion of this point and a case history, see: Lawrence S. Bee, *op. cit.*, pp. 226–228.

mad when I'm around priests." This casual remark was the first indication of ambivalence about Catholicism. The girl in question began to probe and discovered at this point a series of latently hostile attitudes toward Catholicism, attitudes which might well have become serious problems for the couple. Further analysis of this relationship revealed serious religious incompatibilities which eventually resulted in breaking the engagement.

In this case it is clear that the boy was capable of an intellectual commitment, but his thinking and feelings were inconsistent and so this ambivalence and repressed hostility emerged when the circumstances permitted. These people were fortunate since they were able to locate their sources of stress before their marriage. Probably the vast majority of couples involved in relationships of this type become aware of their unsolved problems only after the marriage.

CONFLICT AREAS IN THE MIXED RELIGIOUS MARRIAGE. In the previous section of this chapter we have tried to present a framework within which problems in the mixed religious marriage may be examined. At this point we wish to relate that framework to the difficulties encountered. For example, common problems in the mixed religious marriage include questions which pertain to the religious affiliations of the husband, the wife, and their children, as well as the consequences of these dilemmas for the interpersonal relationship between the spouses. These difficulties, as previously suggested, are outgrowths of socialization experiences, and the ethnocentrism and rigidity which follow. Furthermore, the experiences of each partner impose obstacles to what is acceptable as a solution. In this regard it should be noted that no particular solution for any of these problems appears to be inherently best. Instead it becomes a matter of being able to commit oneself intellectually and emotionally to a given course of action. Satisfactory marriages can result from any possible combination of faiths and from any number of solutions to the problems inherent in mixed religious marriages. The problems which do arise in any of these choices stem from the failure on the part of persons involved to resolve their ambivalence, their doubts, and their repressed resentments which are rooted in inconsistent attitudes and feelings acquired from the past.

Specific Problems of the Mixed Marriage. The objective in discussing specific problems of the mixed religious marriage is to identify the main sources of these problems and to point out alternative solutions to these problems. Through such a procedure we can best call attention both to the potential benefits and to the potential psychological and interpersonal difficulties associated with each alternative solution. A knowledge and understanding of these alternative solutions may enable the individual to resolve his doubts more adequately, so that whatever solution he chooses will have been decided upon in a relatively undivided and whole-hearted manner.

Religious Affiliation for the Spouses.

Both Identify with a Single Religion. One of the most common problems in a mixed religious marriage concerns the religious affiliation of the spouses. Many people believe that a greater degree of religious and marital unity results when one partner gives up his religion and adopts the religion of the other.[17] Others point out, however, that although such unity may emerge, serious problems are frequently encountered. For example, there are those who feel that it is exceedingly difficult for people to give up their religious background without serious internal conflict as well as conflict with the mate.[18] Such potential conflict may result even for people who have not had a formal religious affiliation and who have not attended services prior to their marriage, since, as previously suggested, the issues are not necessarily restricted to religion but also involve a commitment to one's familial and cultural background. Under these circumstances considerable resistance to giving up one's religious identification may emerge, especially if an abandonment of ties to one's background is experienced.

Also it is important to recognize that what is frequently interpreted as a lack of interest in religion when one fails to attend religious services may in reality be a rebellion against religious affiliation and indoctrination. The danger here is that the rebellious partner may not have worked out adequately his religious views. Thus, later in life such an individual may come to regret his rebelliousness and seek a return to the former religious affiliation. Needless to say, the failure to appreciate fully such a possibility may result in much difficulty in the marital relationship.

Each Identifies with His Own Church. A second solution to the religious affiliation of the spouses is agreement to attend separate churches; the following observations are frequently made with respect to this solution. There are those who believe that such an approach is

---

[17] One study showed that marriages in which one spouse changes to the faith of the other do not have as high a divorce rate as mixed religious marriages in which each partner retains his own faith. Judson T. and Mary G. Landis, *Building a Successful Marriage*, 3rd ed., Prentice-Hall, Inc., New Jersey, 1958, p. 249.

[18] Paul H. Landis, *Making the Most of Marriage*, 2nd ed., Appleton-Century-Crofts, Inc., New York, 1960, pp. 230–232.

desirable since it is consistent with unity and the right of the individual to maintain his own beliefs. On the other hand, others point out that by participating in different religious groups value differences are further entrenched; especially since differences in religious values may relate to other basic aspects of family patterns and family planning, particularly planned parenthood and contraception.[19]

Other Approaches. To be sure, there are other attempts at resolving this issue. Some couples decide on a church which is presumably different from their own, but which may in a sense represent a compromise. Thus a Baptist and a Methodist may decide to affiliate with a Presbyterian church. Some Jews and Protestants have attempted to affiliate with a Unitarian church.[20] Further, there are those who become tired of the conflicts and attempt to resolve them by refusing to identify with any religious body.[21] These along with other solutions may be satisfactory but only to the extent that people understand themselves and their basic values well enough to commit themselves to a course of action which minimizes their ambivalence. Ambivalence is responsible for so many of the conflicts in a marriage of this type.

Religious Affiliation of Children. Another problem in the mixed religious marriage is the religious affiliation of the children. To the extent that the parents have committed themselves to a course of action and have resolved any ambivalence, the problem may be minimized.[22] The

---

[19] Even where each partner retains his faith Thomas lists reasons for the Catholic church's opposition to mixed marriages as consisting of ideological differences between: (1) Contraceptives and divorce. (2) Sending children to Catholic schools if they are available. (3) Religious training of children. (4) Loyalties to the Catholic church. (5) Spiritual ideologies. John L. Thomas, *op. cit.*, pp. 152–153.

[20] It is interesting to note, however, that when Jewish-Gentile marriages do occur the chances for success are greatest for the Protestant-Jewish marriage, and the chances for success are least for the Catholic-Jewish marriage, this combination, Catholic-Jewish, is only a slightly better risk than the Protestant-Catholic marriage. Ray E. Baber, *Marriage and the Family*, 2nd ed., McGraw-Hill Book Co., New York, 1953, pp. 100–107. On infrequency of Jewish-Gentile marriage, see: Ruby Jo Reeves Kennedy, "Single or Triple Melting Pot:—Intermarriage Trends in New Haven, 1870–1940," *Am. J. Sociol.*, 49:4 (Jan., 1944), 331–339.

[21] Although there are exceptions, marriages in which the spouses have no religion tend to reflect a higher divorce and separation rate than those in which one spouse converted to the other's religion, or those in which each retained his own religion, see: Judson T. Landis, "Marriages of Mixed and Non-Mixed Religious Faith," *Am. Soc. Rev.*, 14 (June, 1949), pp. 401–407. Paul H. Landis, *op. cit.*, p. 232.

[22] For a discussion of the effect of the mixed religious marriage on the development of the child, see: James H. S. Bossard and Eleanor Stoker Boll, *op. cit.*, pp. 415–416. In one study of Protestant-Catholic marriages in which each partner maintained his original faith it was found that 50 percent of the children were

difficulties loom large, however, in those instances where the choice is still to be made, and the parents are still confused regarding a solution. There are those who believe that the child should make his or her own selection at the proper time. Such an approach has considerable appeal for those with a democratic orientation. Others argue that individual selection of this type can probably best take place only in an environment which is relatively unconcerned with the necessity of identifying people in terms of categories of religious affiliation. This argument indicates that few segments of our society permit children such freedom. Usually through the influence of adults, children acquire definitions of themselves as Protestants, Catholics, or Jews, and come to expect that other children will be so identified. All of this creates confusion for the child of a mixed religious marriage, confusion as to where he belongs and with whom he belongs. It is further indicated that only the most favorable familial environment can overcome these difficulties.

For those parents who are satisfied that they can deal with these factors which impinge on the child's freedom to choose a religion, there are other problems to examine. Many parents, in spite of what they claim, find it difficult to allow the child any real freedom in the selection of a religion. Indeed, there is almost the implicit assumption on the part of each parent that the child will probably select his faith. Thus, when marriage partners agree to allow their children to select their own religious affiliations, there is often a feeling that the child will select his (the parent's) particular religion. This indicates that regardless of the intellectual commitments made, the appropriate emotional response necessary to make the plan work may not be present. Furthermore, it suggests that the parents themselves possess attitudes which will defeat the plan to allow the child individual choice of religious affiliation. In the case which follows we note the husband's ambivalence about his original commitments to have his child reared as a Protestant and his wife's reaction to this situation.

When Mr. A., who was reared as a Catholic, became involved with Miss T., a Protestant, he was so desirous of marrying her that he readily agreed to join her church and to have their children reared as Protestants. Mr. A. considered himself to be a rather objective man, capable of recognizing that "in the long run all religions actually have the same goals," and as a result he was able to fulfill his promise to accept his

reared in the Protestant faith, 45 percent in the Catholic faith, and 5 percent had no faith. The most common tendency seems to be that children follow the faith of their mother. Judson T. and Mary G. Landis, *Building a Successful Marriage*, 3rd ed., Prentice-Hall, Inc., New Jersey, 1958, pp. 246–247.

wife's religion with little obvious difficulty until, after two years of marriage, their first child was born. At this time Mr. A. began to feel quite uncomfortable about having given up his religion and having promised to allow his children to be reared as Protestants. He mentioned this to his wife. The wife appreciated her husband's feelings but she would not agree to rearing their child in the Catholic faith. Considerable tension emerged in the spousal relationship due to the difficulty, and the whole pattern of family life was disturbed.

It is important to recognize that to the extent that there is parental ambivalence about the child's right to choose his religious identification, the child may be bombarded, directly or indirectly, by both parents to join a particular church at a time when the child has little or no understanding of religious views, or of the nature of religious experience. Such confusion results in little clarification of religious affiliation. What the child does understand, however, is that any tendency to favor the church of one parent may result in hurting the other parent, also that parental love may be dependent on how he chooses. All of this may be extremely terrifying to the child, who as a means of escaping this threatening situation, may come to reject both religions. Without being aware of what he is doing, each parent is contributing to the child's insecurity, in that the child is always uneasy about his relationship to his parents.

Needless to say, exploitation of the child is fostered under these circumstances, and in some cases the child himself even comes to recognize his own exploitative powers and develops a pattern of favoring one or the other of the two religions, whichever the case warrants, as a means of manipulating his parents to gain his own wishes.

The mixed marriage of Mr. and Mrs. B. (Protestant–Catholic) is interesting from this point of view. One day during a family discussion Mrs. B. stated that she did not think that their daughter, who was then seven years old, should be permitted to attend the local movie with other neighborhood children. Mr. B. stated that he thought it would be all right. The daughter, immediately sensing her father's approval of something that she wanted very much to do, set out to reward him by stating that she thought her father was right. Indeed, her desire to attend the movie was so great that without actually understanding any of the values involved she went on to reward her father further by announcing that she no longer wanted to be a Catholic like her mother, but instead wanted to be a Protestant like her father!

Such exploitation on the part of the child is most likely to emerge in the midst of parental indecision and ambivalence. The exploitative power which a child can come to experience may well wreck any plan for integrated living and is something which bears watching in families where it develops.

Impact of Religious Differences on Marital Interaction. The third type of problem which may arise in a mixed religious marriage relates to the impact of religious differences on the marital relationship. This difficulty expresses itself in several ways. It may result in a lack of freedom and spontaneity in many areas of the relationship. Thus, areas of the marriage which relate to religion may become topics to be avoided. Despite previous claims to be accepting of the other's faith, a fear of expressing oneself on any topic which directly or indirectly deals with religious issues sometimes develops. This awareness of the need to avoid areas which may embarrass the marriage partner, or which may lead to overt conflict, tends to inhibit the responses of the partners and makes it necessary for each to constantly guard against any expressions which can provoke arguments and misunderstandings.[23] Needless to say, the restrictions which people place on themselves under these circumstances are not conducive to the mutual sharing which is so essential in a meaningful man-woman relationship. In some cases one may become so preoccupied with the need to avoid hostility that the interaction between husband and wife is marked with tension, superficiality, and pretense.

A second expression of difficulty which results from the impact of religious differences on a marriage is that hostility may be displaced on the marriage partner. Such hostility comes about, at least in a general way, from the fact that the persons involved in a mixed religious marriage, who have not really committed themselves emotionally to the relationship, invariably find themselves in conflict with themselves. They worry about whether their choice was a wise one, and about the opinions of relatives and friends. All of this produces discomfort with the ever present tendency to blame the other partner for the discomfort.

For couples who repress discomfort about the marital union there are other considerations. These stem from the fact that the repressed hostility may appear in what seems to be an unrelated form. Much of this occurs with a minimun of conscious awareness on the part of the partners; the repressed hostility may take such forms as nagging or faultfinding which seem to have little to do with religious incompatibilities.

[23] F. Alexander Magoun, *Love and Marriage,* Harper and Brothers, New York, 1948, pp. 259–260.

Thomas points out both dimensions of the problem of hostility in a mixed marriage—the desire to avoid hostility and displaced hostility —in the following:

Religious beliefs by their very nature involve the emotions to such an extent that it is impossible for most people to argue about them with any degree of calm or objectivity. As a result, after a few attempts, most couples give up trying to talk over their religious differences. Finding this approach rather hopeless, they silently agree to disagree. Hence, the unstabilizing effects of religious differences develop in more subtle ways.[24]

In the case that follows we find an instance of displaced hostility. Mrs. G.M., who was involved in a mixed religious marriage, was quite unhappy about her marital relationship although she showed no desire to discontinue it. According to her, the unhappiness of the marriage had nothing to do with the fact that she and her husband held quite opposite views concerning religion. Both she and her husband, according to her, were too objective to quarrel over such intangible things as religious beliefs, rather, she stated, the dissatisfaction with her marriage resulted from the fact that her husband never did anything right! It seemed that when Mr. G.M. smoked his pipe the odor was extremely offensive to Mrs. G.M., and when he didn't smoke it Mrs. G.M. would state that she considered pipe smoking to be a desirable masculine trait. Indeed, when her husband spent Sunday afternoon caring for the lawn, he was regarded as ignoring her, but when instead he spent his time attempting to converse with her she'd claim that he was lazy and unlike others who took an interest in their homes. Nothing Mr. G.M. did was ever quite right. After a gradual deterioration of the marriage, the couple sought professional help. Over a period of time Mrs. G.M. came to learn that her resentments concerning the husband's religion and background were indeed a source of great hostility for her. These resentments were being expressed in nagging and fault-finding.

SOCIAL PSYCHOLOGICAL PREPARATION FOR A MIXED RELIGIOUS MARRIAGE. The fact that there are serious problems to be resolved in mixed religious marriage should not obscure the fact that a solution of these problems is possible. It is again important to note, however, that one's probability of resolving these problems is not dependent upon which specific solution he chooses, but rather upon his ability to fully accept and follow through with whatever solution he chooses. This is to say that the attainment of a meaningful relationship in mixed religious marriage is largely dependent upon the ability

[24] John L. Thomas, S.J., *The American Catholic Family*, p. 161, © 1956. Prentice-Hall, Inc., Englewood Cliffs, N.J.

of the marital partners to commit themselves intellectually and emotionally to a course of action. To make such an intellectual-emotional commitment, however, requires a high degree of personal maturity and integration. Consequently, it is advisable for persons contemplating mixed religious marriage to attempt to assess their personal maturity and integration. In attempting such an assessment, particularly as it pertains to mixed religious marriage, the following two factors might be considered: (1) an examination of one's prejudice, and (2) an examination of one's motivations for the mixed religious involvement.

Prejudice is significant because it is frequently a hidden factor which is nevertheless present and makes the development of a meaningful marriage relationship virtually impossible. The motivations are important because, like prejudice, true motivations for mixed religious involvements are also frequently hidden and, when ultimately discovered, may reveal reasons for becoming involved in the relationship which are not conducive to the development of a meaningful relationship. Let us consider each of these two factors in greater detail.

Prejudice. With regard to prejudice, it should be clear that to agree to be accepting or even sympathetic toward the religious views of an intended marriage partner does not insure the absence of difficulties, religious or otherwise. For, as we have already pointed out, people are frequently so desirous of continuing the pleasurable aspects of dating and courtship that they are likely to delude themselves into believing that they are less prejudiced than they are.

These matters may be hidden. This is especially true of college people who believe that it is academically fashionable not to have prejudices. Thus, a thought such as "I should not be prejudiced" frequently develops into the notion that "I'm not prejudiced." Under these circumstances it is possible for one to become quite broadminded intellectually, and still remain quite prejudiced emotionally.

One way of assessing one's prejudices is to learn to be aware of the responses to certain occurrences. For example, when standing in a checker's line at a crowded supermarket and someone whom you know to be Jewish steps into the line in front of you, does your irritation usually include such thoughts as—"What can you expect of a Jew," or when involved in a lively discussion and you can't get the other person to see your point, it is easier for you to dismiss your resulting anxiety when you can think—"Well, what can I expect from a narrow-minded Catholic"; or "That's a Protestant for you, none of them actually know what they do believe." If under these circumstances, the religion of the person enters your thinking, there is indication that in spite of the fact that you may think that you have no religious prejudice, when called on to behave in a non-prejudicial manner, you are unable to do so; a clear indication of an intellectual commitment to be non-prejudiced with a lack of the intellectual-emotional ability to follow through.

Another occurrence, worthy of attention, pertains to those who feel that they are able to place the religion of their partner and their own religion side by side and treat them equally. Without a doubt there are some people who are capable of doing this. There are others, however, who, although they think they are able to view each religion equally, experience considerable discomfort in any circumstance which forces them to confront the religion of their partner. One young woman, for example, stated that when she and her date were among a group of friends and someone told a joke about her date's religion, she would become extremely embarrassed and think, "why couldn't the joke have involved my religion," even though her date seemed thoroughly amused by the joke. She stated further that although she tried to avoid any discussion involving a comparison of the two religions, whenever such a discussion arose in the group she seemed compelled to bend backwards in supporting her date's religion, although she really didn't believe what she was saying.

While it would seem that this is an example of an attempt to build a relationship in which both religions are viewed equally, failure is inherent because at least one of the partners is categorizing the two religions and treating them differently. Thus, in this case before any equal treatment of the religions involved is possible, an attempt must be made to discover why this young woman feels it so necessary to protect her date's religion. An analysis may uncover certain very negative attitudes which the young woman has toward her date's religion. Thus, the question arises, "Is this woman capable of an intellectual-emotional commitment?"

A second way to assess one's prejudices about members of another faith is to interact in a variety of circumstances with the friends and family of the spouse-to-be. Such interaction makes it possible for one to observe the religious values of the group, to participate in their religious practices, and to observe attitudinal differences that may be present. This interaction may result in the insight that one could adjust very well with members of another religion. On the other hand, such an exposure might enable one to discover that he is less able to accept the differences in religion and background than he had thought. There are those who, on recognizing an inability to accept the differences that confront them, tend immediately to dismiss any further consideration of this potential problem by thinking that their intended mate is different from his friends and family; therefore, their feelings toward his friends and family do not apply to him. What must be realized is that during dating and courtship you are likely to twist the reality of the situation and see the person apart from the underlying prejudices which you might have about his group.[25] Indeed, you may be surprised to discover later that your criticism of his religious group will apply to him also.

Motivations. In addition to questions of prejudice which may interfere with one's ability to build a meaningful mixed religious marriage relationship, there are also questions of motivation for the involvement which may foreshadow difficulty. The motivations which people have for becoming involved in mixed religious marriages deserve careful examination because these motivations are frequently complicated and not necessarily based on a mature love. Several illustrations of this point follow.

A first category of persons who become involved in an interfaith marriage are those who do so primarily because they are ashamed of what they are—ashamed of themselves, their family, friends, relatives, and their religion. This involves a rejection of self. With such negative attitudes toward their background there is a need to make their own religion worse than it is and other religions perhaps better than they are. Such distortion serves the belief that rejection of oneself and acceptance of other values will make things better. These people, like those who think that marriage will solve all problems, are running away from themselves and from their own religion, and looking to an outside source, in this case a union with a member of another religion, to solve their problems. In situations of this type a mixed religious marriage may have much greater appeal than does a marriage with a person of one's own religion. As with all attempts at self-rejection and attempts at making life better by avoiding inner problems, however, disappointment and frustration are inevitable.

A second category of persons includes those who gravitate toward mixed religious marriages because essentially they are rebellious. With these people the mixed religious marriage represents only one aspect of their rebellion. Sometimes these people are in rebellion against parents; often there may be a need to hurt or get back at parents. Others from this category like to think of themselves as non-conformists and frequently they take considerable pride in the mixed religious marriage as a sign of rebellion against their group.

Finally, some people are motivated to become involved in a mixed

[25] F. Alexander Magoun, *op. cit.*, p. 239.

religious marriage by a missionary zeal to change others. This "Pygmalion complex" finds its greatest fulfillment in a relationship where differences exist, thus allowing the person to bring about great changes in his partner. Here, without regard for the feelings of the other person, the individual sets out to remake his partner and the existence of differing religious views offers him a most desirable challenge.

The motivations which we have just discussed have certain elements in common. None of them treat marriage itself as the end goal, but instead marriage is used in an attempt to fulfill needs which are external to marriage. The first case relates to self-rejection and the need to escape, the second to rebel and get back at people, and the third to change and impose one's values on others. Under such circumstances two important points become apparent: (1) in marriages of this type there is little basic interest in the marriage or the marriage partner, instead the marriage is viewed as a means of solving certain personal difficulties and as such is not likely to result in a meaningful relationship; indeed it is likely to produce, not solve, problems, a point which we discussed in a previous chapter concerning motivations for marriage. (2) In marriages of this type it is also quite impossible for intellectual-emotional commitments to be made because the necessary personal maturity and integration are lacking. Consequently, an examination of the motivational factors in mixed religious marriage as well as an assessment of one's deep seated prejudices would appear to be extremely important for all couples contemplating mixed religious marriage.

Before concluding, we hasten to point out that there are many mature and meaningful mixed religious marriages. But the probability that any specific couple will be able to achieve such a relationship is largely dependent upon two factors; first, the ability of the marital partners to understand the breadth of potential mixed religious marriage problems and secondly, the ability of the partners to commit themselves fully to the marriage itself.

SUMMARY

The problems which are confronted in mixed religious marriages, as is true of most types of mixed marriages, tend to be related to differences in the cultural backgrounds of the parties involved. Each religious group, for example, shares a way of life which to a greater or lesser degree differs from other religious groups. And, in this regard, it is important to note that each religious group tends to view its own way of life as being somewhat better than others. Thus, this ethnocentric quality frequently makes it difficult for marriage partners who come from different religious backgrounds to realistically accept differences in each other.

In a democratic society it is often quite easy to delude oneself into thinking that he is less ethnocentric than he is. However, in committing oneself to accept differences in other people, particularly as this pertains to a mixed religious marriage, it is important to be certain that one is not merely making an intellectual commitment, meaning a commitment based on the desire to accept these differences, but that one is capable of making an intellectual-emotional commitment, meaning a commitment based not only on the desire to accept differences but also on the ability to follow through emotionally and behave in accordance with the desire. Once one is capable of making an intellectual-emotional commitment to a mixed religious marriage, it is more likely that he will be able to solve effectively the basic problems which will be confronted, such as deciding on the religious affiliation of the spouses, deciding on the religious affiliation of the children, and dealing with the impact which the religious differences may have on the total marital interaction.

An objective examination of one's prejudices and an analysis of his motivation for becoming involved in a mixed religious relationship are often quite enlightening and frequently can aid the individual to ascertain his ability to make an intellectual-emotional commitment to a mixed religious marriage.

QUESTIONS

1. What in your opinion is the major obstacle confronted in all types of mixed marriages? How exactly does this apply to a mixed religious marriage?
2. Does socialization adequately prepare us to accept differences in people? Explain. Does religion adequately prepare us to accept religious differences in a marriage partner? Explain.
3. In what way do social groups depend on ethnocentrism for survival?
4. What is an intellectual commitment? What is an intellectual-emotional commitment? Give an example of each. Explain how an intellectual commitment can cause difficulty in a mixed religious marriage. How might this be avoided?
5. Is it always possible to commit oneself intellectually-emotionally? What makes this particularly difficult for those contemplating a mixed religious marriage?
6. What are the main problems confronted in a mixed religious marriage? Explain each.
7. What are the dimensions of hostility found in mixed religious marriage? Explain each.

8. What might a person who is contemplating a mixed religious marriage do to attempt to discover whether he has religious prejudice? Consider also other types of prejudice which would be relative to other types of mixed marriage.

9. List and explain the motivations which people sometimes have for a mixed religious marriage. Are people usually aware of their motivations? If not, how may one find help in determining his motivations for a mixed marriage?

PROJECTS

1. Select a mixed religious marriage which you know well and which in your opinion is an unsuccessful marriage. Without identifying the parties involved write a paper explaining: (a) Why you regard this marriage as unsuccessful; (b) What, aside from the couple not having married in the first place, could have been done to avoid the problems of this marriage; (c) What, in your opinion, would be necessary to make this a successful marriage; and (d) What chances for success you feel this marriage has.

2. Select a mixed religious marriage which you know well and which, in your opinion, is a successful marriage. Without identifying the parties involved write a paper explaining: (a) Why you regard this as a successful marriage; and (b) How you account for the success of this marriage.

3. Invite a minister, priest, or rabbi to class to present his views on mixed religious marriage. You may wish instead to interview all three on the topic of mixed religious marriage and present your findings to the class.

4. Interview several students in order to determine under what conditions they would consider marrying outside their religious group. Write a paper concerning what you have found. Do you find that the answers given are realistic or superficial? Do you believe that these people are more or less prejudiced than they think they are?

SUGGESTED READINGS

Bossard, James H. S., and Eleanor Stoker Boll, *One Marriage, Two Faiths*, The Ronald Press, New York, 1957.

———, and Harold C. Letts, "Mixed Marriages Involving Lutherans," *Marriage and Family Living*, 18:4 (Nov., 1956), pp. 308–310.

Golden, Joseph, "Characteristics of the Negro-White Intermarried in Philadelphia," *Am. Soc. Rev.*, 18:2 (April, 1953), pp. 177–183.

———, "Patterns of Negro-White Intermarriage," *Am. Soc. Rev.*, 19 (April, 1954), pp. 144–147.

Landis, Judson T., and Mary G. Landis, *Building a Successful Marriage*, 3rd ed., Prentice-Hall, Inc., Englewood Cliffs, New Jersey, 1958, Ch. 12, "Mixed Marriages."

Peterson, James A., *Education for Marriage*, Charles Scribner's Sons, New York, 1956, Ch. 17, "Achieving Religious Togetherness."

Slotkin, J. S., "Adjustment in Jewish-Gentile Intermarriages," *Social Forces*, 21 (Dec., 1942), pp. 226–230.

Courtship: the prelude to marriage ## 11

In several of the preceding chapters we have been concerned with the factors which prepare people for meaningful relationships in marriage. As we have seen, in some cases these factors lend themselves to maladjustment in marriage while in others such factors facilitate marital adjustment. Another such premarital factor, which (depending on its use) can either aid or hinder the attainment of a meaningful marriage relationship, is the period which precedes marriage, namely, the courtship period.

This period of the man-woman relationship follows the dating period and differs from dating in that it involves a commitment to marry while dating does not. Courtship, therefore, is engagement. However, we hasten to point out that courtship consists of two important phases, the informal and the formal engagements; the difference between these two phases is largely one of the specific purposes involved.

The primary purpose of the informal engagement is to afford the couple an ample period of time to test their relationship and to do so under more serious and realistic circumstances than those found in dating. Further, during the informal engagement, except for the parents and perhaps the very best friends of the couple, no public announcement of the intended marriage is made. This phase of engagement when properly used offers young people the opportunity to learn about each other before publicly committing themselves to marriage.

The purpose of the formal engagement is to announce the intention to marry and to make specific plans for the actual wedding ceremony and honeymoon.[1] In this chapter we will discuss the courtship period in each of its two engagement phases and also consider the circumstances which are involved in breaking an engagement.

INFORMAL ENGAGEMENT—MEANING. The question frequently arises as to whether going steady and pinning constitute informal engagement.[2] This can be answered by stating that in each case the decisive factor in deciding whether or not these are forms of informal engagement is that of intent. When for example, it is the serious intent of the couple that their relationship ultimately result in marriage, then call it what you may it is informal engagement.[3] On the other hand, when going steady means nothing more than a steady dating of one person this month and another next month, and pinning nothing more than having a "claim" on a person until someone better comes along, then neither constitutes informal engagement. The confusion which results from the varying response to pinning is noted in Table 8.

TABLE 8

Answers Given by Men and Women Students to the Statement:
"If a Woman Wears a Man's Fraternity Pin It Means that
They are Engaged." *

Response	Men	Women
Yes	27%	44%
No	47	28
Undecided	26	28

* Judson T. Landis and Mary G. Landis, *Building a Successful Marriage*, 3rd ed., Prentice-Hall, Inc., Englewood Cliffs, New Jersey, © 1958, p. 277.

INFORMAL ENGAGEMENT—FUNCTION. The informal engagement period is a significant phase of the premarital adjustment. It enables the couple to make their adjustments without the formal com-

[1] Harold T. Christensen, *Marriage Analysis*, 2nd ed., The Ronald Press Co., New York, 1958, pp. 333–334. For a discussion of the fact that the functions of engagement are more undefined in our society than perhaps in any other society, see: George Simpson, *People in Families*, Thomas Y. Crowell Co., New York, 1960, pp. 94–96.

[2] For a discussion of going steady and pinning, see: E. E. LeMasters, *Modern Courtship and Marriage*, The Macmillan Co., New York, 1957, Chs. 6–7.

[3] Although here it should be noted that in as much as "formal pinning" may constitute a public announcement of the intent to become "formally engaged," pinning itself does not permit the couple to make their adjustments with freedom from public commitment as does the informal engagement.

mitment to marry. Thus, unlike casual dating, it allows both parties involved to be assured of the serious intentions of the other and may help provide a milieu in which pretense and superficiality are minimized. During this phase of courtship it becomes not only possible to single out the adjustments to be made but to establish a pattern for dealing with problems.[4] To establish a pattern for dealing with problems in a relationship is indeed a worthy objective, since it acquaints the couple with the realities of human involvements and thus minimizes the panic which sometimes comes with the realization that one's relationship is in difficulty.

What kinds of problems and dilemmas ought to be resolved during the informal engagement period? Certainly issues which pertain to personality incompatibilities, differences in values, orientations, and life goals should be discussed. These are some of the significant areas of potential difficulty which ought to be examined.[5] Further, frequently one member of the relationship, or both, may be troubled about some event of the past which they feel could become an issue in the relationship. Sometimes it might be an erotic involvement, or perhaps a serious difficulty with a family member. At this point the question of how much to reveal about the past becomes a problem in the informal engagement period. There are no hard and fast rules that apply here. There is frequently the impulse to blurt out much of this in hope that the slate will be clean and one will have fulfilled the rules of honesty and fair play. It is not that simple, however, since one may serve himself and his relationship best by examining his motivations to tell everything about the past. To some people the impulse to confess the past, so to speak, is merely a form of self-inflicted punishment to relieve guilt feelings. When such is the case, confessing the past may be a way of asking the engaged partner to help carry the burden of guilt and this may accomplish little of a positive nature for the relationship.[6] As often happens with people who feel they ought to be punished for some wrongdoing, there may even be a desire to have the other partner dissolve the relationship as a form of punishment.

There was the case of a young man who had a need to tell his girl friends about the difficulties of his past. These events were frequently so unconsciously distorted that they tended to frighten his girl friends

[4] James A. Peterson, *Education for Marriage*, Charles Scribner's Sons, New York, 1956, pp. 198–199.

[5] Francis E. Merrill, *Courtship and Marriage*, Henry Holt and Co., New York, 1959, pp. 166–168. Merrill suggests that some of the areas in which the couple should explore their attitudes are: (1) love and marriage, (2) marriage and divorce, (3) marital roles, (4) marriage and children.

[6] F. Alexander Magoun, *Love and Marriage*, Harper and Brothers, New York, 1948, p. 187.

away. He always presented himself in the worst possible light as one who took advantage of others and who had little regard for their feelings. Finally, he met a girl who did not react as the others did. She accepted him and his past and looked on him as a challenge for her. At this point the young man became quite perplexed, without knowing why, since his unconscious plan for self-punishment had failed.

A competent counselor can help one to explore his motivations for telling past acts, to separate those which are likely to have bearing on the marriage from those which are not, and to learn how to go about discussing those acts which are regarded as having bearing on the marriage.[7] Certainly a good rule to follow is to ask oneself whether revealing events of the past will in general help the relationship or will place additional stress on it. For one partner to reveal an erotic affair to the other partner prior to marriage would be, for some persons, sufficient reason to dissolve the informal engagement. To talk about the same experience at some time later in marriage might well bring forth a less serious reaction. Much of what one reveals has to be examined in light of the security of the relationship. In general, the more secure people are in the relationship, the more they may tell about the past without precipitation of crises.

Having pointed out some of the real values that may be realized in the informal engagement period we hasten to add that it is unfortunate that young people often tend to run these informal and formal engagement periods together and treat them as one by attempting to work out the difficulties in their relationship after publicly announcing their engagement. When this happens, frequently there is a tendency for the couple to attempt to avoid areas in which adjustments are obviously necessary. They do this because once the engagement is announced there is reluctance to break it, feeling that to do so would be extremely embarrassing socially. Consequently, anything that might cast doubt on the advisability of the marriage tends to be ignored. People who are caught up in this problem often find solace in thinking that it is easier to face doubts after they are married than it is to face them now and run the risk of having to break the engagement.

The episode of Miss C. may help illustrate the point. Miss C. was formally engaged to a young man who behaved in a manner that suggested considerable indifference. Although he stated that he loved his fiancée, he failed to appear for dates, broke them indiscriminately, and was emotionally aloof to a point where he failed to show Miss C. physical demonstrativeness. Miss C. sought professional help and urged her fiancé to do likewise. After some time the counselor presented the

[7] Lawrence S. Bee, *Marriage and Family Relations*, Harper and Brothers, New York, 1959, pp. 254–257.

couple with some formidable problems which needed resolution before the couple could expect a satisfactory marriage. At this point Miss C. became impatient and stated that since wedding plans had been made perhaps she had exaggerated the seriousness of their problems and it might be best to resolve the issues later on.

When problems are avoided during informal engagement, the period becomes a time of superficial entertainment rather than a period of adjustment; many facets of the personalities involved go unexplored and are left to be discovered in marriage itself. Such statements as, "If I had only known about these attitudes before I married her," or "He's a different person from the one I married," are frequently the result of hurried, misspent engagements and could have been avoided if the premarital interaction had been used in a more meaningful way.[8]

It should be clear that the greatest length of time should be devoted to the informal phase of the engagement period since once a satisfactory adjustment is attained, a much shorter period of time is required for the formal engagement.[9] Moreover, by withholding the public announcement until the relationship has been tested, young people may make the necessary adjustments without the social pressure to marry which accompanies the formal announcement. Indeed, if these couples are unable to work out a satisfactory adjustment and wish to discontinue their relationship they can do so with perhaps a minimum of social embarrassment.

THE FORMAL ENGAGEMENT—MEANING AND FUNCTION.

The public announcement of the intent to marry initiates the formal engagement period. And, although the preceding informal engagement is the period during which most major adjustments should have been made, the formal engagement also offers young people plenty of opportunity to further their adjustments.

During this period it is customary to decide on a date for the wedding and also make specific arrangements for the honeymoon and the first home. Deciding such things as whether to be married in

[8] E. E. LeMasters, *op. cit.*, pp. 158–161.

[9] In regard to total length of engagement, one study showed that short engagements (under six months for men and under three months for women) had the poorest chances of resulting in happiness and success in marriage. Lewis M. Terman, *Psychological Factors in Marital Happiness*, McGraw-Hill Book Co., New York, 1938, pp. 198–199. Another study found that the happily married tended to have had longer engagements than those divorced. Harvey J. Locke, *Predicting Adjustment in Marriage*, Henry Holt and Co., New York, 1951, p. 94. And finally Burgess and Cottrell also found that the proportion of good adjustments in marriage increases with increased length of friendship shared by the couple. Ernest W. Burgess and Leonard S. Cottrell, *Predicting Success or Failure in Marriage*, Prentice-Hall, Inc., Englewood Cliffs, New Jersey, 1939, pp. 164–165.

church or at home, how many attendants and guests to have at the wedding, what type of reception to have, and the like, should be determined largely by the specific values of the couple involved.[10] And the exact decisions reached are not nearly as important as the fact that whatever is decided be mutually satisfactory to both parties involved.[11]

Specific plans for the honeymoon are usually made at this time. Although a honeymoon is not essential to the success or failure of marriage it is regarded as being a desirable part of the wedding plans.[12] In the first place the honeymoon has gained an accepted place in the American marriage pattern and as such it serves the purpose of fulfilling what has come to be an important social expectation. More importantly, however, the honeymoon serves the purpose of giving the newlyweds an opportunity to begin their actual marriage relationship without the frequently embarrassing presence of well meaning friends and relatives. Adjusting to the new roles of husband and wife and all the intimacies of interaction that this involves is best facilitated in a milieu which does not constantly remind the couple of their inexperience in these new roles.

With respect to the honeymoon it might be well to simply call attention to some of the common mistakes in planning. It should be clear that excessive expense and involved travel arrangements create tensions which may defeat the purpose of the honeymoon. Furthermore, the tendency to go to resorts which cater to a higher social class than the one to which the couple are accustomed may also be responsible for tensions.

Under these circumstances the newlyweds frequently find themselves in a social environment to which they are not accustomed. This often causes anxieties about such things as proper dress and behavior in accordance with the unfamiliar environment, factors which themselves can defeat the very purpose of the honeymoon. The couple—in adjusting to the plush atmosphere—are all too often detracted from effecting a meaningful adjustment to each other in their new roles of husband and wife, which the honeymoon is supposed to facilitate by providing an environment free from artificiality and unreality.[13]

[10] For an interesting discussion of the wedding by a clergyman, see: "Of Weddings and Funerals," *Harpers Magazine*, 191 (Dec., 1945), pp. 496–499.

[11] Lawrence S. Bee, *op. cit.*, pp. 259–260. It is interesting to note that Bee points out that not only is agreement between the couple necessary but that disagreement between the couple and one or both sets of parents can be painful and divisive in the relationship of the couple themselves.

[12] For a discussion of the wedding and the honeymoon, see: Harold T. Christensen, *op. cit.*, pp. 346–356.

[13] For a discussion of the fact that the honeymoon is not a vacation, see: Lawrence S. Bee, *op. cit.*, pp. 264–267.

BREAKING THE FORMAL ENGAGEMENT. The many factors that have been described in this book in regard to the building of meaningful relationships during dating and courtship are likely to minimize the probability that a formal engagement would have to be broken. Nevertheless, incompatibilities do emerge and many of these cannot be resolved. Thus some couples, after having worked hard at their differences, are faced with the realization that they are not likely to have a successful marriage.[14] When both partners reach such an agreement the relationship should be broken and, although there may be some sorrow because of what might have been, there is also likely to be a sense of relief at having an unsatisfactory relationship ended.[15] Some of the responses of persons to broken engagements are noted in the following table.

TABLE 9
Adjustive Reactions to Broken Engagements *

Behavior	Male (N = 230)	Female (N = 414)
Frequenting places with common associations	11.3%	10.0%
Avoiding places with common associations	2.9	3.4
Avoiding meetings	4.7	5.1
Attempting meetings	5.9	4.3
Remembering only unpleasant things	2.3	3.9
Remembering only pleasant things	15.6	15.8
Dreaming about partner	15.5	11.2
Daydreaming	14.3	11.4
Imagining recognition	6.4	7.9
Liking or disliking people because of resemblance	5.5	5.4
Imitating mannerisms	1.8	2.1
Preserving keepsakes	7.0	10.8
Reading over old letters	6.8	8.7
Total	100.0	100.0

* Clifford Kirkpatrick and Theodore Caplow, "Courtship in a Group of Minnesota Students," *Am. J. Sociol.,* **51** (Sept., 1945), pp. 114–125. The University of Chicago Press.

[14] There are many factors which could lead to this difficulty. Kirkpatrick and Caplow in studying the courtship experience of university students found that among others, such factors as jealousy, possessiveness, criticism, irritability, and dislike of friends played a large part in causing conflict in serious love affairs. Clifford Kirkpatrick and Theodore Caplow, "Courtship in a Group of Minnesota Students," *Am. J. Sociol.,* **51** (Sept., 1945), pp. 114–125.

[15] Ruth Shonle Cavan, *American Marriage,* Thomas Y. Crowell Co., New York, 1959, p. 186.

When, however, one partner is desirous of breaking the engagement and the other is not, this presents a situation which deserves attention. In dealing with the decision about whether or not to break the formal engagement, it first becomes necessary to ascertain whether the difficulty is a result of one's own personal immaturity, suggesting that one might have difficulty in any relationship, or whether it is primarily a matter of value differences which simply do not fit well in a particular relationship. When it is determined that the former is primarily involved, then it might well be wise to reserve judgment on breaking the engagement since the relationship basically could be a sound one. What is necessary for such an individual or individuals is a change in personal orientation, rather than a change in relationships. For example, many immature people are unrealistic and expect too much from a relationship. They may have immature notions about love and distortions regarding the nature of love which will have to be dispelled before a satisfactory relationship can develop. Unless the immature individual can assure himself that he understands his part in the deterioration of a particular relationship he undoubtedly will confront similar difficulties in other relationships.

If, however, after seriously considering his specific role in the relationship he is assured that he has made a serious mistake in his selection of an intended marriage partner, then the engagement probably should be broken. Making a wrong choice is not an uncommon thing and the time to recognize this is during the courtship period. Burgess and Wallin report that in their study of 1,000 engaged couples, about one-third of the men and one-half of the women had one or more broken engagements.[16] Landis suggests that some students of marriage are of the opinion that probably more engagements should be broken than actually are, since this could avoid unstable relationships.[17]

This is not to suggest that breaking an engagement is something to be treated lightly. On the contrary, it is quite the opposite, since a broken engagement often involves personal trauma. Nor is it being suggested that a pattern of broken engagements is to be regarded as reflecting a meaningful approach to marriage because for some people the tendency to break engagements is indicative of unstable and fickle personality characteristics neither of which are regarded as healthy. It is being suggested, however, that becoming engaged in the first place should be regarded as a serious step in the man-woman relationship

---

[16] Ernest W. Burgess and Paul Wallin, *Engagement and Marriage*, J. B. Lippincott Co., Philadelphia, 1953, Ch. 9, "Broken Engagements."

[17] Paul H. Landis, *Making the Most of Marriage*, Appleton-Century-Crofts, Inc., New York, 2nd ed., 1960, p. 312.

and treated as such. However, when under any circumstances one or both of the engaged partners have serious doubts about their ability to adjust in the relationship, a broken engagement may well mean one less broken marriage.

Let us now consider some of the ways of dealing with the engaged partner when it is necessary to break an engagement. The manner in which an engagement is to be broken might well be examined in the light of certain values in the relationship. To begin with, we can assume that the couple have tried to develop a meaningful relationship in which the qualities of trust and respect have been present to some extent. Although perhaps difficult to maintain at the time of breaking a relationship, they are worthy of consideration. They add dignity to the human relationship and have therapeutic value as well. Since the breaking of a relationship is an important aspect of one's socialization, the qualities of respect and trust enable the experience to occur with a minimum of hurt to the self-worth of the members. In light of these values, perhaps the most difficult method at the time, but the best in the long run, is to break the relationship once a decision has been reached that the problems will not be resolved successfully. The realization that one should dissolve a relationship is not without its emotional complications however. There are those who feel guilty and dislike themselves for such a decision since it will involve hurting another person. The fact that more hurt could result were the relationship to continue is, at the time, seemingly unimportant. Thus, many people feel ambivalent especially when it is time for a final break, since the finality arouses severe doubts and conflicts about whether or not one has reached the proper decision.

The ambivalence and the guilt about one's decision become responsible for much inner turmoil. Under these circumstances it is easy to feel not only hostility toward oneself for deciding to dissolve the relationship, but to feel what is experienced as hostility coming from the other person. Thus, the individual who wishes to dissolve the relationship finds his difficulties compounded. For not only does he have to move ahead with a decision about the engagement but he has to cope with hostilities, both those from within and those he feels from the outside. Some people break through the conflicts and discontinue the relationship. A good many, however, who attempt to avoid the conflicts in breaking a relationship often end up creating additional burdens.

One such example is to allow oneself to be talked into prolonging the relationship on some trial basis. This may be aided by pleas from the other member such as, "If you will only give me another chance,

I'll do better." Very frequently the rationale for agreeing to prolong the relationship involves the belief that one has feeling for the other partner. The real reason is often that one wishes to avoid the conflict and possible hostility involved in a definite break. Such a decision to prolong the relationship is responsible for some real difficulties. To begin with, one is giving hope to the other person when really there is no hope. Certainly only an immature person will confront the partner with the intent to break an engagement without having thought through the implications. Thus, to encourage a person to believe that things can work out when in fact one has made up his mind that they will not is cruel to the partner and is also indicative of a gross disrespect for what the relationship meant in the past. Putting off a final decision to break the relationship is one technique used to avoid or minimize the conflicts which one feels about breaking the engagement.

A second example of the need to avoid conflict in breaking an engagement is to engage in statements designed to make it easier for the other partner, thereby minimizing the discomfort which one may feel. For example, one might resort to clichés such as "It isn't that I don't love you, but I love you like a sister (or brother)." What is frequently lost sight of, however, is the fact that far from easing the situation, unintentional pain may be inflicted on the partner since he or she is not desirous of being loved as a sister (or brother). Other types of clichés which may lead to misunderstandings are: "If we can't continue our engagement, I do hope we can continue to be good friends"; or "Now in spite of this I do want to hear from you often." These statements are misleading since the person making them uses them as an attempt, in reality, to soothe his own feelings while the engaged partner on hearing these statements may immediately think that they reflect uncertainty about the desire to break the engagement. These statements tend to create misunderstanding, since, for example, a girl on hearing her fiancé say that, although he wants to break their engagement, he wants to hear from her often and continue their friendship, may easily delude herself into believing that her fiancé is really not desirous of breaking the engagement. This misunderstanding and confusion is further compounded by friends who are eager to sympathize with her and who attempt to do so by agreeing with her faulty interpretation.

A third example of the need to avoid conflict in breaking the engagement is to avoid any formal confrontation at all. Instead, there may be a lessening of the frequency of dates, and even a going away, on one pretense or another, of the person desirous of making the break. Under this method the engagement usually is terminated with the sending of a so-called "Dear John" letter. Because of the vagueness involved in breaking an engagement in this manner the personal trauma created here is probably far greater than it would have been if a straightforward confrontation had been made. We are not suggesting that the engaged partner be approached with arrogance and bitterness but rather, after several unsuccessful attempts have been made to reach mutually satisfactory adjustments, the engaged partner must be confronted tactfully but truthfully with the fact that the engagement is being broken and exactly why it is being broken.

It should be clear that these techniques for the avoidance of conflicts which one utilizes in breaking the engagement are fraught with complications. Rather than solving the difficulties people often find themselves caught up with additional problems which complicate their dealings with the engaged partner; this is probably quite unnecessary.

Up to this point we have been viewing the broken engagement from the standpoint of the partner desiring the break. Let us now look at the broken engagement from the point of view of the person who does not want to terminate the relationship. For this person the breaking of the engagement is often a major emotional crisis.[18] Among other difficulties there is the feeling of being a jilted and discarded lover, and the trauma of explaining the situation to one's friends, not to mention the frequent need of the person himself to understand exactly what happened.

When this results in bitterness and suspicion it is easy to see how one's interaction in future relationships might become warped. Burgess and Locke, however, seem to feel that these reactions to a broken engagement gradually yield to time. They go on to say that there are individual differences in the rate of recovery from a broken love affair and that these differences are due to several factors, including temperament, the number and importance of other interests, and the beginnings of a new attachment. "In retrospect," they continue, "at least after another engagement which is successful, the person tends to minimize the seriousness of the experience and to be thankful that the break took place." [19]

As we already said, each broken engagement may well be one less broken marriage. However, when the person being given up can be made to understand the difficulties which impaired the relationship and made to see the folly in his running headlong into another similar circumstance, then to the extent that he was at fault, learning about

---

[18] For a discussion of emotional reactions to the breaking up of serious love affairs, see: Kirkpatrick and Caplow, *loc. cit.*

[19] Ernest W. Burgess and Harvey J. Locke, *The Family*, 2nd ed., American Book Co., New York, 1960, p. 339.

his deficiencies and doing something to alter them will be of unlimited benefit in his future attempts to develop meaningful man-woman relationships. As Cavan points out it should be remembered that "when a love affair or an engagement breaks, it is only this love relationship that is lost. The capacity to love again and to be loved again remains." [20]

As a final note to this chapter, we would like to state that at some time during the engagement period the couple will undoubtedly consider the economic as well as the medical aspects of marriage. With respect to economic aspects, the couple will be concerned with various consumer problems to be confronted in marriage. With respect to medical aspects, they will be interested in questions of overall health, family planning, as well as sexual adjustment. These problems, both economic and medical, are discussed in the appendices of this text.[21]

SUMMARY

Courtship is that phase of the man-woman relationship which follows dating and precedes marriage. It begins when each partner in the relationship clearly states to the other his intention to have this relationship result in marriage. Courtship, thus, is engagement. There are two periods in the courtship phase, however; the first, referred to as informal engagement, is the period during which the couple have an opportunity to test their ability to adjust to each other, and to establish patterns of working through whatever difficulties they may encounter. At the successful conclusion of this period the couple then announce publicly their intention to marry; this announcement initiates the formal engagement. The formal engagement period consists largely of making the arrangements for the wedding and honeymoon, and preparing the home in which the newlyweds will reside. In this chapter many aspects of the informal and formal engagement periods were discussed and the advantage of having an informal engagement was stressed. Also considered were the conditions under which an engagement should be broken, and the situations which are confronted in the breaking of an engagement.

QUESTIONS

1. What is the difference between dating and courtship? Name and give the purpose of the two phases of courtship.
2. Under what circumstances does going steady and being pinned constitute engagement?

[20] Ruth Shonle Cavan, op. cit., p. 188.

[21] See also: Abraham Stone and Lena Levine, The Premarital Consultation, Grune and Stratton, New York, 1956.

3. How long should the entire engagement last? What proportion of time should be devoted to the informal engagement and what proportion to the formal engagement? Why?

4. What things should a person consider in deciding how much he should "confess" about his past to his engaged partner?

5. What are the common mistakes which people make in planning a honeymoon? Why are these considered to be mistakes?

6. Is the broken engagement an infrequent occurrence in the American society? For what reason do some students of marriage believe that more engagements should be broken? Does this mean that the more broken engagements one has, the more likely he is to be successful in marriage? Explain your answer.

7. What techniques do people use in attempting to minimize the conflict they feel about breaking an engagement? Do these techniques help or hinder the circumstances?

8. What did Burgess and Locke find to be the reaction of people toward their broken engagements? Do you agree with their findings? (See Project 1 in this Chapter.)

9. It has been said that in a broken love relationship only the relationship is lost but the capacity to love again remains. Under what circumstances is this correct and under what circumstances might it be incorrect?

PROJECTS

1. Have each student in the class interview three students who have experienced a broken engagement. Have them find out such things as what were the reasons for the broken engagement; to what extent do the people they interview regard themselves as having been at fault; what, if anything, have they learned from the broken engagement; and finally, what feelings do these people have toward their broken relationship. Summarize the findings in class and have the class analyze the results.

2. Make a survey to find out to what extent going steady and being pinned constitute informal engagement on your campus. Do you find any differences between the answers given by men and those given by women?

3. Take a poll on campus to find out what percentage of engaged and married couples utilized the informal engagement and what percentage went directly from dating into the formal engagement. Find out whether those who utilized the informal engagement period found it helpful and why, and also whether those who did not utilize the informal engagement think they could have benefited from it and why.

4. Interview several married couples and find out in what way engagement prepared them for marriage and in what way, if any, it did not. Ask them whether, if they could relive their engagement period, they would change anything, and if they would, what would they change and why would they change it?

SUGGESTED READINGS

Johannis, Theodore B., Jr., and Karen Many, "Financing Student Weddings," *J. Home Econ.*, **51** (May, 1959), pp. 362–364.

Kirkpatrick, Clifford, and Theodore Caplow, "Courtship in a Group of Minnesota Students," *Am. J. Sociol.*, **51** (Sept., 1945), pp. 114–125.

Mace, David R., *Marriage*, Doubleday, New York, 1952, Ch. 2, "Are Engagements Necessary?"

Magoun, F. Alexander, *Love and Marriage*, Harper and Brothers, New York, 1948, Ch. 6, "Courtship," Ch. 7, "The Period of Engagement," and Ch. 8, "The Honeymoon."

Simpson, George, *People in Families*, Thomas Y. Crowell Co., New York, 1960, Ch. 9, "Some Critical Notes on Weddings and Honeymoons."

Waller, Willard, *The Family* (Revised by Reuben Hill), The Dryden Press, New York, 1951, Ch. 12, "The Engagement: A Bridge to Marriage."

Winch, Robert F., *The Modern Family*, Henry Holt and Co., New York, 1952, Ch. 16, "Courtship and Marriage."

Sexual interaction and adjustment

12

We have already devoted a considerable amount of time to discussions of the issues involved in building a meaningful relationship. The more diligently one pursues the problems which have been pointed out, the less likely that serious marital problems will emerge. Nevertheless, the conditions of intimate and continuous interaction in marriage may bring out aspects of personality and differences in views which were not apparent in the relationship simply because the circumstances which produce them were not present. Although marital partners establish a relationship prior to marriage, it is of necessity limited. In marriage a lifetime of habits, attitudes, and values with respect to the daily patterns of existence emerge. The interaction of these, and the attempt to integrate them are an inevitable source of difficulty. Thus, it becomes necessary to see marital adjustments and conflicts as emerging out of daily interaction, as habits, attitudes, and values are expressed in the interactions of married persons.

SEXUAL ADJUSTMENT. The sexual relationship is one such aspect of marital adjustment.[1] Table 10 suggests that fewer couples reported satisfactory adjustment in sex relations than in other adjustment areas. To be sure there are those couples with sexual experience who

[1] For a discussion of the sex problems of American wives and husbands, see: E. E. LeMasters, *Modern Courtship and Marriage*, The Macmillan Co., New York, 1957, pp. 376–384.

have initiated their adjustments prior to marriage. We can point out, however, that even for these people attitudes and feelings will emerge that had no opportunity to appear previously; these may affect the marital sex union. Let us be specific; there are those persons who seemed to enjoy the sex act before they were married but not after they were married. The reason for such enjoyment may lie in their view of sex. If they looked on sexual relations before marriage as bad and if they were rebels against conventional ideas, then there may be an enjoyment of the act based on taking part in something that is forbidden. When such people marry, however, and sexual relations become a normal, healthy, and conventional aspect of marriage, then the enjoyment has been known to diminish.

TABLE 10

Percentages of Couples Reporting Satisfactory Adjustments From Beginning of Marriage in Six Areas *

Six Areas	Satisfaction from Beginning
Mutual Friends	76%
Religious Activities	74
In-Law Relationships	69
Social Activities	67
Spending Family Income	56
Sex Relations	53

* Judson T. Landis, "Length of Time Required to Achieve Adjustment in Marriage," *Am. Soc. Rev.*, 11 (Dec., 1946), pp. 666–677.

In still other situations, persons who were sexually active with the spouse-to-be or others may become relatively inactive. One example of this concerns a young woman who had led a very active sex life with her fiancé prior to marriage but virtually refused to have sexual relations with him after they were married. It turned out that she had never really enjoyed the sex act but had used it as a means of "getting a husband." [2] As her difficulties increased due to her sexual inactivity she began to realize that some assessment of her behavior was necessary, both for her own well-being as well as for the relationship.

These are simply a few of many possible illustrations which point

[2] One writer points out that among other uses, the sex act can be used as a coin to buy affection, protection, or something from another. Lawrence S. Bee, *Marriage and Family Relations*, Harper and Brothers, New York, 1959, p. 81.

out that new and different attitudes toward sex may emerge in marriage because marriage itself represents a new relationship involving new dimensions of behavior.[3] An understanding of these varying possibilities is especially important in considering the types of problems which may appear when the couple are first married.

Initial Sexual Relations in Marriage. Much has been written about the significance of initial sexual relations in marriage and indeed there is much to be said on this point.[4] The initial sexual experiences in marriage are important for at least two reasons. First, they reveal the approach to the love making process which is important in determining attitudes regarding the sex act. Secondly, and at a deeper level, behavior in the sex act is indicative of the attitudes and feelings which husband and wife express toward one another. We have pointed out earlier that the erotic involvement is but one way in which we relate to others. Thus, it comes as no surprise that the basic attitudes and feelings that we have for one another find expression in our sexual feeling toward each other. For example, contempt, hostility, love, and respect may be expressed in the act. These initial expressions are especially important since they are significant in their effect on the subsequent sexual, as well as interpersonal, adjustment which the couple will have.

One of the problems frequently encountered during initial sexual adjustment is a feeling of disappointment about the erotic experience itself. Both partners may experience less than they expected, there is simply a letdown—"It's less pleasurable than I thought it would be." There may be a lack of, or incomplete, orgasm for either the wife or husband.[5]

An adequate understanding of how people respond to such disappointment in sexual relations is essential since there is considerable ego involvement and feelings of self-worth that should be examined. One of the responses to be watched and understood when the act is not satisfactory is the tendency to hold the other partner responsible

[3] For a discussion of the use and misuse of love in the man-woman relationship, see: Eugenia Elliott, *Growth Through Love and Sex,* (article of) Auxiliary Council to the Association for the Advancement for Psychoanalysis, New York, 1952.

[4] For a discussion of the initial sexual experience, see: F. Alexander Magoun, *Love and Marriage,* Harper and Brothers, New York, 1948, pp. 194–199.

[5] In regard to lack of orgasm, 75 percent of the married women in Kinsey's sample reported that they had experienced at least some orgasm by the end of the first year of marriage. However, 10 percent reported not experiencing orgasm by the fifteenth year of marriage, while others reported experiencing their first coital orgasm after 28 years of marriage or more. Alfred C. Kinsey, et al., *Sexual Behavior in the Human Female,* W. B. Saunders Co., Philadelphia, Pa., 1953, p. 383.

for the lack of pleasure. Often one may feel it was because the partner
failed to respond adequately. Indeed, if the partners do not respond in
a wholehearted fashion, such misunderstanding is very possible. Thus
a feeling of having been rejected sexually may follow. For example,
frequently the husband who suffers disappointment in sexual relations
may blame the difficulty on his wife's reticence or inadequacy in the
sex act. Such reticence may then be viewed by the husband in a personal way and is experienced as rejection. An experience of this type
may bring forth negative reactions in the male either in the form of his
becoming overly aggressive and pursuing sex to demonstrate manliness, or by withdrawal which may take the form of pouting. This in
turn may bring a counter reaction from the wife. She often senses a
kind of inconsiderateness for her feelings and if she grew up with the
stereotype that men are, after all, preoccupied with sexual satisfaction
without regard for the woman's feelings, her stereotype may be confirmed; numerous difficulties can result.

On the other hand if the wife experiences less than she anticipated
in sexual relations, she may believe that her failure to enjoy sex is due
to her husband's inability to respond properly to her and that his failure to do so is a sign of rejection. She may, under these circumstances,
berate or belittle her husband. This in turn may confirm some stereotypes which men hold that women have little rational control over their
behavior and precipitate an argument of significant proportions.

In the examination of illustrations of the behavior just presented, one
has to recognize that personal rejection of the partner may in fact be
involved, but most often disappointment in sexual relations is the result of lifelong attitudes; in all probability they would appear when
they did with any marital partner. Most of us are so ego involved, however, that it becomes difficult to accept this, so reactions become over-
reactions, intensely personal, often with hostility.

The tendency to blame the other person and refuse to assume responsibility for one's role in the sexual disappointment is easy to do
since it is painful for most people to accept the fact that they might in
some way be sexually inadequate. Further, as mentioned in Chapter 8,
our society is one which places considerable emphasis on physical attractiveness. Thus to be sexually desirable is important to members of
both sexes and perhaps especially important for those whose status
and role are more readily tied to marriage, particularly women. For
the wife the feeling of sexual rejection may be devastating, since it
causes a fear about losing the husband.

There is the case of a married woman whose husband was reluctant
to have sexual relations as frequently as she expected. Whenever the

husband refused sexual relations the wife felt rejected and became belligerent, aggressive, and abusive. She stated quite frankly that she felt so rejected that she had to try to prove that she was not "that horrible." Although her husband was reluctant to have sexual relations it had little to do with rejection of her. Instead it was based on the fact that he was a very cold and aloof person.[6] Intimate contact with any woman, emotional or physical, disturbed him, and so this basic sexual union was repulsive for him.

The pattern of berating each other about inadequate sexual performance is very destructive to the relationship and may be responsible for negative attitudes not only toward sexual relations but toward other aspects of the marital relationship as well.

Background Factors in the Initial Adjustment. What are the background experiences which give rise to these sexual disappointments and difficulties at the outset of marriage? Here we are dealing with a variety of personal and social experiences that people have grown up with and which become manifest in the sexual area of the man-woman relationship. Probably one of the most common reasons given by men and women for disappointment or difficulty in the sex act is the notion that one has acquired negative attitudes regarding sexual involvement.[7] This explanation has been used so often and in so general a way as to make it a cliché. Nevertheless, when fully examined and understood it becomes useful with respect to its appropriateness for explaining some sexual disappointments in marriage. Further, negative attitudes toward sex take on the most meaning when we can see how they have evolved out of certain types of experiences, and how they have become integrated as part of one's orientation toward sex. An understanding of any person's reaction to sex is dependent on precisely this type of analysis. At this point let us deal with some common experiences in our culture which contribute to a negative orientation regarding sexual involvement.

[6] For a discussion of aloofness and sexual behavior, see: Abe Pinsky, *Love and Sex in Resigned People,* (article of) Auxiliary Council to the Association for the Advancement of Psychoanalysis, New York, 1951.

[7] For a discussion of the relationship between one's attitudes and his ability to love, see: Antonia Wenkart, *Healthy and Neurotic Love,* (article of) Auxiliary Council to the Association for the Advancement of Psychoanalysis, New York, 1952. One study, however, which attempted to determine the causes of the failure of women to achieve orgasm was unable to find any association with early sex conditioning, type of birth control used, husband's sex technique, or any of the other factors one would expect to be involved. This study finally postulated a neurological factor as being causal. Lewis M. Terman, et. al., *Psychological Factors in Marital Happiness,* McGraw-Hill Book Co., Inc., New York, 1938.

What do we mean when we say that the individual has acquired negative attitudes about sex? We mean first that in the process of growing up in our culture he (or she) has had a variety of experiences which have resulted in attitudes that inhibit sexual pleasure and foster disappointment. In order to appreciate these kinds of experiences which are common in our culture, it is necessary to examine some of the values that operate in society and see how they influence human relatedness and sex. It is probably impossible to grow up in a society which stresses some of the values which ours does and expect healthy attitudes toward sexual relatedness to develop. As indicated in an earlier chapter, the development of mature love is thwarted by the impersonality in society, the commodity orientation, the high degree of destructive competitiveness, and the shallow living. It is safe to say that whenever there are patterns that operate against human relatedness and in fact reduce the worth of the human being as such, difficulties regarding love and sex in the population are bound to be present. An examination of contemporary American family life suggests that the values just mentioned may pervade the entire pattern of relationships in the home. These markedly affect husband-wife relationships, making it difficult for them to understand or relate to each other in any positive way. (See Chapter 6.) These social and familial influences fail to foster a cultural atmosphere which facilitates a satisfactory sexual relationship.

Parental Response to Sexual Curiosity in the Child. In shifting our attention from general social values to the specific reactions of parents we note that the early signs of sexual curiosity which children of both sexes manifest may be misinterpreted by overly anxious, sexually inhibited parents. Thus the child who openly displays his or her sexual organs may find a hostile parent who reprimands severely. Masturbation may be met with threats and fears which can be terrifying to the child. Further the hugging and kissing of another child may be discouraged or anxiously regarded by some parents. These are frequently the reactions of parents who are themselves confused about erotic involvements, and who become very upset about the child's sexual activity since it may arouse in them conflicts and anxieties due to their own unresolved difficulties in this area. It would be a mistake, of course, to assume that the child comes to learn about the negative aspects of sexuality only from the overt negative reactions of parents. Parents may convey a great deal with gestures, with the tone of their voices, and by other acts which reveal their reactions to the child's behavior. For the child, sexual interests are inevitably the result of healthy curiosity and growth, a desire for relatedness, but for the parents they are all too often interpreted as signs of sexual precocious-ness; to these parents what is healthy and natural becomes a sign of the perverse.

The question is, what is the net effect of these experiences on the child? [8] It is easy for the child who is misunderstood because of early sexual curiosity to generalize from the undesirable sexual conditioning to other areas of life. Such generalizations emerge because the child does not possess the intellectual maturity to separate one experience from another. Instead there is a marked tendency to extend the results of one experience to the other experiences. Thus, unfortunate experi-ences in the sexual area are frequently extended to other areas and are often manifest in the following attitudes:

1. To expose feelings means to invite criticism from others.
2. The experiencing of pleasure is followed by punishment.

There are numerous clinical histories of adults who suffer sexual dis-appointment because they still react as they did when they were children. People with such faulty sexual conditioning are anxious about sex as though parental punishment were forthcoming. Thus, they are afraid to let their feelings go or participate wholeheartedly in the sex act. Such people may realize in an intellectual way that their behavior is childlike but they are helpless to deal with the problem because they do not fully understand the impact of their early sexual condi-tioning.

There was the case of one young woman, Miss M., who came to the marriage counselor because she had great difficulty responding sex-ually to her fiancé. She regarded their relationship as satisfactory in every respect except the sexual, due to this difficulty she was con-sidering breaking her engagement. She stated that whenever demon-strations of affection "bordered the least bit on the sexual," she would become extremely uncomfortable, feeling "trapped" and "stifled" and would try desperately to free herself from the situation. In discussing this problem with Miss M. it became apparent that although she had acquired considerable information concerning sex from reading and college courses, she had previously acquired many unwholesome at-titudes from her mother who regarded sex as "something which men need and which women must put up with." Not only did Mrs. M. im-plant this and other ideas in Miss M.'s mind but she also reinforced each attitude by alluding to negative religious interpretations regard-

[8] For a discussion of the relationship between the child's experiences within the family and his psychosexual development, see: Paul H. Landis, *Making the Most of Marriage*, 2nd ed., Appleton-Century-Crofts, Inc., New York, 1960, p. 411.

ing sex. In an atmosphere such as this Miss M., even as a child, soon learned not to ask questions about, or show interest in, anything pertaining to sex, and she learned never to regard sex as pleasurable.

Finally, negative attitudes toward sex may be aided by misunderstandings of religious teachings, unwholesome reading or some traumatic sex experience, either as observer or participant.

Religious Teachings. In regard to religious teachings we note that here is an area in which the influence of religion is not altogether clear. There are those scholars who claim that the early Christian view of marriage was essentially negative.[9] Others, however, believe that this was never the case, that instead such a view is the result of a misinterpretation of early religious teachings. What most church scholars would assert, however, is that religious teachings as interpreted by some churches and some ministers aided the development of a negative view toward sex. Having pointed this out we wish to remind the reader that many churches cognizant of this problem have set about to correct negative views regarding sex through educational programs.

Unwholesome Reading. Unwholesome reading materials can also be a factor in negative views toward sex. Here we are confronted with a large mass of literature some of which is current, some fairly old. As late as the early part of this century there was a considerable body of sex literature, authored by physicians, which fostered an unhealthy view of sex. Irrespective of training, these physicians passed on to the public a distorted view of sex with the implicit notion that although sexual feelings were inevitable they arose from the less desirable components of man. The purpose of knowledge about sex in this framework was to enable one to understand how to deal with man's negative nature.

One is less likely to find sexual indoctrination of this type emanating from professional sources today, but there are other types of literature today which are equally negative. Perhaps the most important in this regard are the published sordid tales of love and violence in which the most destructive components of human nature are revealed and in which sexual relations are devoid of feeling and tenderness. To be sure, such a picture is applicable to some relationships, but it presents a distorted picture of sex, and when the individual views sex in such a manner he almost invariably feels a need to develop protective techniques and mistrust which are manifested indiscriminately.

Sexual Trauma. The role of sexual trauma is difficult to assess. Although it is entirely possible that these are crucial determinants of sexual difficulty, more than likely their significance is exaggerated.

---

[9] Stuart A. Queen, Robert W. Habenstein, John B. Adams, *The Family in Various Cultures*, 2nd ed., J. B. Lippincott Co., Philadelphia, 1961, pp. 183–185.

Invariably those who suffer sexual disappointment point to a dramatic period in their lives when they witnessed or were involved in an unpleasant sex experience. More than likely the impact of such experiences has been distorted. Far more important perhaps is what they do not remember, the daily, ongoing, non-dramatic processes of sexual conditioning which are really at the bottom of most sex problems.

Internalization of Negative Views Toward Sex. These negative views which create sexual disappointment are internalized and become part of the psychic equipment with which people attempt to relate sexually to one another. If one has learned that sex as a human activity is essentially a bad activity, then it tends to remain so, unless serious efforts are made to deal with it. The fact that one is legally and religiously wed does not automatically affect such basic attitudes. Thus, some people are never able to view sexual relations in marriage as a "proper activity." [10] Probably few married people overtly or consciously experience sex as an evil activity. What they do experience repeatedly are the symptoms of negative attitudes in the form of disappointment or dissatisfaction with sex. The large amount of sexually oriented literature and films and the wide audiences which these hold are suggestive of the American's frustration and preoccupation with sex. Further, among the middle class, with whom we are primarily concerned, the problem is even more complex since on the basis of their education they believe that they should know better—that sex is normal and healthy. At the level of feeling and attitudes, however, there may be contradictory attitudes.

Some of these negative views toward sex could be minimized by the functions which the school system could perform. Although many school programs make noble attempts to counteract negative attitudes toward sex, many are lacking in their programs. A good deal of the difficulty would appear to be in the types of courses offered. These stress the anatomy of male and female genitalia along with reproduction; while such knowledge is important it probably has little to do with basic sexual attitudes and feelings.[11]

[10] Francis E. Merrill, *Courtship and Marriage*, Henry Holt and Co., New York, 1959, pp. 300–301.

[11] For a discussion of the implications of a psycho-sociological perspective for a program of sex education in the high schools, see: Jerome Himelhoch, "Sex Education in Sociological Perspective," *Social Hygiene Papers*, Nov., 1957. We are indebted to Dr. Robert A. Harper for suggestion and clarification of three related terms: sexual conditioning, sexual knowledge, and sexual therapy. Harper points out that sexual conditioning refers to the experience and attitudes toward sex which have emerged in the process of growing up. Sexual knowledge consists of formal instruction received in school; while sexual therapy refers to the undoing of faulty sexual conditioning. Harper correctly points out that what we need is much more sexual therapy, if problems in these areas are to be resolved.

For some people their early negative associations regarding sex will diminish, especially if the marriage on the whole is a good one. In such a marriage people discuss their fears and come to understand one another. Perhaps in a majority of marriages people are not so fortunate. They simply plod along with their confusions, expecting little, and probably experiencing less.

SEXUAL COMPATIBILITY AS A PROCESS. Sexual compatibility is in marriage an emergent process.[12] The length of time involved varies: the range of difference with respect to length of time in achieving sexual compatibility will in general depend on how sound the marital relationship is and on the couple's ability to deal with the problems in their relationship, as is shown in Table 11. A meaningful marriage devoid of serious incompatibilities is conducive to sexual compatibility. In addition, a meaningful relationship tends to facilitate sexual compatibility in this way. It fosters attitudes in which people can express themselves sexually with a maximum of freedom and spontaneity, consistent, of course, with the well-being of the relationship. It follows that a meaningful relationship will impose few obstacles on the spontaneous expression of sexual behavior, which is basic for sexual compatibility.

TABLE 11

Length of Time Required to Adjust in Sex Relations and Happiness in Marriage (409 Couples) *

Length of Time Required	Very Happy	Happy	Average
Satisfactory from beginning	53%	36%	11%
1–12 months	61	30	9
1–20 years	43	38	19
Never satisfactory	11	36	53

* Judson T. Landis and Mary G. Landis, *Building a Successful Marriage*, 3rd ed., Prentice-Hall, Inc., Englewood Cliffs, New Jersey, © 1958, p. 378.

Frequency of Erotic Experience. In a meaningful relationship there will be few rules regarding the frequency with which the sex act should, or should not, occur. Such rules lead to frustration. For in addition to disturbing the spontaneity, rules frequently result in individuals evaluating themselves as being either oversexed or undersexed.

[12] Total sexual compatibility may be defined in terms of both partners experiencing orgasm within the sex act. It is clear that a majority of couples only approximate total compatibility.

When people feel that they are undersexed or oversexed they may develop negative self-attitudes and try in some desperate fashion to change their behavior. Such rules may be the result of literature containing statistics on frequency in sexual relations which has been misunderstood, or unconscious ideas which have been acquired from others. What is forgotten is that while there are statistics on the frequency of sex relations for married people, they have been based on limited samples. Furthermore, the range of differences between people may be, and usually is, considerable.[13] To impose rules and restrictions based on artificial or unreal standards is simply to promote frustration. The most sensible measure to use, if one is so inclined, is the satisfaction of the couple. This may mean a high or a low frequency depending on individual differences, needs, and attitudes toward each other. To be sure, in any particular marriage there may be at the outset considerable difference with respect to frequency of interest, with one person desiring sexual relations more, or less, frequently than the other.[14] If there are no deep seated personality problems, this particular difficulty is often easily resolved, especially when the couple are sensitive to each other's needs, spontaneous in their sexual behavior, and a good interpersonal relationship is maintained: that is, where basic personal satisfactions in the marriage are being maintained.

Love Making. In a meaningful relationship there will be few rigidities regarding the nature of sexual experience. By rigidities we mean a pattern of participating in the sex act at the same time in the same way with the same techniques, so that sexual relations become planned. Couples who follow such a pattern often fail to engage in sexual relations when interest develops and indeed may even feel obligated to participate at other times when there is no real interest. There are those, for example, who reject their own spontaneous sex interests because they have become so completely habit bound in their way of life. Among other things this may mean that these people will engage in sexual relations only at night and in the dark. We recognize that such a procedure may be dictated by other activities in the life of the couple. For some couples, however, both the evening and the darkness may be symbolic of secrecy and the forbidden, this is a restriction on

[13] Kinsey pointed out that a great variance of coitus frequency exists among couples. Taking this variance into consideration, however, he presents statistics concerning averages of coitus frequency, see: Alfred C. Kinsey, et al., *op. cit.*, pp. 348–349.

[14] Most studies tend to show that husbands desire coitus more frequently than wives, see: Lewis Terman, et al., *loc. cit.*

spontaneous enjoyment. Couples, of course, are never wholly free to be spontaneous and indeed all patterns, sexual and otherwise, are dictated by other necessities; nevertheless the development of spontaneity in this area may enable the couple to participate in sexual relations at a time which is best for them while avoiding those periods which are not.

Regarding love-making practices themselves, there is still another obstacle to spontaneity and this has to do with the tendency for the married couple to approach each other and to participate erotically in the same identical manner. One of the problems here, of course, is the judgments that couples make about what respectable couples should, or should not, do. With respect to this point there seems to be a variety of love-making practices which physicians and psychiatrists recognize as satisfactory for a large number of people. Appendix A (pages 360–362) by Dr. Lehfeldt could be consulted on this point. To the extent that a meaningful relationship in marriage is present, people feel free to express themselves sexually. Thus, spontaneity is fostered and becomes reflected in experimentation with respect to love making. Many of the relatively less complicated problems in sexual relations can be resolved and pleasure increased by an awareness of these potential difficulties.

The Problem of Communication. Not only does a meaningful relationship minimize obstacles and foster spontaneity, but it enables the couple to communicate difficulties about sexual matters. The importance of communication here is that it enables the partners to reveal their feelings and reactions about what each is experiencing in the sex act. Thus, when handled properly it enables the persons to integrate their differences and build a better sexual relationship. Equally significant, however, is the fact that communication enables the marital partners to reveal those aspects of love making that are disturbing; that is, those which tend to detract from the sexual satisfaction that might be achieved. Likewise, communication enables each to reveal those aspects of love making that are pleasurable. Of particular importance in this regard is the ability to communicate the fantasies which one may have about the sources of sexual pleasure.

Fantasies are common and by their communication to the partner a sexual relationship which is mutually enjoyable may be facilitated. Many people are fearful about communicating their wishes in the sexual area since they feel a sense of embarrassment about them. Many such people go through a lifetime of sexual frustration. We shall deal with a further aspect of communication in a subsequent chapter on handling marital difficulties.

Finally, when rigidities in the sexual relationship are minimized and spontaneity, creativity, and communication are fostered, the less complicated sexual problems may be resolved and, in addition, satisfactory erotic relations may be maintained. A good sexual relationship may have some bearing on the extramarital involvement, a problem to which we now turn our attention.

EXTRAMARITAL SEX INTERESTS. Just as we indicated that a meaningful interpersonal relationship with accompanying spontaneity in marriage will facilitate a good sexual relationship and vice versa, so can we say that the same will minimize the likelihood of extramarital sex interests.[15] Thus, the better the marriage, the less likely the extramarital sex interests, but still possibly some interest of this type exists in most marriages. It is a mistake to assume that even the best relationship will completely insulate a couple from having extramarital sex interests at some point in their marriage. The existence of such interests is understandable in view of the powerful sexual urge which may be controlled but seldom exclusively directed toward one member of the opposite sex. Sexual urges are biological and after all the idea of marital fidelity is a social custom. Extramarital sex interests are considerable as evidenced by the Kinsey reports dealing with both men and women.[16] Our main concern at this point is not with infrequent sex interests; we do feel, however, that when the preoccupation occurs with some persistence, some regularity, and is accompanied by a tendency to become involved, then an examination of the difficulty is in order.

Extramarital sex interests can be examined in terms of three broad sets of factors. First, the difficulties may be due to a breakdown of the interpersonal relationship in marriage. Basic satisfactions are no longer being realized; there is value conflict; and incompatibilities are expressed in the interpersonal relationship. Under these circumstances the marital partners may be belittled by each other, and made to feel that they are less worthy than they are. Such a situation will often alienate people from their marriage with a tendency for them to become erotically interested in others. In short it may be necessary to evaluate the basic marital satisfactions and dissatisfactions.

There is the case of a married man who, after twenty years of happily

[15] Paul H. Landis, *Making the Most of Marriage*, 2nd ed., Appleton-Century-Crofts, Inc., New York, 1960, pp. 416–417.

[16] Kinsey found that about 25 percent of the wives in his sample and about 50 percent of the husbands had had at least one extramarital sexual relationship some time during their marriage, see: Alfred C. Kinsey, et al., *op. cit.*, p. 416; Alfred C. Kinsey, et al., *Sexual Behavior in the Human Male*, W. B. Saunders Co., Philadelphia, 1948, p. 585.

married life, started to develop persistent extramarital interests. Although he had never pursued any of these, he became concerned about their intensity and persistence. He sought professional assistance for this problem, both he and his wife came for help. Over a period of time it was learned that the onset of the husband's sexual interest developed when his wife became preoccupied with furthering her education. Such preoccupation made the husband feel rejected and left out. The fact that he was a relatively uneducated person increased his anxiety and fear that his wife might no longer want him. Thus, the extramarital sex interests were an expression of his fear and a need for reassurance as to his desirability.

A second reason for extramarital sex interests may be a breakdown in the erotic aspect of marriage. Thus, one would have to evaluate the frequency, the discrepancy of interests, the pleasure, or absence of pleasure, present in sexual relations. Also, since general marital and sexual dissatisfactions are so intertwined, it would be wise to examine how unhappiness in one area of marital life may be responsible for unhappiness in another area of marital life.[17]

A third factor in extramarital sex interests relates to personality problems and immaturities that can operate somewhat independently of the marital relationship.[18] Those who are beset by inner problems do not necessarily respond or change in their basic patterns of life even when their marriage is a good one. One such personality type is the individual who displays a long history of insecurity. Such a person comes to think of himself as unloved and unlovable. Thus, we are dealing with a self-image which once constructed does not easily disappear. The fact that a wife or a husband may actually show love to this type of partner may not in itself remove the partner's inner doubts. Such people, therefore, may develop extramarital sex interests which are activated by their need to seek reassurance about their being lovable. The reassurance which they seek is seldom satisfied for any period of time by a new relationship. What is necessary, instead, is an understanding of the negative self-image which creates the insecurity.

A second personality type which is often associated with extramarital

[17] In fact one authority feels that the majority of sexual adjustment problems are largely the result of personality and cultural factors which influence marital adjustment in general, see: Ernest W. Burgess and Harvey Locke, *The Family*, 2nd ed., American Book Co., New York, 1960, p. 437. Another authority clearly points out that sex adjustment is only one of the components of the overall marital adjustment, see: Francis Merrill, *op. cit.*, p. 199.

[18] One student after studying sexual behavior reached the conclusion that sexual promiscuity is a response to emotional and environmental problems and as such is a psychiatric problem, see: Richard A. Koch, "Penicillin is Not Enough," *J. soc. Hyg.*, **36** (1950), pp. 3–6.

sex interests are those who possess a destructive orientation to human relationships. Put simply, this means that their lives are predicated on the assumption that good relationships do not exist and they set out in various ways to prove it. Such people are often flirtatious around the opposite sex. More often than not their involvement ends at the point of flirtation, since their interests are primarily to prove that no relationship can really be counted on. The presence of such types of individuals arouses anxiety in members of the more stable marital unions. The "flirt" is considered a threat to the stability of a marriage, and fear is frequently displayed by the husband or wife who sees the partner becoming ensnared in the flirtatious relationship.

A third personality type, which is often associated with extramarital sex interests, is the one who lives a shallow level of existence. Individuals with such personal deterioration find little meaning to life, and have succumbed to a simple pleasure and pain principle. They pursue what is pleasurable and reject what may involve discomfort or effort. They are amoral and live outside any system of morality. Thus, they are generally unconcerned about their actions or the implications of their actions. Since much of life has lost its meaning these people often thrive on the unusual and the daring, in order that the dullness of their existence be removed. These individuals enjoy becoming involved in extramarital affairs; they take special pleasure in the involvement of others and the complications and excitement to life which this brings.

When married people discover persistent extramarital sex interests, and a tendency toward involvement, a thorough evaluation of the marriage and of themselves is in order. Although discussion and communication are important, it is not recommended that married people discuss their extramarital sex interests unless they have an unusual amount of objectivity. Ordinarily these discussions are very threatening to the marital partner and little objectivity is likely to emerge.

One feasible approach in this regard is to deal with non-sexual marital difficulties with the hope that an alleviation of these will result in a reduction of the extramarital interests. Such an approach may be most fruitful when the difficulties reside primarily in the relationship as such. Such efforts will probably be less rewarding when the difficulties are due to personality problems. For these cases it will be necessary to receive counseling or psychotherapy in order to produce any appreciable change in behavior.

ROLE OF PERSONALITY IN SEXUAL DIFFICULTIES. The role of personality in sexual difficulties is obviously not limited to extramarital sex interests, but instead is rather pervasive in the erotic relationship. It is probably true that whenever personality problems of any type are present, they express themselves in the sexual relationship. For example, there is the husband who may have a need to degrade others, women in particular. Thus he views them as prostitutes. He may be quite unaware of such an attitude but nevertheless treats his wife accordingly.[19] Therefore, essentially he may be indifferent to his wife's sexual needs and wishes. She is there only to satisfy his sexual desires. He is unconcerned with her feelings. Some men of this type may try to control the budget when they are not sexually satisfied. Thus, the amount of money a wife receives becomes a function of her husband's sexual satisfaction. There is on the other hand the wife who looks on herself as a prostitute; she may expect and even suggest that her wishes be ignored. She may see herself as one without any right to wishes, as one who is there only to serve her husband. Some of these women may not even be able to enjoy the sex act unless they are treated without regard for their feelings. The husband and wife in these instances are people who enjoy sexual relations only at the expense of others or themselves. They must degrade, or they must be degraded, before enjoyment occurs.

To continue our analysis, we find other personality types who express their ways of dealing with others in the sex act. There are individuals who are very inhibited and thus circuitous in their approach to sex. These people can never come out and request sexual relations with their partner, instead they have to use great subterfuge to make their feelings known. They hint, they allude, they imply; at times they are so subtle that the other partner misses the cue and disappointment is the end result. Some of these people have to engage in heavy drinking before they can make their feelings known. Such deviant behavior may be frustrating to both of the partners, since the use of alcohol can impair sexual functioning and may result in disturbance when drunkenness is present. The kinds of illustrations we have presented are only samples of the many ways in which personality is expressed in sex, nevertheless they are responsible for many of the sex difficulties in marriage.

It is interesting to note that these types of difficulties are relatively undramatic and frequently are not identified as a source of difficulty in sexual relations, but indeed they are serious since they disturb not only sexual relations but other components of the relationship as well. They are involved problems intertwined with different aspects of personality and they usually necessitate professional assistance before much can be done about them.

[19] See: Eugenia Elliott, *loc. cit.*

Frigidity and Impotency. Perhaps the most complicated and involved expression of personality difficulties in sexual relationships concerns the problems of impotency and frigidity. By impotency we mean the inability to maintain an erection, and by frigidity the inability to experience orgasm. The term impotency is usually applied to men and frigidity to women. Since these problems will also be discussed on pages 362–363 by Dr. Lehfeldt, we will make only a few brief remarks. First, it should be clear that it is very difficult for any untrained observer to tell by outer appearances and behavior whether one is impotent or frigid. Appearances are indeed deceptive. Especially with frigidity it is important to note that behavior may be disguised in order to mask frigidness. Some of the most sexually aggressive and promiscuous women may be essentially frigid. The sexual aggressiveness is both a cover up for the real inadequacies which these people feel and is also an attempt to prove to themselves that perhaps it will be different "the next time."

It is, of course, necessary to recognize that it is no simple task to determine whether orgasm has been experienced by the female.[20] Physicians, in order to ascertain the presence or absence of orgasm, frequently ask the patient whether she felt relaxed or upset after coitus. When the patient reports being upset, presumably orgasm was not experienced. Kinsey at one point in his research suggested the abandonment of the term frigidity since the range of orgasmic experience in the female seemed to be so variable and perhaps difficult to identify precisely.[21] For some women there appeared to be climactic orgasms with a definite high point in the sex act. For other women, there appeared to be a generalized orgasm in which there was no high point but the entire experience itself was pleasurable. In between there are many variations. Unfortunately some women who experience the generalized orgasm think of themselves as frigid. This is an erroneous view which creates unnecessary anguish.

With the exception of what is termed situational frigidity and impotency, the conditions are serious and involved indeed. Situational frigidity and impotency are essentially what the terms imply, they appear with the onset of some stressful situation; financial concerns, loss of a loved one, or hostility projected on the husband (or wife) are examples. When the condition is situational or temporary it disappears once the stress is alleviated.

[20] For a discussion of orgasm, both clitoral and vaginal, see: George Simpson, *People in Families*, Thomas Y. Crowell Co., New York, 1960, pp. 175–177.

[21] Alfred C. Kinsey, et. al., *Sexual Behavior in the Human Female*, W. B. Saunders Co., Philadelphia, 1953.

Causation and Complications. Impotency and frigidity are serious since they markedly impair sexual pleasure. They are involved since they have their origin in the individual's past and have been nurtured for many years. They are difficult to change because they constitute deep seated patterns. For example, in dealing with impotency and frigidity we are dealing with conditions that have developed out of lifelong patterns and problems which have become manifest in sexual relations.[22] There is probably relatively little that can be accomplished by the persons themselves. These conditions require the attention of an expert in psychotherapy. With respect to frigidity the need for a therapist is especially important, since there are those men who take the frigid response reaction as a personal affront to their manliness and assume that if the sex act is repeated often enough the condition will be overcome. The results of such a procedure can be disastrous, since it often exposes the woman to repeated frustration and may only aggravate her condition.

There are perhaps instances where serious dietary deficiencies produced impotent-like reactions in men, and where structural defects in female genitalia have produced frigidity. Nevertheless, it is commonly believed that for the most part impotency and frigidity arise out of social interaction and experience; they are the results of learning.[23] In dealing with the social psychological factors responsible for these conditions, there are a number of variables that are frequently identified as being important causative agents. Impotency has been related to the witnessing of early sex trauma, to being introduced to sex via prostitution and accompanying crudities, to rejection by women in interpersonal or sexual relations which become important in the male's feeling of inadequacy about women, and to fixation upon members of the same sex, expressed as latent homosexuality. Much emphasis has been placed on what Sigmund Freud termed the unresolved Oedipus complex. This refers to repressed sexual feelings which a male may have for his mother, the idea of which is so repul-

[22] For a discussion of the relationship between impotency and personality patterns, see: B. Joan Harte, "The Fear of Love and Sex," (article of) Auxiliary Council to the Association for the Advancement of Psychoanalysis, New York, 1951, p. 3.

[23] One study showed that the vast majority of sexual disturbances in marriage are related to poor social conditioning and a lack of biological and psychological knowledge; while only a minor part of the disturbances are due to biological or organic problems. Ernest W. Burgess and Leonard S. Cottrell, Jr., *Predicting Success or Failure in Marriage,* Prentice-Hall, Inc., Englewood Cliffs, New Jersey, 1939, p. 221.

sive that it serves to produce impotent reactions with women in general.

For the frigid women the variables include some that are similar to men, and some that are different. Sex trauma, including unpleasant sex activity, rejection by the male, latent homosexuality, and an unresolved Electra complex (the opposite of the Oedipus complex, that is, the female has sex strivings for the father).

These sexual factors are considered to be some of the more significant and dramatic variables responsible for impotency and frigidity. There is another view held by many professionals who believe that although faulty sexual conditioning may be a factor producing impotency and frigidity, there are other important considerations. Such considerations center around the view that character and personality determine how one relates sexually.[24] Thus, for example, the background experiences which make one aloof, insecure, or sadistic determine how one relates to another, in all forms of expression, social and sexual. (See Chapter 8.) From this point of view impotency and frigidity at the most fundamental level are basic expressions of how one relates to the opposite sex and how one feels about the opposite sex.

Let us look at the impotent male and visualize in simple terms what he tells us about his relationships with women. It is clear that the impotent reaction may suggest any of the following: a fear of human involvement particularly with women, a need to frustrate women, since in the impotent reaction one involves another erotically only to terminate the relationship at the last moment. Such behavior also involves a frustration of oneself; and indeed such a need may be present. Finally, there may be a marked feeling of inadequacy in relation to women, and such feeling may torment the individual to such an extent that he is unable to complete the act. All these possibilities may be involved in impotency; which one or which combination sometimes becomes an intricate problem.

With respect to the female, the frigid reaction suggests patterns very similar to those discussed for the male. These are extensions of basic attitudes which are expressed in the sex act and there are numerous case histories of sexually disturbed people which are illustra-

---

[24] Freud believed that sexual desire was the source of character formation; however, many modern authorities agree that character determines the particular way in which the sex urge finds expression. F. Alexander Magoun, *op. cit.*, pp. 237–238. One authority, for example, states that: "Sexual attitudes and behaviors are directed by the basic motivations which the human being acquires in the process of being socialized." John J. Honigmann, "Cultural Dynamics of Sex," *Psychiatry,* **10** (Feb., 1947), p. 47.

tive. By way of at least one illustration, there is the case of Mrs. T., a forty-one-year-old married female who had a pattern of frustrating herself in sex and was almost never able to achieve orgasm. The problem as she experienced it was that whenever sexual relations became pleasurable and whenever it seemed as though she were approaching orgasm, certain ideas would come up and these would serve to disturb her enjoyment. The ideas in question had a pattern centering around notions such as—"I should not be enjoying myself." At that point in the sex act, she felt the need to become aloof and terminate the sex act. Indeed, Mrs. T.'s needs for self-frustration was so deep that on the few occasions when she did experience orgasm she became extremely despondent and resentful.[25]

In the life history of this woman the following significant facts emerge. She grew up with an older, neurotic and sadistic sister who always tormented her and gave her the feeling that somehow she was an intruder in the home—she didn't belong. When Mrs. T. attempted new things as a child she was ridiculed, when she was happy her happiness was interrupted by unprovoked attacks from her sister. Mrs. T. grew up with marked feelings of not belonging, of unworthiness, of having no right to enjoyment. In her interactions with people she was self-effacing and replete with self-denial. In sexual relations these same attitudes appeared in the form described above to frustrate her pleasure in sex and these attitudes were deeply involved in her frigidity.

THERAPY FOR IMPOTENCY AND FRIGIDITY. From all that we have said it should be clear that impotency and frigidity are deeply woven into the personality and necessitate professional assistance. Moreover, these are difficult conditions to treat. If we examine the complexity involved in treating impotency and frigidity, we recognize that the therapist not only must go back into the life history of the person to deal with sexual and non-sexual factors which brought these patterns into operation, but he must be even more concerned with how and why these particular experiences resulted in impotency and frigidity and why they are maintained today. The latter is an especially significant and formidable task. Irrespective of what combination of circumstances produced the reactions which cause frigidity and

---

[25] There are also those who, because of their need for self-frustration, on experiencing successful love-making feel marked depression and resentment. Thus, it is an oversimplification to view the achievement of orgasm as the panacea of marital ills, see: Lawrence S. Kubie, "Psychoanalysis and Marriage," in *Neurotic Interaction in Marriage*, Victor W. Eisenstein, Ed., Basic Books, Inc., New York, 1956, p. 26.

impotency, once started they are not easily reversed. They become a component of the overall make-up of the individual and are deeply imbedded in the personality organization.

For any couple a healthy realization of how impotency and frigidity in its various degrees disturbs both the erotic and interpersonal relationship is very basic. Only through such a realization can a couple be motivated to receive the necessary help which will enable them to receive the full benefits of the sexual and marital union.

SUMMARY

The relationships between sexual compatibility and (1) background factors which affect sexual attitudinal development, (2) initial sexual relations in marriage, and (3) patterns of sexual behavior developed in marriage were discussed in this chapter. It was noted that previous experiences regarding sex can result in the internalization of negative or positive sexual attitudes and as such can impair or aid in the development of sexual compatibility in marriage. Also, the initial sexual approaches of the marital couple are of paramount importance in developing sexual compatibility because it is here that one's attitudes toward the sex act and toward the sex partner are likely to emerge. The pattern of sexual behavior developed by the marriage partners is also extremely important in developing sexual compatibility and in this regard an understanding on the part of the spouses concerning (1) the frequency of erotic experience, (2) love making, and (3) freedom of communication becomes a necessity. This is not to say, however, that the understanding must result in an unchangeable pattern of sexual behavior because it is felt that spontaneity in sexual behavior is of vital importance in achieving meaningful sexual compatibility.

Extramarital sex interests were discussed. It was noted that the emergence of a concentrated interest of this type may result from any one of three broad sets of factors: (1) a breakdown in the interpersonal relationship itself; (2) a breakdown in the erotic aspect of the marriage; (3) personality problems and immaturities on the part of one or both of the marital partners. Several types of personality problems were then discussed, not only with regard to extramarital sexual interests but also with respect to frigidity and impotency. It was pointed out that although frigidity and impotency may result from physical structural aspects it is commonly believed that, for the most part, frigidity and impotency arise out of faulty social interaction and exposure.

Finally, it was shown that the presence of extramarital sexual in-

terests and frigidity or impotency in a marriage might be the cause
of or, even more important, the result of marital breakdown.

QUESTIONS

1. In what ways are the initial sexual approaches in marriage important?
   Explain your answer.
2. What are some of the common experiences in the American society
   which can contribute to negative attitudes regarding sexual relations?
   What might be done about correcting this situation?
3. Explain how one's attitudes toward sex can aid or impair his ability to
   achieve a meaningful sexual relationship in marriage.
4. Explain how a breakdown in communication between husband and wife
   can impair the development of a satisfactory sexual adjustment.
5. Discuss the relationship between marital breakdown and extramarital sex
   interests. Give examples.
6. How may personality problems be related to extramarital sex interests?
   Fully explain your answer and give examples.
7. In what way may impotency and frigidity be related to one's past experiences? Explain exactly how impotency and frigidity may be a cause of
   marital breakdown and also how it may be a result of marital breakdown.
   Give examples.

PROJECTS

1. Have a panel discussion concerning the pros and cons of giving children
   information pertaining to sex as a means of developing healthy attitudes
   toward sex.
2. Write your own case history regarding how you obtained information pertaining to sex. Include the means whereby you obtained attitudes toward
   sex which you regard as being unhealthy and the means whereby you
   obtained attitudes which you regard as being healthy. Do you feel that
   your sexual information is adequate and that your attitudes toward sex
   will be conducive to sexual compatibility in marriage?

SUGGESTED READINGS

Bowman, Henry A., *Marriage for Moderns*, McGraw-Hill Book Co., Inc., New
   York, 4th ed., 1960, Ch. 11, "Sex in Marriage."
Ellis, Havelock, *The Psychology of Sex*, Emerson Books, New York, 1938.
Krich, A. M., Ed., *Women, The Variety and Meaning of Their Sexual Experience*,
   Dell Publishing Co., New York, 1954, especially Ch. 4 by Karl A. Menninger,
   "Impotence and Frigidity."
Landis, Judson T., and Mary G. Landis, *Building a Successful Marriage*, 3rd ed.,
   Prentice-Hall, Inc., Englewood Cliffs, New Jersey, 1958, Ch. 16, "Sex Ad-
   justment in Marriage."
Levine, Lena and Mildred Gilman, *Frigidity*, Planned Parenthood Federation of
   America, New York, 1952.
Stone, Abraham, and Hannah Stone, *A Marriage Manual*, Simon and Schuster,
   New York, 1952.

Externalizations and marital incompatibility

13

As the reader has already observed, marital conflicts are complex; they have many dimensions and ramifications. To be sure, marital conflicts are rooted in some form of incompatibility, but incompatibility is after all a general term which does not specify the conditions under which marital conflicts arise. Incompatibility, for example, may arise because the ethnic, religious, or cultural backgrounds of people are different; thus there are difficulties with respect to attitudes, values, and what the partners may wish to achieve in life and marriage. We recognize these as sources of marital difficulty, but there are still other marital problems which, in the opinion of the writers, are of even greater complexity, and probably are less understood. We refer here to incompatibilities which arise because we have the tendency to blame others for our own tensions, and because we tend to impose our difficulties, values, wishes, and goals on those whom we marry. We refer to these patterns of blaming and imposition as externalizations.[1] The tendency to blame others for our problems is a very common characteristic of many human relationships. As we have pointed out earlier, many of us have considerable difficulty in assuming responsibility for the problems we have; and, indeed, we even have difficulty recognizing that most of our discomforts come from our own unresolved problems. With respect to our values and goals, many of us who under-

[1] Karen Horney, *Neurosis and Human Growth*, W. W. Norton and Co., Inc., New York, 1950, pp. 178–179.

stand that there may be different ways of viewing life discover that in our personal relationships we tend to impose our values on—and restrict the choices of—the other member of the relationship. Patterns of blaming and imposition express themselves in numerous ways which defeat the purpose of building a meaningful relationship in marriage. In this chapter we will deal with the various forms which these patterns of externalizing can assume.

EXTERNALIZATIONS WHICH ARISE OUT OF ENVIRONMENTAL STRESS

Blaming the Partner for Our Tensions. Other things being equal, we are likely to externalize and find fault with others when the stresses and tensions which we normally carry become too burdensome.[2] Some of the sources of such stress come from the social environment and are an integral part of modern American life.[3] The nature of life in American society is such that it subjects almost all of us to certain common stresses. There are generalized stresses which arise out of our concern for war or economic security, and from our fears of illness and death. At other levels we find that the competitive nature of our society imposes still another series of stresses.[4] In almost all walks of life the competitive order is in evidence. We compete for dates, for mates, for jobs, for advancement, for popularity, and for prestige.

Men are invariably immersed in competition in their occupational involvements. There is competition for promotion, for salary increments, and for recognition. Inherent in competition is the fact that not all will succeed. Thus, inevitably, stress and frustrations can accumulate not only in the process of competing but as a result of losing out in the competitive process as well.

There is the incident of an engineer who was anxious to get ahead and felt the competition from others in his office quite keenly. Although the man in question worked for a conservative company in which mobility was normally slow and difficult, all the members of the staff did their very best to outdo the others in order to receive what few rewards there were. One year several openings at advanced levels became available due to retirement of older personnel. Competition at this point became intense, and the engineer for a number of months arrived home irritable and anxious. His family suffered con-

---

[2] James C. Coleman, *Abnormal Psychology and Modern Life*, Scott, Foresman and Co., New York, 1950, p. 90.

[3] Jessie Bernard, *Social Problems at Mid-Century*, The Dryden Press, New York, 1957, pp. 79–84.

[4] *Ibid.*, pp. 139–140.

siderably during this period since he was difficult to get along with. When the promotions were made the engineer was not on the list. At this point he became depressed, disillusioned, and began finding fault with his marriage and his family.

Still another aspect of the competitive nature of our society which is responsible for stress concerns the ambitions and goals of power or prestige which people have and the differential outlets available to them for success. For example, people who have internalized certain of these concepts of success may discover that the realization of such goals is not readily available.[5] We see this most clearly with members of minority groups—racial or ethnic—who find opportunities restricted due to their color or religion. There is no reason to assume, however, that only minority groups in our society are subject to these difficulties, since there are many non-minority group persons who are unable to compete successfully for power or prestige because of lack of training, lack of education, or personality difficulties. Furthermore, the concept of success is after all subject to individual definition.[6] For example, how much power and prestige does one have to have in order to be successful? Some people who have internalized success goals may never be at peace with themselves since they are relentlessly driven to acquire more and more power, and they undergo considerable stress in the process.[7]

Finally, it should be pointed out that the inability to cope with the success goals we have indicated through conventional competitive channels, may result in socially disapproved ways of competing.[8] The man who cannot become successful honestly may turn to lying and cheating and a set of questionable ethics. Although such persons may find these patterns necessary, they still may be plagued by inner doubts; doubts which they may wish to hide from their family but which will nevertheless involve their families.

Specialization and Resultant Stress. If we look more closely at the organization of work in modern society, we note the basis of still another series of stresses. We refer here to the development of specialization and the implications of this innovation. Specialization is, of course, functional in the sense that it results in production of better goods and services. In other ways, however, specialization produces

---

[5] Robert K. Merton, *Social Theory and Social Structure,* rev. ed., The Free Press, Glencoe, Ill., 1957, pp. 170–176.

[6] Jessie Bernard, *op. cit.,* p. 76.

[7] Bud Schulberg, *What Makes Sammy Run?,* Modern Library, New York, 1952.

[8] Lawrence Guy Brown, *Social Pathology,* Appleton-Century-Crofts, Inc., New York, 1942, pp. 488–489.

stress for the individual. For example, a high degree of specialization is often accompanied by a reduction of basic skill required for persons performing particular tasks. Such developments which are well recognized in assembly lines are also present in office and managerial functions and even in some of the professions.[9] Thus, there are a number of capable and intelligent persons who are working far beneath their basic capacity. This is a potential source of considerable stress, for indeed it means that large numbers of people are turned into the world of work and for many years will be so located that they will not be able to utilize fully their potentialities.

Thus far we have been discussing the stresses which impinge most directly on men and on those women who are involved in careers. For the woman who remains at home there are other stresses. Today the demands on the housewife are perhaps greater than they were in the past.[10] The tasks often go beyond home management and involve the ability to rear children with good emotional stability and to provide companionship and a favorable emotional atmosphere in the home. Thus many middle-class women today look on the emotional maturity of their children and the general quality of their marital relationship as something for which they have considerable responsibility. Indeed they frequently compare their families with the families of other middle-class women. The achievement of marital success in these terms is no simple task and many women who were—or could have been—successful as homemakers in the past fail today because the demands are more stringent. Since all wives do not in fact have equal opportunity to be successful in this regard, due to the factors of immaturity, or lack of personality integration, or education, considerable stress about failure to meet these goals may emerge.

An additional source of stress and tension for the middle-class woman today arises out of the fact that frequently she may be required to participate in a variety of social roles and each may require different behavior. Social roles are culturally defined expectations of behavior. The typical married woman today, for example, may be expected to fulfill the wife and mother role, the companion role, and the partner role.

(1) The *wife-and-mother* role is the traditional role of the married woman. It implies as its privileges: security, the right to support, alimony in the case of divorce, respect as a wife and mother, a certain amount of domestic authority, loyalty of the husband to one who has borne him chil-

[9] *Ibid.*, p. 489.
[10] Anne Morrow Lindbergh, *Gift from the Sea*, Pantheon, New York, 1955, pp. 25–27.

LAFF-A-DAY

"Welcome to our planet."

Figure 4. Courtesy Jack Markow and King Features Syndicate (May 20, 1961).

dren, and a more or less sentimental gratitude from husband and children. Corresponding obligations include: bearing and rearing children, making a home, rendering domestic service, loyal subordination of self to the economic interests of the husband, an acceptance of a dependent social and economic status, and the acceptance of a limited range of interests and activity.

(2) The *companion* role is essentially a leisure-class phenomenon. The privileges pertaining to this role include: sharing pleasure with the husband, receiving a more romantic emotional response, being the object of admiration, receiving funds adequate for dress and recreation, having leisure for social and educational activity, and the receiving of a certain amount of chivalrous attention. On the other hand, it implies as obligations: the preservation of beauty under the penalty of marital insecurity, the rendering of ego and libido satisfaction to the husband, the cultivation of social contacts advantageous to him, the maintenance of intellectual alertness, and the responsibility of exorcising the demon of boredom.

(3) Finally, there is the *partner* role, corresponding to a new definition of the cultural situation which is gradually emerging. This entails the privileges of: economic independence, equal authority in regard to family finances, acceptance as an equal, exemption from one-sided personal or domestic services to the husband, equal voice in determining locale of residence, and equality in regard to social and moral liberty. The obligation side of the balance sheet would include: renouncing alimony save in the case of dependent children, complete sharing of the legal responsibilities of the family, willingness to dispense with any appeal to chivalry, and equal responsibility to maintain the family status by success in a career.[11]

The existence of these several roles in marriage is responsible for stress and tension on the part of the woman in several ways. First, problems arise because the woman has to make choices about which role she really wishes; is it, for example, a wife-mother role or a partner role? A second problem arises from the fact that she may fulfill a role out of a sense of duty and obligation, such as the wife-mother role; whereas in reality her desire really may be for the companion role—devoid of any responsibility for children.

A third basis for tension arises when husband and wife are both in disagreement about the role which the woman should play in marriage.[12] A fourth source of stress may arise because the woman attempts to combine different elements from each of the three roles. Under these circumstances she may find herself faced with contradictions. Thus for women, as well as men, sources of stress and tension are commonplace in our society.

In the description of potential sources of stress just described it should be remembered that few people in our society can avoid completely these stressful situations. There are, however, individual differences with respect to what can be tolerated. Thus, there are those who are relatively less affected than are others. Other things being equal, the individual with emotional difficulties and immaturities is more likely to have a lower threshold of tolerance for stress than is the person without these problems. The reason for this lies in the fact that the one with problems is already a battleground of inner tensions. Thus, when external stress is superimposed on the existing tensions, balance becomes precarious.

Stress and the Marital Relationship. The effects of continued environmental stress for a marital relationship are always serious and must, therefore, be examined as to their manifestations. Individuals

---

[11] Clifford Kirkpatrick, "The Measurement of Ethical Inconsistency in Marriage," *The International Journal of Ethics* (July, 1936), pp. 444–460. Copyright 1936 by the University of Chicago.

[12] Willard Waller, *The Family*, revised by Reuben Hill, The Dryden Press, New York, 1951, p. 284.

who experience prolonged stress are inclined to function with a certain tenseness and instability; consequently they may be provoked easily for little reason.[13] At the psychological and physiological levels these expressions become a way of releasing pent up emotional feelings associated with stress. Further, the cause of the emotional disturbance may be externalized on the marriage partner. At this point stress, which is unresolved conflict, emerges as conflict; [14] this topic will be dealt with in considerable detail in the chapter on resolving marital conflicts. Under conditions of externalization a husband may identify his irritability as stemming from what he sees as his wife's inability to care for the home adequately, or from her patterns of excessive spending of family income.[15]

There is the case of a married man who had many pressures and responsibilities in his job. Whenever these became excessive he would focus on two difficulties: his wife's cooking and her parents. At these times he humiliated her for the poor way that meals were prepared and for what he termed her ignorant and uninformed parents. His behavior was so patterned that it almost enabled his wife to predict her husband's office problems by his patterns of externalization.

In any marriage in which stress is a factor, there is the ever present danger of incompatibilities and conflicts. Also, the partner engaged in externalizing is often not aware that his fault finding is the result of stress. During these periods remarks are not particularly rational, nor are negative comments necessarily limited to the immediate members of the family but may include relatives and friends. One basic characteristic in marital conflict of this type is the tendency to berate, to humiliate, and to attack the self-worth of the person with whom one is involved. The individual reacting in this way has both the emotional release and the satisfaction of fixing blame on another, thereby avoiding any personal responsibility for the stress and the consequences of stress for the marital relationship.

It is interesting to note that people often engage in such attacks on one another without full realization of the implications. Indeed there are those persons who feel that nothing they say during an argument should be taken seriously. In spite of such well-meaning pleas we must recognize that it is difficult to attack the self-worth of another person without seriously running the risk of provoking him and bringing forth his resentment. We refer to these resentments as residues.

[13] Ernest W. Burgess and Harvey J. Locke, *The Family*, 2nd ed., American Book Co., New York, 1960, Ch. 18, especially pp. 514–516.

[14] *Ibid.*, pp. 510–528.

[15] For a discussion of distortion and externalization, see: Karen Horney, *op. cit.*, pp. 292–294.

Residues are resentments that are repressed after the argument and which become cumulative over a period of time. Thus, when attacks on the self-worth of the marital partner are repeatedly engaged in, there is the serious risk that each partner will repeatedly try to get back at the other in various ways. This "getting back at the partner" may take the form of nagging, frustrating, or taking the daily pleasure out of marriage. When this continues over a period of time tremendous hostility may be built up to a point where the damage to the relationship is difficult to undo.

There is the case of a married couple who had tormented one another with insults and berating for a number of years. During the many arguments they had over a five-year-period each partner developed intense hostility and resentment toward the other. Finally their friends prevailed on them to get professional assistance. When they appeared for counseling they spent almost all of their time expressing their resentments toward each other, and in trying to justify the basis for their resentful reactions. At this stage in their marriage, each was interested in getting back at the other; neither was concerned about understanding how to rehabilitate the marriage.

Finally, we must note that residues may constitute the basis for a rage which seems unprovoked at the moment. The woman who has been berated over an extended period of time may have "a very low tolerance for conflict" and may explode on her husband at the slightest provocation. Thus, in many instances the explosive reaction, which many people have in particular situations, represents an accumulation of resentments and not a response to a specific situation. It is important to have some appreciation of this pattern; otherwise both husbands and wives may be bewildered when one or the other has become markedly provoked at seemingly unimportant remarks.

UNDERSTANDING ENVIRONMENTAL STRESS AND ITS CONSEQUENCES. These stresses which are imposed by the nature of our social order require considerable understanding and handling lest they lead to a deterioration of the marriage. For over a period of time couples who are immersed in conflict which stems from their inability to handle stress may come to believe that there is something fundamentally wrong with their marriage. Some of these people become hopeless and terminate their marriage only to find similar problems in a subsequent marriage.[16] What these people fail to realize is that their tendency to find fault with each other arises out of their

[16] An index of this problem is noted in divorce rates of the remarried, see: Paul H. Jacobson, *American Marriage and Divorce*, Rinehart and Co., Inc., New York, 1959, pp. 150–151.

inability to deal with environmental stress. A first consideration, therefore, in dealing with stress is to separate the basic relationship, which might well be a good one, from these external stresses which result in the externalizations and blaming of one another. This is necessary in order to attain a more positive view of the marriage. When one feels anxious and upset outside the home, and comes home only to discover that he is immersed in conflict there as well, there is almost a complete absence of any secure base in the individual's life. When one can, however, separate the sources of conflict, and recognize, let us say, that it is not the marriage which is at fault, but rather one's inability to handle external stress, the security of the marriage is increased and more effective ways of dealing with stress and its complications may emerge.

Having said all this we recognize that there is considerable reluctance on the part of people to accept the fact that they may be finding fault with their marital relationships simply as a means of releasing pent up feelings of resentments caused by external environmental stress. Many people feel that to accept their inability to handle stress is to admit that they have not adequately organized their lives. Thus, since so many people are perfectionistic about the way they conduct their lives, they are subject to a good deal of self-berating when they sense a personal inadequacy. When, on the other hand, one has accepted the fact that his marital difficulties may be rooted in an inability to deal with stress from the environment, a great deal has been accomplished for the well-being of the marriage. For it is at this point that one has accepted some responsibility for problems; it then becomes easier to isolate the sources of external stress, and perhaps deal with them more effectively. Finally, the berating of the marital partners may be markedly reduced and the relationship strengthened as well as made more secure.

A second consideration which may aid a couple in dealing with environmental stress centers around the couple's values and life goals. Values and goals which are unrealistic and not likely to be attained given the conditions and circumstances of the couple's life will invariably be related to stressful situations.[17] In some instances it may make sense to abandon certain goals and values, in other instances perhaps more effective ways of achieving these goals might be invoked. There are many individuals with good ability but with sights set so high that achievement comes only at a tremendous personal sacrifice.

There was the case of a thirty-five-year-old married man who

[17] For a discussion of values and goals and their relationship to marriage, see: Ernest W. Burgess and Harvey J. Locke, *op. cit.*, Ch. 10, especially pp. 280–282.

entered college in order to become a physician. His wife was of similar age, without children, but very desirous of having a family. As the husband pursued his college work the tensions and stress mounted. He found it difficult to study since he had been out of school for many years. His wife had to work in order to support him and this she resented since she was not in favor of the sacrifices that would be entailed. All of this created much stress in the marriage and both members of the relationship fell into a pattern of arguing. After several years they reassessed their values and goals. The husband realized that at his age acceptance by a medical school was remote. Even if by chance he were accepted he would be forty-five years of age before he could support a family. A shift in occupational choice more consistent with their needs was made and the marital tensions were markedly reduced.

A third consideration in dealing with environmental stress is concerned with common sense remedies which are consistent with certain good health practices. We refer to the pursuit of recreational patterns and hobbies in all their forms which can serve as outlets for stress. These are important, but probably successful only when some more basic understanding of the difficulties has been reached earlier.

EXTERNALIZATIONS WHICH ARISE FROM THE NEED TO IMPOSE OUR VALUES ON OTHERS. We have been discussing sources of stress and tensions that are primarily the result of the nature of our social order. There are other stresses and tensions which are due to personal immaturities and unresolved personality problems rather than due to environmental pressures. One source of such value imposition arises out of the beliefs that one's values are best, coupled with a need to impose these values on others.[18] All of us have known of people who were narrow about their own beliefs regarding tastes in food and clothing, or about ethnic group or religion.

Such narrowness may stem from having lived in relative isolation from people with differing values and beliefs. At a deeper psychological level, however, such narrowness may stem from pronounced feelings of inferiority about oneself and one's background. Under these circumstances people who feel inferior may find new and different tastes and values disturbing, since the new experiences raise questions about the individual's own background. This often results in a need to impose one's habits on others.

A second source of value imposition may result when one fails to realize ambitions or goals. There is the case of the woman who had

[18] Karen Horney, *op. cit.*, p. 208.

been urged by her parents to marry a physician. Although she had accepted these values, she failed to find an eligible physician, but instead found a teacher of biology. The substitute was for her never a satisfactory one and throughout her married life she continued to socialize with physicians' families and to compare her husband with the physicians she knew. The comparison she made was always unfavorable. Since she was frustrated in achieving her values, she urged medical training on her children, tried to control their dating practices, and reminded her husband constantly of his shortcomings. This woman lived in an unreal world in which she could not appreciate the real assets of either her husband or her children. All suffered as a result.

A third source of value imposition is found in the conception of the social roles which we bring to marriage. Social roles as previously noted are culturally defined expectations of behavior. Role conceptions are acquired early in life and seem to persist once developed. With regard to marriage we think of roles as the parts we expect our marital partners to play; the way we expect them to behave; the responsibilities we feel they should and should not assume. One dimension of conflict arises when the concept of the role which each envisages for the other does not correspond with the view held by the other, a point made earlier in this chapter. Under these circumstances there is frequently a tendency to impose one's expectations regarding social role on another and force him to make the necessary adjustments.

A second dimension of role conflict comes when we expect behaviors from ourselves or the spouse that are inconsistent. There was the case of a young professional man who was very interested in changing his class position. Although both he and his wife had come from humble origins, the man had taken special care to equip himself with the attributes that would facilitate his mobility. He went through a university, supported by his wife who worked during this period. While the man in question was circulating with middle-class people with whom he identified and wished to become part of, his wife continued to work, both in and outside the home. After college the husband, who had a definite conception about how his wife could become an asset in the attainment of his goals, imposed his concept of her role on her. This concept included a variety of qualities for which she was neither intellectually nor emotionally prepared. He wanted her to be well read, informed, and intellectual, to be able to entertain well and frequently, to maintain a job, to rear children, and to care for the household. She was also to be submissive.

Figure 5. Reprinted by permission of The Hall Syndicate (June 7, 1961).

If we examine this man's concept of his wife's role, two things stand out. First, there are demands made here which most women would find difficult to fulfill. Further, the demands which are made are inconsistent. Thus, this man expects his wife to be well informed, to be concerned with intellectual matters, but he also expects her to be submissive. Since this was a relatively uninformed girl of very average intelligence, who made little pretense about what she was, the imposition of her husband's values caused considerable conflict.

A good deal of marital difficulty is rooted in role conflict of the type we have described. Thus, prior to marriage or during marriage some of these difficulties may be clarified by exploring, in the most serious and meaningful way, the role concept which each anticipates of the other. Although role concept exploration is a necessity, we recognize that few married persons are prepared to deal with the difficulties in changing role concepts. As noted earlier, each of the members enters the marriage with a concept of role, both for himself or herself, as well as for the other. Such concepts of role are to a lesser or greater extent woven into the fabric of personality and are not easily changed. The reasons for the resistance to change are rooted in several factors.

Resistances to Changes in Concepts of Role. One factor which helps us to understand why role concepts are difficult to change involves the fact that one's concepts of husband, wife, father, or mother have emerged out of interaction with the adults in one's environment; and, indeed, such roles may have been derived from parental models, thus they are frequently associated with deep seated emotional undertones. Very frequently to change a role concept about oneself or a spouse entails a re-evaluation of a parental model from whom the role concept was derived. A husband's giving up of a patriarchal role concept, for example, may entail the realization that his patriarchal father imposed many undesirable decisions on those around him and such realization may be painful to accept.

A second factor which helps us understand why role concepts are difficult to change is related to the idea that one's concept of role is also rooted in one's reference groups, that is, the groups with which one identifies. Such groups may include friends, neighbors, or relatives. Reference groups provide one with a value orientation and set of beliefs about familial duties and obligations, and they also constitute a pressure for conforming to group norms.

There was the experience of a man who entered marriage with the idea that men should not assist their wives with chores around the home; his wife, however, held a different view. After several discussions he agreed to assist his wife with certain household tasks, only to discover, however, that when his friends learned about these interests, they made remarks which cast reflections on his manliness. His need for acceptance by his group was so important that he immediately abandoned his efforts to assist his wife and returned to his privately held notions.

A third factor which helps us understand why role concepts are difficult to change is related to the fact that in the process of growing up in a dynamic society, people seldom internalize one role concept of husband or wife, father or mother; usually different concepts are internalized. For example, a male who has grown up in an authoritarian family will probably internalize a patriarchal concept of his role. It is equally possible that through interactions outside the home, he may also internalize a democratic concept of the father's position in the home. The internalization of two diametrically opposite concepts of role results in a good deal of conflict. At times a man may be both authoritarian and democratic; and he may try to function as though there were no inconsistencies between patriarchal and democratic values. When conflict arises he may be quite confused about what he believes and this becomes manifest in his difficulty in understanding precisely what views have to be changed. Thus there are many men, for example, who are willing to let their wives work or even pursue a career, an indication of a democratic view. Frequently such men are also quite adamant about their right to determine how such additional income should be spent. This attempt to integrate both authoritarian and democratic concepts of role without a clear understanding of how each contradicts the other lends itself to considerable difficulty and confusion.

A fourth factor which helps us understand why concepts of role are difficult to change concerns the fact that role concepts are indicative of our values; and they represent the way in which we come to terms with those around us. For example, the wife who views the husband's role as involving major responsibility for all important decisions is expressing also her view about the position of men and women in the home. This means, therefore, that any change in role concepts involves not only changes in a few items of behavior such as whether one spouse or the other assumes a new responsibility, but very frequently it entails major changes in value concepts regarding even total views of men and women; these involve some basic attitudes which are not easily uprooted.

FLEXIBILITY IN CONCEPTS OF ROLE. The four variables which we have just discussed tend to work in the direction of minimizing change in regard to role concepts. On the other hand, there are the experiences of life, the interactions with different persons, which tend constantly to suggest different and alternative views of husband-wife relationships. In this day and age of mass media and marked personal mobility, almost every marital union is faced with factors which confront a couple with the possibility of revising what each expects of the other. The realization of such a likelihood is exceedingly important. For it can help orient a couple to anticipate changing views of roles as the marital union matures. Whereas in the past with a society concerned with traditions, clinging to fixed concepts of family roles may have insured success, today such a pattern may well be responsible for failure. Thus, one of the major tasks in middle-class marriage today involves the ability to maintain a flexibility in regard to concepts of role, in order that desirable changes may be integrated with a minimum of disruption to the persons and the marital union. It is particularly necessary in this regard to have an understanding of the implications of changes in concepts of role, for both the person and the family. For example, a young woman who had grown up in a patriarchal family was married to a man who was also reared in a patriarchal family. The wife, after engaging in reading and conversation with other women, announced one day that she was tired of being so subservient to a man and that she planned some changes in her home, both for herself and her husband. At that point the woman rebelled against the patriarchal order, abandoned all her responsibilities in the home: the washing, cooking, and caring for the children. During this period she demanded that her husband perform these tasks. After a week of such rebellion she resumed her household responsibilities but became very depressed and was sent for therapy. Her depression, as interpreted by her therapist, was caused by a sense of guilt about her actions. Although she had rebelled, she also felt that she had failed in her responsibilities to her husband and children.

This case clearly suggests that the woman in question, seeking a revision of role for herself and her husband, was not fully prepared to appreciate the complexities involved in producing change. She failed to work through the impact of her desired changes for others in the home and the effects which this might have on her.

Finally, it should be noted that any given marital relationship represents an accommodation between the persons and the experiences which each constantly brings into the marriage. While these external experiences may be threatening to the smooth functioning of a relationship they also may offer the possibility of a creative marriage; that is, a marriage which is sensitive to the needs and wishes of the individuals as they emerge in a dynamic life setting.

Thus far we have dealt with three sources of value imposition; a first source was rooted in the belief that one's values are best, a second source was rooted in unrealized goals and ambitions, and, a third source was based on the need to impose one's concept of role on the other. Let us now turn to a fourth and final source of value imposition.

A fourth source of imposition of values on the mate may come about because one has an idealized image of oneself which is deeply anchored in the personality.[19] The idealized image develops early in life when the circumstances surrounding personal development have not been conducive to the individual's acceptance of himself. Thus, backgrounds in which the individual is rejected or not appreciated for what he is lend themselves to the creation of an idealized image. The image is an attempt to make oneself worthy and acceptable. Thus, the individual rejects what he is and creates an image of what he would like to be in his imagination. The concept is not unlike Reiks' ego ideal, Chapter 5, page 71; we prefer the concept idealized image, because we find it more descriptive. An individual with an idealized image is in a constant state of anxiety because he is straining to fulfill the idealized image, and because he is fearful of not measuring up to the idealized conception. Not measuring up to the idealized image is of special concern since it brings out self-contempt, contempt for what one is. Since the idealized image is always a conception in imagination, it has a mixture of unreal components. For example, one of its major characteristics is perfection.[20] Thus, the individual may think of himself as being all knowing, all kind, all truthful, all moral. Furthermore, he may demand of himself that he behave as though he were all knowing, all kind, all truthful, and all moral without regard for the circumstances involved. Such inner demands which come from the idealized image are impossible to live up to and the realization that one cannot live up to them may cause considerable anxiety and uncertainty about who and what one is. At this point the tendency is to feel that others are not living their lives properly and to find fault with them. At such times one may engage in considerable criticism of the marital partner. If, for example, the wife has an idealized image in which she sees herself as a woman of power and high status, she may focus on factors of power and status in her husband's life. Thus, she may express dissatisfaction about how her husband is progressing in his work even though objectively he may be doing quite well. She might complain that her husband has not received promotion as rapidly as he should, or that he has not received salary advances as rapidly as others. If the wife's idealized image contains the idea of being all knowing, she may externalize this component on her husband and expect him to solve all her problems. If the husband's idealized image contains moral perfectionism, he may externalize this on his

[19] Karen Horney, op. cit., pp. 24–25, 292.
[20] Ibid., pp. 196–197.

wife and expect her never to smoke or laugh at an off-color story under any and all circumstances, or always to tell the truth regardless of circumstances. When the idealized image is imposed on the marital partner shortcomings become readily apparent and criticisms are made about these.

In dealing with externalizations that stem from the idealized image the couple must always assess the kinds of values which are necessary for stability in a marital union. Here there are, to be sure, certain essentials. In general we can say that those values which will ultimately destroy the relationship cannot be tolerated. There must be confidence in the essential honesty, loyalty, and responsibility of the partners. Further, there must be a relative commitment to the mutually agreed on basic goals and values which the couple seek. Aside from these basic values there is an entire area of life in which individual differences in values can function; and it is clearly destructive to a marital union when one imposes values on the other for the sake of maintaining certain immaturities.

Finally it should be noted that the idealized image which one has constructed does not change easily or simply. It has grown out of very real needs in the development of the individual. And it has come over a period of time to give the individual a sense of significance. One will only abandon the idealized image if he can come to feel that he will remain significant and worthwhile without it. When the quality of the marital union is such that acceptance of the individual is present, then it is possible that such an emotional climate will facilitate relinquishing the idealized image. Barring this state of affairs, professional assistance might be sought in order that the implications of the idealized image for the stability of the marital relationship be thoroughly explored and examined.

Finally it is important to recognize that the criticisms in marriage, be they major or minor, are frequently manifestations of the externalizations we have been describing in this chapter. Few people who externalize are aware of what they are doing. People who externalize experience their behavior in terms of attempts to aid the other person to live a more effective life. Mostly they fail to see why they engage in externalizations; and they fail to see the implications of externalizations on the marital relationship.

The patterns described are common in interactions both inside as well as outside marriage. And while externalizations disturb human relationships of all types, they are particularly devastating for marital relationships where the intense and intimate contact brings the externalizations into operation quite early; such reactions to stress and tension can gnaw away at a marriage and make daily living a chore and a battleground for anger.

Externalizations in all their manifestations are seriously disruptive to the marital union since they are subtle and non-dramatic. They are the ongoing, recurrent complaints, accusations, and demands which can work away at the basic foundation of the marital union.

SUMMARY

Externalization is the tendency to blame others for our tensions and to impose on them our difficulties, values, wishes, and goals. Needless to say, when externalization occurs in a marriage relationship it can create a great deal of marital conflict. Certain factors external to the marriage relationship itself, such as the competitive social order, the function of specialization, and the social roles open to women in marriage all tend to create stress and may result in externalization. With respect to the social roles open to women in marriage, for example, it was noted that there are at least three such roles, the wife-mother role, the companion role, and the partner role. The existence of these marital roles can produce a great deal of stress and result in externalizations when a woman (1) is uncertain about the role she would like to fulfill, (2) fulfills one role out of a sense of duty but would prefer to be fulfilling another role, (3) desires one role while her husband demands that she fulfill another, (4) tries to combine several roles and thus confronts contradictions.

Other factors which tend to produce externalization involve personality problems and immaturities. This can be seen, for example, among those people whose need to impose their values on others arises out of their personal narrowness or their failure to have realized certain of their ambitions or goals.

It was suggested that individuals attempt to understand not only the function which external stress plays in their marital incompatibilities, but also the part played by the need to impose one's values on the marital partner. Once each of these leading contributors to externalization in marriage is understood, it is believed that marital incompatibilities can be dealt with more objectively and, consequently, more effectively.

QUESTIONS

1. In what ways may cultural background result in marital incompatibilities? Exemplify.

2. What is externalization? How exactly may it result in marital incompatibility? Give examples.
3. How may the role of specialization in the American society affect marital incompatibility?
4. In what way may the changing role of women in marriage bring about increased stress?
5. Some people feel that nothing they say during an argument should be taken seriously. How might such an attitude be damaging to a marital relationship?
6. What is likely to happen to a person who, not understanding the role which externalization plays in marital incompatibility, simply runs out of one marriage into another? Explain and exemplify.
7. List and discuss the three considerations in dealing with environmental stress in a marriage relationship.
8. List and discuss the four sources of value impositions. Give examples in each case.
9. What type of a marital climate may facilitate the relinquishing of the idealized image? Explain how this is possible.

PROJECTS

1. Write and present a socio-drama which concerns a marital conflict based primarily on externalization factors. After presenting the drama have the class discuss it.
2. Have a debate on the following topic: The Modern American Wife-Mother Confronts More Stress than Did the Early American Wife-Mother.

SUGGESTED READINGS

Burgess, Ernest W., and Harvey J. Locke, *The Family,* American Book Co., New York, 1960, 2nd ed., Ch. 18, "Family Conflicts and Accommodations."

Hill, Reuben, *Families Under Stress,* Harper and Brothers, New York, 1949.

Hollis, Florence, *Women in Marital Conflict,* Family Service Association of America, New York, 1949.

Jacobson, Alver Hilding, "Conflict of Attitudes Toward the Roles of the Husband and Wife in Marriage," *Am. Soc. Rev.,* 17 (April, 1952), pp. 146–150.

Magoun, F. Alexander, *Love and Marriage,* Harper and Brothers, New York, 1948, Ch. 10, "Emotional Adjustments."

Waller, Willard, *The Family,* revised by Reuben Hill, The Dryden Press, New York, 1951, Ch. 14, "Bases of Marriage Conflict," Ch. 15, "Processes of Conflict."

Parents and in-laws

14

In several sections of this book we have dealt with the role of parents in the various stages of one's personal and social development. That parents play a crucial part in what happens to us as individuals should be abundantly clear. In the course of our development our parents come to deal with us in particular ways and we in turn learn to respond to them in particular ways. Thus characteristic patterns of relationships emerge between parents and children. These patterned relationships are an outgrowth of several factors including the dependency needs of the child on the mother and vice versa, the quality of the relationship between the parents, and the emotional maturity of the parents. In this chapter we will deal with some of the implications of these parent-child relationships as they pertain to one's personal development and to the development of one's marriage.

FAMILY VARIABLES AFFECTING OUR RELATIONSHIPS WITH PARENTS. At the outset we should note that there are certain factors in the mother-child relationship which almost always offer the possibility of each becoming overly dependent on the other for the gratification of needs. The human infant has probably the longest period of dependency on its mother of any single member of the animal kingdom. It is inevitable that under these circumstances the infant becomes conditioned to depend on its mother for the gratification of its basic physical and emotional needs, and for the mother to look forward to the pleasure which she may derive from being in-volved in the satisfaction of the infant's needs. Although the develop-ment of some dependency between mother and child is perhaps in-evitable, the likelihood that the extent of such dependency will reach an unhealthy point, that is, where each will become overly dependent on the other, is increased when the husband-wife relationship is lack-ing in basic satisfactions.

When the husband-wife relationship is unsatisfactory for whatever reasons, there is a tendency for one or both parents to compensate by an excessive preoccupation with their children. Although the husband-father may become excessively involved with his children, most often it is the wife-mother who does so; [1] we will discuss this point presently, but before doing so let us look more closely at the problem of marital dissatisfaction.

The reasons for marital dissatisfactions may run the gamut of all types of incompatibility described in the past several chapters. A common factor producing marital dissatisfaction among the American middle class, however, centers around the value orientation of many middle-class husbands and wives. Frequently these people are con-cerned with acquiring and maintaining position and wealth. Thus, the husband who has the major involvement in these pursuits may spend a great deal of time away from home at his business or office in order that he consolidate his socio-economic position and improve it when the opportunity presents itself. Considerable time and energy may also be spent in cultivating desirable social contacts and belonging to the proper clubs, since these are important assets for the male who wishes to "get ahead." The middle-class woman who is often not adverse to the male's orientation faces certain consequences as a result. Fre-quently she finds herself living a lonely and dissatisfied life with a husband who is seldom home. When the home is located in the suburbs several hours removed from the husband's place of employment, the extent and frequency of the husband's absence may be aggravated still more. A woman who finds herself in this plight, and who experiences marital dissatisfaction as a result, may well be at a loss to understand her difficulty. For, indeed, in terms of her own middle-class orientation, her husband's preoccupation with social status fulfills many of her own social expectations; and she has often been taught that happiness is after all often dependent on social and material success. At a deeper interpersonal level, however, she senses that something has happened to her marriage but is at a loss to identify the difficulty; she may also

[1] Geoffrey Gorer, *The American People*, W. W. Norton and Co., New York, 1948, p. 54.

be quite confused about whether her personal dissatisfactions should be verbalized to her husband. Her husband, on the other hand, may be equally confused if he is accused of failing in the family responsibilities, since in his own view his socio-economic pursuits are precisely the concerns which a good husband should have. He sees himself as a self-sacrificing, hard-working husband who is trying to provide his family with all they need. Thus he may be unable to see the full impact of his behavior on his family; and he may be unresponsive and unsympathetic to complaints from his wife, or his family, about his failure to fulfill the emotional component of his role as husband and father. When these problems are compounded by personal immaturity, life in such families becomes even more difficult. This condition in the more economically secure families may be related to the emotional disturbances which some children growing up in these families experience.

Maternal Overprotection—a Prelude to In-Law Difficulties. As a result of the kind of marital relationship which has just been described, certain consequences ensue. First, the mother may become so absorbed in the lives of her growing children that she may, for all practical purposes, reject the possibility of re-examining her relationship with her husband. (To re-examine one's relationship is no simple task, to be sure, since it usually involves a drastic revision of values and perspectives; nevertheless, some people are able to make such revisions in their way of life and thereby improve the quality of their marriages.) The mother may become so preoccupied with her children that she abandons herself as a person. Thus, she may neglect her health and abandon her own interests in order to please her children.

Why does the mother abandon herself and become excessively preoccupied with her children? All emotionally healthy people desire recognition and a place of some importance in the lives of those dear to them. The areas where the mother or woman, however, may seek such recognition are usually much more restricted than are a father's or male's opportunities. He may find recognition in his occupation and profession, and he has less restriction on his personal behavior and may find socially acceptable diversions from an unhappy marriage. In our society there are few compensations for the middle-class mother who is unhappy and dissatisfied. She can seldom pursue a career unless she is properly trained and so oriented. She may become an active "joiner" and "club woman," but even here the satisfactions are limited since competition for status in these organizations may be keen and quite intense. One of the most feasible roles, therefore, into which she can pour all her energies is the role of mother; it is the one role in which she is most likely to achieve success and a sense of significance in the lives of her children.[2] As such it becomes a compensation for a poor marital relationship. Although such preoccupation may assume healthy and responsible proportions at first, it often develops into maternal overprotection, especially when the mother herself may have had an unhappy childhood.[3] Such overprotection results in a pervasive effort to restrict experiences for the child by taking over many of the responsibilities which should be the child's. Why does the mother, who has had an inadequate relationship with her husband, overprotect? First, these mothers often feel trapped in a marriage without very much understanding of its problems. Thus, there is a tendency for them to become quite hopeless about their ability to deal with the circumstances of life; this hopelessness is manifest in their treatment of their children. There is therefore a tendency to feel that the adversities of life are so overwhelming that without excessive parental protection the child will come to some disaster. Secondly, the mother has the belief that her efforts will bring affirmation and give her a sense of importance and significance. In all of this activity on the child's behalf, there is an unconscious agreement which the mother often expects the child to fulfill. It goes something like this, "I have sacrificed for you and it is, therefore, your responsibility to repay me by continued affirmation, by affording me a significant place in your life, and by abiding by my wishes." With such views it is easy to see how an overprotective mother becomes excessively concerned with what the child does, how he performs at school, does he eat, what does he eat, and on and on. When the child begins to demonstrate an interest in the opposite sex more parental anxiety may be aroused since this signifies a concern for relationships which will ultimately remove the child from the home. Thus, interference in dating patterns and discouragement of involvements with members of the opposite sex are common. In one study the attempts of parents to interfere with the courtships of their sons and daughters were examined and it was found that it is not only quite common for such interference to occur but when it does occur it is the mother who is more likely to do the interfering.[4]

At best many parents who have not emancipated themselves from their children interpret a love interest of their son or daughter as a

[2] Marvin B. Sussman, "The Help Pattern in the Middle-Class Family," *Am. Soc. Rev.*, **18** (Feb., 1953), pp. 22–28.

[3] David M. Levy, "Maternal Overprotection and Rejection," *Arch. Neurol. Psychiat.*, **25** (Apr., 1931), pp. 886–894.

[4] Alan Bates, "Paternal Roles in Courtship," *Social Forces,* **20** (May, 1942), pp. 483–486.

threat to the perpetuation of the family unit and they react with apprehension. Frequently such apprehension takes the form of hyper-
criticism toward those with whom an involvement takes place. When a
serious involvement which may lead to marriage appears, such a parent
may become unusually disturbed; this requires understanding. A
parent who has built her life around a child may be faced with a ter-
rible void when the child leaves; such a parent may be faced with
boredom and disinterest. This is particularly the case where a mother
has neglected to revitalize her own relationship with her husband. Thus,
upon the marriage of her son or daughter, she may be faced with the
need to re-establish a union with a husband that she no longer cares
for. She may find it necessary to undo many personal habits that have
been responsible for alienating her husband. All of this may be quite
formidable and painful.

Some women of the type we have described behave quite childishly
when confronted with the marriage of their child. In one instance for
example, at the wedding of her daughter, a woman was told by her
pastor that, "this is a happy occasion for all; especially for you and your
husband, since now you will have an opportunity to do many things
with one another that you were not free to do before." Since the pastor
had been unaware of the deteriorated state of the marital relationship,
he was very surprised at the hostility which was forthcoming from the
woman. She replied rather indignantly that she had always done things
with her husband and she resented the insinuation that she had not.
Having blurted this out she sensed the inappropriateness of her reaction and apologized profusely. Those who knew the woman more
intimately understood why she was so touchy and defensive. For, indeed, she reacted precisely as she did because she was now without
any appropriate diversion and would be forced to confront the rather
meaningless relationship that she shared with her husband.

The small middle-class family may be particularly vulnerable to the
pattern of unhealthy emotional involvement since the mother con-
centrates all of her attention on one or two children. This is quite different from larger family units where the possibility for emotional involvements of mother and child with a greater number of children is
likely, thereby restricting the likelihood of an excessive attachment to
only one child. Unless children are unusually astute and can see the
consequences of such maternal interference they are likely to confront
two things: first a feeling of helplessness with respect to doing things
on their own; and equally significant, a pervasive feeling of guilt when
their wishes run counter to the wishes of their parents, since they have
been impressed with the sacrifices which their mothers have made on

their behalf. In the process of growing up, young people may deal with this problem in one of several ways. There are those who sense the unhealthy component and fight it off. Thus, after some struggle, the child emancipates himself in a healthy way. He comes to have a healthy realization of his rights and those of his parents. There are other people who simply react with rebellious behavior and reject the parent. They become hostile in varying degrees, and, in extreme cases, may have nothing to do with their parents. Finally, there are those who accept the overprotection; they accept the idea of being helpless; they abandon their own wishes and feel perpetually guilty when they have wishes of their own which are different from their parents. Neither of the two latter adjustments, rebellion or acceptance of overprotection, is likely to lead to successful resolutions and each is fraught with difficulty in subsequent marriages. The rebellious person may attempt to reject his parents, but generally there is a pervasive guilt about having done this, and such guilt can plague the individual for many years. This not only creates inner conflict but may disturb his relationship with his spouse as well.

There is the case of a young married man who had openly rejected both his parents. He saw his mother as one who was interested in "tying him to her apron strings." After a series of violent arguments he left home and married without inviting his parents to his wedding. After the wedding he went to a location far removed from his parental home; he claimed that he was very satisfied with this arrangement and refused to answer mail from home. After his first child was born, he began to become ambivalent about his decision to reject his mother. He wanted his parents to see his first child. For a number of months he was quite depressed, anxious, and prone to pick fights with his wife. The general domestic situation had deteriorated considerably before the husband and wife both agreed that a solution to the parental problem was mandatory if the marital arguments were to diminish. At this point professional assistance was sought, which over an extended period of time aided the husband in understanding his difficulties in relation to his parents.

Accepting the overprotection without any effort to emancipate oneself is even more devastating, since it dooms one to a life of feelings of inadequacy and feelings of guilt whenever parental wishes are not adhered to. Such an existence can be quite crippling and restricts the assumption of responsibility for oneself. Thus, there are numerous cases of individuals who have learned to think of themselves as inadequate. Frequently they feel entitled to be excused from the demands which life makes. Moreover, since they feel helpless they may consider it unfair when requests are made that they work and support themselves or their families. They may even consider it unfair that they are expected to assume responsibility for their mistakes and errors in judgment.

It should be pointed out that once the individual feels helpless, his demands on a mother and others may become so excessive that the mother's life and the lives of others become increasingly chaotic.

If neither rebellion nor the acceptance of overprotection is satisfactory, how does one come to terms with his overprotective parents? First, by accepting the fact that one's parents are as they are, not necessarily because of their own choosing but because of the way in which life has dealt with them. Second, by avoiding complete rejection of one's parents through an accepting of those things that further a mature relationship with the parent and rejecting only those aspects of behavior that restrict the development of a mature relationship. This can only be done, however, when the parents and children have some measure of autonomy; that is, when each feels that he has a right to choose the course of action that he wants rather than finding it necessary to be compliant to the wishes of the other.

Maternal Rejection—Another Prelude to In-Law Difficulties. In our discussion up to this point we have concentrated on how an inadequate parental marriage may lead to maternal overprotection and all the consequences thereof. Nevertheless, it is important to remember that an inadequate parental marriage may also result in a parent's rejection of the child. What are the consequences here? In some instances the parent, or mother, who recognizes this tendency in herself may out of a sense of guilt immediately attempt to compensate for this by becoming overly concerned with the child. Thus, overprotection may result here also. However, even in cases where compensation is not the major mechanism involved, the rejection of a child is seldom total. Instead, it usually takes the form of ambivalence, with alternate feelings of rejection and efforts at trying to make up; this might be regarded as a partial compensation for the rejection. Needless to say, all of this can be very devastating for the child since it leaves him with a pervasive feeling of doubt and uncertainty as to where he stands. The child who feels uncertain about his parental relationship may react with a compulsive need to please them which results in abandonment of his own wishes. But, parents who are ambivalent toward their children are, indeed, difficult to please.

IN-LAW DIFFICULTIES. Any individual who has not resolved the interpersonal problems with his parents which we have described will carry them into his marriage; at this point they involve one's husband

"I'm afraid poor George is in for a lot of mother–in–law trouble."

PARADE

Figure 6. Courtesy Bill Polvogt and Parade Publications, Inc. (June 11, 1961).

or wife and result in what we commonly identify as in-law problems.[5] Where both husband and wife have unresolved parental problems, the situation may become extremely complicated and aggravated.

The Nature of In-Law Involvements. If a parent still needs to control the life of his grown, married offspring, one can expect a good deal of parental involvement in several areas of the young adult's married life. Furthermore, such involvement will actually be encouraged by the offspring who has not achieved emancipation from his parents. In this regard recent studies show that the tendency to bring the mother into marital conflicts is more frequent among young wives, since they are found to be less emancipated from their mothers than are their husbands.[6]

The in-law involvements may center around what kind of a place

---

[5] All of this may be aggravated by the fact that young people tend to enter marriage with extremely negative attitudes toward the mother-in-law, attitudes which in themselves may be the result of the American stereotype of a mother-in-law as being mean, meddlesome, and miserable. See: Evelyn Millis Duvall, *In-Laws: Pro and Con*, Association Press, New York, 1954, Ch. 2.

[6] Mirra Komarovsky, "Continuities in Family Research: A Case Study," *Am. J. Sociol.*, **62** (July, 1956), pp. 42–47.

TABLE 12

The In-Law Named Most Difficult by 1,337 Persons *

Most Difficult In-Laws	Percent
Mother-in-Law	36.8
Sister-in-Law	20.3
Brother-in-Law	5.4
Father-in-Law	5.0
Daughter-in-law	2.8
Other Female in-Laws	1.6
"All in-Laws"	1.5
Son-in-Law	0.7
Other Male in-Laws	0.1
No Difficult in-Laws	25.8
Total	100.0

* Evelyn Millis Duvall, *In-Laws: Pro and Con*, Association Press, New York, 1954, p. 188.

the couple reside in, and how the home is furnished, or they may center around how the couple spend their time, how they entertain their friends, how they spend their money, the style of clothes each wears, how often they visit parents, and how long they stay.

In order to fully understand the nature of in-law involvements, however, it is less important to concentrate on the types of symptomatic problems they can produce and more important to consider the sources from which these involvements emanate. In this regard, we have already discussed at some length the relationship between faulty parental marriages and in-law involvements. There are additional sources of in-law involvements, however, which for the most part are described in the psychological and psychiatric literature. Let us look at some of these.

Mothers or fathers who are themselves emotionally immature, fearful about relating to people, often lead very sheltered lives. Such parents become emotionally attached to a son or daughter and find it very painful to sever the psychic ties between themselves and their children. Due to this inability to make such a break, these parents often regard the marriage of their child with utmost anxiety. Indeed, if they are unable to prevent the marriage itself they will tend to keep a critical eye on the marriage and will frequently make excessive demands on their daughter-in-law or son-in-law so that all the wishes of their son or daughter will be fulfilled as adequately as they had been in the past.

Moreover, some psychoanalysts report that an insecure mother may actually become jealous of her daughter because she, the mother, may find herself romantically attracted to her son-in-law. Such attraction, however, is so socially unacceptable to her that she must reject it, turning it into a strong dislike for the son-in-law.[7]

Finally, if a parent is one with frustrated professional ambitions, he may make excessive demands of his child whom he has come to regard as a means of vicariously fulfilling his own ambitions. Thus, when his child marries, there may be a good deal of berating of the son-in-law or daughter-in-law by the parent and a tendency to constantly remind the son or daughter about the spouse's shortcomings.

Parental dissatisfactions of this type are especially likely because of the high degree of upward mobility in our society today. The existence of social mobility in general also makes possible the selection of a mate who represents a different cultural background and different values from one's own. This means that not only will differences in the value patterns held by the marital partners have to be accommodated but also those differences between the individual and his in-laws will have to be considered.

All of these difficulties should suggest the greatest caution in living with in-laws for any period of time, since all of the problems we have described may become intensely aggravated when young couples live with their in-laws.[8] Furthermore, several aspects of the newlyweds' marital adjustment may be delayed by living with parents and in-laws. The opportunity to reach decisions independently may be greatly retarded. The sexual adjustment, which requires freedom and spontaneity for maximum enjoyment, may be blocked when the environment cannot be properly controlled. Thus, in general the speed with which a couple mature in terms of marital obligations and responsibilities is reduced.

In one case a young man brought his wife home to live with his mother, a woman obsessed with the dangers of sexual intercourse, since she believed that it depleted one's energies. Whenever the couple could not be found for any period of time, the mother became quite inquisi-

---

[7] For a full discussion of the psychoanalytic factors involved, see: John C. Flugel, *The Psychoanalytic Study of the Family*, International Psychoanalytic Press, London and New York, 1921.

[8] Simpson, *op. cit.*, pp. 204–205. We do not imply that this would be true in all cultures. Indeed one study dealing with another culture refutes the idea in that it not only reports that no association was found between living with in-laws and marital adjustment but it also suggests that in certain cases having an in-law in the house may be advantageous to the young couple. Georg Karlsson, *Adaptability and Communication in Marriage*, Uppsala, Almqvist and Wiksells Boktryckeri Aktiebolag, 1951, p. 106.

tive about the cause of the absence, and was always certain that her son was sexually involved. The mother so plagued the couple that within a matter of weeks, the wife threatened to obtain a divorce if the husband did not make some provision for their residence elsewhere.

AN ATTEMPT TO DEAL WITH THE PARENT AND IN-LAW PROBLEM. There are those who believe that problems with parents and in-laws are less evident today than in the past, since today there is a much greater likelihood that the young couple may not reside in the community of the parents. For some individuals with parental and in-law difficulties movement to a new locality facilitates the adjustment. On the other hand, we recognize that involvements with parents and in-laws are charged with the deepest of feelings. Thus, while separation may facilitate the adjustment in some cases, in others it may intensify any problems of overdependency that are present. There are no simple solutions or remedies for these difficulties but there are perhaps certain considerations which are worth examining. In this regard, it is of the greatest importance to be able to identify prior to marriage those patterns in the parent-child relationship which are likely to result in a restriction of the young person's maturity in his marital relationship. A realization of such restrictions and efforts to resolve such possibilities by both parents and children can do much in avoiding some of the difficulties we have discussed.

For a parent the acceptance of the emancipation of his grown, married child is made excessively difficult by the fact that an entire way of life consisting of specific attitudes and a sense of significance and purpose has become intimately rooted in his relationship with his child. To give this up, particularly when there may be no real substitute, is very disquieting. It is because of this that a son or daughter who wishes to help a parent with these problems must have considerable understanding of the parent.

For the son or daughter there is an equally serious problem. Emancipation from one's parents necessitates the relinquishing of some of the satisfactions which one has come to enjoy. Such satisfactions, as having another assume responsibility for one's life, may be much more enticing than the goals of maturity which require both the development of a philosophy about the meaning and responsibility inherent in living, and also constructive efforts to attain such goals.

Finally, it should be noted that it is questionable whether one ever gives up the satisfactions derived from immature relationships without some hope that the alternative will be more rewarding. For parents and their grown children, such a hope may come from the realization that there is far greater stability and personal happiness to be derived from personal autonomy than there is from the endless waste of energies tied to the maintenance of an immature way of life.[9]

SUMMARY

The relationship between parent and child is an important factor in understanding the complexities which surround in-law problems. When the parent-child relationship is mature and meaningful there is little likelihood of its becoming a factor in creating in-law problems. However, when the parent-child relationship is unhealthy (consisting either of overprotection or rejection) it may become a major factor in bringing about in-law difficulties. In the case of overprotection, for example, unless the young adult is able to emancipate himself from his parents and in turn cause his parents to free themselves from using him as their major source of satisfaction, this overprotection may become a concern in his marriage, and as such it may bring about many serious difficulties in his interactions with his wife.

The nature of in-law involvements and the sources from which these involvements emanate were discussed. In addition to faulty parental marriages, other sources of in-law involvements considered were the inability of parents to sever the psychic ties between themselves and their children, and also parents' use of their children as a means of vicariously fulfilling their own frustrated wishes.

It is important to recognize the complexity of in-law involvements because the development of successful in-law relationships requires an understanding on the part of both the parents and the children who are involved.

QUESTIONS

1. State briefly but clearly the relationship between child-parent interaction and in-law problems. Give examples.
2. What is maternal overprotection? Discuss how a woman involved in an inadequate relationship with her husband may become overprotective with her child.
3. List and discuss the ways in which young adults may deal with maternal overprotection. Which of these ways are likely to lead to successful marriage and which are likely to lead to unsuccessful marriage? Explain your answers.
4. What is parental rejection? How does this affect a parent-child relationship? What effect might it have on one's subsequent marriage? Explain your answers.

[9] Evelyn Millis Duvall, *op. cit.*, Chs. 3 and 6.

5. How might living with in-laws increase the potentiality for in-law problems? Is this always true? Explain your answers.

PROJECTS

1. Select two marriages with which you are acquainted, one that you regard as reflecting successful in-law relationships, and one that you regard as reflecting unsuccessful in-law relationships. Make an objective analysis of each marriage, attempting to show how the successful relationships differ from the unsuccessful, and also how each type develops.

2. Write a paper concerning the circumstances under which you would consent to live with your in-laws, and also the circumstances under which you would consent to have them live with you. Attempt an objective analysis of your answers.

SUGGESTED READINGS

Duvall, Evelyn Millis, *In-Law: Pro and Con*, Association Press, New York, 1954.

Duvall, Sylvanus M., *Before You Marry*, Association Press, New York, 1949, Ch. 10, "The Family You Marry."

LeMasters, E. E., *Modern Courtship and Marriage*, The Macmillan Co., New York, 1957, Ch. 15, "In-Laws: Friends or Enemies."

Levine, Lena, *Modern Book of Marriage*, Bartholomew House, New York, 1957, Ch. 5, "Getting Along with Parents and In-Laws."

Stryker, Sheldon, "The Adjustment of Married Offspring to Their Parents," *Am. Soc. Rev.*, **20** (April, 1955), pp. 149–154.

Wallin, Paul, "Sex Differences in Attitudes to In-Laws—A Test of a Theory," *Am. J. Social.*, **59** (March, 1954), pp. 466–469.

Marriage and the pursuit of a college education

15

In previous chapters we have been dealing with particular dimensions of marital difficulty, which included sexual adjustment, sources of marital conflict, role conflicts, externalizations of various kinds, and parent and in-law difficulties. In this chapter we plan to examine marriage in a particular setting in which several of the difficulties previously discussed play a significant role.

Not so many years ago it was customary for the middle-class male to complete his education, become established in a job or profession, and then marry. As shown in Table 13, however, since World War II there has been a marked increase in the number of married people

TABLE 13

Percentage of Married Undergraduate Students at the University of Oregon *

Year	Men	Women
1941	5.5%	2.2%
1946	23.5	7.9
1951	23.9	7.7
1956	27.1	10.9

* Lester A. Kirkendall, "Married Undergraduates on the Campus: An Appraisal," *The Family Life Coordinator,* **5:2** (Dec., 1956), pp. 54–63 by permission of E. C. Brown Trust.

who are pursuing an education.[1] Many of these marriages present special difficulties which we will examine.[2] Before doing so, however, it should be noted that there are at least three types of college marriage: those in which the couples were married for a considerable period of time before either or both of the partners entered college, those in which the couples were married just prior to entering college, and those in which the couples married while attending college.

In this chapter our concern is with the latter two types, and although there are undoubtedly some differences between them, they are each faced with two eventualities for which some preparation may be warranted. The first is that many of the marital conflicts to be faced may emerge much earlier than would be the case in the non-college marriage. The second eventuality is that these marital conflicts may come with such rapidity that the couple can be thrown into more turmoil than usual, since they do not have an adequate opportunity to resolve one conflict before another starts. In this sense married persons attending college may be faced with conflicts in the first two years of marriage that others might not have to face for a considerably longer period of time. The reason for this state of affairs stems from the unique atmosphere of the college setting. To a lesser or greater extent institutions of higher education are dedicated to the examination of ideas and the exploration of new and different values. In such an atmosphere the opportunity for intellectual stimulation and growth is such that its impact, while not significant for all, is significant for many of the individuals involved. It is because of this unique opportunity for new experiences and growth that changes in the marital partners are often imminent and these must be coped with. In this sense the college atmosphere is not easily matched by non-university situations in which a couple may find themselves. Let us examine some of these possibilities for new experiences and trace the implications which these have for conflicts in the marital relationship.[3]

[1] For a discussion of the effect which wartime anxiety and military service have on the growing number of college marriages see: James A. Peterson, *Education for Marriage*, Charles Scribner's Sons, New York, 1956, pp. 175–176. For a discussion of reasons and pressures for early marriage see: James H. S. Bossard and Eleanor Stoker Boll, *Why Marriages Go Wrong*, The Ronald Press Co., New York, 1958, pp. 103–111.

[2] For a discussion of college marriages see: Ruth M. Hoeflin, *Essentials of Family Living*, John Wiley and Sons, New York, 1960, pp. 231–233. For a discussion of the special stresses confronted by college marriages see: Henry A. Bowman, *Marriage for Moderns*, McGraw-Hill Book Co., Inc., New York, 1960, pp. 490–498.

[3] For a discussion of the problems involved in the "too early" college and high school marriage see: Paul H. Landis, *Making the Most of Marriage*, 2nd ed., Appleton-Century-Crofts, Inc., New York, 1960, pp. 274–278.

DIFFERENTIAL CHANGE AND GROWTH IN MARRIAGE.

One major potential source of conflict in the college marriage stems from the fact that one partner may change and grow more rapidly than the other. Such changes emerge quite early out of the dynamics of college living and frequently have their origin in the broad impact of the university experience on the marital partners.

For a husband who attends school there is the opportunity for growth which may come about through his participation in an academic program, or perhaps through his interaction with different persons in the university setting who open new vistas for him. Out of such circumstances differential growth between him and his wife may appear. This frequently presents a problem of considerable significance since many wives under these circumstances find the husband's education and personal growth so threatening that they may impose obstacles in regard to his education.

In one instance a wife became so concerned that she might lose her husband that she exaggerated the seriousness of even her minor ailments. This resulted in her husband staying at home, missing classes, and receiving poor grades. It was some time before the husband saw what was happening and realized the necessity of reassuring his wife of his love for her. Frequently, the woman who regards the education of her husband as a threat may become competitive and try to outdo him, either by attending school herself or by developing other skills. Competition of this type, if not recognized, may lead to serious conflict because the emphasis here is not only upon surpassing the other but there is envy of the success of the other without any healthy identification in regard to his accomplishments. When, however, the achievements of the husband awaken in the wife a healthy desire for new experiences, the results may be extremely beneficial to the marriage.

Although we have assumed that it is the husband who attends school, it may be that the wife decides to attend the university. Here we also have the ever present opportunity for new experiences, her entire outlook may undergo change. In such instances the husband may experience the university as a threat to his marriage. There was the case of a husband who did not possess a college education and who became very upset after his wife started to attend school. He complained bitterly about how the home had "gone to pieces." He accused her of being selfish and threatened to leave her, if she did not stop attending school.

When each partner undergoes a process of change, new views may enter the marriage, views regarding what the goals in marriage should be and what values are worth pursuing. Often such reassessment of values and goals leads to a sounder and more meaningful relationship. Usually, however, even when change involves both partners, it may still result in some difficulty between the spouses for at least two reasons. A first reason has to do with the fact that when people do change they do not necessarily change at the same pace or in the same way. A second reason why difficulty may emerge even when both marital partners are involved in change stems from the fact that in change, core elements in the personality are involved and these elements do not change easily. One of the core elements in the personality of each spouse has to do with perception of roles in marriage; and we wish to turn our attention to this problem briefly.

ROLE CONFLICT. A second major source of potential conflict in the college marriage which is interrelated with the change and growth just described has to do with role conflict. As a result of their exposure to the academic setting each partner in a college marriage may envision a new and different role in marriage. A subservient wife or husband may perceive new capacities. Often this may lead to a new definition of role which may be in conflict with the role expectations of the spouse. Furthermore, frequently the realization of such new capacities may be so exciting for the moment that the individuals become narrowly selfish. Thus a husband who discovers a new talent in himself may temporarily ignore his responsibilities to his wife and children; or the wife who believes that she possesses acting ability may ignore her responsibilities in the home and spend her time at the local playhouse. The realization of capacities, although intrinsically worthwhile, is frequently associated with conflict and confusion in the home. In one situation, a woman who had discovered a new asset in herself was exploited by her friends to the detriment of her family. This young married woman discovered that she had a great capacity to organize social affairs. She was so delighted at this discovery that she allowed her friends to shift an unusual amount of responsibility on her. Her friends accomplished this by flattery in which the young lady was told her unusual abilities. As a result the young lady found her time completely taken up with the organization of church picnics, school lectures, and the like. Her husband recognized what was happening and began to complain bitterly in the hope that his wife might take stock of how she was being manipulated by her friends.

In all matters dealing with realization of new capacities a sense of perspective is necessary. Personal talents and interests have to be woven into the broader fabric of the marriage; otherwise chaos and imbalance are likely to characterize the marriage.

MULTIPLICITY OF ROLES. A third major source of conflict in college marriages arises out of the fact that the partner may be required to fulfill several social roles, and each role may be in conflict with the other. The husband, for example, may discover that he must be a husband, a father, an employee, and also a student. Thus, he may have to be fairly passive in the classroom and at work, and more assertive at home with his wife and child. Furthermore, in regard to his role as a student he has to study, but his wife may demand more social life than they have. He also may feel a sense of obligation to spend time with his children, if he has any.[4] All of this may be aggravated by the fact that the wife is seeking to complete her education as well. Her potential for tension is also great, since she may be for the moment wife, mother, student, and employee.[5] The obligations inherent in each role may be equally important and none may be satisfactorily abandoned. Thus, life for such couples can often become grim with the difficulties involved in the growth of each individual, the conflict with one another, and the conflicting nature of the new social roles; tension is ever present. The pot is always on the verge of boiling over, so to speak.

EXTERNALIZATIONS IN COLLEGE MARRIAGE. Under these circumstances externalizations of tensions may be a regular occurrence in college marriages, and such externalizations constitute a fourth major source of conflict in the college marriage. As has already been noted, when externalizations are operating, it is easy for people to aggravate each other, to find fault, to nag and berate one another. The particular focus of the externalization—that is, what a spouse singles out as a target—will vary with the particular relationship. For example, it may be an economic problem, a sex problem, or an in-law problem, particularly when there already is some basis for one of these problems. Indeed, all of these problems may be sources of conflict in any marriage. The point is that when a person externalizes his tension and hostility, and begins to focus on problems, even minor problems are distorted, and their seriousness and significance are exaggerated. It is important that the tendency to distort the seriousness

---

[4] For a discussion of the effect children have on a college marriage see: Theodore B. Johannis, "The Marital Adjustment of a Sample of Married College Students," *The Family Life Coordinator*, 4:4 (June, 1956), p. 29.

[5] James A. Peterson, *op. cit.*, pp. 169–172.

of a problem (which is a by-product of externalization) be noted, since a tremendous amount of energy can be wasted in conflict about relatively unimportant matters.

THE PARENT AND IN-LAW RELATIONS. A fifth source of conflict in the college marriage has to do with parents and in-laws. We recognize, of course, that such problems are frequently a function of the externalizations that have just been described. Thus, under some circumstances, parents and in-laws may be blamed for difficulties that they have little to do with. On the other hand, there are several factors intrinsic to the college situation, which do make certain types of conflicts with parents and in-laws a common occurrence.

Parental and In-Law Ambivalence. A first factor which is related to parental and in-law conflict is the fact that from the beginning of the marriage each partner may have been faced with negative reactions from his parents. Middle-class parents are generally very concerned with the social and economic well-being of their children. Thus, they may view the marriage of their children in college as potentially disruptive to the plans which they have for their children. Middle-class parents may feel uneasy about a son who marries while still in college since there is the danger that he may become so burdened with economic responsibilities that he will abandon college. For a daughter who seeks such a marriage there may be the concern that she will abandon her education and the years attended may be wasted. Thus often there may be a reservoir of ambivalence on the part of parents and in-laws.

Economic Difficulty and Resulting Patterns of Interaction. A second factor involved in the possible rise of conflict with parents and in-laws relates to economic difficulties, a problem fairly common in the college marriage.[6] Of significance here is not the economic problem per se, but rather the patterns which tend to be used for dealing with the problem under these circumstances. For in these patterns much about how the married pair deal with parents and in-laws and vice versa is revealed. A knowledge of such patterns may prove to be significant in enabling all of the involved persons to understand the nature of their conflicts with each other.

The economic problem which has been singled out for analysis

[6] For a discussion of economic support from parents in regard to college marriages see: Judson T. Landis and Mary G. Landis, *Building a Successful Marriage*, 3rd ed., Prentice-Hall, Inc., Englewood Cliffs, New Jersey, 1958, pp. 188–190.

may be divided into two parts; one involves the married pair,[7] the other pertains to parents and in-laws. For the married pair in need of economic help, there is often conflict about how the problem ought to be resolved. The couple may wish to be independent and solve their own problem or they may decide to seek assistance from their parents. Either of these two courses of action, however, involves calculated risks for the married pair. If, for example, one or the other member of the relationship is too independent, both may suffer from this aloofness. On the other hand, if the couple is inclined to be dependent, then the economic help received from the parents may increase the dependency and involve the parents in the marriage to a greater extent than is wise. Thus the course of action that couples decide to follow when economic help is needed should be given a great deal of consideration.

The second dimension of conflict in regard to the question of economic assistance is concerned with the parents and in-laws. If they are middle-class persons, they may be concerned with having their children maintain a particular standard of living. At the same time, as middle-class parents they may also feel that individualism and a spirit of self-reliance are necessary if their children are to manage their affairs properly. This conflict may be complicated by the fact that they desire a place of importance in the lives of their children and feel that economic assistance will insure such a place. Here the several courses of action open also involve calculated risks. If the parents refuse to give economic help, there is the fear that they will endanger their relationship with the married pair and hurt their children in a very material way. If they extend help they may encourage dependency on the part of the married pair; and as parents they may become involved in a way which hurts their relationship with the young couple. This would be the case especially where parents and in-laws are led to a pattern of frequently visiting the couple, ignoring their own interests and becoming completely absorbed in the relationship of their children. Thus, for both the married pair and the parents or in-laws there are conflicting motivations that are brought into play when questions of economic assistance arise.

Masking Emotional Dependency. The precarious balance between emotional dependence and independence may be so uncomfortable, both for parents and children alike, that it is often masked. One way of masking it is to act on the basis of one motivation and repress the

[7] For a study of student opinion concerning financial assistance from parents in college marriages see: Rex A. Skidmore and Anthon S. Cannon, *Building Your Marriage,* Harper and Brothers, New York, 1951, pp. 226–227, 638–639.

other. When motivations are sufficiently mixed and complicated in this way, there is always the danger that they will not be fully explored or fully understood either by parents, in-laws, or the married pair. For example, a son who has needs both for independence and dependence may block out momentarily his need for independence and seek the financial aid. With an equally strong repressed need to be independent, however, and without being aware of what he is doing consciously, he may become very sensitive and resentful about any advice he receives from his parents since he already feels uneasy about depending on them for economic aid. Thus, such repression brings with it added complications.

Parents or in-laws, likewise, may feel a need both to help their children and a need to leave them on their own. Thus, due to this ambivalence, frequently when parents do extend economic assistance it is accompanied by a need to control its use; parents may become moody and pout when they are not consulted on purchases which the married pair make. In one instance a married daughter, who borrowed money from her mother, found her mother very unhappy whenever she was not consulted on purchases. The mother's reaction troubled the daughter so much that she cleared all purchases with her mother, a pattern that robbed the daughter of her autonomy and caused much conflict in her marriage.

Approaching the Need for Economic Assistance with Hidden Intent. Situations in which economic help is being sought are frequently complicated by the fact that both the married pair and the parents or in-laws may be sensitive to rejection. Often such sensitivity may lead to the hiding of actual intent. A married son, for example, may allude to the many material possessions of his friends hoping that his parents pick up the cues and offer assistance. On the other hand, parents may talk about the spirit of adventure and the excitement of building one's own future, thereby indicating that they have no intention of giving help. In each of the above situations there are two points to keep in mind. First, the hiding of intent is in many instances done unconsciously, so that persons are unaware of what they are doing. A second point is that by hiding intent a good deal of face-saving becomes possible. Thus, if a father appears unreceptive to the idea of help, the son may hide consciously or unconsciously behind the idea that he never really wanted help. If the father recognizes that he has really hurt his son by refusing to help, he may declare that he really did not understand his son's request and at that point offer assistance.

The patterns of interaction which emerge during questions of economic assistance, including the masking of emotional dependency and the hiding of intent, make whatever problems are present between parents, in-laws, and the married pair immensely complicated. Reactions of the sort we have described keep all participants from actually dealing with their responsibilities to one another, and can only be averted when all concerned attempt to understand the situation more clearly than is often the case.

CONFLICT AND SEXUAL ADJUSTMENT. The disturbances in the interpersonal relationship which can come from all of the conflict sources just described very often find their expression in the sexual adjustments that are to be made in the college marriage. Some individuals who are hostile may become indifferent to sex; they may suddenly experience less pleasure, or refuse to participate, particularly if it will enable them to get back at the spouse.

Further, as persons undergo changes in concepts of role, their part in sexual relations may undergo change as well. Thus, a woman who believes she has no choice other than to engage in sexual relations when her husband so indicates, may come to feel her wishes are also important and refuse sexual relations. Or a husband who feels that he has no right to indicate his interest in sexual relations may suddenly come to feel that he has every right to do so, and make such feelings known. Thus, new definitions of one's role produce conflict.

Finally, each partner may become so absorbed with the demands of college and his other responsibilities that he experiences periods of marked indifference regarding sexual activity. Here the sexual withdrawal is not a matter of expressing resentment but stems from the fact that energies are completely absorbed by the many demands and responsibilities which are present.

There was a married male college student who found his work exceedingly difficult and had to spend tremendous amounts of time preparing for examinations. He experienced such anxiety about doing well in his exams and maintaining other responsibilities that for a couple of weeks before midterms he experienced temporary or situational impotency when he tried to perform the sex act. Such impotence remained until the examinations were completed, then he was able to become sexually responsive once more.

POSITIVE FACTORS IN COLLEGE MARRIAGES. Although our focus has been on the problem areas in the college marriage, the reader must not conclude that beneficial aspects are not present.[8] First,

[8] For studies involving success and happiness ratings of college marriages see: Judson T. Landis, "On the Campus," *Survey Midmonthly*, **84:**1 (Jan., 1948),

it should be noted that the possibility of both satisfaction and disappointments which emerge out of sharing interests and goals may provide the couple with a solid foundation for dealing with the future. Second, there are the erotic satisfactions which may be realized, devoid of the difficulties which confront the unmarried. Both of these features help orient the individuals more clearly as to purpose in life, and may become important factors in their commitment to serious pursuits in life. In fact, a study by Svend Riemer has affirmed one beneficial result: the grades of college people improve after they are married.[9]

To be sure, conflict may also emerge out of the pursuit of marital satisfaction. Conflict, however (as will be indicated in a subsequent chapter), does not have to be negative; it can be quite beneficial. For in conflict there are many opportunities for reassessment of values and goals, and for the subsequent growth of the marital relationship. In college marriages, the successful are those who have been able to detect the sources of conflict, who have learned to deal with conflict, and who have been able to profit as a result.

SUMMARY

The college marriage is much more prevalent today than it was in the past. Because of this, and because of the unique conditions which surround the college marriage, it is felt that giving special consideration to this area is warranted.

With respect to the conditions in which the college marriage is found, it is recognized that persons involved in college marriages not only tend to confront the "normal" marital conflicts earlier than those involved in non-college marriages, but they also confront these conflicts much more rapidly than persons involved in non-college marriages. The early and rapid conflict confrontation and its accompanying need for adjustments on the part of members of a college marriage frequently create more than the usual amount of turmoil.

In this chapter, in addition to discussing the place of conflict in college marriage, some of the sources of the conflict were also discussed. These sources of conflict are: (1) differential change and growth in marriage, (2) role conflict, (3) multiplicity of roles, (4)

---

pp. 17–19. Harold T. Christensen and Robert E. Philbrick, "Family Size as a Factor in the Marital Adjustments of College Couples," *Am. Soc. Rev.*, **17** (June, 1952), pp. 306–312.

[9] Svend Riemer, "Married Veterans are Good Students," *Marriage and Family Living*, 9 (Feb., 1947), pp. 11–12. See also Judson T. Landis and Mary G. Landis, *op. cit.*, pp. 179–180.

externalizations, and (5) parents and in-laws. Special attention was also given to such patterns as the masking of emotional dependency, and hiding the intent of asking for, giving, or receiving economic assistance; it was suggested that these patterns add complications to the problems that may already be present in the college marriage.

It is not our intent to reflect negatively on college marriages—it goes without saying that many of them are happy and successful ones. We have intended, however, to point out very clearly the complexity of the conflict which may confront persons involved in, or contemplating, college marriage. This is done in the hope that a clearer understanding of conflict may eventuate in more successful marriages of this type.

QUESTIONS

1. Describe briefly the three types of college marriages. Analyze each type from the standpoint of probable problem areas and show how these marriages may be similar to or different from one another in regard to the amount and type of conflict confronted.
2. What is meant by differential change and growth in marriage? Is differential change and growth more likely to occur in a college marriage than it is in a non-college marriage? Explain your answer.
3. Discuss role conflict in marriage. Does this potential problem area apply more to college marriages than to non-college marriages? Explain your answer.
4. Explain how externalizations occur in college marriage. Cite examples.
5. Discuss parent and in-law relations as potential sources of marital conflict. Do you think that there is a difference between college marriage and non-college marriage with respect to how this potential source of conflict unfolds and its probability of occurrence?
6. What is meant by masking dependency? What is meant by hiding intent? How can each of these patterns compound the difficulties in effecting adjustments in college marriage?

PROJECTS

1. Hold a panel discussion concerning the pros and cons of marrying while in college.
2. Interview several married college students. Divide these subjects into two groups: those who were married before attending college, and those who were married while attending college. Attempt to determine what each group regards as the advantages and disadvantages of combining marriage and college attendance. Do you find any difference between the two groups? Do you find any differences in the answers given by men and the answers given by women? If you find differences, how do you

account for these differences? Report your findings and your analysis to the class.

SUGGESTED READINGS

Bowman, Henry A., *Marriage for Moderns*, McGraw-Hill Book Co., New York, 4th ed., 1960, Ch. 15, "Young Marriage Today."

Johannis, Theodore B., "The Marital Adjustment of a Sample of Married College Students," *The Coordinator*, 4:4 (June, 1956), pp. 24–31.

Kirkendall, Lester A., "Married Undergraduates on the Campus: An Appraisal," *The Family Life Coordinator*, 5:2 (Dec., 1956), pp. 54–63.

Landis, Judson T. and Mary G. Landis, *Building a Successful Marriage*, 3rd ed., Prentice-Hall, Inc., Englewood Cliffs, New Jersey, 1958, Ch. 10, "Marriage Under Special Circumstances."

Riemer, Svend, Married Veterans are Good Students," *Marriage and Family Living*, 9 (Feb., 1947), pp. 11–12.

Resolving marital conflict

16

In previous chapters we discussed some of the major areas of marital conflict. In this chapter we will examine the nature of marital conflict, and deal with those understandings which may contribute to a resolution of marital problems.

SOME BASIC IDEAS REGARDING THE NATURE OF MARITAL CONFLICT. It is important to appreciate certain basic ideas which surround marital conflict. There is a common assumption that conflict is inherently bad for a marriage. In this regard it should be pointed out that not all marital conflict is necessarily undesirable or destructive.[1] Whether or not conflict is destructive depends on the extent to which it involves an attack on the self-worth of the marital partner; as previously indicated, such an attack is replete with difficulties for the marital union. When the self-worth of the marital partner is not the focus of the conflict, however, there may be beneficial developments.

A first useful purpose of conflict occurs when the conflict leads to a redefinition of the marital difficulty. This may be achieved when issues are brought out into the open, extraneous issues dispensed with, and misunderstandings about the real issues clarified. As a result, each partner may be able to think more clearly about the difficulty in-

[1] See: Willard Waller, *The Family*, revised by Reuben Hill, Dryden Press, New York, 1951, pp. 309–312.

volved; and a resolution for the difficulty may be found more readily.

A second useful purpose of conflict occurs when the marital partners develop a realistic understanding of one another, and the basic values of each are delineated. There was the case of a married woman who saw her husband, a college student, as being much brighter than he actually was. She had an idealized image of her husband which kept getting in the way of seeing him realistically. For several semesters the husband's grades were very average, and the wife became resentful and brooded. One day when she could no longer contain her resentment she expressed her sense of disappointment toward her husband and this led to a series of quarrels. In the process of quarreling, the husband pointed out the strain under which he had been operating trying to live up to his own, as well as her, expectations. The quarrels were quite intense but they resulted in the wife's coming to have a deeper sense of appreciation of her husband's plight. The husband, on the other hand, grew in his understanding of his wife's behavior and her needs. A closer and more meaningful relationship emerged as a result. In this instance, and in many others, conflict may clarify the different values at work and remind the marital partners of their obligations; it may well be that in any relationship some conflict is essential, if it serves to sharpen beliefs, and continues to alert the partners to the expectations of the other.

A third useful purpose which can result from marital conflict comes about when the partners appreciate the extent of their emotional commitment to the marriage. As disagreements which lead to conflict emerge in the marital relationship, there is a tendency for each to become alienated from the other and to assume that the entire relationship is negative. Often conflict may create an awareness of the positive emotional involvement.

There was a married couple who were engaged in conflict which had its origins at least fifteen years in the past. During the quarrels they brought up many hurts from the past: insults that were made, interference from parents in their marriage, even difficulties from courtship. It became increasingly clear to each, however, that while there were many hurts from the past, they also found themselves thinking about the enjoyments: the restaurants they had eaten in, the movies they had seen, the places they visited, the sentiments and feelings surrounding all of these experiences. Thus, there was the realization that not only was there much that was positive about their marriage, but that deep personal feelings were also associated with their marriage.

FORMS OF MARITAL CONFLICT. At the outset we should note that probably much marital conflict originates with competition between the persons about some aspect of their life. When competition is not resolved it lends itself to rivalry. Rivalry brings with it tension which, if not dealt with effectively, emerges into conflict. Conflict most often results in accommodation, with each agreeing to grant some concession in order that an adjustment be reached. The interplay between competition, rivalry, conflict, and accommodation over an extended period of time results in each marital partner accepting some of the values of the other. When this occurs understanding and acceptance have taken place and the difficulties between the marital partners are minimized.[2]

Exterior Forms. In dealing with marital conflict one has to differentiate the broad exterior forms of conflict from the inner dynamics of conflict, the actual interplay between the persons. In regard to exterior forms, we recognize particular forms such as concealed and overt conflict, acute conflict, chronic conflict, progressive conflict, and habitual conflict.[3] In concealed conflict the feelings are kept under wraps, so to speak. Conflict takes the form of frustrating the other or dropping subtle remarks designed to belittle. A wife, for example, may develop a pattern of cooking food the husband does not like, she may neglect the home, she may make unfair comparisons between her husband and others who are perhaps more successful in occupation or profession.

In overt conflict the difficulty is out in the open, there is no attempt to deny the problem by either of the marital partners. One form of overt conflict may be acute conflict in which tension builds up over a period of time and then bursts forth when neither of the partners can contain it. Sometimes in patterns of acute conflict a particular problem subsides, but as new problems appear tension mounts and acute conflict may again be imminent.

When the basic marital difficulties are not resolved we may have chronic conflict; it is recurrent. There may be temporary solutions but little is resolved. The feud goes on with nagging and belittling. Chronic conflict often emerges into progressive conflict. In progressive

[2] *Ibid.*, pp. 298, 306–307.
[3] *Ibid.*, pp. 296–298. Joseph K. Folsom, *The Family and Democratic Society,* John Wiley and Sons, New York, 1943, Ch. 13. Ernest R. Groves and William F. Ogburn, *American Marriage and Family Relationships*, Henry Holt and Co., New York, 1928, pp. 85–87.

conflict the marriage continues to deteriorate, and each new problem is added to the unresolved problems of the past. Progressive conflict can develop into habitual conflict—a point where the couple cannot, or will not, agree. The toll on the mental health of the marital partners in habitual conflict is perhaps greater than in any other form of conflict, since it is often characterized by a high degree of tension with much berating.[4] The marital partners become increasingly hopeless and demoralized.

Inner Dynamics of Conflict. Thus far our analysis has been limited to the outer dimensions of marital conflict. More important, and of greater concern for us in the present treatment, are the inner dynamics of marital conflict; that is, what actually goes on between the marital partners during conflict.

The inner dynamics in any marriage are not haphazard but are to a large extent a function of how the couple, with their individual personalities, have come to relate to each other. Each couple during courtship and on into the formative period in their marriage come to understand the way they can best deal with one another. This learning process in each marriage involves a type of verbal sparring, some of this is conscious but a good deal of it is unconscious. The term sparring generally applied to boxing is defined by Webster as "skirmishing for advantage." The function of such verbal sparring in a marriage is to see what the opponent is like, what the points of vulnerability and sensitivity are, what kinds of statements bring what types of reactions.

Thus, a husband married to a woman who is insecure about her educational background may attempt to intimidate her with ideas he obtained from school in order to win an argument. He senses her vulnerability here and tries to take advantage of the situation. If his plan works, he now has a plan for subsequent marital difficulties.

Thus, a strategy for dealing with one another develops; such strategies are important in understanding how conflict is resolved in any particular marriage.

Strategies. One such strategy in marital conflict is the throwing out of "feelers or trial balloons" to see what responses will occur, then plotting further strategy from there. A husband, for example, may wish to join a country club in order to play golf but he knows that his wife does not approve of his golf playing. In his discussions with his wife he may talk in vague generalities about people whom his

[4] Waller and Hill, *op. cit.*, p. 306.

wife thinks highly of, who also happen to be members of the club. The subject of golf, which is the most important element in the conversation, may not even be introduced. His main concern is to observe his wife's response. Thus, after each comment the husband makes, he waits for a reaction from his wife for these reactions give him his cues as to which strategies to employ.

A second strategy in marital conflict is the introduction of behaviors designed to engender guilt in order to control the behavior of the marital partner. There was the case of a married woman who, whenever faced with marital conflict, presented herself to her husband as a sweet, innocent, misunderstood, and helpless female. By presenting herself in this way, she aroused such guilt in her husband about fears that he could be mistreating her, that usually he abandoned his own wishes and gave in to hers.

A third strategy in marital conflict is to "needle" the partner. This is accomplished by presenting what seem to be compliments which on reflection turn out to be insults. The purpose of the "needle" is both to berate for the purpose of berating, that is, to hurt the marital partner, and also to undermine the self-confidence of the marital partner in order that he will abandon his views.

There was a married man who, when in conflict with his wife, had a habit of comparing her with other wives. He would always select a person with virtues, a hard worker, or a devoted wife. These attributes he would praise. The women he selected for comparison also possessed some obvious limitation, such as being known for poor judgment, or a tendency to gossip, or homeliness. This man's wife would at first feel complimented but on further reflection sense the invidious comparison. She was sensitive enough so that her confidence was indeed undermined. As a result she withdrew from the conflict and would give in to her husband.

These are not the only strategies employed in marital conflict. Sometimes flirtatious behavior at social gatherings may be employed in order to make the marital partner jealous and insecure so that he will become more agreeable. At other times temper tantrums are employed as strategies; sexual unresponsiveness may also appear.

Consequences of Strategies. The first consequence of the strategies we have discussed is that they tend to result in a marked complication and confusion about the real issues in marital conflict. This is to say that the marital partners may become so confused that they do not really know what the real issues are. Indeed, the basic points of disagreement and the strategies employed in dealing with the conflict become so intertwined, involved, and complicated that many married people do in fact become hopelessly bogged down because they do not know what their basic marital problems are.

A second consequence of the use of strategies in marital conflict has to do with their direct impact on the members of the marriage. Strategy diverts energies into deviant and non-constructive channels. Each partner involved in strategies expends a considerable amount of energy in planning strategy; energy which perhaps could be more profitably employed in a more straightforward and constructive approach to the marital conflict.

Although strategies to some extent characterize almost any marriage, there are relationships in which one member employs strategies much more than the other. Such marriages pose interesting problems in terms of which partner is in control of conflict situations. At first glance there is some reason to suspect that the partner who relies heavily on strategy frequently controls the relationship. Nevertheless, there is a price involved. Like all people who have to rely on strategies, there is often a basic insecurity and tenuous feeling about the control. This creates not only anxiety but the need for additional strategies to cope with the anxiety. Thus, the price of control would appear to be high in terms of psychic energy. The member of the marriage who uses fewer strategies can also at times control conflict by simply being aware of the strategies of the other marital partner. However, such an awareness may at times also usher in counter strategies. Regardless of who controls conflict, both partners pay a price since they have to be on guard in their dealings with one another and cannot relate to one another with their true feelings.

A third consequence of strategies for the marital relationship has to do with their resistance to change. The strategies employed in conflict over a time become an integral part of the personality; thus the strategies themselves become important. By importance in this sense we refer to the feeling of pride and significance which the person derives from employing them. One may come to feel, for example, that the powers of strategy and manipulation are clever, subtle, deceptive; the strategies give to the person a feeling of mastery over others. There are some persons who enjoy creating marital conflict in order that they have an opportunity to employ strategies. Indeed, some marriages are held together primarily because each partner finds the use of strategies an exciting diversion. In such marriages the pride which surrounds strategies is more important than the actual issue in the conflict. Finally, we must add that being proud of the strategy not only complicates conflict, as indicated earlier, but makes the resolution of marital conflict excessively difficult.

RESISTANCES WHICH INTERFERE WITH RESOLUTION OF CONFLICT. Thus far we have presented to the reader a general discussion regarding the nature of marital conflict, including its exterior forms, the internal dynamics in the form of strategies, and the resultant complications. There is still another important dimension of marital conflict with which we have to deal. We refer here to particular tendencies which keep people from recognizing their conflicts and dealing with them effectively; we regard these tendencies as resistances and we deem them important enough to warrant special attention.

Not Accepting the Existence of a Problem. One major resistance which interferes with a couple's abilities to handle their marital conflicts is their reluctance to admit that a marital problem exists.[5] Although such admission sounds simple enough, there is resistance on the part of one or both members of a marriage to admit to themselves and to each other that all is not well, even when obvious signs of difficulty are present. Almost all counselors have at one time or another encountered the husband or wife who appeared for help—not because they felt any need but only to satisfy their mate.[6] These kinds of people are very difficult to work with since they find it necessary to provide a façade of marital well-being.

Furthermore, there are well-developed ways of thinking which block out a couple's awareness about themselves and their marital problems. For example, there are those people with marital difficulties who state that since all couples have problems there is little that is different or unusual about any incompatibility which they might possess. To be sure, to have marital problems is to be like other married people; problems are inherent in living. What is important here, however, is the manner in which this point of view is employed. The danger is that such a philosophy is employed to rationalize doing nothing about one's marital problems. The logic goes something like this: all couples have some marital difficulty, we also have marital difficulty, therefore we are like others. This means that since the couple believe that they are like other couples there is really nothing to be concerned about. If one shifts this same analysis to questions of physical illness, however, the logic would no longer hold. If the

[5] Paul H. Landis, *Making the Most of Marriage*, 2nd ed., Appleton-Century-Crofts, Inc., New York, 1960, p. 643.

[6] For a discussion of this point and also of the motives behind decisions to consult an analyst, see: Lawrence S. Kubie, "Psychoanalysis and Marriage," in Victor W. Eisenstein's *Neurotic Interaction in Marriage*, Basic Books, Inc., New York, 1956, pp. 10–43, especially pp. 32–33.

THE GIRLS   By Franklin Folger

"There's nonsense for you, Henry — 'the American
housewife spends so much time watching television
she's completely unaware of her husband's presence.' "

Figure 7. Courtesy Franklin Folger and the Sun-Times–Daily News Syndicate
(June 7, 1961).

average couple in our society suffered from tuberculosis, few couples
would feel comfortable about the thought that they were like other
couples in this regard. Instead, they would try to remedy the condition
as early as possible. Since, however, many people view only medical
problems as worthy of time and consideration, problems in interpersonal relationships are persistently avoided and rationalized as being
unimportant. It is clear that unless a couple can overcome the resistance involved in accepting that all is not well with their marriage
little can be done to bring about change.

The Lack of Communication. A second area of resistance which interferes with the handling of marital problems results from an inability to communicate problems, resentments, and feelings. In the most positive sense communication between the marital partners enables feelings, resentments, and hostilities to come out into the open. Ideas, distorted or otherwise, when brought into the open may be tested by reality. Some problems can be avoided and many can be resolved when the lines of communication between husband and wife are kept open; there is much that is positive and therapeutic in this. A breakdown in communication negates these possibilities; and the greater the breakdown in communication, the greater the likelihood that people will distort, imagine, and twist grievances, since it is so easy for the imagination to run off in all directions when a basis for testing reality in interaction is not present. It should be pointed out that regardless of the therapeutic values involved, there is considerable resistance to communication; instead there are patterns among people which restrict the communication of marital grievances.

One such instance is found in the pattern of hopelessness, a pattern which some people use in dealing with their marital problems. They accept marital difficulty as part of fate, this is what life has "dished out." Thus, they believe that there is little that they can do in order to change things, so it makes little sense to complain about grievances.[7]

Consider this example of a married woman whose husband was an alcoholic. He usually built up to his drinking sprees slowly, but once started they would last for about a week, climaxed by some kind of violence that necessitated imprisonment. During one of these sprees the husband came home, beat his wife, and knocked out her upper front teeth. Since such drinking and violence in some form had characterized their marital life, the woman's friends encouraged her to go to a marriage counselor. She resented the idea and became angry at her friends. Finally, she consented, but came to the counselor in a very hostile and defensive mood. Her attitude was one of defending her husband, she was certain that the counselor wanted to break up her home; and in one moment of stress she blurted out, "He only knocked out my uppers, he did leave the lowers."

This was a woman who was quite hopeless about the possibility of change and who was therefore willing to put up with considerable abuse. More important, she was not only hopeless about making her life a happier one, but by avoiding professional assistance she also sentenced her husband to a life of gradual deterioration.

A second instance of a pattern which limits the communication of

---

[7] Francis E. Merrill, *Courtship and Marriage*, Henry Holt and Co., New York, 1959, p. 380.

marital grievance is found in the person who is fearful of the conflict and hostility which may emerge if there are complaints about dissatisfactions. These people have great difficulty in handling situations in which conflict is involved. At such times they usually become anxious and upset. They will go to great lengths to avoid conflict even when this means withholding marital grievances from their spouses. These are often people who are self-effacing, afraid to assert themselves, or to stand up against abuse and mistreatment. In order to avoid anxiety and conflict, some of these people are even prone to minimize the importance of their dissatisfaction and over a period of time may reach the conclusion that they attached too much significance to their grievances.

Thus, there are individuals who appear for professional assistance in their marriages and talk quite openly and readily about their problems. However, when they sense that a resolution for their difficulties may involve conflict and the confrontation of their spouse on particular issues they often become passive. At this point they will frequently terminate their counseling and indicate that they had perhaps exaggerated the seriousness of their difficulties.

A third instance of a pattern which limits communication of marital grievances is found in people who refrain from complaining because they are insecure about their marriage. These people believe that any expression of dissatisfaction with the marriage will produce rejection by the other partner, resulting in the termination of the marriage. Thus, they prefer to hold on, no matter how bad things are rather than run the risk of losing the marriage.

Fourth and finally, we have the person who has learned that there is value to holding onto a grievance until it can be used strategically against the marital partner at some opportune time.[8] Thus, grievances can be built up as ammunition to be used in an argument to attack the marital partner. These grievances may also be held back and employed later to justify demands for material possessions or favors from the marital partner.

Here then we have several instances of patterns which keep people from communicating their problems. They constitute serious resistances to the solution of marital difficulties, and as such must be dealt with if solutions to marital problems are to be reached.

Dealing with Symptoms Rather than Causes. A third major resistance which interferes with a couple's abilities to handle marital

---

[8] For a discussion of the self-pitying individual and the use of marital grievance, see: F. Alexander Magoun, *Love and Marriage*, Harper and Brothers, New York, 1948, p. 251.

conflicts is the tendency of couples to deal with superficial aspects of their marital problems: thus little is resolved. There are, to be sure, many reasons for this tendency. In some instances a problem may have many facets and thus only certain parts are seen. In other instances individuals may be genuinely ignorant or unaware of the real issues involved.[9] In a great many instances, however, there is something far more serious at work. We refer here to an unconscious tendency to substitute a superficial problem for the basic problem. This tendency is present since frequently the real or basic problem or problems may be painful or difficult to face. Counselors readily report that the problems which couples present are seldom the basic difficulties, and that an important aspect of counseling has to do with bringing into focus the real issues so that these may be dealt with effectively. The particular superficial problem employed will vary with a couple or with an individual. Often people who have dabbled in psychological literature, and have encountered the belief that sexual problems are at the root of all difficulty, will assume that their marital difficulties are rooted in sex, when indeed they may not necessarily be.[10] When such people come for counseling they may discuss sexual difficulties, giving the impression to the counselor that they are presenting significant information about their marriage. One of the authors has encountered in counseling many people who were perfectly willing to talk about sexual problems, but who were quite unwilling to discuss, let us say, the way they maneuver their mates.

For very conventional people, on the other hand, something like a sexual problem might be covered up with something more socially acceptable, such as an economic problem.[11] This tendency may be illustrated with the case of a very conventional middle-aged couple who appeared for counseling complaining about conflicts concerning economic matters. In talking to the couple about their marriage they reported that in general, aside from money squabbles, all was well. They refused to accept the possibility that other problems could be present. Nevertheless, the counselor's impression was different. It was difficult for him to believe that a seemingly intelligent couple could not solve a budgetary problem unless there were underlying involve-

[9] Emily H. Mudd and Malcolm G. Preston, "The Contemporary Status of Marriage Counseling," *Annals of the American Academy of Political and Social Science*, **272** (Nov., 1950), pp. 102–109.

[10] One study indicated that financial problems are often the focus in marital disagreements but not usually the cause of such difficulty. Lewis M. Terman, et al., *Psychological Factors in Marital Happiness*, McGraw-Hill Book Co., New York, 1938, p. 169.

[11] *Ibid.*

ments which had not been brought out. Over a period of time the underlying complications were revealed. The husband reported that for a considerable period of time he had been dissatisfied with the frequency of sexual relations but that his wife was quite unsympathetic about this. At this point in the marital history we discover that the husband started to nag and to complain to his wife about the amount of money she was spending. The wife in turn resented her husband's behavior and arguments would ensue. When these patterns were brought out into the open, the question of a sexual interpretation was raised for the first time by the wife, who wondered whether her husband's concern about how much money she spent was really an attempt to get back at her for his sexual frustration. At that point, however, the wife herself rejected such an interpretation and the husband could see little validity to it. Over a period of time the significance of the wife's interpretation emerged. The problem was sexual in nature but not exclusively so. For there were feelings of personal rejection on the part of the husband who was already insecure. Whenever he felt rejected by his wife, who was herself an emotionally aloof person, he would become vindictive; he would try to get back. In this particular marriage the husband's attempt to get back at his wife took the form of controlling the wife's spending habits; in other marriages a mate's vindictiveness might have another outlet.

The case we have just described is significant since it illustrates several important points. The tendency to deal with the superficial aspects of a problem is frustrating and self-defeating. The people in our example could never arrive at a satisfactory solution to their problem by simply making budgetary arrangements, and yet their conventional outlook enabled them to see only an economic problem. Furthermore, by dealing with a superficial dimension of their difficulty their frustration increased since it exposed them to the same problem, or similar ones, with the likelihood that eventually they might become quite hopeless about reaching any sort of a solution.

Avoidance of Responsibility. A fourth major resistance which interferes with a couple's abilities to handle marital difficulty is the tendency to avoid responsibility for one's part in the difficulty. We hear a great deal about the need to be objective and to see all sides of a question, but often such advice, although well intended, represents an oversimplification and does not come to grips with those forces which keep people from assuming responsibility for what they do or for what they believe. There are several aspects to the problem of avoidance of responsibility. Nevertheless, an essential component found in all such people is a fear of accepting unfavorable notions about themselves. To accept patterns which may enable one to change and grow is, of course, a positive step. For many perfectionistic people, however, to accept responsibility for their part in a difficulty means to realize that they have not handled their lives with perfection; this makes them very vulnerable to self-hate and self-berating, which upsets them greatly. In order to avoid these possibilities of attack on self, such people are really fearful, and understandably so, about admitting their responsibility in the problems of marriage.

An interesting illustration of this point concerns a young wife who had become involved with other men. Although extramarital sexual relations had never occurred, they might easily have. The marriage had deteriorated to a point where the husband saw no point in continuing the relationship unless both of them were willing to get professional assistance. But the wife stated that she could never go to a counselor since this would entail admitting and accepting some responsibility. She stated, "I simply couldn't stand admitting I was wrong."

Overintellectualization. A fifth resistance to overcome is the tendency for couples to deal with their problems at the level of thinking only, without regard for underlying feelings. People are often told to discuss rather than to argue, to be objective rather than subjective. This is not bad advice but it often misses the point. Certainly we can say that it is better to discuss than to argue, since in the argument you are out to win, regardless of tactics and you are not really after a resolution. Advising a couple to discuss and to be objective does not go far enough, however, and is therefore likely to be unrewarding. Many couples who wish to resolve their difficulties sit down with a list of clichés in anticipation that by maintaining a reasonable, objective attitude, no problem will be insurmountable.[12] In reality, however, the most rewarding way to deal with marital difficulties is to try to come to grips not only with the reasonable and objective remarks which people make but also with those underlying attitudes and values of which people frequently are not aware. It is unlikely that anything which is only verbal or intellectual will bring about lasting change. But when people can emotionally integrate new views, their behavior changes. (Our distinction between intellectual and intellectual-emotional commitments discussed earlier in this book developed this point of view.)

[12] One author calls this discussion without communication. Henry A. Bowman, *Marriage for Moderns,* McGraw-Hill Book Co., New York, 1960, p. 317.

RESOLUTIONS. It is apparent that resistances have to be over-come if marital difficulties are to be resolved. Whenever a couple can overcome the resistances which keep them from dealing with their marital difficulties they have certainly not resolved their problems, but they have taken an important step toward the solution of their problems. These resistances obscure difficulties and hinder solutions: resistance keeps people from admitting that anything is wrong; for those who can feel that something is wrong there may be a fear about communicating; for those who communicate, there may be avoidance of responsibilities for the problem. Only when all these resistances are worked through can there be much hope of satisfactorily resolving marital conflicts. When resistances are removed then it is possible for a couple to develop some comprehension about the underlying attitudes and feelings which lurk beneath the surface remarks that they make about their problems. These hidden feelings and attitudes are the real indicators of our motivations and go to the heart of the issues. If, in the course of a discussion about a marital problem, a couple can capture the real indicators of thinking and feeling, they can, indeed, do much about their problems. The following dispute between a husband and wife about her mother is a case in point.

Husband: Whatever you may think, I have a lot of respect for women.-
Wife: I hope that's the way you feel.
Husband: Yes, you know that's the way I feel; I give them every con-sideration at the office and at home.
Wife: Why do you react to my mother as you do?
Husband: Your mother, well that's different. She's a woman, that's right, but she's also a mother-in-law; and that's something you don't fully under-stand. A mother-in-law is a special case.
Wife: Well, doesn't the idea of respect apply to her?
Husband: Yes, it does and it doesn't. It depends; now sometimes your mother is as sweet as can be; she keeps quiet and never says anything. You never know she's there. I respect her then.
Wife: You mean when she doesn't disagree, you respect her?

In the illustration we have just presented, part of a lengthy discus-sion between husband and wife, several interesting aspects were re-vealed. First, it should be noted that regardless of what this man says, his respect for women is conditional. By that we mean that respect depends on whether women threaten him or not. It is also clear, there-fore, that he can be quite inconsistent in his attitudes toward women; he behaves different ways at different times. What might be quite beneficial for this husband would be the realization that he may be-lieve things other than what he states. Indeed, some of his beliefs may be contradictory and inconsistent. The realization that he believes equally opposite things might enable him to understand some of his difficulties in relation to women, as well as his mother-in-law.

There is no intent to convey the idea that the resolution of marital conflict can be achieved through any single or simple technique. A good deal of our analysis in this book runs counter to such an idea. On the other hand, if one can assume that many of the marital conflicts that we have are the result of conflicting personal views which are neither readily known to the marital partners nor easily observable, then the ability to capture the underlying impact of marital discussions makes it possible for many couples to be of considerable assistance to each other in resolving some of their marital difficulties.

The capacity to come to grips with marital conflict through an understanding of the deeper levels of personality of the partners is perhaps one of the most essential attributes if a marriage is to develop and grow.

SUMMARY

Marital conflict is not necessarily undesirable or destructive. Indeed, when the focus of the conflict does not involve an attack on the self-worth of the marriage partner, conflict can, and frequently does, serve some useful purposes in marriage. Conflict can, for example, (1) lead to a redefinition of the marital difficulty, (2) help the partners to develop a realistic understanding of one another, and (3) help them to appreciate the extent of their positive emotional commitments to the marriage.

The exterior forms of marital conflict, such as concealed, overt, acute, chronic, progressive, and habitual conflict, as well as the inner dynamics of marital conflict, were defined and discussed. In regard to the latter, it was noted, for example, that when marital conflict involves the use of certain conflict strategies, such as the "feeler" strategy, the "needle" strategy, and those strategies designed to create feelings of guilt in the partner, it is least likely to serve a useful purpose in marriage. Also involved in those patterns of inner dynamics which keep people from dealing effectively with conflict are what were referred to as resistances. Resistances consist of patterns of thinking and behaving which are illustrated by the following: (1) not accepting the existence of a problem; (2) lack of communication, (3) dealing with symptoms rather than causes, (4) avoidance of responsibility, and (5) overintellectualization.

It was suggested that an understanding of these inner dynamics of marital conflict, as well as an understanding of conflict itself, can do much to facilitate the resolution of marital conflict.

QUESTIONS

1. List and describe three useful purposes which marital conflict can serve. When is marital conflict most unrewarding and damaging to a marriage?
2. Define and give an example of each of the following forms of marital conflict: overt, concealed, acute, chronic, progressive, and habitual conflict.
3. What is a strategy as it pertains to marital conflict? List and discuss the consequences of the use of strategies in marital conflict.
4. What is a resistance as it pertains to marital conflict? List and discuss the five major resistances discussed in this chapter.
5. List and discuss the patterns which impair communication of marital grievances.
6. Under what circumstances do you believe that couples can solve their marital conflicts without professional assistance? Under what circumstances do you feel that professional assistance is necessary? Discuss in full.

PROJECTS

1. Write, and have members of the class enact, a two part skit depicting a couple involved in a marital conflict. In the first part bring out as many of the factors as possible which impair the resolution of conflict, as discussed in this chapter; for example, an attack on the personal worth of the partner, the use of strategies, and the presence of resistances. In the second part of the skit show how these impairments might be avoided and the conflict resolved. Have the class as a whole discuss the skit.
2. Write two brief case histories involving marital conflict. For your first history use a case which involves marital conflict which you think was successfully solved; for your second history use a case involving marital conflict which you regard as unsolved. Analyze each case in terms of the discussion found in this chapter.

SUGGESTED READINGS

Benson, Purnell, "The Interests of Happily Married Couples," *Marriage and Family Living*, **14** (Nov., 1952), pp. 276–280.

Bowman, Henry A., *Marriage for Moderns*, McGraw-Hill Book Co., Inc., New York, 1960, 4th ed., Ch. 10, "Adjustment in Marriage."

Duvall, Evelyn M., and Reuben Hill, *Being Married*, D. C. Heath and Co., Boston, 1960, Ch. 14, "Coping with Conflict," and Ch. 15, "Facing Crises."

Kenkel, William F., *The Family in Perspective*, Appleton-Century-Crofts, Inc., New York, 1960, Ch. 15, "Developmental Tasks of the Married Pair."

Landis, Paul H., *Making the Most of Marriage*, Appleton-Century-Crofts, Inc., New York, 2nd ed., 1960, Ch. 21, "Marriage Adjustment," Ch. 22, "Patterns of Adjustment," Ch. 23, "The Issues of Marriage: Happiness and Unhappiness."

Simpson, George, *People in Families*, Thomas Y. Crowell Co., New York, 1960, Ch. 11, "Marital Accommodation and Discord."

Parenthood

Throughout this book we have stressed the significance of a meaningful relationship in marriage. In this regard we have pointed out not only how such a marriage may be nurtured but how it may be maintained. It should be clear that the quality of the marital relationship which a couple have established is intimately related to questions regarding parenthood. In this chapter we will deal with several topics which relate to parenthood, including motivations for parenthood, family planning, the emotional climate necessary for successful parenthood, the conditions of parenthood in America today, and finally some factors which affect our roles as parents.

Parenthood is highly valued in the American society. Pity for those who are unable to have children and the setting aside of special days to honor mothers and fathers are but a few of the indications of the importance accorded parenthood. The majority of people entering marriage desire to have children; few enter marriage expecting to have no children. Some married couples plan to have children early in their marriage while others plan to postpone parenthood. Few couples, however, are fully aware of the factors which can disrupt their plans. For example, couples who engage in sexual relations with some frequency and regularity must face the fact that a pregnancy can occur earlier than they anticipate.

UNANTICIPATED EARLY PREGNANCY. Some couples have such complete confidence in methods of child spacing that they fail to realize the limitations of such control, natural or mechanical. In this respect it is important to emphasize that in spite of widespread use of birth control, unplanned pregnancies in marriage do occur. And of all periods in marriage unplanned pregnancies are perhaps more likely to occur during the early period than at a later time due to the probability of high intensity of sex desire, the probability of high fertility, and the probability of inadequate knowledge of child spacing and of birth control techniques on the part of the couple during this period. It was found, for example, that in one group of college marriages in which birth control techniques were used, two-thirds of the pregnancies were unplanned.[1] One-third of the unplanned pregnancies (or half) were admittedly due to carelessness on the part of the couple in their use of the technique; but in the remainder of unplanned pregnancies the couples were unable to explain the occurrence. Consequently, young married couples, regardless of their desire to have an early pregnancy, should at all times be prepared emotionally to accept this situation. There are those couples, for example, who make elaborate plans for the initial years of married life, prior to parenthood. Such plans must always be made with the realization that pregnancy may not always be controllable. When such couples fail to accept emotionally the possibility of parenthood, the disruption to their lives and to that of the child can be serious indeed. For at best the anticipated introduction of a child into the family milieu necessitates a basic reorientation of the couple's way of life. Thus, when a pregnancy occurs before the marital partners are willing to accept it, they suffer, and the infant finds himself in a disturbed family atmosphere.

Although we have stressed the fact that marriage partners must prepare themselves for an early pregnancy, it is perhaps equally important that they give some consideration to the possibility that they may never be able to have children, and to the resolution of whatever problems they might have in regard to the acceptance of this possibility.

CHILDLESS MARRIAGES. With all of the attention which is given to the topic of avoiding pregnancy, the fact that some couples attempt again and again to effect pregnancy is frequently overlooked. Throughout the world, for example, 10 to 15 percent of all marriages are childless.[2] In the U.S. approximately 9 percent of the marriages in

---

[1] Shirley Poffenberger, Thomas Poffenberger, and Judson T. Landis, "Intent toward Conception and the Pregnancy Experience," *Am. Soc. Rev.*, **17** (Oct., 1952), pp. 616–620.

[2] See: Abraham Stone, "World Conference on Human Infertility," *Marriage and Family Living*, **15** (Aug., 1953), pp. 231–233.

rural areas are childless and 17 percent of urban marriages. Admittedly, we do not know exactly what percentage of these marriages are childless by desire; but we do know that at least some of these marriages are childless in spite of attempts on the part of the couples to have children. Young couples should, therefore, be prepared to face the possibility of a barren marriage; and certainly some attempt should be made to assess the attitudes of each toward the possibility that a pregnancy may never take place. For many, barrenness is extremely difficult to accept. In some instances the attitudes and behavior of parents and in-laws become an important aspect of the problem, as in this example of an involuntarily childless couple: the parents of the wife were certain that the inability to have children was due to some deficiency on the part of the husband; they reasoned that they, the wife's parents, had no problem having children, and, therefore, why should their daughter. In the same case the husband's mother, using the same reasoning, assured her son that the sterility was not his but his wife's. When this occurs and the desire for children is strong enough, it is possible for the husband and wife to begin to blame each other for their childlessness. Thus, the relationship may become disturbed.

Certainly if either partner has knowledge of his or her sterility, withholding this information can be potentially damaging to the relationship, as it was for one woman who married late in life at the insistence of her mother who was fearful that the woman would become "an old maid." Although the woman had known that she would be unable to bear children, her mother insisted that this not be revealed to the prospective husband since it might bring about a change in his attitude. The woman complied and said nothing to her prospective husband. After several years of trying to have children, the husband insisted on a medical examination for each. At this point the woman revealed the fact that she could not have children. The husband became furious, accused his wife of being a liar, threatened divorce, and was on the verge of initiating proceedings. The family and friends prevailed on him to reconsider his decision. Although he has remained married, he has never forgiven his wife for withholding this important information, nor has his wife forgiven him for his hostile attitude toward her.

Whenever there is suspicion that a couple are unable to have children, it is probably best to consult a physician as early as possible. If, after proper examination and treatment, a pregnancy seems unlikely, then the couple might decide whether they wish to accept their childlessness or whether they would prefer to try to adopt a child. Adopting a child is, of course, a serious undertaking, and should, therefore, be considered carefully by the couple before being attempted. In considering adoption, the couple will recognize that due to the limited number of children and the strict requirements made by legally sanctioned agencies, adoption is not always possible. In the event that a couple are unable to adopt a child it then becomes necessary for them to accept their childlessness and to set out to maturely build their relationship on bases other than parenthood.

FAMILY PLANNING. For the majority of couples, however, plans for child spacing will be feasible and practical; for such couples, consideration will undoubtedly be given to the advantage of either having a baby during the first year of marriage or delaying the first pregnancy until sometime later in marriage.

In regard to these two possibilities, opinions differ. Some authorities claim that early pregnancy may have adverse effects on a young marriage. Such authorities believe that the adjustments which husband and wife have to make to one another are more readily achieved without the additional complications imposed by parenthood. There is some evidence that having a child during the first year of marriage does make the early period of marriage unnecessarily difficult and according to Christensen[3] interferes somewhat with the happiness of the couple. Furthermore, early pregnancy may detract from the spouses' initial adaptation to their marital roles; this detraction may create difficulties especially in those cases where young couples do not recognize and are not yet prepared to accept the responsibilities which pregnancy and parenthood involve.

Not all authorities view early pregnancy unfavorably, however. In fact it is strongly favored by some. Mace,[4] for example, along with the authors, suggests that postponing pregnancy is associated with certain risks since the likelihood of infertility increases with age; thus prolonged postponement may ultimately make pregnancy impossible. Further suggestions have been made to the effect that the tendency for physical complications arising from pregnancy increases with the age of the mother. (See Dr. Lehfeldt's discussion in Appendix A.)

Indeed, because of the likelihood of a minimum number of medical complications present for the woman when births occur at younger ages, many gynecologists have even abandoned the previously held

[3] Harold T. Christensen and Hanna H. Meissner, "Studies in Child Spacing: III—Premarital Pregnancy as a Factor in Divorce," *Am. Soc. Rev.,* **18** (Dec., 1953), pp. 641–644.

[4] David R. Mace, "Should You Have a Baby the First Year?" *Woman's Home Companion,* **76** (Dec., 1949).

notion that children should be spaced at least two years apart; they now suggest that in order to get the childbearing period over earlier, pregnancy can occur at more frequent intervals depending on the general health of the woman involved.[5] It may well be that such advice is being followed; as Table 14 indicates, there has been a drop in the median age of women at first births.

TABLE 14

Median Age of Mother at First Live Birth, United States, 1940–1958 *

Year	Median Age
1940	23.0
1950	22.7
1957	21.9
1958	21.8

* Abstracted from Vital Statistics of the United States, 1958, Vol. 1, Washington, D.C., U.S. Government Printing Office, 1960, pp. 3–20, Table 3K.

VOLUNTARY CHILDLESSNESS. Finally, we must recognize that there are some marriages in which one or both persons do not desire a child at any time in their marriage. Some men, for example, are so opposed to becoming fathers that they refuse to accept the reality of pregnancy when it occurs in their marriages; and in so doing they may withhold the emotional support necessary to women during pregnancy. These men, when confronted with the physical signs of pregnancy during its later stages, may refuse to be seen publicly with their wives, thus making the entire period of pregnancy an unwholesome and grotesque thing.[6]

Some of the reasons given for not wanting a child are: it limits freedom, it ruins the figures of women, and, in general, the rewards are not commensurate with the efforts involved. Some women remain childless because there is an extreme fear of pregnancy and childbearing. Read points out that the fear of childbirth is not surprising in view of the fear-ridden and unwholesome attitudes which society has toward it. In fact, he goes further and states that much of the physical pain of childbirth is actually rooted in fears created by society. He describes the process by which this occurs as a fear-ten-

[5] Paul H. Landis, *Making the Most of Marriage*, 2nd ed., Appleton-Century-Crofts, Inc., New York, 1960, p. 504.

[6] F. Alexander Magoun, *Love and Marriage*, Harper and Brothers, New York, 1948, p. 291.

sion-pain syndrome. Thus, fear causes physical tension which in turn is largely responsible for unnecessary pain during childbirth.[7]

Other authorities believe that while many people think that their motives for avoiding parenthood are simply financial or are based on fears of childbirth, they are really motivated by deeper psychic processes. These authorities claim, for example, that a woman who identifies with an unhappy mother, might, in attempting to avoid parenthood, really be attempting to reject her femininity. In other words, parenthood for some may become symbolic of conflicts which that person is not prepared to deal with.[8] Certainly a couple should try to understand their motivations for avoiding parenthood, just as it is useful to understand one's motivations for parenthood. Having said this, it should also be clear that there are many couples who refuse to have children for other kinds of reasons. There are some persons who have decided to pursue careers and have rationally examined the alternatives of having or not having children. Such people believe that since their career pursuits are so important and time-consuming, any children they might have would not have the proper home environment. Furthermore, there are also those persons whose marriages are so unstable that they question the wisdom of having children—at least until the conditions causing the marital difficulties are alleviated. Thus, the decision to remain childless can be a very proper and sensible adjustment to one's life circumstances.

Although the decision to remain childless may not be indicative of deeper emotional involvements, it should be pointed out that the research available in this area indicates that the absence of desire to have children is associated with marital unhappiness.[9] Thus, marriages in which children are desired, whether they appear or not, have a greater chance of success than do those in which there is no desire for children, as noted in Table 15. The reason for this association

[7] Grantly Dick Read, *Childbirth without Fear,* Harper and Brothers, New York, rev. ed., 1953.

[8] For an extensive discussion of psychogenic sterility and case histories, see: George Simpson, *People in Families,* Thomas Y. Crowell Co., New York, 1960, pp. 420–426.

[9] Robert B. Reed, "Social and Psychological Factors Affecting Fertility. VII: The Interrelationship of Marital Adjustment, Fertility Control, and Size of Family," *Milbank Memorial Fund Quarterly,* **25** (Oct., 1947), pp. 383–425. Another finding which may reflect the importance of being able to control the size of family is that of Christensen and Philbrick, it states that marriage happiness tends to decrease with an increase in family size. Harold T. Christensen and Robert E. Philbrick, "Family Size as a Factor in the Marital Adjustment of College Couples," *Am. Soc. Rev.,* **17** (June, 1952), pp. 306–312. See also: Ernest W. Burgess and Leonard S. Cottrell, *Predicting Success or Failure in Marriage,* Prentice-Hall, Inc., Englewood Cliffs, New Jersey, 1939, p. 414.

between the desire to remain childless and unhappiness in marriage is not altogether clear; but it has been suggested that the desire to remain childless may be indicative of an emotionally immature personality, which, in general, has difficulty adjusting to the demands of marriage. Thus, it may be that the personal immaturities are the factors responsible for both the unhappiness which occurs, and the lack of desire to have children. Under these conditions, these might be the very individuals who are least capable of being effective parents.[10]

TABLE 15

Desire for Children and Marital Adjustment *

	Poor	Fair	Good
No children present but children desired	9%	27%	64%
One or more children present and desired	20	33	47
No children present and none desired †	55	24	21
One or more children present but none desired †	67	22	11

* Adapted from Burgess and Cottrell, *Predicting Success or Failure in Marriage,* Prentice-Hall, Englewood Cliffs, New Jersey, 1939, p. 414.
† Not desired by husband or wife or both.

Indeed, Magoun [11] states that when an unwanted child appears in a marriage, in addition to adding to the emotional confusion which already may be present in the marriage, one of two things is likely to happen. Either the child is rejected by loading him with feelings of humiliation, inferiority, helplessness, stupidity, unattractiveness, guilt, and fear, or the parent becomes over-solicitous, hating the child with all his "love." The falseness of such love, says Magoun, is betrayed by a series of traumatic inconsistencies such as exaggerated expressions of affection followed by acts like forgetting the little one's birthday. Magoun claims that children are not spoiled by too much love, but they are spoiled by a false love.

Having considered childless marriages and the motivations behind them, let us now consider the motivations which often underlie the desire for parenthood.

MOTIVATIONS FOR PARENTHOOD. The fact that a person desires to become a parent does not in itself insure adequacy in parent-

[10] Paul Wallin and Howard M. Vollmer, "Marital Happiness of Parents and Their Children's Attitudes To Them," *Am. Soc. Rev.,* 18 (Aug., 1953), pp. 424–431.

[11] F. Alexander Magoun, *op. cit.,* pp. 289–290.

hood. Instead, this latter objective will be accomplished only when the motivation for parenthood is mature, when the marriage itself is sound, and when the prospective parents are mature and integrated people. In regard to motivations it is evident that some motivations for parenthood are mature and others immature. Immature motives for parenthood are present when the child is used to aid the parent in the resolution of a personal difficulty such as loneliness, or as a source of fulfillment for frustrated personal wishes. Under such circumstances restrictions on the child's capacity and direction of growth are pronounced since the child must always fit into parental needs and requirements, irrespective of what may ultimately be in the best interests of the child himself.

Immature Motivations for Parenthood. Immature motives for parenthood may be categorized into the following types:

Those Who Desire Parenthood as a Means of Holding Together a Poor Relationship. This motive for parenthood is immature since parenthood here is viewed as a method of holding together a man-woman relationship which is in the process of deteriorating. In addition to the problems which may arise from the inability to appreciate the responsibilities of parenthood, this motive is further fraught with difficulty in that parenthood is not a cure for an unhappy marriage.[12] Not only is parenthood an unlikely solution for marital problems but also the responsibilities which it entails will more than likely add further problems to a relationship already overburdened with difficulty. It is possible that parenthood for some people operates somewhat like a "trap," holding one or both of the partners to a poor relationship. But this type of restriction does little to make the relationship more satisfying; indeed as has already been noted it tends to create further unhappiness for the marriage partners.

There is the case of a twenty-eight-year-old woman who was married to a successful professional man. The marriage was poor from the outset. The woman's solution to the marital difficulties was to become pregnant in the hope that her husband would not then wish to abandon her. Although there was every indication that the relationship with her husband was deteriorating the woman continued in her belief that children would preserve her marriage. By the age of thirty-three this woman had three children, all conceived with the same motive. The parents were in continual conflict and the children experienced considerable neglect. Shortly after the third child was born the husband became involved with another woman and left his wife.

[12] Paul H. Landis, 2nd ed., *op. cit.*, p. 518.

Those Who Desire Parenthood to Keep from Being Lonely. In some marriages the relationship is so poor that the wife, husband, or both, feel a profound sense of loneliness and distance from one another. Although such people may feel hopeless about the relationship becoming better, they believe that they might be less lonely if a child were present. To be sure, children can and do add a great deal to the life pattern of the parents but the attempt to use children to overcome personality deficiencies, or marital deficiencies, results in considerable harm for the child. Such a parent, or parents, may make excessive demands on children, perhaps expecting them never to leave home, to marry, or to have a life of their own in any context. This point was discussed in some detail in a previous chapter concerning parent and in-law involvements.

Those Who Desire Parenthood as a Means of Realizing Unfulfilled Goals. In some cases a child may be desired so that a parent may realize through the child the goals he was unable to achieve by himself. Thus, the son of the frustrated baseball player might be expected to be a successful participant of the Little League. To the extent that the parent's projection of his frustrated desires does not take into account the talents, skills, interests, and experiences of the child himself, this becomes a pattern of the parent's exploitation or using the child for his (the parent's) own benefit. As such, the motive for parenthood as a means of achieving exploitative ends is regarded as being immature.

Those Who Desire Parenthood as a Means of Attaining Security. There are those whose desire for parenthood stems from a need for security. To greater and lesser degrees, security is behind the motive for parenthood in at least three kinds of cases. First, those who derive security from the ability to carry on the family line. To these people the child is valued as a means of continuing the family name (in cases of a boy) and as a means of living up to, and, indeed, even adding to, the family's already "splendid" achievements.

Second, there are those who see parenthood primarily as a means of deriving security (financial and otherwise) in their old age. We are not referring here to those cases in which elderly parents receive emotional and/or financial support from their children, given and accepted with the love and understanding which characterizes a meaningful parent-child relationship. We are referring to those cases in which the parent initially regards the child as an investment which can be called on later to yield returns; the obligation to do so is at the parent's bidding.

Third, there are those whose desire for parenthood stems predominantly from the fact that they derive a sense of security from knowing that they, by becoming parents, have fulfilled an expectation which society makes of married couples. To these people it is "normal" and "right" to have children; and thus in order to be counted among the "normal" and "right" they too must strive to be parents.

These three motives identified with attaining security may be present to greater and lesser extents in many couples' desires for parenthood. When, however, they become the predominant motives for parenthood they are regarded as being essentially immature because in these cases the child is not viewed as an end in himself, but rather as a means to an end.

Mature Motivation and Meaningful Setting for Parenthood. Now that we have discussed some of the immature motivations for parenthood, let us consider motivations which would be considered to be mature. The motivation for parenthood is mature when the child is not viewed as a means to a parental end but rather as an end in itself. Parents under these circumstances desire children because of what children intrinsically represent. In such an atmosphere the child will feel free to grow and develop in terms of his own interests, talents, and wishes.

The Significance of the Marital Relationship for Successful Parenthood. In addition to mature motivations, successful parenthood is also dependent on other factors in the marital environment. When the husband and wife share a meaningful relationship with basic satisfactions, a favorable emotional climate is present which is conducive to the growth of the child.

One author, in pointing out the reciprocal nature of the love which characterizes meaningful family life, states that when both spouses derive gratification from each other a "psychological reservoir (is created) from which the emotional security of the child is nourished." [13] Another author sums it up this way:

> The family atmosphere surrounding the child in early infancy and childhood is the most important single factor in personality development for he absorbs the atmosphere of the life about him. Impressions and attitudes resulting from these early experiences carry over through the individual's lifetime, affecting many other relationships.[14]

Personality Factors in Successful Parenthood. In addition to the quality of the marital relationship, the personality make-up of the pro-

---

[13] Therese Benedek, *Insight and Personality Adjustment*, Ronald Press Co., New York, 1946, pp. 32, 123–124.

[14] Paul H. Landis, 2nd ed., *op. cit.*, p. 527.

spective parents is significant in successful parenthood. There are several problems which the prospective parents have to deal with and to resolve before they are ready to assume the task of parenthood.

The Insecure Parent. Parents who are insecure in their marriage, or in their person, may view the child as a threat rather than as a pleasure. For each marital partner, parenthood may mean that affection will have to be shared with the infant. Insecure people may react with resentment toward the infant in these instances.

The Egocentric Parent. Parents who are egocentric may view the child as a disturbance to personal plans. The personally pleasurable activities of mixing and socializing, and of participation in clubs may have to be curtailed and such curtailment can be experienced as an imposition. Further, the daily routine of marriage may be disturbed. These changes involve some personal reorientation which may be trying and difficult for egocentric people.

Although most people consider themselves emotionally equipped for parenthood, few probably are. Significant evidence for this is found in the high incidence of emotional instability in our society which is marked in childhood and adult psychological disorders. Much of this reflects a failure on the part of parents to provide a healthy climate for the development of mature and emotionally stable personalities.

PARENTHOOD IN CONTEMPORARY AMERICA. The insecurity, egocentricity, and rigidity in the parents just described was perhaps less serious in the past than it is today. The shift in roles of parenthood and child rearing emphasizing the intellectual and emotional development of children today demand a level of personal and social maturity on the part of the parent which perhaps was not so essential in the past. The extent and nature of these demands on parents may be appreciated by examining the changes as described by Professor Evelyn Duvall. Professor Duvall, who has studied the changes which have occurred in parental roles, as well as those which have occurred in the role of the child, dichotomizes the changing concepts of the role of mother and child into the traditional (i.e., previously accepted ideologies concerning the roles) and the developmental (i.e., contemporary ideologies concerning the roles).[15]
She finds that a good mother in the traditional conception was one who:

—— kept house—washing, cooking, cleaning, mending, sewing;
—— took care of child physically—keeping child healthy, guarding his

[15] Evelyn Millis Duvall, "Differential Concepts of Parenthood," Ph.D. dissertation, University of Chicago, 1946, pp. 40–41. See also Daniel R. Miller and Guy E. Swanson, *The Changing American Parent,* John Wiley and Sons, New York, 1958.

safety, feeding, clothing and bathing him, and seeing that he rested;
—— trained child to regularity—providing a schedule, seeing to it that regular hours were given to performing important functions;
—— disciplined—correcting child, demanding obedience, rewarding good
behavior, keeping promises, was firm and consistent;
—— made the child good—teaching obedience, instructing in morals, building character, praying for the child and seeing to his religious instruction.

Whereas a good mother in the developmental conception is one who:

—— trains for self-reliance and citizenship—trains for self-help, encourages
independence, teaches child how to adjust to life and how to concentrate;
—— sees to emotional well-being—keeps child happy and contented, makes
a happy home in which the child feels welcome and secure, thereby
overcoming his fears;
—— helps child develop socially—provides toys, companions, plays with
child, supervises child's play;
—— provides for child's mental growth—gives educational opportunities,
provides stimulation to learn, reads to child, tells stories, guides reading, sends child to school;
—— guides with understanding—sees child's point of view, gears life to
child's level, answers questions freely and frankly, gives child freedom to grow, interprets, offers positive suggestions;
—— relates self lovingly to child—shows love and affection, spends time
with child, shares with child, is interested in what child does and
tells;
—— is calm, cheerful, growing person herself—has outside interests, is
calm, gentle, humorous.

In describing the changes which have occurred in the role of the
child this same author finds that a good child in the traditional conception was one who:

—— kept clean and neat, obeyed and respected adults, pleased adults, respected property, was religious, worked well, and fitted into the
family program.

A good child in the developmental conception is one who:

—— is healthy and well, shares and cooperates with others, is happy and
contented, loves and confides in parents, is eager to learn and grows
as a person by developing an ability to handle himself and to handle
different situations.

Thus, it is evident that the changes which have occurred in the role
of the mother are primarily the result of a movement away from an
emphasis on fitting the child into the family program toward that of
emphasizing the worth and importance of the child himself. This
trend is further evident in the following description of the changing

role of the American father as described by another author who, using the same dichotomy of the traditional and developmental roles, found that the traditional father was one who: [16]

—— was a strong individual, always right, and regarded the child as his ward;
—— knew what the child should be so he did not have to seek to understand the child as an individual;
—— was interested only in activities which he determined were his responsibility for the child's good;
—— placed emphasis on giving things to and doing things for the child;
—— was interested in child's accepting and attaining goals set by the father;
—— found satisfaction in child's owing father a debt which could be repaid by the child's obedience and by bringing honor to the father through achieving the goals established by the father;
—— felt that parenthood was a duty which the church, family and/or society expected him to discharge, or which was forced on him as a biological function.

A good father in the developmental conception is one who:

—— sees himself and the child as individuals and therefore seeks to understand the child and himself;
—— concerns himself with all the activities and needs of the child;
—— places emphasis on the growth of the child and of himself;
—— is interested in child's determining and attaining goals which the child himself has selected;
—— finds satisfaction in child's becoming a mature individual and in the child's contribution to his (the father's) growth;
—— feels that parenthood is a privilege which he has chosen to assume.

Once parents assume the developmental goals rather than traditional goals, they have assumed a burden of considerable magnitude. For it is probably more difficult to be an adequate parent in the developmental sense than it is, and was, in the traditional sense. As noted in Chapter 2 the traditional parent was authoritarian. Thus, he operated on the basis of rules and norms which were dictated by tradition. The authoritarian role enabled the parent to cover up or obscure his personal inadequacy. He could possess all kinds of personal problems, he could be aloof and distant, rigid and inflexible, unsympathetic and inconsiderate. The presence of these parental traits, moreover, did not make the parent incompetent to fulfill his role since the goals of parenthood were different in the past. Much greater emphasis was placed on integrating the child into the family and society without regard to the child's own wishes and values.

The modern, middle-class parent, who is concerned with develop-

---

[16] Rachel Ann Elder, "Traditional and Developmental Conceptions of Fatherhood," unpublished masters thesis, Iowa State College, Ames, Iowa, 1947.

mental child-rearing goals, is confronted with a series of objectives which demand of him or her a degree of maturity and integration which is often difficult to meet. To begin with, one has to be committed to the concept of personal development and to self-realization in terms of one's emotional and intellectual potentialities. Parents who are emotionally disturbed themselves, and who have serious inhibitions about their own development, may be blocked in appreciating the need for self-realization. Furthermore, the parental commitment to developmental goals requires the parent to possess the integration to create an atmosphere in which the full potentiality of the child may be realized. In the authors' view, such a development can best occur in a home where the affectional function is adequately fulfilled.[17]

DEVELOPMENTAL GOALS IN PARENTHOOD AND THE AFFECTIONAL FUNCTION. In the final section of this chapter we will deal with the affectional function (which was introduced in Chapter 3), and discuss its significance in the achievement of the developmental goals just described. With respect to the affectional function, we emphasized earlier the significance of a family atmosphere conducive to the development of patterns of interaction characterized by feelings of dignity and respect for individual members, and an emotional climate where each partner lives with warmth, emotional acceptance, and the possibility of self-realization.[18] At this point, however, we wish to deal with the affectional function in a more detailed manner. The purpose for our doing so is to show how the achievement of the previously discussed developmental goals is exceedingly dependent upon the fulfillment of three characteristics of the affectional function which follow:

1. Affective dimensions
2. The emergence of individuality
3. The development of interpersonal relatedness

[17] See also Nelson N. Foote and Leonard S. Cottrell, Jr., *Identity and Interpersonal Competence*, University of Chicago Press, Chicago, Ill., 1955. An excellent statement of a related framework with respect to the goals of family life. Also Orville G. Brim, Jr., *Education for Child Rearing*, Russell Sage Foundation, New York, 1959, pp. 56–75. For a discussion of the fact that middle-class family behavioral patterns tend to be the norms of the society and that lower-class children, despite their socialization, tend to be expected to live up to these norms, see: George Simpson, *op. cit.*, pp. 290–292.

[18] Karen Horney, "The Neo-Freudian View: Man for Himself," in *Sociology: A Book of Readings*, Samuel Koenig, Rex D. Hopper, and Feliks Gross, Eds., Prentice-Hall, Inc., Englewood Cliffs, New Jersey, 1953, pp. 65–67. See also: Reuben Hill, "The American Family: Problem or Solution?" *Am. J. Sociol.*, **53** (Sept., 1947), pp. 125–130.

Affective Dimensions—the Development of the Capacity for Positive Feelings. The first significant characteristic of the affectional function, namely, affective dimensions, pertains to the development of human relationships characterized by positive feelings. From the points of view of both husband and wife, this involves an interpersonal relationship characterized by empathy, understanding, respect, and appreciation. When a marital relationship of this type is present the emergence of positive feelings in the child toward himself and toward others (empathy, understanding, respect, and appreciation) becomes a possibility. The emergence of this affective component is intimately tied to the second characteristic of the affectional function: individuality.

The Emergence of Individuality. Individuality is the right of the person to be the active agent in his own life and to select his own values out of the array which are available (as was discussed in Chapter 2). Mature individuality is cognizant of, and has respect for, the rights and dignity of others, and is not to be confused with indiscriminate rebelliousness (to be discussed later in this chapter).

The realization that one is accepted for what one is, as evidenced by the emergence of satisfying affective relationships, is a significant determinant for the development of individuality. The desire and courage to be oneself emerges from a respect for what one is. Individuality, therefore, emerges out of a set of human relationships which engender in the person a fundamental respect toward himself. This self-attitude may include the courage to trust one's judgments, form opinions, express oneself without fear, and choose insofar as possible the values which are meaningful to one. From these self-attitudes there emerges an inner core of strength to which the individual can turn in adjusting to the problems inherent in living.[19] The answers to personal problems may then be sought from within the individual rather than from exclusive reliance on others, or the conflicting opinions of family and friends. The person who has no confidence in his own judgment, in our sense, lacks individuality because he must compulsively rely on the judgments of others.[20]

The achievement of individuality is no simple task, however, for the capacity to appreciate individuality in oneself and others is unfortunately not a common experience. The most serious obstacles to

[19] Karen Horney, *Our Inner Conflicts*, W. W. Norton and Co., New York, 1945, Chs. 3 and 4.

[20] At the marital level individuality is nurtured when the partners possess a recognition and appreciation for the healthy differences which exist between them and when they make efforts toward integration of these differences.

the development of individuality are overprotection and rejection.[21] Overprotection retards individuality; it leaves the child with a pervasive feeling that personal security can only be found in giving oneself up to others and their wishes. The phenomenon of rejection, on the other hand, fosters the feeling that one is unacceptable to others; from this, fears of expressing healthy convictions emerge.[22]

In persons who have not had the opportunity for individuality to emerge, there is hopelessness and despair which emanates from the realization that one has little control over his personal destiny. For the person who achieves individuality, however, one of the most fundamental processes in human development has been experienced.[23]

The significance of individuality for human development may be more fully appreciated when compared with the phenomena of indiscriminate, "blind" conformity and indiscriminate rebelliousness.

Indiscriminate, Blind Conformity. Conformity is a necessary ingredient of group life and is present within the framework of individuality. The nature of conformity in individuality and in indiscriminate, blind conformity, however, is essentially different. One in whom individuality has emerged has developed the capacity to rationally assess a course of action with respect to whether conformity in a particular instance should or should not be followed.[24] Thus, when a per-

[21] Herman Lantz, "Problems of Social Class," in Caldwell and Foster, Eds., *Analysis of Social Problems*, Stackpole Co., Harrisburg, Penna., 1954, pp. 544–596. Also Leo H. Bartemeier, "The Practical Application of Basic Mental Hygiene Principles by the Cornelian Corner," *Bulletin of the Menninger Clinic*, 12 (July, 1948), pp. 113–116.

[22] Arnold W. Green, "The Middle-Class Male Child and Neurosis," *Am. Soc. Rev.*, 11 (Feb., 1946), pp. 31–41.

[23] Karen Horney, "The Neo-Freudian View: Man for Himself," *loc. cit.*

[24] "The sociological meaning of individuality: when we extend the meaning of individuality to man we find it essential to use the term in its sociological reference. Here we say that a social being has more individuality when his conduct is not simply imitative or the result of suggestion, when he is not entirely the slave of custom or even of habit, when his responses to the social environment are not altogether automatic and subservient, when understanding and personal purpose are factors in his life activities. Individuality in the sociological sense is that attribute which reveals the member of a group as more than merely a member. For he is a self, a center of activity and responses expressive of a nature that is his own. This conception stands behind the admonition we often give to others—or to ourselves—"be yourself." Being oneself need not mean just originality; it certainly does not mean eccentricity. A strong individuality may, in fact, express more fully the spirit or quality of his country or his time, but he does so, not because he is quickly imitative or easily suggestible, but because of his sensitivity to the age itself.

"It is true that when members of a group are more individualized they will reveal greater differences and they will express themselves in a greater variety of

son of this type conforms, he does so because he believes in what he is doing.

The blind conformist, on the other hand, has learned to view individuality and self-expression with fear. In his life history, his early efforts directed at individuality were met with ridicule, rejection, and humiliation, and one available adjustment for him was the indiscriminate taking over of all group values. Thus, when this person conforms, he does so merely for the purpose of conforming, without having given his behavior any thought. Such a development may not only become a blight on the individual's integrity, but may drive him to act against his best interests.

Indiscriminate Rebelliousness. Individuality must also be distinguished from indiscriminate rebelliousness. Like the blind conformist, the rebellious person lacks the capacity for rational assessment of group norms and personal modes of conduct. In this instance, however, instead of a compulsive need to accept group norms, there is a compulsive need to reject them. For these persons, family life may have been characterized by the enforcing of very strict standards of conduct, thus creating rebellion. Moreover, the development of individuality represents one of the fundamental problems in democratic social organization. This problem centers on how best to achieve a system of integrated social values while providing for individual selection and interpretation of social norms.[25]

Development of Interpersonal Relatedness. By interpersonal relatedness, the third constituent of the affectional function, we mean the ability to engage in interaction with a minimum of fear, hostility, and anxiety. Interaction based on fear and anxiety stems from needs to

---

ways. But the criterion of individuality is not how far each is divergent from the rest. It is, rather, how far each, in his relations to others, acts autonomously, acts in his own consciousness, and with his own interpretation of the claims of others upon himself. When the possessor of individuality does as others do, at least in matters he deems important, he does it not simply because others do it, but because his own self approves that particular behavior. When he follows authority, except in so far as he is compelled to, he follows it partly because of conviction, not only because it is authority. He does not superficially accept or echo the opinions of others—he has some independence of judgment, some initiative, some discrimination, as we often say, some 'strength of character.' The degree in which he exhibits these qualities is the degree in which he possesses individuality." From R. M. MacIver and Charles H. Page, *Society: An Introductory Analysis,* Rinehart and Co., New York, 1949, pp. 50–51.

[25] R. M. MacIver, *The Ramparts We Guard,* The Macmillan Co., New York, 1950, pp. 51–53. Also Kimball Young, *Personality and Problems of Adjustment,* F. S. Crofts and Co., New York, 1940, Ch. XXIII.

be envious of others, to prove oneself to others, and to use others for affirmation. Only in a family in which positive feelings, related self-acceptance, and individuality have emerged can the individual be given the stability which will enable him to interact with a minimum of anxiety. Why is this so? The need to prove oneself to others stems from a rejection of oneself and fundamentally a need to prove oneself to oneself. The need to be envious of others and the need to use others stems from a hopelessness about one's ability to attain accomplishments with any measure of success. Thus, one may feel resentful about the accomplishments of others and believe that only by using others can anything worthwhile be achieved. When, however, one's individuality has had an opportunity to emerge, then a feeling for what one may be able to accomplish can occur; this realization will tend to negate the need to use and manipulate others or resent their accomplishments.[26] Under these conditions interaction may be characterized by an identification with—and a feeling of happiness about—the success of others.

PARENTAL PROBLEMS IN THE FULFILLMENT OF THE AF-FECTIONAL FUNCTION. The task of developing relationships in which husband and wife are capable of fulfilling the affectional function is no simple matter, for it usually requires that the parents come from backgrounds in which the three characteristics of the affectional function have been an important part of their personal experience. That one can more readily experience toward others what one feels toward oneself is a well-recognized psychological axiom.[27] Thus, the person who has been nurtured in a social milieu which has fostered the development of positive affective dimensions, individuality, and interpersonal relatedness has had the opportunity to realize the significance of these qualities. An intellectual appreciation for these characteristics of the affectional function is by itself insufficient, however, because although an intellectual understanding permits one to verbalize about the significance of the affectional function, it does not necessarily prepare him to effect the affectional factor. For example, when the proper familial background has not been present, parents may encounter real difficulty in their attempts to create the emotional atmosphere necessary for the unfolding of the affectional function. In view of our analysis, therefore, it becomes obvious that

[26] MacIver and Page, op. cit., p. 52. Also Karen Horney, "The Neo-Freudian View: Man for Himself," loc. cit.

[27] George Herbert Mead in Mind, Self, and Society, Charles W. Morris, Ed., The University of Chicago Press, Chicago, Ill., 1934, p. 138.

some parents, in terms of their socialization, have greater difficulty in fulfilling the requirements of the affectional function than do others. It is of the greatest significance that individuals appreciate their shortcomings in this regard, and attempt to do something about them in order to be able to realize their fullest potential as wives, husbands, and parents.

SUMMARY

All young married couples should be prepared to face the possibility of unanticipated early pregnancy. For some couples, however, it is the inability to achieve pregnancy that will be confronted. Both of these possibilities and their effects on the marital relationship were discussed in this chapter.

In fact, the entire area of family planning was considered; including motivations which people have for desiring to remain childless, and the motivations which people have for desiring to become parents. In regard to the latter, it was noted that certain motivations for parenthood are regarded as immature. These include such motivations as desiring parenthood: (1) as a means of holding together a poor relationship, (2) to keep from being lonely, (3) as a means of realizing unfulfilled goals, and (4) as a means of attaining security. Mature motivations for parenthood, on the other hand, are those in which the child is not viewed as a means to a parental end but rather as an end in himself. Mature motivations for parenthood, as well as a healthy atmosphere for child rearing, tend to be based on secure and meaningful marital relationships, consisting of marital partners whose personalities are devoid of insecurity, egocentricity, and rigidity. This is particularly true in the American society where the emphasis is not on the traditional roles of parenthood but rather on the developmental roles of parenthood. Such a setting is conducive to the emergence of the affectional function and its three characteristics: (1) affective dimensions, (2) the emergence of individuality, and (3) the development of interpersonal relatedness.

QUESTIONS

1. Discuss the pros and cons concerning (a) having a baby during the first year of marriage, and (b) postponing pregnancy until later in the marriage.
2. Discuss the reasons offered by voluntarily childless couples for wishing to remain childless.
3. List and discuss the four immature motivations for parenthood described in this chapter. Explain exactly what a mature motivation for parenthood is.

4. In what ways do insecure parents and egocentric parents affect child rearing? Give examples.
5. Describe the difference between traditional and developmental roles for the mother, the father, and the child.
6. List and describe in full the three characteristics of the affectional function.

PROJECTS

1. Make an analysis of your own parent-child relationships, noting those aspects which you regard as having resulted in a successful relationship, and those you regard as having resulted in an unsuccessful relationship.
2. Interview a number of male and female students to learn:
   a. Whether or not, when married, they desire to become parents.
   b. Their reasons for desiring to become parents, or their reasons for desiring to remain childless.
   c. For those who desire parenthood, how soon after marriage would they prefer to begin their family?
   Analyze your results in order to determine whether you find any differences between the answers given by men and those given by women.

SUGGESTED READINGS

Bee, Lawrence S., *Marriage and Family Relations*, Harper and Bros., New York, 1959, Ch. 14, "Parenthood."
Boss, Helen, and Carl Boss, *If You Adopt a Child*, Henry Holt, New York, 1957.
Himes, Norman E., and Donald L. Taylor, *Your Marriage*, Rinehart and Co., New York, rev. ed., 1955, Ch. 20, "Preparation for Parenthood," Ch. 21, "Sterility," Ch. 22, "Shall We Adopt A Child?" Ch. 23, "Learning to Live with Children."
Landis, Judson T., Thomas Poffenberger and Shirley Poffenberger, "The Effects of First Pregnancy Upon the Sexual Adjustment of 212 Couples," *Am. Soc. Rev.*, 15 (Dec., 1950), pp. 766–772.
Merrill, Francis E., *Courtship and Marriage*, Henry Holt and Co., New York, 1959, Ch. 17, "Reproductive Roles," Ch. 18, "Prenatal Roles," and Ch. 19, "Parental Roles."
Read, Grantly Dick, *Childbirth Without Fear*, Harper and Brothers, New York, rev. ed., 1953.

Divorce and remarriage

18

Throughout the book we have discussed the man-woman relationship as it emerges and matures; in this chapter marital dissolution will be the subject. It should be clear that in spite of all that a couple may endeavor to do to resolve their marital conflicts, they may be faced with the realization that there is no longer any basis for the continuance of the relationship; thus breaking the marriage becomes a consideration. A broken marriage may be viewed as the discontinuance of a previously existing marriage relationship, and although this discontinuance may come about either from death, or from the decision of one or both of the marital partners to end their marriage relationship, we will be concerned with the latter—that is, the voluntary termination of a marriage relationship. With this end in view the discussion will center on such specific topics as: the means through which marriage relationships may be terminated, the legal and causal factors associated with divorce, the social factors and implications of divorce, who the divorced are, the predivorce and postdivorce stages, those who don't divorce, and remarriage.

THE MEANS BY WHICH MARRIAGE RELATIONSHIPS MAY BE DISSOLVED.

Desertion. In dealing with dissolution of the marital relationship, we note the existence of several common methods. First, marriage may be dissolved through desertion. In desertion one partner simply leaves and no longer functions in the marital role. This "poor man's divorce," which desertion is sometimes called because it appears to be more common at the lower income levels,[1] may be more traumatic than divorce itself because it is unannounced and more often than not comes as a surprise to the unprepared party remaining in the marriage. Desertion usually presents further trauma since it occurs more frequently in the lower social class which has a relatively high birth rate. This means that these children must be cared for by the marital partner who remains in the marriage and who receives no help from the partner who deserted.

Annulment. A second way in which marriages are sometimes terminated is through annulment. An annulment of a marriage is a legal decree stating that no valid marriage was contracted because the legal requirements of marriage had never been met. This may involve fraud or deception, present at the time of the marriage on the part of one or both of the marital partners. One or both partners may have been under legal age; one or both might not have legally dissolved a previous marriage. The annulment is frequently used as a means of terminating marriage relationships in states where it is very difficult to obtain a divorce due to the limited grounds on which a divorce can be granted; in New York, for example, a divorce will be granted only when adultery is proved.[2] Information on grounds for annulment is included in Appendix C.

Separation. A third means whereby a marriage relationship may be terminated is through legal separation. Legal separation means that the marital partners have agreed to live separately and not function together as husband and wife; legal separation does not grant the partners the right to remarry. In other words, although the marital partners are not living together, in the eyes of the law they are still regarded as being married and, consequently, are not free to remarry. In spite of the fact that legal separation does allow those persons whose religion prohibits divorce a means of severing the marriage re-

---

[1] William M. Kephart and Thomas P. Monahan, "Desertion and Divorce in Philadelphia," *Am. Soc. Rev.*, 17 (Dec., 1952), pp. 719–727.

[2] In New York state the only ground for which a divorce can be obtained is adultery. Consequently many marriages are terminated through annulment. In fact since 1946 one-third of the marital dissolutions in New York state were annulments and in several New York counties the number of annulments exceeded the number of awarded divorces. Kingsley Davis, "Statistical Perspective on Marriage and Divorce," *Annals of the American Academy of Political and Social Science*, 272 (Nov., 1950), pp. 9–21.

lationship, it frequently leads to major problems particularly in cases where one or both of the married partners become emotionally or erotically involved with another, whom they cannot marry because of their legal marital status.

Divorce. The fourth and most common method of terminating a marriage relationship is through a divorce. Divorce is a legal means for dissolving a legally recognized union of marriage for some cause that arose after the establishment of the marriage. Through divorce the marital partners are legally returned to their single statuses and are free to remarry if they so desire. With regard to divorce there are certain pertinent facts regarding how the law functions which should be pointed out.

Wronged and Wrongdoer. Theoretically, divorce is almost never granted when both marital partners agree that they have contributed to the marital difficulty. Instead, divorce can be granted only in cases where one partner proves to the state that he has been offended by the other marital partner. This means that in most divorce proceedings there is one who is identified as the "wronged" and another who is identified as the "wrongdoer." In some instances this concept has led to rehearsals in the attorney's office prior to a court hearing. The object of the rehearsal is to be certain that the person suing for divorce, the wronged, knows how to respond in court. In some instances the "wronged" has become upset during the actual court proceedings and in the confusion of the moment revealed information concerning his or her personal contribution to the marital difficulty. Such cases are frequently dismissed, since both parties have now admitted their contribution to the marital difficulty.

Grounds for Divorce. With respect to the legal grounds for divorce, there are vast differences among the states concerning what constitutes a basis for divorce. In some states divorce can only be granted when it is proved that one of the marital partners has committed adultery, whereas in other states divorce can be obtained on the grounds not only of adultery, but cruelty, desertion, non-support, alcoholism, committing a felony, impotence, pregnancy at marriage, and drug addiction as well. A list of the grounds for divorce in each state is found in Appendix C.

Difficulty in Obtaining Objective Statistics. Because of the two factors discussed above, namely that one marital partner must be the wrongdoer and the other the wronged, and also because of the differences which exist between the state laws constituting grounds for divorce, it is exceedingly difficult to study objectively the causes of divorce by means of the data obtained from court records. The concepts of the wronged and wrongdoer obscure the real causes of divorce. In a vast majority of cases the party being sued for the divorce, the wrongdoer, does not contest the divorce; [3] consequently this person appears in the court data as the partner solely responsible for the difficulties in the marriage.[4] Moreover, it is generally easier for the wife to obtain the divorce than for the husband. The court is inclined to protect the woman and more likely to be conservative in granting a divorce to a man. When the wife applies for divorce, the court often assumes that a woman has considered the social and economic consequences and is prepared to accept them. Thus, the fact that a woman sues for divorce does not imply that she necessarily desires a divorce. It may only indicate that she, her husband, and the attorney decided it would be the simplest way of attaining the divorce. An objective study of divorce on the basis of court statistics is also made difficult by the need to fit marital offenses into the grounds for divorce permitted within the specific state. In this regard, people seeking a divorce (irrespective of their reasons for doing so) frequently permit legal counsel to couch their reasons to suit the laws of the state. Indeed, the lawyer himself, regardless of the conditions involved in the particular marriage, will probably select to use grounds which will insure that the divorce is obtained with a minimum of difficulty.

Consequently, even though some students compile statistics in the attempt to show what percentages of divorces are granted on the grounds of cruelty, desertion, neglect to provide, adultery, drunkenness, and the like, it is highly questionable just how accurately these statistics depict the real causes of divorce.[5]

DOMESTIC RELATIONS LAW—SOCIAL IMPLICATIONS. It is obvious to observers of the legal scene that there are many problems associated with domestic relations law. It frequently places clients in the position of having to distort the truth in order to obtain a divorce. This often results in personal and social embarrassment where the evidence is "trumped up" in order to meet requirements acceptable to

[3] Alfred Cohen, *Statistical Analysis of American Divorce,* Columbia University Press, New York, 1932, p. 43.

[4] For a discussion of the "guilt" criterion in American divorce laws, see: Paul W. Alexander, "The Follies of Divorce—A Therapeutic Approach to the Problem," *Law Forum,* 1949, pp. 695–711.

[5] For a study which attempts to get to the real reasons for divorce and desertion, see: Ernest R. Mowrer, "The Variance Between Legal and Natural Causes for Divorce," *Social Forces,* 2 (March, 1924), 388–392.

the court as may be the case where the only acceptable grounds are mental cruelty or adultery. Periodically the public becomes disturbed at the inconsistency, and sometimes cruelty, of domestic relations law, but usually such concern is of short duration. The American Bar Association, on the other hand, has given considerable attention to the problems involved in the hope of working out some of the difficulties.

In order to understand some of the current problems in facing up to the difficulties with domestic relations law it becomes important to deal with two considerations. First, although the basic reasons for divorce have changed, the legal grounds for divorce have remained essentially the same.[6] The legal grounds for divorce in America, which go back to early English law, are concerned with whether or not the marital obligations have been adhered to. These obligations are essentially moralistic in nature, involving such things as mental cruelty, impotency, adultery, drunkenness, and neglect. These grounds for divorce may have been reasonable when the basis of marriage was more narrowly construed as centering around procreation and economic considerations. Under these circumstances the grounds for divorce listed above were the only types of violations that could become a basis for marital dissolution. Today, however, the basis for marriage is rooted in several other affectional considerations previously discussed. Thus, the real basis for divorce is often more generally found in some form of interpersonal incompatibility. Domestic relations law, for the most part, fails to take into account the change in the basis of marriage and the resultant causes of marital failure.

A second consideration affecting revisions in domestic relations law concerns the political ramification for those individuals who would recommend change. Members of legislative bodies, and others concerned with such change, are invariably fearful of attacks either from those who wish to maintain the law as it is, or from those who wish to liberalize and change the laws. Fears of antagonizing some section of the populace have resulted by and large in a "hands off policy" with respect to domestic relations law.[7]

DIVORCE: SOCIAL IMPLICATIONS. In spite of the fact that throughout history more American marriages have been broken by death than by divorce, the divorce trend has shown an increase over

[6] W. Freidman, *Law In a Changing Society,* University of California Press, Berkeley and Los Angeles, Calif., 1959, pp. 207 and 225.

[7] Fowler V. Harper, *Problems of the Family,* Bobbs-Merrill Co., Indianapolis, 1952, pp. 771–775.

the years.[8] Indeed, of all marriages taking place in 1900 only about one in twelve resulted in termination through divorce, and in 1922 about one in eight; whereas it is believed that of all marriages taking place currently at least one in four will be terminated by divorce.[9] Further, an increase in the American divorce rate is occurring even among couples who have children.[10]

/ It is believed that the increased rate of divorce is the result of the vast social changes which have been taking place in the American society, and the marital incompatibilities which are related to these changes. The reader will recall that in Chapter 2 we stressed the significance of the change from the rural to urban society, along with the economic emancipation of women, the increased secularization of American social life, the resulting decline in religious sanctions, the individualistic basis for mate selection and the individualistic basis of marital expectations. All of these have been responsible for a new basis for family life which has not yet had sufficient opportunity to stabilize itself. It is axiomatic that whenever social systems of any type go through change, instability will result. It is important, therefore, to view the current instability of the American family in proper perspective. There are some people who see the high divorce rate as an indication that the institution of marriage and the family is becoming individualistic and atomistic; they see a grim future for the family, and predict ultimate disintegration of family life as we know it today. For the vast majority of professionals, however, the current crisis in family life is seen as one phase in the process of social change. Thus, the current crisis is viewed as stemming from the fact that while the traditional basis of family has disappeared, a new basis for family living has not yet fully emerged. When such emergence is complete it is believed that families will be integrated around the concept of democratic-individualistic values. Under these conditions people will remain married not because society expects them to, but because they so desire, since their most cherished values are to be found in family living.[11] Until such time we can expect a continuation of instability—

[8] In 1890, 33 marriages per 1,000 were terminated annually; of these 3 by divorce and 30 by death. In 1957, 27 marriages per 1,000 were terminated annually; of these 10 by divorce and 17 by death. Paul H. Landis, *Making the Most of Marriage*, 2nd ed., Appleton-Century-Crofts, Inc., New York, 1960, p. 25.

[9] *Ibid.*, p. 612.

[10] Paul H. Jacobson, "Differentials in Divorce by Duration of Marriage and Size of Family," *Am. Soc. Rev.*, 15 (April, 1950), pp. 235–244.

[11] Mabel A. Elliott, "The Scope and Meaning of Divorce," in Howard Becker and Reuben Hill, Eds., *Family, Marriage, and Parenthood*, 2nd ed., D. C. Heath and Co., Boston, Mass., 1955, p. 669.

an instability, however, that may be avoided in some instances and stabilized in others through marriage education, marriage counseling, and the like.

DIVORCE—PERSONAL IMPLICATIONS. Divorce is a procedure which enables those who are involved in an unhappy marriage to legally start over again in the pursuit of marital happiness. Nevertheless, for many people divorce may solve little. Those who are divorced for neurotic reasons may not be capable of benefiting from the second chance which divorce offers them. For the neurotic it is possible that the use of divorce merely results in a series of unsuccessful marital ventures. One authority, for example, claims that divorce is merely a temporary respite and strategic retreat in the great battle of neurosis.[12] By this he means that many neurotics seek a divorce when their neurotic way of life is questioned or disturbed.

There was the case of a middle-aged man with an excessive need to dominate. For years he was able to dominate his wife, much to the amazement of the immediate family and close friends. At one point in their marriage the wife decided to go to a university in order that she develop whatever potential she might possess, and pursue the esthetic values that interested her. Such action on her part resulted in a prolonged series of arguments in which the husband attempted to discourage his wife by disparaging remarks regarding her goals. He was unsuccessful in his attempt to discourage her and discovered that she was becoming increasingly self-reliant. At this point the husband forbade his wife to continue attending school. After a series of violent disputes in which the wife refused to stop attending school, the husband threatened and finally arranged to divorce her. Two years later the husband remarried. This time he married a woman very similar to the way his former wife had been during the early part of their marriage; she was insecure, timid, and very self-effacing. He divorced his first wife because she no longer fitted in with his neurosis, and he sought another woman who would. If his second wife were to mature, the husband would be faced with a similar set of problems.

It should be noted that many people who are married to neurotics and emotionally immature individuals make the necessary adjustments so that life is tolerable. Nevertheless, these adjustments are usually made at a considerable sacrifice in terms of the personal happiness which can be derived from marriage; acceptance of the sacrifices entailed should only be done after serious deliberation.

[12] Edmund Bergler, *Divorce Won't Help,* Harper and Brothers, New York, 1948, p. 27.

From all that we have said it should be clear that individuals in marital conflict should attempt to make some effort to assess their motivations for seeking divorce; particularly they need to have some understanding of the variables, personal and social, which have produced the deterioration of their relationship. Only then is there hope that these individuals will have some appreciation of what has happened, and some vision regarding how to avoid similar involvements.

WHO THE DIVORCED ARE. In earlier chapters we discussed certain factors which were found to be associated with successful marriage and certain other factors which were found to be associated with unsuccessful marriage. An understanding of these factors will not only give the reader a general picture of divorce, but may also provide him with an understanding of certain aspects of his own marriage. In the first place, it should be pointed out that those factors which were discussed in Chapter 9 as being related to unsuccessful marriage tend to be found to a large extent among the divorced population. These include, among others, such factors as the marital partners coming from markedly different cultural backgrounds, educational levels, and social classes; displaying domineering, pessimistic, or overly sensitive personality characteristics; lacking self-confidence or being overly self-sufficient; having inadequate sexual knowledge and training; having unhealthy attitudes concerning sexual relations; and using inadequately the courtship stage of the man-woman relationship.

In addition to these findings derived from marriage prediction studies, there are other significant factors which have been reported, such as the findings in regard to: ethnic origin, rural and urban environments, race, age at marriage, duration of marriage, economic status, educational level, childless marriage, and size of family.

Ethnic Origin. The American divorce rate is highest among those people born in this country whose parents are also native Americans. The next highest rate is found among those native Americans whose parents were (or at least one parent was) foreign born. Those who show the least rate of divorce are the foreign born Americans. The fact that the foreign born show the least rate of divorce probably reflects a number of factors. For example, it may be that divorce as a means of solving marital difficulty is simply not a part of the cultural heritage of these people. Or, as one sociologist notes, perhaps the expectations of the foreign born regarding marriage are less demanding and hence these people may experience fewer of the frustrations and disappointments which might lead them to seek divorce; also, many of them are likely to be followers of Roman Catholicism and, therefore, not likely to divorce.[13]

Rural and Urban Environments. Urban areas reflect a higher divorce rate than do rural areas. This might mean that marital expectations are higher and more individualistic among urban dwellers, thus more marital frustration would be experienced; or this higher urban divorce rate could also point to a predominance of occupational frustration in the urban setting, causing some people to attempt to displace their hostility in the man-woman relationship.[14]

Race. When the divorce rates of negroes and whites coming from the same community background are compared, the negro grouping reflects the higher divorce rate, although the proportion of divorced persons among all negroes is relatively small.[15] This apparent contradiction is explained by one sociologist, interested in the study of divorce, as resulting from the fact that the negro grouping is predominately found in rural areas; and, as we have already seen, rural areas produce fewer divorces than do urban areas.[16] It should be noted, however, that the negro divorce rate itself may be of questionable significance since, particularly among the lower-class southern negroes, many marriages tend to be informally contracted (common law) and require no formal divorce for their termination. Consequently, marital disorganization among the negroes may be even higher than would be apparent in the divorce statistics.

Age at Marriage. One study, which tends to be representative of other similar studies, showed that the divorced, both men and women, tended to marry at a younger age than did the non-divorced (those still married). The average age of first marriage for divorced females was 19.9 years, for non-divorced females 21.5 years; while for divorced males it was 23.2 years, and for non-divorced males 24.1 years.[17] This may imply that those who marry at an earlier age tend to be less socially and psychologically mature than are those who marry later. Or it could mean that earlier marriages are associated with lower

---

[13] Jessie Bernard, *Remarriage,* The Dryden Press, New York, 1956, p. 79.

[14] George Simpson, *People in Families,* Thomas Y. Crowell Co., New York, 1960, p. 355.

[15] See: Jessie Bernard, *loc. cit.* See also: William J. Goode, *After Divorce,* The Free Press, Glencoe, Ill., 1956, Ch. 4.

[16] Jessie Bernard, *loc. cit.*

[17] Harvey J. Locke, *Predicting Adjustment in Marriage,* Henry Holt and Co., New York, 1951, pp. 101–104.

educational and income groupings, because each of these, as we will see presently, tends to be related to high divorce rates.

Another interesting finding concerning age and divorce is that among the divorced the difference in the age of husband and wife is greater than it is among the non-divorced.[18] In this regard, although the risk of divorce is present when the husband is quite a bit older than his wife, it is even more apparent in marriages where the wife tends to be quite a bit older than her husband.[19] The relationship between age differential and divorce is probably best explained in terms of differences between the marital partners in regard to such items as sexual adequacy and social values, since both of these tend to be affected by age.

Duration of Marriage. The first five years of marriage are the most hazardous years in that the majority of the divorces which occur do so during this period.[20] The high divorce rate during this period probably results from the fact that this is the period of marriage during which the majority of incompatibilities appear; and adjustments between the spouses are made. Some couples may be able to accommodate and adjust to each other; these couples remain married. Other couples, however, may be unable to effect satisfactory adjustments; these marriages tend to become the potential divorce cases.

Economic Status. Contrary to common belief, divorce is most frequent at lower income levels.[21] This finding might imply that, although all marriages require adjustments on the part of the spouses, the added strain of financial burdens decreases the desire to work at making such adjustments for those in low-income brackets. Thus, these people may have less incentive to effect marital happiness.

Educational Level. In spite of the above findings pertaining to economic status and divorce, the divorce rate tends to increase as the level of education increases up to and including graduation from high school; however, the divorce rate for college graduates is lower than the divorce rate for any other educational level.[22] This drop in the divorce rate for college graduates may be the result of the education received; or it may mean that due to college attendance

---

[18] *Ibid.*

[19] See: Mabel A. Elliott, *op. cit.*, p. 686.

[20] Paul H. Jacobson, "Differentials in Divorce," *loc. cit.*

[21] Harvey J. Locke, *op. cit.*, p. 283.

[22] This study pertains only to native white American men. William F. Ogburn, "Education, Income, and Family Unity," *Am. J. Sociol.*, 53 (1947–1948), pp. 474–476.

marriage occurred at a later age. The significance of this latter point was discussed previously.

Children and Divorce. In a previous chapter we noted that the presence or absence of children in a marriage does not tend to be related to marital success, but rather the desire to have children is found more frequently among the successfully married, and the lack of desire for children is found more frequently among the unsuccessfully married. Now regarding divorce and children, couples with no children tend to have a higher divorce rate than do couples with children; this is particularly true for those who have been married for five years or less.[23] After five years of marriage, however, the divorce rates between those with children and those without children tend to become more similar; and by the eighteenth year of marriage the divorce rate for both groups is very similar.[24] This could imply that the inability to have children might be an area of marital conflict during the earlier years. Or that the decision to have children reflects a satisfaction with the marriage relationship, whereas in unsatisfactory marriage relationships there may be a reluctance to have children.

In regard to the number of children and divorce the findings suggest that the greater the number of children, the less the divorce rate.[25] This could reflect the presence of large families among Roman Catholics for whom divorce is prohibited; or it could imply that "the inseminatory success manifested to the father by the presence of his large brood may be a compensation to the husband and father for conditions which might otherwise lead to divorce." [26]

It is particularly interesting to note the fact that the low divorce rate for large families when coupled with the high divorce rate for low-income levels would seem to suggest that in the low-income grouping those with few or no children are extremely susceptible to divorce. It would also appear to suggest that persons in the higher income levels who have large families are extremely well protected from divorce. But, indeed, more research, with combinations of various factors included, is needed before we will be able to understand more fully the conditions of divorce.

Finally, we wish to add that although the reasons for the association between divorce and the social variables we have discussed are not completely understood, they do provide a couple with potential in-

---

[23] Paul H. Jacobson, "Differentials in Divorce," *loc. cit.*
[24] *Ibid.*
[25] *Ibid.*
[26] George Simpson, *op. cit.*, p. 352.

dices of vulnerability, and such awareness may enable the couple to understand with more clarity some of their difficulties.

Having discussed briefly the factors which have some relationship to divorce, we now consider the psychic and social circumstances which precede and follow divorce.

PREDIVORCE AND POSTDIVORCE. Contrary to the widespread notion that people go through a divorce with a minimum of psychic disturbance, divorce is generally an emotionally, psychologically, and socially traumatic experience which leaves its marks and scars on the personalities involved. To begin with, many individuals experience a sense of personal rejection which is painful. Even when there is mutual consent that the divorce is necessary, each may feel that he was not wanted or desired by the other. Furthermore, there may be a profound feeling of having failed in a personal sense. It is as though they "should have made it work" in spite of any obstacles in their path. The extent to which one is disturbed by a divorce is frequently increased when one member of the former marriage decides to remarry. For the remaining individual the remarriage of his former spouse may prove to be rather traumatic. This is particularly so when one member of the relationship continued to hope, as many do, that somehow even after the divorce "they would get back together." Sometimes these people become martyrs, waiting for the mate to return. In other instances they may desperately plunge into a new relationship prematurely in order to prove that they are still lovable and desirable.

DIVORCE AND THE MIDDLE CLASS. Among the middle class, especially, divorce may come as a crisis. Middle-class people are frequently insecure about their positions in the community and are usually very eager to be thought well of by others. Thus, they are particularly vulnerable to the negative definitions which others in the community might have regarding divorce. These negative reactions from the community may be based on several factors. For some people divorce represents the dissolution of a unit which is the basis of orderly group life; for others it has sinful connotations which are rooted in religious conviction. For a good many others, however, divorce is upsetting because they see it as a potential solution for their own inadequate marriage; nevertheless, because of personal fear or pressure from community or church, they attempt to drown out the temptation by denying any valid basis for divorce and by condemning persons who do divorce. Often the marriages of these people who do not divorce are fundamentally far worse than many marriages which end in separation or divorce.

There is the case of a couple who had been married for twenty years; these people had never been happy in their marriage, and throughout most of it they had been involved in serious marital conflict. Whenever they interacted with each other for an extended period of time they ended up arguing about even minor issues. Thus, over a period of time their relationship deteriorated until they had almost nothing to do with each other. It is interesting to note however, that this couple, with an exceedingly poor relationship, were the most outspoken members of their community with respect to the divorce of others.

In spite of the personal and social complications involved, people do adjust to divorce, and the degree of trauma in achieving this adjustment decreases as the mutuality in desiring the divorce increases. Where, for example, there has been a prolonged period of estrangement or the partners may have not seen one another for an extended period of time, divorce is much less of a crisis. Although some divorces appear to be sudden and without a prior history of marital discord, there is most often a process through which the couple pass before reaching a final decision. Let us consider this process in greater detail as we discuss the predivorce and postdivorce stages outlined below.[27]

Some Disturbance of the Affectional-Sexual Life. This usually involves the withholding of affectional response due to some unsatisfactory marital condition; or it could involve more subtle forms of attempting to compensate for lack of rapport in other areas of marital life by an overemphasis on the demands made in the affectional-sexual area. It is not uncommon for one or both members of the relationship to become involved with someone outside the marriage during this initial stage. The outside affair may be a variable in initiating the marital disturbance, or may be an impetus in furthering the deterioration of the marriage, or both. Although vigorously denied by some, a good many of those who become divorced have either already established a relationship outside of marriage, or at least they believe that the possibilities of doing so are promising.

The Mention of the Possibility of Divorce. Just as the declaration of love and the intent to marry initiates the courtship period, so the

[27] Willard Waller and Reuben Hill, *The Family*, rev. ed., The Dryden Press, New York, 1951, pp. 513–515.

mention of divorce by one or both marital partners indicates the presence of rather marked difficulties in the marriage relationship.

The Appearance of Solidarity Is Broken. At this point the couple begin to openly admit to friends that their marriage is in difficulty and increasingly they come to take the world into their confidence. This may include more emphasis on blaming the marital partner for the crisis. During this stage parents and friends in attempting to help may either agree with each marital partner in turn, or even set out on their own to try to "patch things up" for the couple; usually a series of homespun lectures based on clichés are offered.

The Decision to Divorce. The decision to divorce is sometimes made in haste and anger, but more frequently it tends to be the result of a continued state of extreme dissatisfaction with the marriage, which one or both partners simply decide to terminate. The fact that in most cases it is the wife who files for divorce does not necessarily mean that wives are more desirous of divorcing than are husbands. In some cases this may be so, but in cases where there is an equal desire to divorce, it is usually the wife who files for the divorce. Also, in certain cases where the husband may actually be the partner who first desires divorce, he may create a series of circumstances which make it ultimately necessary for the wife to desire and to file for divorce.[28]

Crisis of Separation. During this stage the marital partners live apart. This often tends to be a traumatic phase since it involves the realization that a new way of life must be established. However, the extent of the trauma may be markedly reduced in those cases where the partners are already involved in new love relationships.

The Divorce. This is the final severance of the marriage relationship; and although both partners by now have had time to prepare emotionally for the reality of divorce, the finality of divorce at this point still tends to be difficult to accept, unless, of course, a new love affair has emerged.

The Period of Mental Conflict. The stage following the divorce is generally a difficult one. One student of divorce found that most people regretted their divorces feeling that perhaps they had acted too hastily.[29] This finding, however, has been questioned.[30] It is at this time that the reconstruction of one's new life pattern must crystal-

[28] William Goode, *op. cit.*, Ch. 11.

[29] Willard Waller and Reuben Hill, *The Family* (revised edition), Dryden Press, New York, 1951, p. 514. See also Willard Waller, *The Old Love and the New*, Liveright Publishing Corp., New York, 1930.

[30] William Goode, *loc. cit.*

lize; this is never worked out simply. The reconstruction usually calls for establishing a new social pattern and a new circle of friends. For despite the soundness of previous friendships, the individual frequently discovers that he no longer feels comfortable with the married couples of his previous acquaintance.[31] Also, one has to break established patterns with regard to eating, sleeping and sexual behavior.

Women have particular problems in this regard since the divorcée may discover that other married or engaged women may consider her a threat to their own relationships. The belief is that since the woman has already been divorced she is less governed by conventional patterns and may seek involvement with other men. Furthermore, with regard to her relationships with men she has certain related difficulties. Many men, married or single, look on the divorcée as one who has already participated in sexual relations, is now without sexual activity, and is therefore "a pushover" for the right individual. Thus, many divorced women complain that it is exceedingly difficult for them to establish relationships in which men are not out to exploit them sexually.

One divorced woman reported that she had received numerous proposals of marriage, but all of them were contingent on sexual involvement before the marriage would occur. In each instance refusal to participate in sexual relations resulted in a decline in interest on the part of the male.

At any stage in the alienation pattern a couple may decide to attempt a reconciliation and to remain together as husband and wife.[32] For some couples reconciliation seems to work, but for many others it tends to lead to a series of reconciliations necessitated by the repeated occurrence of crises, which themselves tend to become increasingly serious in nature.

DIVORCE AVOIDED AFTER SUIT HAS BEEN FILED. Not all people who file for divorce end up getting a divorce. Indeed, one study found that between 20 and 45 percent of all divorce cases filed were dismissed.[33] This study notes that the reason for nearly all dismissals

---

[31] In one study of divorced women, however, it was found that they did not regard themselves as social outcasts but instead were able to retain their previous circle of friends. William Goode, *loc. cit.*

[32] Indeed some couples even attempt a reconciliation after they have been divorced, for as one study points out a significant proportion of the divorced persons who take mates of like marital status involves persons who had been married to each other previously; they marry each other again. Paul H. Jacobson, *American Marriage and Divorce*, Rinehart and Co., Inc., New York, 1959, p. 67.

[33] Quentin Johnstone, "Divorce Dismissals, a Full Study," *Kansas Law Review*, 1:3, May, 1953.

was reconciliation, but it also notes that in a large percentage of these cases reconciliation did not last and the couples eventually divorced. Dismissal was more likely to occur in cases where there were children, the partners claiming that their attempted reconciliation was for "the good of the children." Advice on the desirability of dismissing a divorce suit is sometimes but not generally sought from the lawyers and judges involved in the cases.[34]

In many cases where reconciliation has occurred, little improvement in the marriage actually occurs. Instead the couple, although very unhappy, decide to accept their state of unhappiness. The relationship for these people has lost its meaning and it is held together because of other considerations. There are some people who prefer to remain together in spite of marked incompatibility because of religious considerations. Others fear being left alone. Finally, there are those persons who remain together because of neurotic needs. For example, a vindictive person who has a need to "get back" at the mate will cling to a bad relationship in order to inflict suffering on the partner. A masochistic person will remain in an undesirable marriage in order to punish himself. An individual with a need to dominate will remain in a marriage in order to satisfy that need. Thus, some people actually enjoy the unhappy state of their marriage because it fulfills for them certain neurotic needs which they have developed.[35]

EFFECTS OF DIVORCE ON CHILDREN. The relationship between the occurrence of divorce and the consequences which this has upon the children who are involved has always interested the layman and the professional. The traditional view has been that such family dissolution was devastating for the children, involving an uprooting from relationships with family and friends. This view is based on the assumption that before divorce the children involved had a set of warm, stable and dependable relationships which were suddenly dissolved. Although such is possible, in general this is probably an unwarranted assumption. For indeed in many cases the relationships prior to divorce were devoid of any stability and predictability. In such cases the actual occurrence of separation or divorce might prove to be less traumatic for children than a continued existence in a family atmosphere of hostility and distrust.

[34] Some authorities feel that many lawyers and judges are not capable of performing such counseling in spite of the fact that this would appear to be not only a desirable but also an important aspect of their roles. Paul W. Alexander, *loc. cit.*

[35] We have discussed, in an earlier chapter, the immature needs on which a love relationship may be based.

One authority feels, for example, that divorce is frequently over-estimated as the factor most harmful to children because in reality the state of unhappiness and family trauma which precedes divorce may play an equally, or even more, damaging part than the divorce.[36] Thus, it is conceivable that the continued exposure to family trauma may prove more harmful to children than the actual severing of the family relationship through divorce. This suggests that just as divorce offers marital partners "another chance" for marital happiness, so too may it offer children "another chance" of being exposed to a more secure and meaningful family atmosphere.[37]

Having pointed this out it is also necessary to indicate that divorce under any circumstances does involve some trauma for the child. Even in those instances where there is already marked insecurity, the final act of divorce can create, at least for the moment, even more insecurity than before. In this regard we must remember that particularly for young children with limited understanding divorce may be interpreted as a sign of rejection in an intensely personal way. Thus, a young child may come to feel that a father who left the family has really abandoned him and may come to feel that for some reason his father no longer loves him. The fact that young children cannot always communicate such fears raises the possibility of unintended but nevertheless undesirable personality consequences for the child. Responsible parents must always be alert to this in order that they be able to cope with these destructive interpretations which children may come to believe.

Divorce in any event is a serious step usually affecting the lives of several people. Thus, it is important to understand when divorce will constitute a solution to one's difficulties, and when the dissolution of a family will present even more problems than it will solve.

REMARRIAGE. For the final section in this chapter we would like to discuss the question of remarriage. Such a discussion may prove of general interest since it will help orient the reader to certain pertinent facts about those who remarry. It may also be of personal interest to those who have terminated their marriages and who contemplate remarriage.

Remarriage after divorce is a common experience and the chances for happiness in these subsequent marriages are fair. Most persons

[36] J. Louise Despert, *Children of Divorce*, Doubleday and Co., Inc., New York, 1953.
[37] F. Ivan Nye, "Child Adjustment in Broken and in Unhappy Unbroken Homes," *Marriage and Family Living*, 19 (Nov., 1957), pp. 356–361.

who remarry after divorce do so in a relatively short period after their marriages are dissolved.[38] Women tend to remarry approximately 4.6 years after divorce, and men 2.5 years after divorce.[39] In fact, it is interesting to note that divorced people tend to remarry sooner than the widowed. In one study it was reported that three-fourths of all divorced persons were remarried within five years; however, of those who had been widowed for five years, only one-half of the men and one-fourth of the women had remarried.[40] In regard to contemporary community attitudes toward the remarriage of divorced people, it appears that the trend is toward greater receptivity and the attitudes at present seem to be more favorable than they are unfavorable.[41]

Who Remarries.[42]

The Remarried Woman—a Statistical Average. The remarried woman was at first marriage in her very early twenties. Her marriage lasted approximately 5.8 years, which means that she was in her later twenties when divorced. She remained unmarried for a period of about 4.6 years, and remarried in her early thirties. She had, on an average, slightly more than one child. She retained sole custody of the child after divorce. Her child's attitude toward her remarriage ranged from that of favoring it to that of showing indifference toward it; and toward her new spouse the attitude of her child tended to be friendly. This attitude was reciprocated by the new spouse (new father) who felt affection for her child; however, the remarried woman's attitude toward her spouse's children although affectionate, was less affectionate than was her new husband's attitude toward her child. On the latter point it should be noted that the custody of the children tends to fall to the mother; and therefore the remarried woman does not usually live with the children of her new husband. The attitude of the parents of the remarried woman tend to be more favorable toward her second marriage than they were toward her first marriage.

The Remarried Man—a Statistical Average. The remarried man at first marriage was approximately twenty-four years old, his marriage lasted for about seven years. This means that he was in his early thirties when divorced. He remained unmarried for only 2.5 years and remarried in his middle thirties. He did not get the custody of his child

[38] Paul H. Jacobson, *American Marriage and Divorce, op. cit.,* pp. 69–70.
[39] Jessie Bernard, *op. cit.,* p. 11.
[40] *Ibid.,* pp. 65–66.
[41] *Ibid.,* pp. 12, 37.
[42] *Ibid.,* pp. 11–12.

(average children 1.39) and the attitude of his child toward his remarriage was largely one of indifference, and toward his new spouse the child's attitude ranged from neutral to friendly. As we have noted, his wife's attitude toward his child ranged from affectionate to neither affectionate nor rejecting, but his attitude toward her child was more affectionate. The attitudes of the parents of the remarried man, very similar to the attitudes of the parents of the remarried woman, were more favorable toward his second marriage than they were toward his first marriage.

Having presented a brief sketch of the remarried woman and the remarried man, let us now examine the findings in regard to marital success or failure for these groupings. Although it is noted that the divorce rate for remarried persons is higher than it is for the first marriage—and incidentally this tends to increase with each successive remarriage— [43] in most studies it is found that over half of the remarriages are reported to range in happiness from above average to extremely successful.[44] This would seem to uphold clearly the statements made earlier that many people are capable of utilizing the opportunity which divorce offers them to begin a new marital relationship in which they can find happiness. However, the data also suggest that for others remarriage is associated with marital unhappiness similar to that of the first marriage. In such cases, until the personality problems and immaturities involved are dealt with, these people will be unable to participate meaningfully in any marriage relationship.

SUMMARY

Marriages may be dissolved involuntarily by death or voluntarily by desertion, annulment, separation, or divorce. In this chapter consideration was given to marriages which are dissolved by divorce and to the resulting social and personal implications. The relationships between divorce and ethnic origin, rural-urban residence, race, age at marriage, duration of marriage, economic status, educational level, and the presence or absence of children were described. Predivorce and postdivorce stages were discussed. The predivorce and postdivorce stages include the following: (1) some disturbance of the affectional-sexual life; (2) the mention of the possibility of divorce; (3) the appearance of solidarity is broken; (4) the decision to divorce is made; (5) crisis of separation begins; (6) the divorce takes place; and (7) the period of mental conflict which follows divorce.

Also discussed were the effects which divorce has on the marital

[43] *Ibid.*, pp. 66–67.
[44] *Ibid.*, pp. 108–113.

partners and on the children who are involved. In this regard it was noted that when both marital partners are desirous of obtaining a divorce, a minimum of psychic trauma results. However, if only one of the partners desires the divorce, the trauma may be increased tremendously. With regard to children, it was noted that a parental divorce always involves some amount of psychic trauma. However, it was suggested that in some cases the harmful effects of this trauma may be less than those experienced by the child who is forced to live in a parental environment saturated with hostility and anxiety.

Remarriage was then discussed and a description was given of the remarried man and woman in the United States today.

QUESTIONS

1. List and define the four ways in which marriages may be voluntarily dissolved.
2. What are the difficulties confronted in attempting to obtain objective statistics concerning causes of divorce?
3. What is the relationship between social change in the American family and divorce rates? Explain your answer and give examples.
4. Discuss the relationships between divorce and the following factors:
   (a) ethnic origin
   (b) rural-urban residence
   (c) race
   (d) age at marriage
   (e) duration of marriage
   (f) economic status
   (g) educational level
   (h) presence or absence of children
5. List and describe the stages which one tends to go through prior to, and after, divorce.
6. For what reasons do some couples, although unhappily married, select to remain married? Explain your answer.
7. Under what circumstances does remarriage tend to be successful, and under what circumstances does it tend to be unsuccessful? Explain your answer.

PROJECTS

1. Interview several clergymen to learn about the attitudes of their churches toward divorce. Check particularly on any changes in the attitude of the churches which may have occurred in the past 100 years.
2. Have a panel discussion concerning whether or not divorce is harmful to marital partners, and also whether or not it is harmful to the children involved.

SUGGESTED READINGS

Bergler, Edmund, *Divorce Won't Help*, Harper and Brothers, New York, 1948.

Bernard, Jessie, *Remarriage*, The Dryden Press, New York, 1956.

Goode, William J., *After Divorce*, The Free Press, Glencoe, Ill., 1956.

Monahan, Thomas P., "Divorce by Occupational Level," *Marriage and Family Living*, **17** (Nov., 1955), pp. 322–324.

Nye, F. Ivan, "Child Adjustment in Broken and in Unhappy Unbroken Homes," *Marriage and Family Living*, **19** (Nov., 1957), pp. 356–361.

Waller, Willard, *The Old Love and the New*, Liveright Publishing Co., New York, 1930.

Obtaining
professional assistance

19

You will recall that in Chapter 1 we indicated that this book has a problems orientation. Thus, throughout our treatment we have focused much of our attention on the many dilemmas of the man-woman relationship. Some of these as we have indicated may be dealt with by the marital partners themselves. Many of the marital conflicts that we have discussed, however, are sufficiently complex to require the services of a professional. In this final chapter, therefore, we wish to turn our attention to a discussion of such services.

Our society is very much concerned with the development of professional counseling and therapy. This interest in the growth and development of professional services to aid persons involved in marital conflict is the result of several factors. One such factor is society's concern for the plight of marriages as well as its concern for the plight of the individual caught in family conflicts. Society recognizes that it has a stake in what happens to families not only from a humanitarian point of view but also because any concentration of disturbed familial relations ultimately has its broader ramifications for the total society. A second factor which has spurred the growth of professional services is society's recognition that social forces play an important part in creating marital conflicts. (In Chapter 2 and other chapters we discussed the part that social changes have played in marital and family conflict.) Thus, society believes that it has a responsibility to make help available for those families and individuals in need of help. As a re-

sult of these concerns, there are now in existence numerous public
social work and family agencies which offer services. For those who
desire and can afford to pay for private assistance there are numerous
private practitioners who are available to help individuals and families caught in conflict.

The development of professional services, public or private, to assist
the person with marital conflict does not mean that people necessarily
seek out such services. Indeed, many turn to non-professional assistance; some, for example, go to friends and relatives. Unless the friend
is professionally competent such a procedure is not likely to be rewarding.[1] Friends can be notoriously unobjective, in a positive or negative direction. On some occasions they may praise a person for certain
actions, in other instances they may be judgmental and fix blame too
readily. The danger of gossip is also something to be reckoned with.
Moreover, to go to friends may place a burden on the continuation of
the friendship, since one may feel embarrassed about what was revealed under stress even to a friend. The friend, in turn, may feel embarrassed about what was heard and may find continuation of the relationship difficult. The motivations which underlie the need to tell
friends about one's marital difficulties should be examined. For indeed, quite apart from any desire for help, there may be a need to injure the spouse by distorting the nature of the difficulty.

In addition to seeking aid from friends, other non-professional
sources include the newspaper as well as the radio, where marital difficulties are aired to a public audience. It should be clear that while the
advice given through such media is not altogether bad, it is limited and
often superficial, since it is of necessity based on insufficient knowledge, half-truths, and distortions. Furthermore, as is true with so many
marital difficulties, the solution is not to be found in well-meaning advice, but is instead dependent on the marital partners' understanding
of the complexities involved.

It should be evident that great sums of money are spent each year
on these non-professional sources of information; and it is equally evident that people in trouble are much more prone to consult the persons and sources of information just described than they are to go to
professional counselors for help.[2] Why is this so? One aspect lies in
the need to avoid responsibility for the problem. Let us be specific;

[1] Lawrence S. Bee, *Marriage and Family Relations*, Harper and Brothers, New
York, 1959, pp. 315–316.

[2] For a discussion of the use and misuse of the marriage manual, see: George
Simpson, *People in Families*, Thomas Y. Crowell Co., New York, 1960, pp. 524–
525.

when anyone consults a professional counselor, he has usually, although not always, accepted the fact that there is a problem which has to be examined. Furthermore, if the counselee is evasive he will usually be informed that the counseling relationship can only be successful when there is a spirit of examining difficulties in an open, direct, and straightforward manner. Counselor and counselee are in face-to-face interaction and the business at hand is out in the open. There are many people with problems who are emotionally unable to deal with their difficulties this way; they have to be evasive and circuitous. While any good counselor would not encourage the avoidance of responsibility for problems, other media inadvertently do, since there is no face to face confrontation on issues. So the woman who writes to the newspaper can present her version of how she has been wronged, and while she admits to having a difficulty, she can avoid responsibility for her actions. To be sure, people often are informed by the newspaper consultant that all is not well with them, but this is always done in an impersonal and rather light fashion so that the impact may be of little consequence.

A second factor which keeps people from seeking professional assistance for their problems concerns the anti-intellectual, anti-scientific attitude which pervades much of our time. We have noted earlier the tendency to compartmentalize so that we accept science as applied to the physical, chemical, and biological, but science in human affairs is frequently rejected. Thus, many people feel that problems in human relations are part of the unknown and unknowable, and as such are not susceptible to scientific inquiry.[3] Such people avoid professional counselors.

A third factor which keeps people from seeking professional assistance with their marital problems has to do with the view that people with problems are weak people; those who do not have problems are therefore strong people.[4] These are naïve views to say the least. To begin with, problems are inherent in life. Thus, all of us have difficulties, although some people have more than others. Many of the so-called people of strength turn out frequently to have many problems, often well covered by arrogance and aggressiveness. Perhaps the real test of strength of character is the ability to face up to what is true about

[3] One author states that many people are skeptical about the use of marriage counseling in any romantic realm. Francis E. Merrill, *Courtship and Marriage*, Henry Holt and Co., New York, 1959, p. 380.

[4] For a discussion of a similar point, namely the reluctance to see a counselor because doing so is an admission of failure, see: Norman E. Himes and Donald L. Taylor, *Your Marriage*, rev. ed., Rinehart and Co., New York, 1955, p. 338.

MARTHA BLANCHARD

"Guess who our marriage counselor says is
causing all the trouble around here."

Figure 8. Courtesy Martha Blanchard and *Look* magazine.

oneself; this means the recognition of problems and of the personal consequences that have emerged. Such recognition is not for weaklings, for there is much pain in self-examination and in stripping away delusions. From a professional point of view, the prognosis is always much more favorable with the person who appears for counseling because he accepts the fact that he has problems and feels that an examination and resolution is necessary, than is the person who comes to counseling through coercion and self-deception implying that he is not in need of help.

SELECTION OF THE PROFESSIONAL. The selection of a professional person for help with one's marital difficulties is not simple, however, and is complicated by at least three factors. One factor has to do with certification of qualified personnel. As the professions of counseling and therapy grow there is a very real problem of developing standards of certification so that unqualified persons are not allowed to tamper with marriages and human personalities. The official professional societies representing the different counselors and therapists are making very strenuous efforts to make certain that persons engaged in counseling and therapy have been properly trained and understand all of the ramifications involved in dealing with personality and relationship difficulties. To achieve the goal of keeping unqualified persons from engaging in counseling is a difficult task requiring perhaps legislation and an alert and well-informed public. The laws in this country regarding who may and who may not provide counseling and therapy have been exceedingly lax.

A second factor which complicates selection of a professional person for assistance has to do with where such persons locate. There has been a marked tendency for therapists and counselors to locate in relatively large urban centers, so that large sections of semirural and rural America are virtually without their services. Part of the reason for the neglect of such areas has to do with the greater demands which heavily populated centers make for such services. The fact that qualified counselors and therapists are not plentiful makes the situation even more difficult.

Perhaps another reason for the few counselors and therapists found in small communities has to do with the fact that counselors and therapists are inclined to feel that persons from the smaller population centers with an individualistic spirit are inclined to look on marital problems as best resolved by the individuals concerned. Thus, many professionals feel that the small community is not likely to be a rewarding place in which to practice.

A third factor which complicates the selection of a professional for assistance concerns the differences in training even between professionals. For example there are different kinds of professionals with wide differences in training and professional maturity; there are psychiatrists, psychologists, and marriage counselors. Some of these devote full or part time to public and private agencies; others are engaged exclusively in private practice.

PSYCHIATRY AND PSYCHOANALYSIS. Psychiatrists are physicians who have specialized in the handling of deep-seated emotional difficulties. The most highly trained group of these people are those who have been certified by the American Board of Psychiatry and Neurology; the Board's standards are accepted as being exceedingly high. Within this group there are further subdivisions. One group practices general psychiatry, and this may include psychotherapy as well as physical and chemical therapies. Another group is devoted to the practice of psychoanalysis. Although most psychoanalysts are also physicians, there are analysts who are not physicians. They are presumably well trained. These are people who have received training in non-medical psychoanalytic institutes, and have been certified by them to engage in the practice of psychoanalysis. Psychoanalysis differs generally from psychotherapy in that its goals involve attempts at a total change of personality and orientation, rather than the removal of specific symptoms or problems. Further, psychoanalysts will use physical or chemical therapies only in extreme emergencies. The psychoanalyst functions with certain premises which often distinguish him from other therapists. Some of these premises may be stated as follows:

1. The strong reliance on the unconscious from which source personality conflicts may be revealed.[5]

2. The belief in the significance of dreams as an expression of conflicts.[6]

3. The belief in the importance of free association as a means for assisting the patient to understand his difficulties. Free association may be defined as a technique in which the patient reports all of the associations which enter consciousness, irrespective of content. The analyst, with the assistance of the patient, attempts to interpret the meaning of the associations in the context of the patient's difficulties.

Psychoanalysis is both costly and long. A complete analysis runs for several years, and during this time the patient is seen three to four times per week.

Although psychoanalysts have much in common, there are psychoanalytic schools which differ from one another in several respects. One of the most basic distinctions between the analytic schools relates to how far they have deviated from the original teachings of Sigmund Freud, the founder of psychoanalysis. Freud himself, and

[5] Indeed, not only is the unconscious an important source for revealing personality conflict, it is also viewed by one analyst as the important level in which conflict is solved. "Like good intentions, self-knowledge is of little value unless it penetrates to the unconscious levels of the human spirit. On this depends the future of marriage." Lawrence S. Kubie, "Psychoanalysis and Marriage," in Victor W. Eisenstein's *Neurotic Interaction in Marriage,* Basic Books, Inc., New York, 1956, pp. 10–43, especially p. 31.

[6] For case histories involving dream analysis, see: Martin H. Stein, "The Unconscious Meaning of the Marital Bond," in Victor W. Eisenstein's *Neurotic Interaction in Marriage,* Basic Books, Inc., New York, 1956, pp. 65–80.

those who have clung to his original views, minimized the role of social and cultural factors in personality disturbances. Those analysts who have deviated from Freud have generally accorded much more significance to the role of society and culture in creating human difficulties. These deviant analytic schools of thought have been identified as Neo-Freudian and represent the followers of such persons as Karen Horney, Harry Stack Sullivan, Franz Alexander, and others. For readers interested in the differences between these Neo-Freudian schools as well as between the orthodox and Neo-Freudian schools in general, there is now a great deal of literature to be consulted.[7]

Now that we have briefly discussed psychiatry and psychoanalysis, we might ask about its relevance for marital conflict. When the marital conflict is primarily the result of deep-seated personality problems of long-standing nature and the individuals involved seek a basic change and reorganization of personality they may wish to investigate the possibilities of either psychiatry or psychoanalysis. Qualified psychiatrists and psychoanalysts are listed in standard medical directories with statements of training and experience included. Non-medical psychologists trained in psychoanalysis are also certified by their respective associations.

PSYCHOLOGISTS. Practicing non-analytic psychologists represent different orientations. Many of these practitioners have been markedly influenced in their thinking by Freud and the Neo-Freudians, although they are not personally engaged in the practice of psychoanalysis. Their practice is concerned with enabling the individual to overcome specific personality difficulties, perhaps shyness, feelings of inferiority, or marked aggression, which interfere with his ability to get along with others. The goal of such therapy is not to bring about a reorganization of personality but is more limited in scope. Psychological counseling is generally of much shorter duration than psychoanalysis, and usually much less expensive.

When the marital conflict is primarily the result of personality difficulties and such difficulties are few and not deep seated, the individual may wish to seek psychological counseling. It should be noted in this regard that some psychologists experimenting with short forms of psychotherapy have reported much success.[8, 9]

[7] Joseph Jastrow, *Freud, His Dream and Sex Theories*, Pocket Books, Inc., New York, 1954.

[8] Perhaps the best known of these persons is Albert Ellis, a practicing psychologist in New York, who has developed a theory of "Rational Psychotherapy." Albert Ellis, "Rational Psychotherapy," *J. gen. Psychol.*, **59** (1958), pp. 35–49.

[9] Qualified psychologists and marriage counselors are sometimes hard to find.

"PERHAPS YOU HAVEN'T GIVEN YOUR MARRIAGE A CHANCE."

PARADE

Figure 9. Courtesy Joseph Zeis and Parade Publications, Inc. (June 11, 1961).

MARRIAGE COUNSELING. Marriage counseling services represent another source of professional help for disturbed relationships.[10] Medical people frequently engage in marriage counseling, but most certified marriage counselors tend to be non-medical persons who are trained in the behavioral sciences. Although all marriage counselors

The American Psychological Association certifies psychologists and the American Association of Marriage Counselors certifies marriage counselors. In addition to such certification one might look for an advanced degree in the science of human behavior, the Ph.D. or its equivalent. Universities are often in a position to recommend counselors and are usually happy to assist persons from the community in this respect. See also: Rex A. Skidmore, Hulda Van Steeter Garrett, and C. Jay Skidmore, *Marriage Consulting,* Harper and Brothers, New York, 1956, pp. 233–234.

[10] For a study of professional attitudes toward marriage counseling see: Richard K. Kerckhoff, "The Profession of Marriage Counseling as Viewed by Members of Four Allied Professions: A Study in the Sociology of Occupations," *Marriage and Family Living,* **15** (Nov., 1953), pp. 340–344.

are vitally interested in the marital relationship, they differ in their view in regard to the role of the marriage counselor. One group of marriage counselors believes that the function of the counselor is to deal primarily with matters of value incompatibility. These persons believe that the marriage counselor should avoid dealing with deep-seated personal difficulties including the unconscious. A second substantial body of professional opinion on marriage counseling believes that personality problems and immaturities are the basis of most marital conflict.[11] Professionals who hold this view believe that marriage counseling itself is really a form of psychotherapy and that the marriage counselor, if he is to function adequately, must at times deal with the deeper personal disturbances as they relate to marital difficulties.

Although the couple themselves may have some difficulty deciding what type of professional aid to seek, they can have confidence that any qualified psychiatrist, psychologist or marriage counselor will be able to determine the extent to which personality difficulty is involved in marital conflicts. Hence, when the therapist or counselor does not feel competent to deal with a case himself he will usually make the necessary referral to someone else. Appendix D carries a list of agencies from which accredited persons may be sought, and any of these agencies would constitute reliable starting places for help.

FUNCTION OF THERAPISTS AND COUNSELORS. There is considerable confusion regarding the kinds of things therapists and counselors attempt to do; it would seem appropriate therefore to outline some of the essential functions. To begin with, probably the main difference between psychotherapy and counseling, in the ideal sense, is that the former deals with deep-seated attitudes. The counselor, on the other hand, works primarily with conscious material only. Both psychotherapy and counseling do have certain common elements, however, which should be pointed out. To begin with, it should be clear that therapists and counselors, if competent, are not back slappers whose prime function it is to pass on clichés to make you feel better; nor are they people who simply sit around telling you what you ought or ought not to do. Competent counselors are not going

---

[11] Robert W. Laidlaw, "The Psychiatrist as Marriage Counselor," *Am. J. Psychiat.*, **106** (April, 1950), p. 736. One noted psychiatrist defines marriage counseling as a form of short-term psychotherapy dealing with interpersonal relationships in which problems relating to marriage are the central factors; quoted by Emily H. Mudd in *The Practice of Marriage Counseling*, Association Press, New York, 1951, p. 206.

to waste their time or yours with these superficial approaches to the complexities of human behavior.

Furthermore, therapists and counselors do not possess a preconceived view that all marriages must be saved regardless of the personal sacrifice involved. Therapists and counselors are primarily interested in revealing the real problems in the marriage, including their ramifications and complications, in order that the patient or counselee be in a position to deal with them effectively. This may be accomplished only when the individual understands his difficulties. Thus, competent therapists and counselors are persons who, through training and experience, can create a climate in which the counselee or patient can examine his problems. This process is facilitated by permitting the counselee to talk at some length about his marriage; this enables him to unburden himself, a process that is sometimes referred to as catharsis.

A second important component in the therapeutic and counseling process is the ability of the professionally trained person to accept individuals and their problems. This does not mean that he condones all behavior, neither is he likely to blame, or create guilt in the marital partners. For, indeed, he recognizes that the life experiences of the counselee have resulted in certain values or personal immaturities which have now emerged in marital conflict. The task is to see how the circumstances of life have, in a sense, created behaviors which the individual did not necessarily select himself.

Over a period of time and under favorable circumstances the counselee comes to see his problems, the attitudes associated with these problems, and the disturbances which these bring to his marriage. Only when the counselee knows what his problems are is he in a position to employ his intellect to do something about them.[12] This is an important point, since many laymen are under the erroneous impression that the solving of one's problems is simply a matter of common sense (by this they mean a matter of intelligence). The woman who continues to remain in love with an alcoholic whose chances for rehabilitation are very slim knows better, but she feels emotionally compelled to continue her love. Only when she can come to understand why she needs to love an alcoholic, when she has some appreciation of the underlying needs and emotional forces which are operating, can she make some rational choice—or use her intelligence.

[12] Marie W. Kargman, "The Clinical Use of Social System Theory in Marriage Counseling," *Marriage and Family Living*, 19 (Aug., 1957), pp. 263–269, especially p. 263.

Importance of Counseling and Therapy. There is much benefit which may be derived from competent counseling and therapy. For it is not only the total marriage which is involved but the lives of the marital partners which are perhaps even more important than the relationship. With successful professional assistance it becomes possible for the partners to clarify the values and goals they seek in marriage, the incompatibilities that may have had their origin in those pursuits, and the personal contribution each partner has made to the marital conflicts which have emerged. After that, they may be in a position to choose whether they desire to dissolve the present relationship, or whether it is feasible and possible to attempt to rehabilitate the present relationship. In any event, competent professional assistance will enable the couple to clarify these issues and minimize future problems whether they arise in the relationship they now have, or in some future involvement.

Professional counselors and therapists certainly cannot solve all marital complications. There are still gaps in knowledge and techniques which must be overcome and understood. Gradually, however, more and more of the complexities of the human relationship are better understood. What was once part of the mysterious is now part of the knowable. And, as we continue to study and engage in research, many of the areas of the human relationship that were inaccessible to understanding will be understood. Such accomplishments will be the result of human efforts; for human beings possess not only the ability to complicate their lives but the capacity to understand and build their lives as well.

SUMMARY

The simple solutions to marital problems which tend to be found in soap operas and fairy tales unfortunately are rarely found in the realities of living. For, indeed, the complex nature of marital conflict frequently makes it necessary for individuals not only to expend much time and energy in solving their problems but also to seek professional assistance in resolving their conflicts. Some people, however, although in need of professional assistance, turn to the non-professional (friends, relatives, newspaper columns, etc.) for help with their problems. They do this for a number of reasons: (1) they may wish to avoid assuming any responsibility for their problems, and, consequently, they may fear that the direct face-to-face confrontation with a professional person will make such avoidance impossible; (2) they may feel that problems in human relationships are part of the unknowable, and as such are not susceptible to the scientific inquiry of the professional realm; (3) they may feel that to admit that they have problems and to seek professional help in solving them implies that they are very weak people. Needless to say, the authors cannot accept these views. But what is more important, particularly since these views keep people who are in need of professional assistance from receiving it, the authors regard the existence of these views as being extremely unfortunate.

In this chapter various types of professional assistance available to couples to help them in resolving marital conflict were discussed; these are psychiatry, psychology, and marriage counseling. Also discussed were the similarities and differences which exist between the function of therapists and counselors, each of whom is trained to assist people in resolving marriage problems.

QUESTIONS

1. For what reasons is the United States society very much concerned with the development of professional marriage counseling and therapy? Discuss.
2. Why do some people try to avoid a face-to-face confrontation with a professional counselor, and instead seek other sources to get advice concerning their marital problems?
3. List and discuss the three factors which complicate the selection of a professional counselor.
4. When couples are receiving marriage counseling, who actually solves the marital conflict, the counselor or the counselee? Discuss this in full.

PROJECTS

1. Check all agencies in your community which might be doing marriage counseling and report to the class what facilities are available in your community.
2. Invite someone who is trained in the area of marriage counseling to speak to your class about counseling as a career.

SUGGESTED READINGS

Bowman, Henry A., "A Critical Evaluation of Marriage and Family Education," Marriage and Family Living, 15 (Nov., 1953), pp. 304–308.

Foster, Robert G., "How A Marriage Counselor Handles A Case," Marriage and Family Living, 16 (May, 1954), pp. 139–142.

Mudd, Emily H., et al., Eds., Marriage Counseling: A Casebook, Association Press, New York, 1958.

Rutledge, Aaron L., "Marriage Counseling Today and Tomorrow," Marriage and Family Living, 19 (Nov., 1957), pp. 386–390.

Vincent, Clark E., Ed., Readings in Marriage Counseling, Thomas Y. Crowell Co., New York, 1957.

Appendices

In dealing with the material in this book our concern has been with the man-woman relationship and the essential features of this relationship. There are two other important areas of information that have bearing on the man-woman relationship in marriage that were not formally discussed in this book; these include the medical and consumer problem areas. The discussions to follow are designed to supplement the several areas of the marital relationship with information on medical and economic facts in order that the reader be in a position to understand more clearly some of these problems.

Medical aspects of marriage

appendix A

Hans Lehfeldt, M.D.

The medical section was contributed by Hans Lehfeldt, M.D. Dr. Lehfeldt is a physician of wide professional experience, both in Europe and in the United States. His major medical interests are in gynecology and obstetrics. Dr. Lehfeldt's approach to his specialty in medicine suggests an appreciation and sensitivity for the psychological and sociological factors which may be implicated in obstetric and gynecologic problems. Furthermore, his many years of teaching experience have put him in close touch with the kinds of medical information which those about to be married need. A brief statement of Dr. Lehfeldt's experience and interest follows. Private practice, Berlin, 1928–1935; private practice, New York, 1936 to date; cofounder and codirector, Birth Control, Marriage Counseling Clinic of Gesellschaft for Sexual Reform. Coeditor of popular-scientific periodicals of "Sexual-Hygiene," 1932–1933 and "Die Geburtenregelung," Berlin, 1933. Member of Arbeitszentrale fuer Geburtenregelung, Berlin, 1931–1933. Assistant of Gynecological Clinic, New York University, 1937–1945. Clinical assistant of Lenox Hill Hospital, OPD, 1936 to date; adjunct, obstetrics and gynecology, Grand Central Hospital, 1958 to date; clinical assistant visiting obstetrician-gynecologist, 3rd division, Bellevue Hospital, 1958 to date; chief of contraceptive clinic, New York University Bellevue Medical Center; teaching assistant in obstetrics and gynecology, New York University, College of Medicine. Past Officer of the Rudolf Virchow Medical Society. Cofounder and member of executive committee of the Society for the Scientific Study of Sex. Member of medical committee, Planned Parenthood Federation of America. Author of Buch der Ehe, Berlin, 1930; translator of "Gynecologic Radiography" by Dalsace and Garcia-Calderon, Hoeber-Harper, 1958. Numerous contributions to German, French, and American scientific journals. American correspondent for the British Journal of Sex Education, 1949–1952. Lectures at Broca Hospital, Paris University, 1952 and 1954. Mission to Barbados, BWI, 1957, for lectures and instruction in contraception.

Dr. Lehfeldt's material is organized into several parts; each is designed to deal with one major medical aspect of the man-woman relationship in marriage. In Part 1 which follows, the concern is with the anatomy and physiology of sex organs, which includes details of structure and descriptions of functions as well. Dr. Lehfeldt deals with the phenomena of menstruation, puberty, and menopause. Masterbation is also discussed in this section.

PART 1: ANATOMY AND PHYSIOLOGY OF SEX ORGANS

ANATOMY OF THE FEMALE SEX ORGANS. The female generative or reproductive system can be divided into the external and the internal genitalia. Whereas the external organs are in general outside of the body, the interior organs are situated within the pelvic cavity.

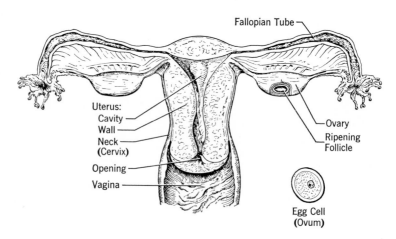

Figure 10. Female sex organs—front view.

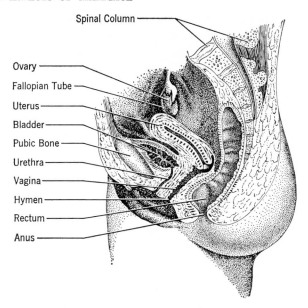

Spinal Column

Ovary
Fallopian Tube
Uterus
Bladder
Pubic Bone
Urethra
Vagina
Hymen
Rectum
Anus

Figure 11. Female sex organs—side view.

The external organs are the vulva and the vagina. The *vulva* consists of the labia, the clitoris, the openings of the urethra and the vagina and the hymen. The labia or lips consist of two symmetrical pairs of skin-folds, of which the outer lips (labia majora) are larger, and the inner lips (labia minora), smaller. The skinfolds start below the pubic hair and extend toward the region of the anus. The clitoris is located in the center of the upper part of the labia minora and is usually the shape and size of a pea. A little below the clitoris is the urethral opening. Still further down is the vaginal opening or the introitus (Latin for entrance). Each of the labia majora contains a gland, called Bartholin's gland, whose secretion lubricates the introitus. In a virgin, a thin, bandlike membrane, called the hymen, narrows the introitus. The hymen is usually ruptured during the first cohabitation. At their pos-terior or lower part the labial folds unite again, forming the "four-chette." The anatomical structure situated between the vulva and anus is called the perineum.

The *vagina*, although invisible without an instrument (speculum), is nevertheless considered part of the external female genitalia. It is situated between the bladder and the rectum. In the nulliparous woman (one who has never borne a child), the vagina is a tubular structure with a closed end. At its upper or proximal terminus lies the uterus or womb, the lowermost part of which forms the cervix. The cervix is a finger-like structure which dips into the vagina, causing it to form pouches, called fornices, one in front of the cervix (anterior fornix) and one behind (posterior fornix). The posterior fornix is deeper than the anterior one. The vagina is remarkably elastic, and during the birth process, stretches sufficiently to become a part of the birth canal. During menstruation, the vagina also serves as the passageway for the blood that flows from the uterus. (For the coital function of the vagina, see Part 2 of this appendix—Marital Relations.)

The internal organs consist of the uterus, two fallopian tubes, and two ovaries. In shape and size the *uterus* resembles a pear. The small, lower end of this pear-shaped organ has already been described as the cervix; the upper part of the uterus is called the body, corpus, or fundus. The uterus is a hollow organ. Its inside cavity is shaped like an inverted triangle. At the cervical end of the uterus is a small opening, the external os (mouth), which connects with the vagina. Two still smaller openings link the upper part of the uterine cavity with the *fallopian tubes*, which curve from the upper end of the uterus toward the ovary on each side extending in a funnel-like shape called the fimbrial end. Thus a system of canals connects the ovaries via the tubes, the uterine cavity, and the cervical canal, with the vagina. The *ovaries* are the female sex glands, the size and shape of an almond.

PHYSIOLOGY OF FEMALE SEX ORGANS. The function of the female sex organs (as well as of the male) is governed by the *pituitary gland,* a small structure situated at the base of the brain. In the woman, hormones secreted by its anterior lobe (follicle-stimulating hormone—FSH, and luteinizing hormone—LH) bring about a ripening of the eggs in the ovary. Furthermore, these hormones induce the ovary to secrete two hormones of its own, estrogen and progesterone, which are responsible for ovulation and menstruation. No function of the sex organs is possible without the pituitary; this gland has therefore been described as the "motor of sexual function."

In the mature woman the *ovary* has two functions: production of eggs (ova) and secretion of estrogen and progesterone. In the newborn female baby, the ovaries contain about a quarter of a million egg cells. In the mature woman the monthly ovarian cycle begins with the growth of "follicles," groups of cells arranged circularly around the ovum. These follicles grow and mature by multiplication of their cells, by enlargement of the ovum itself, and by accumulation of fluid inside the follicle. Every month one of the many follicles ripens in this manner and the enlarged ovum assumes an eccentric position in the follicle. This so-called *graafian follicle* rises to the periphery of the ovary; the fluid inside the follicle increases until finally the follicle bursts, and the ovum is expelled into the lateral or fimbrial end of the fallopian tube. This process, called ovulation, takes place in midcycle, i.e., half-way between two menstrual periods. A few days after ovulation, the ruptured follicle is transformed into a yellow body, the "corpus luteum." If the ovum is not fertilized, the corpus luteum degenerates into a pale scar, the corpus albicans; if the ovum is fertilized, the corpus luteum continues to grow until about the seventh month of pregnancy when it is finally absorbed. The growing follicles secrete estrogen, while the corpus luteum produces progesterone in addition to some estrogen.

Estrogen is produced mainly during the first three weeks; progesterone, during the fourth week of the menstrual cycle. These hormones, secreted into the bloodstream, affect the lining of the uterus, the endometrium. During the first three weeks of the cycle, the endometrium enters the so-called proliferative phase by gradually growing thicker under the influence of estrogen. In the fourth and last week of the cycle, the endometrium, now under the influence of progesterone, enters the so-called secretory phase, preparatory to either menstruation or implantation (nidation) of the fertilized ovum. If the egg is not fertilized, the superficial layers of the endometrium are pushed off, thereby reducing the thickness of the uterine lining to one-fourth. This process opens blood vessels, and menstrual bleeding ensues. A few days later the loss of layers in the endometrium is compensated by the cells of its basic layer which grow at the beginning of the next cycle, again forming first another proliferative, and later, a secretory endometrium.

These cyclic changes in the uterus are subject to cyclic changes in the ovary, which in turn are dependent upon the hormones produced by the anterior pituitary. As the pituitary is dependent on normal functioning of the thyroid and of the adrenal glands, it becomes obvious that only women with a normal general endocrine system will have a physiological and regular menstrual cycle.

Menstruation, or the periodic flow of blood from the uterus, occurs at fairly regular intervals of 28 days. Individual variations of the cycle, however, are not necessarily abnormal. The length of the cycle, i.e., the interval between the first day of the last and the first day of the following menstruation, may range from 21 to 35 days. A normal menstruation lasts three to five days. Some pain during menstruation is not unusual. Severe and incapacitating pain, however, indicates dysmenorrhea. Medical treatment with hormones or pain relieving drugs is usually beneficial. Some instances of dysmenorrhea are psychogenic and require psychotherapy. Many women are moody, tense, or depressed during the week preceding the period. This "pre-menstrual tension syndrome" can also be alleviated by medical treatment or psychotherapy. For protection during the menstrual flow many women wear tampons, such as Tampax, instead of sanitary napkins, a practical and harmless convenience. Much is said in advertisements about "female hygiene," involving douching with disinfectants, particularly after sexual intercourse or after menstruation. Most modern gynecologists consider douching completely unnecessary for a healthy woman, as the normal vagina has a self-cleansing faculty far superior to any chemical preparations.

Puberty. Puberty, the transition period between childhood and adult life, usually extends over several years. Its first physical signs are appearance of secondary sex characteristics, which, in the female, are growth of pubic hair and development of the breasts. The first menstruation (menarche) usually occurs between the ages of twelve and fourteen, but its onset may vary widely. Menarche before the age of nine, or after the age of seventeen, is considered abnormal.

In the past hundred years, there appears to be a tendency toward an earlier onset of puberty, which has been attributed to improved hygienic and nutritional conditions. For one to two years after menarche, the quantity of flow, as well as the intervals between periods, may vary widely. Often menstruation is regularly established, but no ovulation takes place; in other words, many adolescent girls produce the phenomenon of anovulatory menstruation, i.e., menstruation without a preceding ovulation. This explains the *relative* infertility of adolescent girls. Gradually, there are fewer anovulatory menstruations, until finally every menstrual period is preceded by ovulation.

Psychic phenomena accompany these physical changes. Adjustment to adolescence entails a variety of moods which require understanding by parents, teachers, and adult friends.

Menopause. Menstruation ceases between the ages of forty-two and fifty-two (average, forty-seven). As a rule, the earlier the menarche, the later the menopause. Concurrent with the "change of life" are retrogressive changes in the breasts and the generative organs. As in puberty, a number of anovulatory menstruations occur, lowering the fertility. However, conception may take place, even after a period of several months of amenorrhea. Menopause is caused by the cessation of the ovarian function. During this period, the ovary gradually loses its follicles and is transformed into non-functioning tissue, while the anterior pituitary gland shows signs of hyper-activity. In the aging male, however, this gland exhibits signs of decreasing function. The overactivity of the anterior pituitary gland in women during change of life causes endocrine disturbances, affecting several other glands —the thyroid and the adrenals. This pluriglandular disturbance probably accounts for some of the vasomotor disorders occurring during this period. Although three-fourths of all women experience some disturbances during menopause, 90 percent of them pursue their usual activities. In general, the *symptoms* are mild, consisting of flushes, or a prickling sensation in the fingers or toes. They respond well to hormonal therapy, which is harmless and, if given under medical supervision, does not produce cancer. Psychological alterations in menopause are sometimes pronounced, such as, anxiety syndromes and depressions; they may be ascribed partly to the fear of aging or to the fallacious assumption that menopause signifies loss of sexuality. Actually libido and sex enjoyment often increase during and after menopause with the elimination of the fear of pregnancy.

ANATOMY OF MALE SEX ORGANS. The male sex organs consist of external structures: the penis and scrotum; and of internal structures: the vas deferens, the seminal vesicles, and the prostatic gland. The penis has the double function of serving as an implement for

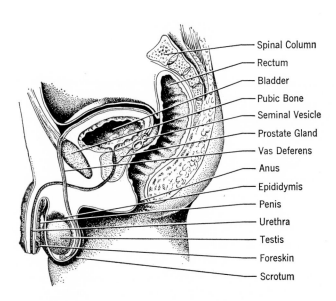

Figure 12. Male sex organs—side view.

urination and for coitus. The *penis* consists of head (glans), rim (corona), and shaft. The shaft lies below the symphysis to which it is firmly attached. A cross section of the penis shaft reveals three structures: a single structure surrounding the urethra, called corpus cavernosum urethrae, and two symmetrical structures, the right and left corpus cavernosum of the penis.

Underneath and behind the penis is the *scrotum*, a sac containing the two *testicles* and the two *epididymides*. From each side of each epididymis, a small tube, the vas deferens, runs through the inguinal canal and into the pelvic cavity behind the endopelvic segment of the urethra. At the point where the bladder continues into the urethra and attached to the posterior surface of the bladder lie two symmetrical sacs, the *seminal vesicles*. The *vas deferens* conducts the secretion of the testicles, the spermatozoa, from the epididymis, through the inguinal canal into the seminal vesicles. Behind the two seminal vesicles, the bladder, and the pelvic portion of the urethra, is a large structure, the *prostatic gland,* which encircles the uppermost part of the urethra.

PHYSIOLOGY OF MALE SEX ORGANS. The main mass of the semen derives from the seminal vesicles where it is stored. The prostatic gland produces a part of the seminal fluid, which activates the spermatozoa. During erection they continue into the urethra where, mixing with the prostatic secretions, they form into the final ejaculate. It may be seen that the anatomical pathway of the mature sperm is a complex one.

The testicles are about 4 to 5 cm long and about 2½ cm thick. They have a double function: in addition to producing spermatozoa, they are endocrine organs which control secondary male sex characteristics, such as, male type of hair growth and voice, and the virile structure of the body. The typical eunuch characteristics of high voice and beardlessness, produced by castration before puberty, illustrate the endocrine function of the testicles.

In contrast to the female whose production of ova ends in the menopause, the male produces *spermatozoa* from puberty into old age. The development of the spermatozoon is long and complicated. It originates as a round cell, the spermatogonium, and passes through several stages of transformation before assuming its final form. Full spermatogenesis, a continuous process in man, usually starts at the age of sixteen. The spermatogonium has a total of 46, i.e., 23 paired, chromosomes, of which one pair, the XY chromosome, is dissimilar in size and shape. This pair is determinative for sex.

Examination under an ordinary microscope shows the normal spermatozoon divided into four sections: head, neck, middle section, and tail. The head is oval in shape and the tail is approximately 10 to 12 times the length of the head. The quantity of an ejaculate is subject to great variations; 3 to 5 cc of seminal fluid may be considered an average amount. Each cc of seminal fluid contains about 100 to 120 million spermatozoa. If there are only 60 million per cc, or less, fertility is lowered. However, men with even lower sperm counts may be able to impregnate.

Erection originates in the central nervous system. Under sexual stimulation, the reflux of blood from the corpora cavernosa in the penis is blocked, and the penis distends and becomes rigid. If the stimulation continues, erection is eventually followed by ejaculation.

As in the female, the endocrine, as well as the gamete (sexual) producing testicular functions, depend on the function of other endocrine glands, particularly the anterior pituitary. Good testicular function is also dependent on a well-functioning thyroid.

Puberty. Puberty in the male usually starts a couple of years later than in the female. Its most significant signs are hair growth and change of voice. While erections may and frequently do occur during early childhood, ejaculation generally begins in puberty. Nocturnal erections during dreams followed by ejaculation, called pollution, or nocturnal emission are not infrequent during this epoch. Such physiological phenomena may have a frightening effect on a child or an adolescent boy, unless explained. Early sex education is therefore of great importance.

Masturbation is a frequent practice in adolescent boys, as well as in people of all ages and both sexes. It is not dangerous—contrary to the beliefs still held by some adults.

Is There a Male Menopause? This question is raised again and again by physicians and laymen. Some psychological and somatic phenomena occurring in middle age have been attributed to a "male climacteric." Actually, there is no anatomical or physiological basis for this assumption. Male potency and fertility continue into old age, although potency diminishes somewhat in older men.

PART 2: MARITAL RELATIONS

In Part 2 Dr. Lehfeldt turns his attention to marital relations. In this part the purpose of the author is to provide the married couple with a knowledge of physiological and psychological facts necessary for successful performance of the sex act; and of pathologies when the sex act is not consummated successfully. Dr. Lehfeldt gives particular attention to the nature of orgasm and its psychological manifestations. In addition he deals briefly in this section with the physiology of coitus, coital behavior, and the technique of defloration.

PHYSIOLOGY. Coitus, also called cohabitation, copulation, or sexual intercourse, consists of insertion of the erect penis into the vagina, followed by more or less vigorous thrusts of the penis in the direction of the cervix. The cohabitation ends with ejaculation; most of the seminal fluid is deposited around the cervix and into the posterior fornix of the vagina. Recent studies show that spermatozoa reach the cervical canal a few minutes after unprotected intercourse.

The frequency at which individual couples have intercourse is subject to great variations. Two or three times a week is considered average. In the later years of marriage, and with advancing age, the coital frequency decreases gradually.

The duration of the coital act also varies, 2 to 5 minutes is an average length of time. Healthy men of normal potency can extend the act to about 20–30 minutes. There are many different techniques of cohabitation; the choice depends on experience and individual preference, as well as on the somatic and psychologic condition of the partners. Sex play, which frequently precedes cohabitation, includes lip kissing, and stimulation of the sex organs.

VARIOUS COITAL POSITIONS. In the most commonly known coital position, the male lies above the female who faces him. In other frequently used positions, the female lies above the male, or the male and female lie on their sides facing each other. A wide variety of positions are described in the extensive literature on the subject, for instance, in the famous *Kama Sutra* by Vatsyayana, published in India more than 1,600 years ago, and in the Roman literature by authors like Apulaeus, Ovid, and Lucian. One of the best-known modern writers on sex techniques is Van de Velde, whose books were first published some thirty years ago.

Technique of Defloration. In the female's first sexual intercourse, the hymen must be penetrated. If the hymen is thin and elastic, it will break or dilate with little or no discomfort; if it is rigid, entry may cause pain. Understanding and gentleness on the part of the male will greatly help to relax the female and thus to overcome, or at least soften, the pain. The breaking of the hymen usually causes a slight bleeding, which may recur during a few subsequent cohabitations. In the rare instances where full penetration is not possible, or where coitus continues to be painful for the female as late as two weeks after the first cohabitation, medical advice should be sought. Usually a simple procedure, such as stretching a rigid hymen, or dissection, will straighten out the difficulty.

Tactful behavior during a couple's first coital experience is of the greatest importance for marital sex adjustment. If the first cohabitation precipitates an inexperienced young woman into a state of anxiety, serious marital difficulties may result. A honeymoon, therefore, should be regarded not solely as a time for lighthearted pleasure and happiness, but also as a decisive period leading to greater understanding and happiness.

Orgasm. The peak of sexual activity is called orgasm. The partners suddenly become tense, experience muscular spasms for a number of seconds, and then return to a normal, or sometimes subnormal, physiological state.

Orgasm is the prototype of a psychosomatic reaction. Physical changes during orgasm include an increased heart rate, elevated blood pressure and respiration, and an increased flow of blood into the genital organs. These symptoms are followed by spastic contractions of the muscles surrounding the genital area. At the time of orgasm, the male ejaculates seminal fluid while in the female orgasm no discharge of gametes occurs, but there is some secretion produced by the Bartholin and cervical glands. Electroencephalograms taken during intercourse show significant changes resembling epilepsy. Orgasm is usually coupled with a short loss of consciousness, preceded by a feeling of elation, and followed by a sensation of complete relaxation. This peaceful sensation after orgasm is one of its notable aspects.

With the exception of ejaculation, the phenomenon of orgasm is precisely the same in both sexes. The studies of Kinsey and his group seem to indicate that the length of time needed to achieve orgasm is also approximately the same for both sexes. Up to that time, the assumption had been that women were slower in reaching orgasm, and, in general, had a different orgastic curve. In the male, relaxation after orgasm was believed to set in almost immediately, while the female was supposed to return to normal after some delay (Kehrer, Van de Velde).

The psychoanalytic school of thought emphasizes the importance of vaginal versus clitoral orgasm. According to the Freudians, only vaginal orgasm can provide full sexual satisfaction. Physiologically there is no difference between the two forms of orgasm; individual couples may alternate clitoral and vaginal orgasm in various cohabitations.

The preceding paragraphs have dealt mainly with the technique of sexual relations. Technique can be learned by inexperienced couples, either from books or through expert advice, but technique is not all. Satisfactory sexual union for both husband and wife can be achieved only if the two have an intimate psychologic relationship, dominated by love, devotion, and deep understanding. All too often frigid women or impotent men consult their physician, in the vain hope that reading a few chapters on sex technique in the right book will cure their ills. Although the doctor can successfully advise couples whose failure to adjust sexually is based solely on inexperience, he cannot always cure other, more deeply rooted inadequacies.

PATHOLOGY. The foregoing remarks about orgasm clearly indicate that no woman capable of clitoral orgasm, or of any orgasm, should be considered frigid. Frigidity can be described as the inability to achieve orgasm; in its absolute form it is rare, while relative frigidity, i.e., occasional inability to achieve orgasm, is not infrequent. This condition may be due to a difference in the sexual "appetites" of the partners.

Males seem to have a more frequent desire for intercourse than females. When the drive for cohabitation is absent in the woman, she will frequently not achieve orgasm. If there is mutual understanding, this situation need not endanger the marital relationship.

Generally, frigidity has no organic or endocrine cause, although it may be produced temporarily by a severe disease. In most cases, frigidity is a psychological disorder caused by deep-seated conflicts. The logical treatment is therefore some form of psychotherapy, including psychoanalysis. Pseudo-frigidity—not to be confused with frigidity—is generally due to sexual inexperience of one or both partners and can often be cured by marriage-counseling. It may also originate in an aversion of the woman for her partner, in which case neither psychotherapy nor marriage-counseling is likely to help.

The counterpart to female frigidity is impotence in the male. In mild cases, the erection time is shortened and ejaculation occurs early, at times before insertion of the penis (premature ejaculation). In more severe forms of impotence, the erection is impaired and intercourse becomes impossible. In another form of impotence there is failure of the male to achieve ejaculation.

Impotence is rarely caused by a physical disorder, consequently hormonal therapy is of little value. The treatment for impotence is psychotherapy. Frequently men are impotent with one woman, but highly potent with another, a fact that clearly points to the psychological origin of this condition. There is a physiological lowering of potency with increasing age, but even octogenarians do not entirely lose their capacity for sexual intercourse.

PART 3: FAMILY PLANNING

Part 3 deals with the important problem of family planning and should be of considerable interest to the reader irrespective of religious persuasion. Some of the significant problems dealt with in this section include those associated with planning of pregnancy for different age groupings, child spacing methods, infertility, and sterility. Medical methods for dealing with these problems are described.

Planning a successful marriage and planning pregnancies is much more important than planning the wedding. Two different personalities must adapt their ways of life—always a difficult change, even if one or both partners have had previous marital experience.

Family planning is not synonymous with limiting pregnancies. Most couples have definite ideas about the number of children they want, even though they may modify their plans later. All pregnancies should be desired and planned. No couple should have their children before being ready for them. Thanks to modern methods of contraception, it is unnecessary to bring children into the world haphazardly. In some cases, for instance after a severe illness, the physician may advise postponement of pregnancy; or he may favor early pregnancy, or a rapid succession of pregnancies, as in the case of endometriosis, the presence of endometrial tissue in abnormal locations, or in the presence of uterine fibroids. Elderly couples also should have their children early in marriage, for several reasons: (1) pregnancy complications are more frequent in elderly mothers, as will be discussed later, (2) the incidence of fetal deformity is higher in older parents, particularly the incidence of mongoloid children, and (3) fertility in women definitely decreases with age. Of twenty-year-old females, only 3 percent are sterile, while by the age of thirty the percentage reaches 12, and by age forty, it is 32 percent.

Medical experience has emphasized the merits of child spacing, particularly in the case of young parents, where an interval of about two years between deliveries is often desirable for physical and psychological reasons. In making a decision, each family must of course consider its individual situation. The situation might be discussed with a physician, a marriage counselor, or a spiritual adviser. The Catholic Church, while prohibiting all mechanical methods of contraception, permits the rhythm method, by which intercourse is avoided during the fertile days of the cycle. However, many of the Catholic users of contraceptive methods in the United States avail themselves of the mechanical methods condemned by their church.

The two "appliance" methods most commonly used in this country are the condom for the male and the diaphragm combined with jelly or cream for the female. A less frequently used method is the cervical cap. If made of plastic material, the cervical cap can be worn throughout the entire cycle, thus providing prolonged protection, but it cannot be prescribed for women who have any pathology of the cervix. Special creams and jellies have been developed for use alone, i.e., without a diaphragm. This method provides a slightly lower degree of protection than the diaphragm-jelly combination method. Coitus interruptus (withdrawal) is a contraceptive method used by many couples with considerable success; however, the abrupt arrest of the sex act often interferes with satisfactory marital relations.

Recently oral contraceptive tablets have been developed. These "pills"—synthetic hormones—prevent conception by suppression of ovulation. They are only available with a doctor's prescription and should be taken only under medical supervision. This method is harmless and most effective.

It is good advice to a young couple not to attempt to cope with the complex problem of family planning unassisted, but to obtain expert counsel. The physician should not limit himself to one single method of family planning; for if this method proves unacceptable to a particular couple, they will discard it after a short while. The physician who is successful in prescribing a technique suited to individual needs will obtain the highest rate of acceptance and thus will be most helpful to his patients.

INFERTILITY AND STERILITY. Two types of impaired fertility exist: infertility and sterility. Infertility can be defined as the inability to produce living children; in this condition conception occurs but the pregnancy is terminated before the baby is viable, ending either in spontaneous abortion or in premature delivery. In sterility, no conception takes place. The expressions sterility and infertility are frequently erroneously used as synonyms.

In antiquity, and in some primitive civilizations even today, barrenness is blamed exclusively on reproductive failure in the female. Actually, we should not think in terms of infertile or sterile men and women, but of barren couples. In general, it may be said that males are the cause of sterility and infertility as often as are females. In many instances, both partners are responsible for the failure to conceive.

Infertility and sterility present delicate problems of diagnosis and treatment because the process of reproduction, as shown in the foregoing chapters, is such a complicated one. Usually, any dysfunction in the male is much easier to diagnose. An examination of the semen will reveal deficiencies in motility, abnormal forms, a low sperm count— or in cases of male sterility, absence of motility or no sperm at all. Any investigation of a barren couple should therefore start with the examination of the male.

For the examination of the female, a number of procedures are necessary. First, we need to determine whether ovulation takes place. A few physicians have been able to observe the process of ovulation in the living woman by means of a culdoscope, an instrument similar to the cystoscope, inserted into the peritoneum through a vaginal incision while the patient was under anesthesia.

In the majority of cases, however, physicians have to rely on indirect signs of ovulation, i.e., the effects produced in connection with ovulation. Menstruation, as has been stated previously, is not in itself proof of ovulation. Cyclic changes in the endometrium, which occur in the ovulating woman, can, however, be used to determine indirectly whether ovulation has occurred. Through endometrial biopsy (an office procedure) small parts of the endometrium can be removed and examined after the presumed ovulation time; they will show, or fail to show, secretory changes which are indicative of ovulation. A simpler method is taking the basal temperature every morning. A typical basal temperature chart shows the so-called dip, the temperature reaching its lowest point on the 12th day of the cycle, followed by a sustained, elevated temperature curve from the 14th to the 27th day of the cycle. Among laboratory tests to determine ovulation are vaginal smears, examination of the cervical mucus, and special urine tests.

Another important method used in the investigation of female sterility is the utero-tubal insufflation, the Rubin test, also an office procedure. Carbon dioxide gas is inflated under pressure by means of a canula through the cervical canal into the fallopian tubes. The escape of the gas through the tubes can be heard by the physician. When the patient assumes the erect position after the test, she will experience shoulder pain, if the tubes are open. Another technique to determine tubal patency is hysterosalpingography: a contrasting material is injected through the cervical canal in order to obtain a radiologic picture of uterus and fallopian tubes. This method, usually employed after utero-tubal insufflation has failed to demonstrate tubal patency, frequently helps to localize the site of tubal obstruction. Both the Rubin test and hysterosalpingography are not only diagnostic but therapeutic procedures as well, and often help to restore tubal patency and to cure sterility.

The results of operations aiming at restoration of tubal patency are still rather discouraging; the success rate is very low.

PART 4: PREGNANCY

In Part 4 the phenomenon of pregnancy is presented in detail. Dr. Lehfeldt's purpose here is to provide the reader with an understanding of pregnancy in its many aspects. Thus the signs of pregnancy are discussed, including laboratory tests for pregnancy. The physiology of pregnancy is fully described. Finally Dr. Lehfeldt addresses himself to the subject of proper prenatal care and pathology of pregnancy.

PHYSIOLOGY. Pregnancy begins at the moment when a mature ovum, expelled from the ovary and having entered the fallopian tube, is fertilized by a spermatozoon. As mentioned before, a single ejaculate contains several hundred million spermatozoa. Most spermatozoa perish in the hostile secretion of the vagina, but some reach the cervical canal and ascend from there into the uterine cavity and into the lumen of the fallopian tubes. Here they encounter the ovum, but only a single spermatozoon will penetrate the membrane of the ovum and fertilize it. After the head of the spermatozoon has entered the ovum, the tail disappears; head and neck migrate towards the center of the ovum and unite with its nucleus into one cell. This cell divides into two cells, which again subdivide to form more and more cells, arranged in circular fashion. Some of these, the so-called auxiliary cells, multiply faster than the center cells and form a layer around them. The center cells, the so-called formative cells, are the ones from which the embryo later develops. A fluid, probably secreted by the auxiliary cells, soon appears in the center of the cell accumulation so that the entire structure looks like a small balloon filled with water. At the same time that the cell divisions and modifications take place, the fertilized ovum moves toward the uterine cavity, taking from six to seven days to complete its migration. The endometrium then enters the so-called secretory phase, characterized by wide and tortuous glands and a thickened mucus membrane full of blood vessels. In this condition the endometrium constitutes an ideal medium for the nesting (nidation) of the fertilized ovum in which the development of the fetus now begins. The nutrition of the ovum is effected through the affiliation of maternal endometrial cells and of some of the auxiliary cells of the fertilized ovum. The cells at the periphery of the ovum form into villous structures (worm-like processes) which facilitate the alimentation of the growing embryo. The entire mass of villi is called the chorion. The cell-membrane covering the inside of the embryonic sac is called the amnion. The fluid in which the embryo is suspended is called the amniotic fluid, or baby water, and is contained in the amniotic sac. From the chorionic villi, the afterbirth (placenta) develops.

In this space we cannot discuss in detail the full development of embryonic life, but will have to limit ourselves to a few basic facts. In the fourth week the embryo is about 1 cm long and already shows rudiments of eyes, ears, and nose. In the second month of pregnancy, the embryo is about 2½ cm long, and the external genitalia start to develop. In the third month, the fetal length is about 8 cm, fingers and toes are visible. In the fourth month, the fetus measures about 16 cm, in the fifth month 25 cm. Already in the third month the fetus starts to move, but its movements are not noticeable yet. Usually, fetal movements, called "quickening," are noticed by the expectant mother in the fifth or sixth month of her first pregnancy, and earlier in subsequent pregnancies.

Usually the first indication of pregnancy noticed by the woman is the discontinuation of menstruation. Other subjective signs are a tendency to urinate more frequently, swelling of the breasts, nausea, or a slight feeling of faintness. A woman who observes any of these symptoms usually consults her physician. It is advisable to have such a consultation about a week or ten days after the first missed period. Even in the early phase, the physician may be able to diagnose pregnancy: the uterus is slightly enlarged, somewhat softer, and more congested; the breasts are fuller, and frequently a fluid, the so-called colostrum, can be expressed from the breasts. These diagnostic indications differ only slightly from findings in the non-pregnant uterus shortly before the onset of the next period. If re-examination one or two weeks later shows more pronounced changes, the diagnosis is more certain.

A number of biological tests have been developed which help the physician diagnose pregnancy at an early stage. The best known is the so-called A-Z test, developed by Aschheim and Zondek. For this test urine from the expectant mother is injected into immature female mice. In case of pregnancy, the mice react with swelling, congestion, and hemorrhages into their ovaries. In modifications of the A-Z test, rabbits, rats, and frogs are used. All of these tests show a high degree of accuracy, but it must be emphasized that no test is 100 percent reliable. An accurate diagnosis at an early stage can be made only through physical examination combined with observation of the woman. Another important point is that any result of such a pregnancy test, be it positive or negative, must be regarded as unreliable if the test is made earlier than 10 days after the first missed period. A simple test for determination of early pregnancy is the fern test, which is based on examination of the cervical mucus, for the so-called crystallization phenomenon. This test, which is done in the doctor's office and can be interpreted immediately, is accurate only in a negative way, i.e., as a method of ruling out pregnancy. Its advantage is that it can be performed as early as a few days after the missed period, at which time the A-Z test or its modifications fail to give adequate information.

While clinical as well as biological tests usually enable the physician to arrive at a comparatively early diagnosis, they are not 100 percent reliable. A definitive diagnosis is possible only by observation of the clinical symptoms produced by the fetus. By the third month, the fetal bone formation is advanced enough to be detected by X ray, but today such an examination is considered harmful. In the fourth or fifth month the fetal heart can be heard in a soundproof room by means of sound amplification; at this time the mother herself will begin to feel fetal movements or "quickening."

The question whether the sex of the baby can be determined before birth has preoccupied people from time immemorial. Theoretically, it can be done today by puncturing the amniotic sac and by aspirating some amniotic fluid; this fluid contains cells from the fetus which will reveal its sex under microscopic examination. As puncture of the amniotic sac is dangerous, it is in most cases advisable to abstain from sex determination before birth.

PRENATAL CARE. Prenatal care, which today is a routine procedure in the United States, has been instrumental in lowering maternal and infant mortality. Early in pregnancy the woman is given a complete physical examination, including blood count, urinalysis and blood serology (Wassermann). In addition, the patient's—and if necessary, her husband's—blood type and RH factor are determined. The bony pelvis is measured, a fairly reliable method to determine whether the pelvis is wide enough to allow smooth passage of the baby at birth. Until a few years ago, many obstetricians took pelvic

X rays of every patient expecting her first baby. In the light of modern knowledge concerning possible harmful effects of radiation on the baby, X-ray studies during pregnancy are now done only if there is a compelling reason, and then only very late in pregnancy.

Pregnancy lasts roughly 40 weeks. During the first 20 weeks the expectant mother should not gain weight; the physician, who sees the patient about once a month during this period, will prescribe caloric restrictions, if necessary, and will see her more frequently if she tends to gain weight. During the second 20 weeks, an average gain of one pound per week is normal; but many women gain more, even on an apparently normal diet. Stricter medical supervision during the second half of pregnancy is necessary; the patient is seen every two to three weeks, and usually once a week during the last month. The prevention of abnormal weight increase is one of the most important prophylactic methods in the fight against late toxemia. Besides weight, blood pressure and urine are checked at each visit—another safeguard against late toxemia.

During the second half of pregnancy, supplementary vitamins and minerals, among them iron, are usually prescribed. Occasional blood counts are taken to check possible development of pregnancy anemia.

The prenatal visits are important not only from the medical but also from a psychological point of view. They help physician and patient to get thoroughly acquainted and to establish confidence, so that the expectant mother will face childbirth optimistically and fearlessly.

PATHOLOGY OF PREGNANCY. Nausea and vomiting in early pregnancy are rather common disturbances; they are more frequent during the first pregnancy. This condition, called *early toxemia*, has also been described as morning sickness, since the patient often suffers from it in the morning, even on an empty stomach. Nausea may also occur in the later hours of the day, and may continue until late in pregnancy. In most instances, this condition is alleviated by a number of available medications. Only rarely, in cases of severe nausea and vomiting, suppositories or injections are required. Dietary measures are helpful; they must be adapted to individual needs. Some patients fare better on a liquid, others, on a solid diet. Cold food is often tolerated better than hot meals. Some pregnant women have a definite aversion against, others a craving for, particular foods.

A far more serious condition is *late toxemia*, characterized by extreme weight increase and by swelling of ankles and legs. In severe cases, the patient has an elevated blood pressure, and sometimes kidney and liver damage. The best method to fight this condition is prophylaxis. Regular visits to the doctor's office facilitate early detection and treatment.

Ankle or leg swelling is not always caused by toxemia, but may be due to varicose veins, which sometimes form during pregnancy. Another cause of ankle and leg swelling is water retention, which is easily checked by restriction of liquid intake and by proper medication. However, when ankle swelling is associated with elevated blood pressure and albumin in the urine, the condition must be considered serious. A strict diet must be maintained, including not only liquid but also salt restriction; often bed rest may be necessary. If no quick improvement results from such treatment, hospitalization becomes necessary. The mortality from late toxemia has greatly decreased in the United States due to these precautions.

Bleeding during pregnancy is always an ominous sign. Early in pregnancy it may be the first indication of a threatening miscarriage. It is therefore important in case of bleeding that the pregnant woman notify her doctor immediately. Bleeding occurring late in pregnancy may be indicative of an even more dangerous situation: while slight staining is not infrequently an early sign of impending childbirth, any stronger bleeding must be considered a danger sign, and the doctor must be notified immediately.

Often such bleeding is due to abnormal implantation of the placenta, called *placenta previa*. If there is the slightest suspicion of placenta previa, the woman must be hospitalized immediately and kept under strict observation. If bleeding caused by placenta previa occurs around the 34th or 36th week of pregnancy, or later, the baby is usually viable and can be saved by cesarean section. Maternal death as a consequence of placenta previa has become a rare occurrence, due to modern precautionary measures, such as, the availability of blood for transfusion, and to generally improved obstetrics.

ERYTHROBLASTOSIS. Erythroblastosis is sometimes confused, by lay people, with "blue baby." A blue baby is one who is suffering from a congenital heart condition which produces the blue discoloration of the skin and mucus membrane. In erythroblastosis the baby is not blue but turns yellow. Erythroblastosis of the newborn is caused by the incompatibility of maternal and paternal blood groups. Besides the four main blood types (O, A, B, AB) there are blood factors which also exist in the Macacus and Rhesus monkey and which are called Rhesus or RH factor for short. Eighty-five percent of the entire population are "RH positive," which means that their blood contains this rhesus factor. Erythroblastosis can occur only in that 15 percent of women who are both RH negative and married to RH positive men. Even for these couples the risk of having an erythroblastotic baby is practically nil for the first-born child and only 5 percent for subsequent children. It has become established practice to test RH negative women for RH antibodies repeatedly during pregnancy. An increase in these antibodies may be a sign that the expected baby may be erythroblastotic. It is important to be prepared for such a possibility, as many erythroblastotic babies can be saved by exchange transfusion, by which their own blood is replaced by blood from a donor, soon after birth, sometimes within hours after delivery.

PART 5: CHILDBIRTH

In Part 5, the final section of this appendix, Dr. Lehfeldt introduces the subject of childbirth. Here he deals with several pertinent issues that are of concern to prospective parents. The author is much interested in ways of orienting the expectant mother so that she may enter childbirth with confidence and a minimum of anxiety. As part of such orientation he provides a careful description of the signs of impending childbirth, the birth process, cesarean section, the puerperium, and postpartum care.

Childbirth, like pregnancy, is a physiological process. In the great majority of cases, childbirth produces no complications; in a very small fraction, however, mothers as well as babies are faced with a potentially dangerous situation. The danger can be minimized by hospitalization. The generally accepted practice in the United States of hospitalization during childbirth has greatly contributed to the lowering of the rate of maternal mortality. Hospitalization has also caused some decrease in neo-natal mortality, even though the loss of newborn babies is still considerable.*

While the advantages of hospital delivery are obvious, it must be conceded that hospitalization at this time and during the puerperium creates a number of psychological difficulties for some mothers, sometimes even for the entire family. The expectant mother is removed from her own environment into an unfamiliar atmosphere; she is often

---

* In 1935, more than 60 mothers lost their lives in giving birth to every 10,000 babies; in 1958, fewer than 4 mothers in 10,000 failed to survive childbirth. Likewise, there has been a marked reduction in the hazard of birth for the baby. In 1935, more than 60 babies in every 1,000 deliveries failed to survive; in 1958, this figure has been reduced by more than half.

exposed to cries of pain from women in active labor; the bare hospital room and the unknown faces of nurses, interns, or residents—all these circumstances may produce a feeling of isolation and even anxiety. The newborn baby usually is not allowed to stay with the mother but is transferred to the hospital nursery; only during feeding time does the mother have a chance to see and enjoy her baby. In most hospitals she can see her husband only during visiting hours. A few progressive hospitals have initiated the so-called "rooming-in" procedure to overcome the effects of separation of mother and child during the puerperium. Unfortunately, rooming-in requires additional medical personnel and is therefore the exception rather than the rule. The modern practice of shortening the hospital stay after childbirth to five days (formerly ten to fourteen days) has somewhat mitigated this problem.

If the expectant mother can be relieved of her fears, she will be more relaxed and more cooperative during labor. In former years, many deliveries were performed in twilight sleep, induced by injections or oral or rectal medication. Women who are delivered in twilight sleep experience a retrograde amnesia, so that they do not remember either labor or delivery. They may wake up without even knowing that they had their baby. This method of delivery deprives the mother of a wonderful experience. In addition, instances have occurred where the drugs given for induction of twilight sleep have affected the baby's respiratory center. For this reason, physicians have become more cautious in using these drugs. Today we have new drug combinations to relieve labor pains which have little or no influence on the baby. Nevertheless, many physicians prefer to use the "natural childbirth" method, where no drugs are administered, whenever possible.

Preparations for natural childbirth start during pregnancy. The expectant mother must thoroughly understand the mechanism of the birth process; it is then that she learns the different breathing techniques, aimed at relaxation, which she has to use in the various phases of the delivery. If adequately prepared, a woman will be able to help actively the progress of labor; if, however, in spite of such preparation, she experiences intolerable pain, she most certainly should get analgesics or anesthesia. In normal deliveries, the necessity for using drugs seldom arises, provided patient and physician have confidence in the method of natural childbirth.

SIGNS OF IMPENDING CHILDBIRTH. While there are variations in the length of time, childbirth is expected to occur in nine months plus seven days after the first day of the last menstrual period. Around this time, the expectant mother will know that delivery is impending, from one of three signs, or from a combination of the three: (1) the start of regular uterine contractions, (2) the breaking of the bag of waters (the amniotic sac), (3) some staining. Irregular contractions usually occur during the last weeks of pregnancy; contractions signifying the beginning of labor are regular, occurring at intervals of 15 to 20 minutes, and each must last for 30 to 60 seconds. If contractions of this type recur for one hour, it is necessary to notify the physician. The patient should also get in touch with her doctor if she notices staining, or if she feels the loss of baby water, even if she has no regular contractions. The loss of baby water is not always easily detected, as the patient may confuse it with profuse discharge or the escape of urine. In case of doubt it is always advisable to discuss the question with the obstetrician.

THE BIRTH PROCESS. The birth process is divided into three stages. In the first stage, the lowermost part of the uterus, consisting of cervix and lower third of the uterine body, dilates to form part of the birth canal. When this dilatation is accomplished, the second stage starts, during which the baby is expelled by contractions of the uterus, assisted by the abdominal muscles. In the third stage, the afterbirth or placenta follows 10 to 15 minutes after the birth of the baby, or is expressed by the obstetrician.

Ninety-five percent of all deliveries are vertex presentations, which means that the presenting part—i.e., the part first appearing at the mother's perineum—is the vertex or head. In slightly over 3 percent of the cases, the buttock or breech is the presenting part. Very shortly after the presenting part has passed the perineum, the rest of the baby's body is expressed through the birth canal, formed not only by the cervix and the lower uterine segment, but also by the vagina. The obstetrician now cuts and double-ties the umbilical cord. The baby usually cries immediately under the influence of the atmospheric air, and will thereafter breathe normally and regularly.

CESAREAN SECTION. Approximately 5 percent of the deliveries in the United States are done by cesarean section, for which there are various medical indications. One, placenta previa, has already been mentioned; in extreme cases, the location of the placenta actually blocks the baby's passage through the birth canal (*placenta previa centralis*); toward the end of the first stage of labor, with increasing dilatation, the placenta separates from the uterus and bleeding occurs, endangering the baby's and even the mother's life. The situation is less dangerous when the placenta is not centrally located and when only part of it reaches into the lower segment of the uterus; then the bleeding is generally less profuse. After rupture of the membranes, the baby's head may compress the placenta during the descent and stop the bleeding, thereby eliminating the need for cesarean section.

Another indication is cephalo-pelvic disproportion, which exists when the baby's head is too big to pass through the bony pelvis of the mother. Severe cases of late toxemia and fetal distress may also require section.

The decision to perform this operation should not be made lightly; while it is nowadays a very safe procedure, its mortality rate, although very low, is slightly higher than that of vaginal deliveries. Another point to be considered is that, according to the opinion prevailing among obstetricians, women who have had one abdominal delivery should also be sectioned in subsequent deliveries. Most obstetricians recommend tubal sterilization at the time of the third cesarean section. For a woman with many preceding abdominal deliveries, each pregnancy becomes more hazardous. For this reason, this procedure must be considered as one lowering the woman's fertility.

The pregnant woman's age may yet be another indication for section: in the elderly primigravida—women thirty-five years of age or older who give birth for the first time—conditions which complicate delivery, such as hypertension, uterine fibroids, or uterine inertia (failure to produce strong contractions) are more frequent than in the younger woman. The above-described risk of repeated abdominal deliveries is greatly reduced for older women, as their fertility is lowered and their chances of successful future pregnancies are smaller.

It has become common practice in this country for obstetricians, contemplating delivery by cesarean section, not to make this important decision alone but only after consultation with another specialist.

THE PUERPERIUM. The German expression for puerperium, "Wochenbett" (week-in-bed), translates the age-honored habit of letting the newly delivered woman stay in bed for at least one week. Modern obstetricians make young mothers get up 12 or 24 hours after delivery. Due to this new regimen, vascular complications, such as, trombophlebitis and embolism, have been reduced to a minimum. Physical activity early after childbirth must therefore be considered as desirable. Nevertheless, a period of rest of several weeks after delivery is still as important as ever.

Until recently, bottle feeding, a safe and easy method, was used by

United States city populations as an almost exclusive method. Today, nursing has again become somewhat more popular. There is a new awareness in women that breast feeding is a more natural method than bottle feeding. It also has definite advantages. The sucking action of the baby, through a reflex mechanism, produces uterine contractions which help the uterus resume its normal size much faster. More important still is the psychological advantage that both mother and baby derive from nursing. Nursing actually provides sexual enjoyment of which non-nursing women deprive themselves; they also deprive their baby, for the bottle is a poor substitute for the intimate contact established between mother and child through nursing.

For young mothers who resume professional life soon after childbirth, nursing is, of course, impossible. Breast feeding is contraindicated in a few rare situations, such as anemia after cesarean section, erythroblastosis of the baby, and acute infectious disease of the mother. It is a myth that nursing impairs the mother's figure; no excessive eating is necessary for the nursing mother, and the shape of her breasts is not affected by nursing.

POSTPARTUM CARE. Modern obstetrical care includes supervision during the first few months after the delivery. Usually, the patient is re-examined in the doctor's office two weeks after childbirth. About six weeks postpartum, during the second visit, the cervix is also examined for possible lacerations or minor infections, which are rather common. If attended in time, they are completely harmless.

Intercourse can be resumed six to eight weeks after childbirth; at the second postpartum consultation, the planning of further pregnancies should also be discussed.

SUGGESTED READINGS

Part 1
Dickinson, Robert L., *Human Sex Anatomy*, Williams and Wilkins, Baltimore, 1933.
Eastman, Nicholson, J., *Williams Obstetrics*, Appleton-Century-Crofts, New York, 1950.

Part 2
Ellis, Albert, *The Art and Science of Love*, Lyle Stuart, New York, 1960.
Kinsey, Alfred C., et al., *Sexual Behavior in the Human Male*, W. B. Saunders Co., Philadelphia and London, 1948.
———, *Sexual Behavior in the Human Female*, W. B. Saunders Co., Philadelphia and London, 1953.
Oliven, John F., *Sexual Hygiene and Pathology*, J. B. Lippincott, Philadelphia, 1955.

Stekel, Wilhelm, *Frigidity in Woman*, Liveright Publishing Co., New York, 1926.

——, *Impotence in the Male*, Liveright Publishing Co., New York, 1927.

Van de Velde, T. H., *Ideal Marriage*, Covici, Friede, Inc., New York, 1930.

Part 3

Dickinson, Robert L., and Louise S. Bryant, *Control of Conception*, Williams and Wilkins Co., Baltimore, 1932.

Freedman, Ronald, et al., *Family Planning, Sterility and Population Growth*, McGraw-Hill Book Co., New York, 1959.

Guttmacher, Alan F., et al., *The Complete Book of Birth Control*, Ballantine Books, New York, 1961.

Knaus, Hermann, *Woman's Fertile and Infertile Days and How to Compare Them*, Ivan Obolensky, New York, 1962.

Ogino, Kyusaku, *Conceptive Period of Women*, Medical Arts Publishing Co., 1934.

Portnoy, Louis, and Jules Saltman, *Fertility in Marriage*, Signet Books, New York, 1951.

Sanger, Margaret, and Hannah M. Stone, Eds., *The Practice of Contraception*, Williams and Wilkins Co., Baltimore, 1931.

Stone, Hannah M., and Abraham Stone, *A Marriage Manual*, Simon and Schuster, New York, 1953.

Parts 4 and 5

Calderone, Mary S., Ed., *Abortion in the United States*, Hoeber-Harper, New York, 1958.

Eastman, Nicholson J., *Expectant Motherhood*, Little, Brown, and Co., New York, 1947.

Gebhard, Paul H., et al., *Pregnancy, Birth and Abortion*, Hoeber-Harper, New York, 1958.

Guttmacher, Alan F., *Having a Baby*, Signet Books, New York, 1950.

Levine, Milton I., and Jean H. Seligman, *A Baby is Born*, Simon and Schuster, New York, 1949.

Spock, Benjamin, *The Pocketbook of Baby and Childcare*, Pocket Books Inc., New York, 1950.

Consumer problems of married people

appendix **B**

Donald S. Longworth, Ph.D.

Professor Longworth is a sociologist by profession, and has for many years been keenly interested in consumer problems as they relate to family living. The author has been a teacher of family sociology and a marriage counselor for many years. As such, he has been close to the kinds of adjustments which persons starting out in marriage are called on to make. Professor Longworth has accumulated a vast range of knowledge in the area of consumer problems; some of this knowledge is offered in the presentation which follows. Professor Longworth's background and experience include: B.S. and M.A. from Bowling Green State University in Bowling Green, Ohio; and Ph.D. from Ohio State University in 1952. He has been at Bowling Green State University since 1949 as a member of the Sociology Department, and he has been Chairman of that department since 1958. Professor Longworth has also served as Visiting Professor at Western Michigan University.

In this section Professor Longworth will discuss the consumer problems of married people in all phases of the family cycle. Special attention will be given to the newly married couple with college training. The discussion covers the cost of maintaining a home and the general problems of family finance, methods of coping with financial shortages, and family security needs.

SPENDING THE FAMILY INCOME. Most young people want and need a realistic picture of what their future financial situation is likely to be. Ignorance or wishful thinking often leads to plans and hopes that reality can never fulfill. In a study dealing with several areas in which marital couples had to make adjustments, the financial area was one of the areas found to be of major importance.[1] Balancing available income against the needs of the family is frequently a difficult adjustment. The couple who have a realistic conception of the cost involved in maintaining a family and the probable income that will be available have a decided advantage. In planning for the future, one way to approach the problem is to estimate what the family will need.[2] A minimum requirement for launching a marriage is that the couple be free of extensive debts at the time of marriage; it is helpful if some cash savings are available. Generally speaking, the larger the sum saved the better, because during the early years of marriage many families discover that there is a shortage of money. The cost of furniture, a car, and the expense of maintaining a home all add up to a large amount of money. In many instances the situation is further complicated by the arrival of a baby. The actual cost, however, is partially determined by the values of the couple and the cultural pattern to which they have grown accustomed. If a family lives in a so-called two-car neighborhood, they may be under considerable social pressure to own two cars even though they have little need for a second car for transportation purposes.

Because of the differences involved in specific cultural patterns, it is difficult to predict the actual expense for supporting a family; but a sufficiently realistic estimate can be made to expedite successful planning. In this regard the construction of a plan of specific anticipated expenses is helpful. However, in constructing such a financial plan it must be noted that newlyweds frequently tend to exaggerate probable income and underestimate the cost of maintaining a family. The findings in the following table are very interesting on this point.

The earnings of most American males are comparatively small while they are in the twenties; this is true even for college-trained men. However, as we have already pointed out, this is the time when most families are expanding, and in comparison to income expenses are very high. The adjustment is further complicated by the fact that some people are motivated to marry in the hope of improving their economic position. These people apparently do not recognize that it has taken approximately 25 years for their parents to establish their present

[1] Judson Landis, "Length of Time Required to Achieve Adjustment in Marriage," *Am. Soc. Rev.*, 11:6 (Dec., 1946), 666–667.

[2] Howard F. Bigelow, *Family Finance*, rev. ed., J. B. Lippincott Co., New York, p. 322.

TABLE 16

Earnings of American Men, 1950 *

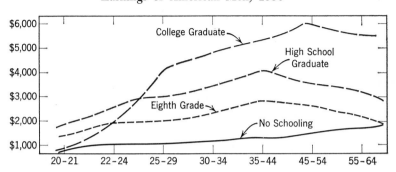

* "Education," Special Reports, Vol. 4, U.S. Census, 1953.

level of living. Thus it is reasonable to expect a somewhat lower level of living during the early years of marriage than that to which one has been accustomed in the parental home.

In some instances the bride and groom have been reared in homes where the general level of living is markedly different. This condition adds to the complexities of marriage adjustment. When the income is $4,200 in a family with three children, a pattern of purchasing and consumption gradually emerges. It is taken for granted, for example, that dresses and suits will be worn for several seasons. Likewise the purchase of such items is limited to the type of store that stresses maximum quality at a medium price. Style and the type of store are of secondary importance. On the other hand, in a family with three children where the income is in excess of $10,000 a year, the style of the item purchased and the exclusiveness of the store in which it is purchased become important considerations.

It is interesting to note that in two families of the same size with the same income, it is possible that one family will maintain a considerably higher level of living than the other. This difference in the level of living may be due to the types of financial management employed. Proper management of funds can greatly raise the level of living for a family. The elasticity in terms of stretching available funds is not unlimited, however. In all probability, the elasticity is greater in those families where the income is above the minimum level.

About the time that the children reach high school or college age the expense of maintaining a family reaches its highest level. At this time the resources of most families are seriously taxed. Fortunately, this is also the time when earnings reach their maximum level in many instances. Savings accumulated in earlier years can reduce some of the strain.

In the "empty nest" phase of the family cycle—that is, the phase during which all of the children have grown up and left the home leaving only the father and mother—income usually declines. Sometimes health needs and service functions performed for the family produce a financial burden. The numerous private and public retirement benefit programs have materially reduced the strain at this phase in the family cycle. However, some people do not reserve sufficient savings for their later years. The current emphasis on the improvement of retirement programs and provision for part-time employment after retirement portend better prospects for retired persons in future years.

METHODS OF COPING WITH THE FINANCIAL SHORTAGE.
When a family discovers that its wants exceed its available funds, what are the possibilities? In the first place, there are several things the members of the family can do to increase the benefits from funds available; and secondly, in some instances it is possible to increase the available funds. The more common and practical methods of realizing these two possibilities will be discussed.

When a family is confronted with financial difficulty someone invariably suggests that the way to cope with the problem of inadequate funds is to live by a budget. A popular misconception relative to a budget, however, is that it will increase the funds available. A budget will enable a family to spend existing funds in such a manner that they will get more of the goods they really want, but it will obviously not increase the number of dollars available to the family.

Some families are capable of managing their affairs much more successfully when they employ a budget while others become "budget slaves." The proper use of a budget is essential if it is going to contribute to the welfare of the family. In its most elementary form a budget is nothing more than a written record of the income and expenses of a family. There are several budgetary possibilities that may be employed by a family.

One approach is to start at the beginning of the month and allocate available funds to the various areas of anticipated expense. For example, $60.00 would be reserved for food. Purchases are made as long as funds are available. If funds are exhausted by the 28th of the month, no more purchases are made even though there might be a need for additional food. This approach has several overtly impractical features, but for some families it seems to work better than any other plan.

Another approach is to utilize one of the prepared budget books. Space is provided for entries relative to income and expenses in the more common areas. Usually two columns are provided under the general heading of expense, one entitled "estimated expense," and the other "actual expense." Some books provide suggestions as to the proportion of a family's income that should be spent for housing, food, and the like.

The following table shows a long list of items which might be included as budget headings and subheadings.[3] No family will need to use all these headings. The list is intended to suggest a great variety of possible items which a family may wish to include in working out its own set of budget headings.

TABLE 17

Suggestions for Budget Headings

Food	Insurance
Groceries	Repairs
Meats	Depreciation allowance
Baked goods	House operation
Fresh fruits and vegetables	Public utilities
Butter	Water
Eggs	Gas
Milk	Electricity
Meals purchased outside home	Fuel
Clothing	Telephone
For husband	Garbage removal
For wife	Services
For each child	Resident maid service
Housing	Non-resident service
Charges on rented home	Supplies
Rent	Home cleaning supplies
Repairs paid by tenant	Stationery and postage
Other expenses paid by tenant	Furniture, furnishing and
Rent for garage	equipment
or	Repairs
Charges on owned home	Payments
Payments on principal	Laundry service and dry cleaning
Interest charges	Automobile maintenance
Taxes	Initial purchase
Special assessments	Upkeep and operating expense

[3] *Ibid.,* p. 502.

TABLE 17 (*Continued*)

Automobile maintenance (*Cont.*)	Recreation
Insurance	Amusements for the family
Allowance for depreciation	Entertainment of others
Monthly payments	Children's toys and play equip-
Transportation Expenses	ment
Car rental	Vacation expense
Bus	Organization memberships
Taxi	Church
Railroad	Professional organizations
Personal expenditures	Labor unions
Personal supplies	Fraternal orders
Allowances	Social clubs
Health	Savings and Security
Medical doctor	Real estate
Hospital	Savings account
Drugs	Life insurance
Dentist	Property insurance
Eye glasses	Expenditures for others
Nursing	Charity
Education	Gifts
School expenses	Taxes
Reading matter	Income tax
Private lessons	Property tax
	Sales tax

The use of a budget enables a couple to live within its income. Generally, a family should plan to operate with a balanced budget. A family can experience a deficit for brief periods without jeopardizing marital happiness. An extended period of deficit spending however can lead to marked difficulty, for in addition to the personal trauma it entails (although some people are much less annoyed by bill collectors than others), repeated inability to meet financial obligations will ultimately impair the credit rating of the family.

Much has been written relative to the proportion of the income that should be spent for each of the items in the budget. It is difficult to make specific suggestions that have practical value when applied to the individual family. The following table is an abbreviated budget for a newly married couple with one child five months old. The wife is not employed. You will note that actual expenses generally exceed estimates. This table may also suggest the proportion of the income that should be spent in each area.

TABLE 18

Thirty-Day Budget for a Newly Married Couple with One Child, on an Income of $379.00 per Month

Item	Estimate	Actual Expenditures
Food	$ 55.00	$ 67.00
Clothing		
Husband	20.00	22.00
Wife	10.00	9.00
Child	5.00	6.20
Housing		
Rent	70.00	70.00
House operation	35.00	48.00
Furniture	20.00	20.00
Transportation		
(New Ford—plan to trade cars every 2½ years)	45.00	104.00
Personal expenditures		
Husband's	5.00	5.00
Wife's	5.00	5.00
Health	12.00	12.00
Education	6.00	6.00
Recreation	20.00	25.00
Organization memberships		
Church		
Clubs		
Union, etc.	12.00	17.00
Savings and security	5.00	0.00
Other expenditures	12.00	14.00
Taxes	42.00	42.00
Totals	$379.00	$472.20

To a person unaccustomed to assuming the responsibility of operating a home, $379.00 per month seems like a more than ample amount. The estimated expense for the couple whose budget was presented in Table 18 totaled $379.00. It is obvious that when expenses exceed available income ($472.20 — $379.00 = $93.20), the family has a problem.

The largest discrepancy occurs in connection with the expenditure for transportation. A new car may be much more expensive than the couple had anticipated. A car is thought to be a necessity by most families in the United States, although it really is not required in every location. Public transportation, when available, is usually more economical than private transportation. Many people reason that it is more economical to buy a new car every two or three years and avoid the high cost of repairs on an aging vehicle. This kind of reasoning was more applicable in times past, when repair costs were very important in the operation of a car. Today, however, although repair costs are still high, they have not advanced as rapidly as other costs in the operation of an automobile: two of the largest costs for the modern car owner are depreciation and finance costs. A family wishing to reduce transportation costs should (1) pay cash for the family car, thus eliminating finance charges; and (2) buy a good used car. If a new car is purchased then it should be kept at least five or six years in order to reduce the depreciation loss.

The family budget is a spending plan. It is a tentative estimate of the family's income and the family's expenditure for a realistic list of items. It is a guide to intelligent spending. In the final analysis it is a tool that provides a service for the family. If the use of a budget seems to create more problems than it solves, the plan should be altered or abandoned altogether.

One approach that sometimes works in those instances where the usual budget seems to produce added tension is for the couple to keep an accurate record of all expenditures during the course of the month. This at least enables a family to know how its money is being spent. At the end of the month, family members can review the spending pattern for the previous month and possibly alter their behavior in the following months. This plan seems to work better, at times, than a more formal budget.

The budget should never be thought of as a means to force the marriage partner "into line" on the matter of spending money. If this attitude exists, something more fundamental is wrong in the relationships of the couple, and the budget keeping will not correct the difficulty.

Few people have economic means that they consider entirely adequate. The family with an income of $4,100 may think their problems would be solved if they could double the income. Additional income, although it has advantages, frequently brings with it additional problems in adjustment. There are many families of limited means that are happy and well adjusted. Whatever the actual dollar income, careful management and agreement with regard to purchases produces its rewards. A couple can learn much about buying and borrowing which will help in family financial management.

Buying on a cash basis has some advantages. The chief advantage is that the policy of paying cash tends to prevent overbuying. Buying for cash makes it possible to shop around and buy where quality and prices are most satisfactory.

One disadvantage of operating entirely on a cash basis is that no credit ratings are kept on cash customers; then if it does become desirable or necessary for these people to use credit, it takes them a little longer to establish a credit rating. This is probably a more important disadvantage in urban centers than in rural areas. Cash buyers often complain that in many stores they are not treated with the consideration that is accorded to the charge customers. Sometimes they have more difficulty in returning merchandise or securing repairs.

The chief advantage of charge accounts is their convenience. The charge account offers a further advantage in that it represents a complete record of expenditures. All the conveniences offered by the charge account, however, are reflected in the prices paid for goods. To operate a charge account system, delivery service, and the many other conveniences provided by the modern store costs money. Thus when you trade at a store that provides these services, you usually pay higher prices for comparable merchandise because the cost of these services must be added to the purchase price.

Borrowing is sometimes necessary in order to purchase the required goods for a family. Unexpected expenses may arise due to illness or accident before there has been an opportunity to accumulate savings. In other situations, people may decide they want the immediate use of a new refrigerator, car, or furniture and they mortgage their future income to do so.

Several sources of credit are open to people who want to borrow. The interest rates that are charged vary greatly from one agency to another. The rates are charged according to the risks involved in the lending. College-trained people generally fall in the low-risk group. Many school teachers, however, are notorious for their inability to take advantage of the lowest interest rates available. Credit is a commodity, the same as any other goods that might be purchased. Thus the intelligent course of action is to shop for the lowest interest rate available. Because of a lack of information, many people with a good credit rating borrow money from agencies that specialize in lending to people who have a poor credit rating. In so doing these people pay unnecessarily high interest rates.

The small loan company, for example, charges a very high rate of interest because very little collateral is required. In some instances the interest rate is as high as 36 percent per year. It is a mistake to be misled by the 3 percent per month appeal. This type of loan company has its place in the economy, but the point we are making here is that many people who employ its services could borrow more advantageously at another type of lending service.

Let us consider a hypothetical case which will enable us to review much of what we have said this far. Let us assume that a couple lacks the cash to purchase a desired item—what might they do? The first step they might take is to "muster up" all of the buyer resistance possible. In so doing the following questions might be raised. Is the item really needed? Is it possible to manage without the item until a future time when it is easier for the couple to make the purchase? If it is decided that the item is not needed immediately and that its purchase can be postponed, the problem is solved. If, on the other hand, the purchase of the item is deemed necessary in spite of the lack of immediate funds, then the next step that the couple might take is to go to a commercial bank or credit union and attempt to borrow the necessary money. If this is not possible then the couple might attempt to purchase the item on a charge basis. Some stores do not make an additional charge if the item is paid for within a limited period of time. If your credit rating is favorable (and this is determined by whether or not you have paid your previous bills when you said you would) it is fairly simple to open a charge account. We might point out that in regard to maintaining a favorable credit rating you should be prompt in paying your bills; and if at any time you cannot make a payment when it falls due, you should call or go to the credit office and explain your circumstances.

As we have already noted, purchasing goods on the installment basis involves the paying of somewhat higher costs. In spite of this, you will be urged in advertisements to purchase on a time basis at a small additional charge. The purpose of these advertisements is to attract more customers for the business of selling credit. Credit is one of the largest businesses in the United States, and when properly understood and properly used it plays a very functional part in the economy. It must be recognized that the people who sell credit, just as the people who sell anything else, expect to earn a profit.

In determining the amount to be paid under the installment sales contract, a regular service charge is added to the unpaid balance. This charge, which is too often confused and compared with pure interest rates, must cover interest on the money lent, credit and collection expense of the lending agency, a reasonable allowance for bad debt losses, allowance for expenses involved in repossession and reconditioning, and certain types of insurance as specified. This charge is quoted in terms of nominal simple interest percentages (the amount of service charge expressed as a percentage of the total amount borrowed on a per annum basis, on the total initial unpaid balance). The actual effective rate of interest is generally about twice the nominal rate because the borrower is constantly decreasing the outstanding balance by monthly payments made throughout the loan period.

To further illustrate the difference between nominal and actual interest rates, an example is in order. Assume that you contract to buy a $3,000.00 car for 25 percent down or $750.00 and assume that the balance is to be paid in 24 monthly payments at a nominal interest rate of 8 percent. The dealer would grant you credit of $2,250 with an interest cost of $180.00 per year, or a total cost of $360.00 for interest (.08 × $2,250.00 × 2). Therefore, you will pay monthly payments of $108.75 for a period of 24 months. This appears to be an interest rate of 8 percent, but the real rate of interest you pay each month will be substantially more than 8 percent: you pay $15.00 interest per month ($\frac{1}{12}$ × .08 × $2,250.00) throughout the two year period, but you owe the seller or lender the full amount of interest for the first month only. For the rest of the period you have borrowed less than $2,250, the amount decreasing to $93.75 the last month.

To further illustrate installment buying costs let us assume that a couple with income of $375.00 per month wished to make many of their purchases on a cash basis, although we recognize that this might entail some inconvenience. The following items are not normally purchased on an installment basis.

Items for which the majority of families pay cash:

Food	$ 67.00
Rent and operation of home	118.00
Personal	10.00
Health	12.00
Education	6.00
Recreation	25.00
Organizations	17.00
Savings	5.00
Taxes	42.00
Total	$302.00

The amount of income available for installment purchases is $375.00 — $302.00 = $73.00 per month. If the average rate of interest paid on installment purchases was 22 percent per year, the cost each month is 1.8 percent × $73.00 = $1.32; on a yearly basis the cost is $15.84. This is one way that a family can grant itself a cash increase which is tax free.

Getting the most for each dollar spent should be the goal of every family; and to achieve this goal, the cultivation of buyer resistance on the part of each member of the family is extremely helpful. Other suggestions which will help to achieve the stretching of available funds are:

1. The purchasing of goods in quantity, where the family's needs are such that this is a practical procedure.
2. Trading at stores that sell strictly on a cash basis.
3. The purchasing of goods on an off-season basis.
4. Buying used items when they will adequately serve the needs of the family.
5. The proper care and repair of clothing, tools, and equipment.
6. Home processing of food.
7. Wearing the proper clothing for activities.
8. "Do it yourself" where the necessary skills and tools are available.
9. Having a garden, if you have gardening "know how" and can use the fruits and vegetables produced.
10. Eating at home as much as possible.
11. Devising recreational activities that require a minimum cash outlay.
12. Trying to purchase items that will have multiple usage, and select things that can be used by more than one member of the family.

Several consumer guides are available to assist families in securing the maximum value for cash spent. These guides are of the greatest value to the family that is contemplating purchasing an item with which they have had no previous experience. For example, if a family wishes to purchase an automatic washer but they have never owned or operated an automatic washer, they can obtain information relative to capacity, efficiency, and price of the various washers from consumers' guides.

The best known of the consumer guides are *Consumers' Research, Inc., in Washington, New Jersey, and Consumers Union,* 17 Union Square West, New York, New York. These two organizations work similarly. They are independent of all business organizations; secure their income from sales of books, reports, and reprints; do not accept money or articles to be tested from manufacturers; and put the items they test on the open market. No one can pay in money, goods, or services to have any product recommended, or any unfavorable comment made, modified, or omitted from the reports. These guides give a rating of many types of articles and explain the basis of the rating. One of the chief values of this type of service is that it will stimulate the buyer to study values and to buy intelligently.

The most important limitation of the consumer guides is that sometimes an item given the highest rating is not available in the area where the buyer wishes to make a purchase. Aware of this problem, the consumer guides try to concentrate their ratings on items that are distributed nationally. It is not desirable to follow blindly the recommendations made by these organizations, but their discussions of the various considerations which determine the quality of specific items are helpful.

Sometimes a couple who wants to marry but feels that there is an insufficient income to maintain a home decides to share a home with in-laws. There are several reasons, as indicated in the text, why it is difficult to work out a satisfactory adjustment when a home is shared with in-laws. These reasons may be summarized in the following way. (1) Most homes do not provide the necessary privacy when two families occupy the same dwelling. This is especially true in the area of the sexual and affectional adjustment. (2) A part of the satisfaction in marriage comes from being confronted with problems, and then solving these problems. The in-laws frequently volunteer suggestions as to how the problems of the newlyweds can be resolved. As a result the newlyweds miss the thrill and satisfaction of solving their problems. To the in-laws, the newly married couple appear to be dangerously idealistic about coping with marriage adjustment. (3) A third source of tension is misunderstanding on the part of the two families with regard to their respective roles and responsibilities. In the United States the social roles of two families in this type of situation are not clearly prescribed. The result is a considerable amount of confusion and tension on the part of the two families.

Although it is possible to reduce the cost when two families share a home, and in some instances a pleasant adjustment is attained, it is generally true that the two families will find it advisable to establish separate dwellings even though the income available is very limited.

Every additional member in a family increases the pressure on the family income. If both husband and wife want a baby and they are ready to assume the responsibilities of parenthood, the arrival of a child can add considerably to the happiness of the home. Some authorities estimate the cost of rearing one child to adulthood—in situations where the parents are college trained—at approximately $20,000.00. In all probability, many families, especially middle-class families, spend more cash than is necessary to promote the welfare of the child. To postpone having children for a brief period in order to stabilize the family's economy is feasible; but for the couple to intentionally avoid for years the arrival and responsibility of children may ultimately impair the welfare of the home.

When a wife is employed outside the home there is usually some increase in the cash income of the family. However, in order for the wife to be employed, there are certain additional necessary expenses (and the amount of income tax a family will have to pay is increased when the wife is employed). There are more expenditures for transportation, food, dues, clothing, laundry, and other items when a wife is employed. These items may total over $100.00 a month and they are seldom less than $50.00 per month. Whatever this amount happens to be, it should be subtracted from the gross income of the wife to obtain the net increase. If there are children that must be cared for while the mother is working, there may be an additional cash outlay. If the earnings of the wife are modest, it is possible that her employment could result in a financial loss for the family. If the members of the family as a whole are happier, however, when the wife is employed outside the home, then the net income increase may be a secondary consideration. Of course, it is also possible that whatever additional income is available as a result of the wife working may relieve some of the financial pressure on the family.

PROVIDING FOR FAMILY SECURITY. Economic security is a very important factor in the happiness of a family. As has already been discussed, in most families expenses will exceed income for some periods, and emergencies may occur which will severely tax the resources of the family.

A family economic plan is not complete until some provision has been made for savings. It is important to establish the principle that something will be saved from each pay check. Some families decide that they will save whatever is left when the bills have been paid. This approach usually is not very productive. The months and years pass and the family tends to have nothing to show for its efforts. A very definite savings plan should be effected and this plan should be reviewed periodically, with the amount put into savings increased whenever practical.

Another very important part of a family's security is making provision for adequate housing. The newly married couple will be faced with the decision of whether to rent or to buy a home. Before a couple make a final decision, they should seriously consider their needs and the advantages and disadvantages of renting and buying a home.

When renting a house, you should be certain just what is to be included in the rental price. In furnished apartments, water, electricity, and sometimes gas are supplied. Whether garbage and rubbish collection are included or not may be a point about which to make inquiry. In most houses that are rented unfurnished you pay all the utilities on a metered basis to the city. It may be more economical for a couple to rent a furnished apartment than to own their furniture if it is necessary to move frequently from one location to another.

In those instances where a family decides that it is desirable to purchase a home, a program of finance will have to be worked out. In the majority of instances, a down payment is made which may range from a few hundred dollars to several thousand dollars. The balance or remainder of the indebtedness is paid out of income over a period of years.

Selecting a house, old or new, requires considerable skill and good judgment. The location of a house is a matter of great importance. Many hours of time can be wasted in getting to jobs, school, and church if the family makes an unwise choice of location. The social status of the family is also in part determined by the area of residence.

It is no longer practical to think of a home purchase as a one time only expense. The mobility of our society and the needs of a family contribute to change with regard to housing, so that lifetime residence in one location is not usually the pattern. For the most part, it is probably unwise to purchase a home if the family does not expect to live in the same area for at least three years. The couple should always ask their real estate agent these questions: "If we found it necessary to sell the house next month, who would be interested? Who could buy? What would be the probable selling price?"

When a house is found that meets the needs of the family, is generally of sound construction, and is available below the prevailing price for similar construction in the neighborhood, it represents the best buy for the family. Good value and reasonable purchasing price are always assets; then if it becomes necessary to dispose of the house, the seller will be protected against a loss.

A real estate agent can be helpful in locating a suitable home and in arranging the financing of the home. Generally a real estate agent can provide more assistance if he knows the family's needs and preferences, the amount of available funds, and probable income.

It is sometimes possible to buy directly from the owner without buying through a real estate agent. The agent receives a commission of several hundred dollars for selling a house. It is obvious that the price of the home must be somewhat higher if an agent is involved. However, many times the agent will provide helpful information that is worth the fee he is paid. A real estate agent can be especially helpful in providing assistance for arranging the financing of the home— which is the next step once you have found a home for sale that appeals to you and meets your needs. The family must decide what they can pay as a down payment. Remember, there will be expense in connection with moving previous belongings and furnishing the home. The down payment may be very small, or it can be as much as 40 percent of the purchase price. Never pay anything, or sign anything, until you are absolutely certain you want to purchase the home.

The interest rate that you will have to pay will vary depending on general economic conditions and the lending agency. Credit is a commodity and the borrower should attempt to get the lowest possible interest rate. The difference in an interest rate between 5 percent or 6 percent is very important when the loan is large and it extends over a number of years.

You might consider mortgage payments on a house very much as you do installment payments on a car, a TV set, or the like. The larger the down payment, the smaller will be the monthly installments, and the less the actual cost of the item. It may be something of a shock to see in black and white how much it costs to pay the interest on the principal borrowed for a number of years. The total number of dollars needed to pay for a home will greatly exceed the stated purchase price. The following example illustrates the desirability of paying for a home as quickly as possible.

TABLE 19

The Cost of Borrowing $8,000 at 5 Percent Interest for Various Numbers of Years

Number of Years to Pay	Monthly Payments	Amount Paid for Interest
15	$63.27	$3,388
20	52.80	4,672
25	46.77	6,031
30	42.95	7,462

You will note that if the loan runs for thirty years the amount you have to pay for interest is nearly equal to the stated purchase price. In some instances it will be to the financial advantage of a couple to buy a very modest home initially. When an equity has been established in this home, it can be sold and a better home purchased. This pattern can be repeated several times in a twenty year period. The advantage of this plan is that the interest cost for home financing is kept to the minimum. At about the time the children reach high school a family can own a home and the monthly payments of the family will have been within their means. The family will experience less inconvenience in moving if they purchase the so-called lifetime home initially. It will, however, require from eight to twelve years longer to pay for a home using this plan.

A family may decide that available housing is unsuitable or that it is too costly. The "do-it-yourself" pattern has been extended to include housing. It should be recognized that many hours of labor are necessary to construct a home and it is necessary to possess many professional skills. The modern home represents engineering refinements that were not available at any cost a few decades ago. A major cost in building a home is the labor. This can be saved if a family has lots of time and multiple skills. Financing the home becomes somewhat more complicated when the family does most of the work in building its home.

Since World War II, an increasing proportion of the population has elected to live in mobile homes. Modern trailers are well constructed and possess many of the features of modern homes. A trailer has the advantage of providing furniture and shelter for a family. The rental charge for parking a trailer should be included with the purchase price in the housing cost.

Family security is not complete without provisions for meeting fire loss, automobile accidents, and possible death. The purpose of an insurance plan is to enable a family to cope with those emergencies that they would otherwise lack the necessary financial means to handle. The primary purpose of insurance is to provide protection.

One of the first items a couple usually purchases is a car. Should the car be damaged in an accident or stolen, the loss to the family might cause considerable inconvenience. There is also the possibility that the dirver of the car might contribute to the damage of another car or the injury of its passengers. This is known as liability damage. In some states all drivers are required to carry liability insurance. Even though you never expect to cause an accident, you should never drive a car without carrying liability insurance. A comprehensive automobile policy will cover all possible accidents. Those drivers that are less likely to be involved in accidents are able to get their insurance at lower rates.

If any property is owned the family should consider carrying protection against loss by fire, theft, or natural causes. This type of protection is not very expensive. It is important that the policy provide comprehensive coverage.

During the last decade, so-called health insurance has become very popular. Some plans pay only a part of the hospital expenses and others pay the doctor bills. Sometimes a couple will purchase this type of insurance in the hope that they will be able to reduce at least their medical costs. If a family should have unusually heavy medical expenses, it is advantageous to have medical insurance. The main advantage of medical insurance for a typical family is that they can pay their medical bills on an installment basis. In fact, families who do not have cash savings that can be used in meeting medical emergencies probably cannot afford to be without medical insurance.

There is always the possibility that some member of a family will die or be physically incapacitated. In the event of death, there will be expense in connection with the burial and the last medical bills. If the individual is a "bread winner" in the family the future welfare of his dependents may be impaired. An insurance program that provides protection against economic loss can be of great value in assisting the family to make adjustments.

Much of the confusion relative to insurance can be avoided if it is recognized that the primary purpose of insurance is protection. If a family has the necessary economic means to meet all emergencies, there is little need for an insurance program. In an insurance program you buy protection to cover the financial losses that you could not handle with resources available.

The first step in establishing an insurance program for a family is to determine its needs. Usually a minimum of $1,500 worth of protection is needed for each marital partner; the $1,500 would be necessary to pay last medical expenses and burial debts in the event of death. The expense might be much larger. The bulk of the insurance should be carried by the primary "bread winner" of the family; for purposes of illustration, we are assuming that this is the husband and that $1,500 is the only insurance carried on the life of the wife. On the life of the husband, however, over and above the $1,500, an additional minimum of $1,000 protection should be provided. This additional protection is designed as an adjustment fund for the wife in the event of the death of her husband who was her sole support. The approximate figure of $1,000 is based on the assumption that the wife is employable and that she will be employed within a 90 day period following the death of her husband. A much larger sum may be necessary in other instances.

In all probability, the family will have some indebtedness for a car, furniture, or installment purchases. This indebtedness should be covered by insurance. A representative newly married couple might need $2,000 worth of protection in this area. If there is indebtedness on a home, the mortgage should be covered by either mortgage insurance or additional life insurance. If there are children, at least $3,000 protection should be carried on the life of the father for each child in the family. Most newly married couples will need at least $5,000 worth of protection. In some instances the necessary protection will exceed $20,000. The next step is to select the proper type of insurance.

There are several types of policies to choose from and many different companies. All of the major companies charge essentially the same rate so that the choice of a company is largely a matter of individual preference for a particular plan or agent. Three basic types of life insurance are available. The first type in term insurance which provides the maximum protection for the smallest premium. The insurance policy is written for a stated period of time, such as one year. The protection provided is stated in the policy, and as an example here, we will say that it is for $5,000. The rate or premium is determined by the age of the person insured. A man needing $5,000 protection for one year who is twenty-two years of age could buy $5,000 of term insurance for approximately $50 a year. Many times when the family income is low, this is all that the family can spend for insurance. Term insurance does not have loan value or cash surrender value and the rate becomes progressively higher as the insured grows older. These are, of course, the distinct disadvantages of this type of insurance. A family with a very low income in the early years of the marriage, however, might find it desirable to use term insurance for a few years to provide the necessary protection and then gradually convert to other types. In these cases it is important that the person buying term insurance buy the type of contract that can be converted to another type policy at any time without a physical examination.

For the family that is interested in protection and some other additional insurance benefits, a second type of life insurance, namely a limited or ordinary life policy, may be the most desirable. On this type of insurance the rate or premium remains constant throughout the years the policy is in force and the insured pays premiums for a stated period of years, such as 20 or 30 years. If the insured dies at any time after the policy is in force, his estate will receive the amount stated on the face of the policy plus any dividends that might have accumulated. It is desirable, in the majority of instances, to have an insurance plan paid up at the time the "main bread winner" reaches age sixty-five. And it is most desirable to begin such an insurance plan at an early age. A man wanting $5,000 protection who is twenty-two years of age, for example, could purchase a limited payment life plan that would cost approximately $110 a year. The same man desirous of the same amount of coverage would have to pay more per year if he initiated the policy at a later age.

Besides a constant premium rate, ordinary life insurance has these advantages: the policy has loan value and cash surrender value. The loan value of a policy is the amount of money the insured can borrow from an insurance company. This amount is usually somewhat lower than the total premiums that have been paid to date. The interest rate charged is generally lower than that charged by banks. The cash surrender value is the amount paid by the insurance company to the insured if it becomes necessary to drop the policy prior to its normal termination date. Many companies have a plan whereby if it becomes necessary to drop a policy, the premiums that have been paid are not lost. The insurance company permits the policy holder to take paid up insurance. The amount stated on the face of the policy is reduced proportionally to the premiums that have been paid. No further payments are made.

The third type of life insurance is the endowment policy. An endowment policy enables a person to accumulate a fund of money which will become available to him on a future date named in the policy. Because the policy includes a savings program, the premium rate is higher than that of a comparable term of an ordinary life insurance policy.

The endowment policy is designed for those who need not only life insurance protection for dependents but also a definite sum of money or income at some future date to supplement or replace their earnings. An endowment policy might be used to provide funds to send a child to college. If the insured dies prior to the maturity date of the policy, his estate receives the full amount stated on the face of the policy. The loan value of endowment insurance is very high.

Endowment insurance can usually be converted to paid up insurance if it is necessary to drop the policy prior to maturity. A man twenty-two years of age needing $5,000 could purchase an endowment policy at an approximate cost of $250 a year for a 20-year period. An annual expenditure of this amount, however, might be prohibitive in some families.

The core of most family insurance programs should be built around ordinary life or limited payment life policies. The various plans available may incorporate more than one type of policy. There are so many policies issued by the various companies that a family should be able to find a plan that fits its needs. Most insurance agents are professional people who have a sincere interest in serving the needs of the client. An insurance plan for a family should be reviewed periodically to determine if the necessary protection is provided.

In recent years group insurance has become increasingly popular. The hazard to the company and the administrative cost are reduced in this type of plan. Generally the premium rate will be lower, especially for older people. In some instances a part or all of the cost of this type of insurance is paid by the employer. When available, group insurance is usually a good buy.

It is the privilege of each policy holder to designate a beneficiary. In the majority of instances a husband would designate his wife and children as beneficiaries. Where the option is available it is generally best to arrange for the payment of life insurance benefits on a monthly basis over a period of years because many people lack the necessary financial skill to manage a large sum of money.

If you are eligible for Social Security survivorship and old age insurance benefits, these will help provide the protection that you and your family need. The local office of the Federal Security Agency of the United States Government nearest to you will be glad to give you information about Social Security.

What I have presented in this section of the appendix is an analysis of the consumer problems that are likely to be encountered in marriage. A careful consideration of these potential difficulties and their solutions will enable a couple to get the most out of their financial resources and perhaps minimize relationship disturbances which emanate from consumer problems.

SUGGESTED READINGS

Bergler, Edmund, *Money and Emotional Conflicts*, Pageant Books, Paterson, New Jersey, 1959.

Bigelow, Howard F., *Family Finance*, Lippincott, Chicago, 1953.

Consumer Reports published monthly by Consumers' Union of the United States, Inc., 256 Washington St., Mount Vernon, N.Y.

Feldman, Races Loman, *The Family in a Money World*, Family Service Association of America, New York, 1957.

Gordan, Leland J., *Economics for Consumers*, American Book, New York, 1953.

Institute of Life Insurance, *Life Insurance Fact Book*, 488 Madison Ave., New York, annual publication.

Landis, Judson T., and Mary G. Landis, *Building a Successful Marriage*, 2nd ed., Prentice-Hall, Englewood Cliffs, New Jersey, 1953.

Lasser, J. K., and Sylvia F. Porter, *Managing Your Money*, Henry Holt, New York, 1956.

Locke, Harvey J., *Predicting Adjustment in Marriage: A Comparison of a Divorced and a Happily Married Group*, Henry Holt, New York, Ch. 13.

National Manpower Council, *Work in the Lives of Married Women*, Columbia University Press, New York, 1958.

Troelstrup, Arch E., *Consumer Problems*, McGraw-Hill Book Co., New York, 1952, Chs. I, II, III, and IV.

U.S. News and World Report, "New Ways to Use Insurance," March, 1958, pp. 80–91.

Tables
on marriage laws
and divorce grounds

appendix **C**

The following tables are from Council of State Governments, *The Book of the States* (1960–1961 edition), Chicago, pp. 389–391.

MARRIAGE LAWS*
As of January 1, 1959

State or other jurisdiction	Age at which marriage can be contracted with parental consent		Age below which parental consent is required		Common-law marriage recognized	Physical examination and blood test for male and female		Waiting period	
	Male	Female	Male	Female		Time limit between examination and issuance of marriage license	Scope of medical examination	Before issuance of license	After issuance of license
Alabama.......	17	14	21	18	★	30 da.	(a)	....	......
Alaska.........	18(b)	16(b)	21	18	.....	30 da.	(a)	3 da.	......
Arizona........	18(c)	16(c)	21	18	.....	30 da.	(a)	....	......
Arkansas.......	18	16	21	18	.....	30 da.	(a)	3 da.	......
California......	18(b,d)	16(b,d)	21	18	.....	30 da.	(a)	....	......
Colorado.......	16(b)	16(b)	21	18	★	30 da.	(a)	....	......
Connecticut....	16(b)	16(b)	21	21	.....	40 da.	(a)	4 da.	......
Delaware.......	18(c)	16(c)	21	18	.....	30 da.	(a)	....	(e)
Florida.........	18(c,d)	16(c,d)	21	21	★	30 da.	(a)	3 da.	......
Georgia........	(f)	14	17(g)	18(g)	★	30 da.	(a)	3 da.(h)	......
Hawaii.........	18	16(b)	20	20	.....	30 da.	(a)	3 da.	......
Idaho.........	15	15(b)	18	18	★	30 da.	(a)	....	......
Illinois........	18	16	21	18	.....	15 da.	(a)	....	......
Indiana........	18(c)	16(c)	21	18	.....	30 da.	(a)	3 da.	......
Iowa...........	16	14	21	18	★	20 da.	(a)	....	......
Kansas	18(b)	16(b)	21	18	★	30 da.	(a,i)	3 da.	......
Kentucky......	16	14	21	21	.....	15 da.	(a)	3 da.	......
Louisiana......	18(b)	16(b)	21	21	.....	10 da.	(a)	....	72 hrs.
Maine.........	16(b)	16(b)	21	18	.....	30 da.	(a)	5 da.	......
Maryland......	18(c)	16(c)	21	18	.....	.....	...	48 hrs.	......
Massachusetts.	18(b)	16(b)	21	18	.....	30 da.	(a)	5 da.	......
Michigan......	(f)	16(c)	18	18	.....	30 da.	(a)	3 da.	......
Minnesota.....	18(b)	16(b)	21	18	.....	.....	...	5 da.	......
Mississippi.....	17(b)	15(b)	21	21	.....	30 da.	(a)	3 da.	......
Missouri.......	15(b)	15(b)	21	18	.....	15 da.	(a)	3 da.	......
Montana.......	18	16	21	21	★	20 da.	(a)	....	......
Nebraska......	18	16	21	21	.....	30 da.	(a)	....	......
Nevada........	18	16	21	18	.....	.....	...	....	......
New Hampshire	(j)	(j)	20	18	.....	30 da.	(a)	5 da.	......
New Jersey.....	18(b)	16(b)	21	18	.....	30 da.	(a)	72 hrs.	......
New Mexico....	18(c)	16(c)	21	18	.....	30 da.	(a)	....	......
New York......	16	16(b)	21	18	.....	30 da.	(a)	....	24 hrs.(k)
North Carolina.	16	16(c)	18	18	.....	30 da.	(l)	(m)	......
North Dakota..	18	15	21	18	.....	30 da.	(n)	....	......
Ohio...........	18	16	21	21	★	30 da.	(a)	5 da.	......
Oklahoma.....	18(c)	15(c)	21	18	★	30 da.	(a)	....	......
Oregon........	18	15	21	18	.....	30 da.(o)	(p)	3 da.	......
Pennsylvania...	16(b)	16(b)	21	21	★	30 da.	(a)	3 da.	......
Rhode Island...	18(b)	16(b)	21	21	★	40 da.	(q)	....	(r)
South Carolina.	16	14	18	18	★	.....	...	24 hrs.	......
South Dakota..	18	15	21	18	★	20 da.	(a)	....	......
Tennessee......	16(b)	16(b)	21	21	.....	30 da.	(a)	3 da.(s)	......
Texas..........	16	14	21	18	★	15 da.	(a)	....	......
Utah...........	16(d)	14(d)	21	18	.....	30 da.	(a)	....	......
Vermont.......	18(b)	16(b)	21	18	.....	30 da.	(a)	....	5 da.
Virginia........	18(c,d)	16(c,d)	21	21	.....	30 da.	(a)	....	......
Washington....	(t)	15	21	18	.....	.....	...	3 da.	......
West Virginia..	18(d)	16(d)	21	21	.....	30 da.	(a)	3 da.	......
Wisconsin......	18(c)	15	21	18	.....	15 da.	(a)	5 da.	......
Wyoming	18	16	21	21	.....	30 da.	(a)	....	......
District of Columbia ...	18	16	21	18	★	.....	...	3 da.	......

*Prepared by the Women's Bureau, United States Department of Labor.

(a) Venereal diseases.
(b) In special circumstances statute establishes procedure whereby younger parties may obtain license.
(c) Statute establishes procedure whereby younger parties may obtain license in case of pregnancy or birth of a child.
(d) Parental consent is not required if minors were previously married.
(e) Residents, 24 hours; non-residents, 96 hours.
(f) No provision in law for parental consent for males.
(g) If parties are under 21, notice must be posted unless parent of female consents in person.
(h) Unless parties are 21 years or more, or female is pregnant.
(i) Feeblemindedness.
(j) Below age of consent parties need parental consent and permission of judge.

(k) Marriage may not be solemnized within 3 days from date on which specimen for serological test was taken.
(l) Epilepsy, idiocy, imbecility, mental defectiveness, unsound mindedness, tuberculosis and venereal diseases.
(m) 48 hours if both are non-residents.
(n) Feeblemindedness, imbecility, insanity, chronic alcoholism and venereal diseases.
(o) Time limit between date of examination and expiration of marriage license.
(p) Venereal diseases, epilepsy, feeblemindedness, mental illness, drug addiction and chronic alcoholism.
(q) Tuberculosis and venereal diseases.
(r) If female is non-resident, must complete and sign license 5 days prior to marriage.
(s) Does not apply when parties are over 21 years of age.
(t) No minimum age set.

(a)

DIVORCE LAWS AS OF JANUARY 1, 1959*

State or other jurisdiction	Residence required before filing suit for divorce	Adultery	Mental and/or physical cruelty	Desertion	Alcoholism	Impotency	Non-support	Insanity	Pregnancy at marriage	Bigamy
Alabama	(a)	★	★	1 yr.	★	★	★	5 yrs.	★	..
Alaska	2 yrs.	★	★	1 yr.	★	★	★	18 mos.	..	..
Arizona	1 yr.	★	★	1 yr.	★	★	★	....	★	..
Arkansas	2 mos.	★	★	1 yr.	★	★	★	3 yrs.	..	★
California	1 yr.	★	★	1 yr.	★	..	★	3 yrs.	..	..
Colorado	1 yr.(h)	★	★	1 yr.	★	★	★	5 yrs.	..	★
Connecticut	3 yrs.(h)	★	★	3 yrs.	★	..	..	5 yrs.	..	..
Delaware	2 yrs.(h)	★	★	2 yrs.	★	..	★	5 yrs.	..	★
Florida	6 mos.	★	★	1 yr.	★	★	..	....	..	★
Georgia	6 mos.	★	★	1 yr.	★	★	..	3 yrs.	★	..
Hawaii	2 yrs.	★	★	6 mos.	★	..	★	3 yrs.	..	..
Idaho	6 wks.	★	★	1 yr.	★	..	★	3 yrs.	..	..
Illinois	1 yr.(h)	★	★	1 yr.	★	★	..	....	..	★
Indiana	1 yr.(p)	★	★	2 yrs.	★	★	★	5 yrs.	..	..
Iowa	1 yr.	★	★	2 yrs.	★	..	..	....	★(r)	..
Kansas	1 yr.(s)	★	★	1 yr.	★(t)	★	★	5 yrs.	★	★
Kentucky	1 yr.	★	★	1 yr.	★(t)	★	..	5 yrs.	★	..
Louisiana	(w)	★	..	....	..	..	..	....	..	..
Maine	6 mos.(h)	★	★	3 yrs.	★	★	★	....	..	..
Maryland	1 yr.(h,z)	★	..	18 mos.	..	★	..	3 yrs.	..	..
Massachusetts	5 yrs.(h)	★	★	3 yrs.	★	★	★	....	..	..
Michigan	1 yr.(h)	★	★	2 yrs.	★	★	..	....	..	..
Minnesota	1 yr.(h)	★	★	1 yr.	★	★	..	5 yrs.	..	..
Mississippi	1 yr.	★	★	1 yr.	★	★	..	3 yrs.	★	★
Missouri	1 yr.(h)	★	★	1 yr.	★	★	..	....	★	★
Montana	1 yr.	★	★	1 yr.	★	★	★	5 yrs.	..	..
Nebraska	2 yrs.(h)	★	★	2 yrs.	★	★	★	5 yrs.	..	..
Nevada	6 wks.(h)	★	★	1 yr.	★	★	★	2 yrs.	..	..
New Hampshire	1 yr.(h)	★	★	2 yrs.	★	★	★	....	..	..
New Jersey	2 yrs.(h)	★	★	2 yrs.	..	..	..	....	..	..
New Mexico	1 yr.	★	★	★	★	★	★	5 yrs.	★	..
New York	(ah)	★	..	....	..	..	..	....	..	..
North Carolina	6 mos.	★	..	....	..	★	..	5 yrs.	★	..
North Dakota	1 yr.(p)	★	★	1 yr.	★	..	★	5 yrs.	..	..
Ohio	1 yr.	★	★	1 yr.	★	★	★	....	..	★
Oklahoma	1 yr.(s)	★	★	1 yr.	★	★	★	5 yrs.	★	..
Oregon	1 yr.	★	★	1 yr.	★	★	..	3 yrs.	..	..
Pennsylvania	1 yr.	★	★	2 yrs.	..	★	..	....	..	★
Rhode Island	2 yrs.	★	★	5 yrs.(al)	★	★	★	....	..	..
South Carolina	1 yr.	★	★	1 yr.	★	..	..	....	..	..
South Dakota	1 yr.(h)	★	★	1 yr.	★	..	★	5 yrs.	..	..
Tennessee	1 yr.	★	★	2 yrs.	★	★	..	....	★	★
Texas	12 mos.	★	★	3 yrs.	..	..	..	5 yrs.	..	..
Utah	3 mos.	★	★	1 yr.	★	★	★	★	..	..
Vermont	6 mos.(z)	★	..	3 yrs.	..	..	★	5 yrs.	..	..
Virginia	1 yr.	★	..	1 yr.	..	★	..	....	★	..
Washington	1 yr.	★	★	1 yr.	★	★	★	2 yrs.	..	..
West Virginia	2 yrs.(h)	★	★	1 yr.	★	..	..	....	..	..
Wisconsin	2 yrs.(h)	★	★	1 yr.	★	★	★	....	..	..
Wyoming	60 days(h)	★	★	1 yr.	★	★	★	2 yrs.	..	..
Dist. of Columbia	2 yrs.(h)	★	..	2 yrs.	..	..	..	....	..	..

*Prepared by the Women's Bureau, United States Department of Labor.
(a) No specific period required except 1 year when ground is desertion or defendant is non-resident, or 2 years if wife sues husband for non-support.
(b) May be enlarged into an absolute divorce after expiration of 4 years.
(c) Crime against nature.
(d) Court may forbid remarriage.
(e) Incompatibility.
(f) Crime before marriage.
(g) Final decree is not entered until one year after interlocutory decree.
(h) Under certain circumstances a lesser period of time may be required.
(i) Interlocutory decree is issued providing that parties shall be divorced 6 months after date of decree.
(j) Female under 16, male under 18, complaining party under age of consent at time of marriage not confirmed after reaching such age.
(k) In the discretion of the court.

(l) Habitual violent and ungovernable temper.
(m) Defendant obtained divorce from plaintiff in another state.
(n) Mental incapacity.
(o) Loathsome disease.
(p) Five years if on ground of insanity.
(q) Two years where service on defendant is by no other notice than publication.
(r) Unless husband had an illegitimate child and this fact was unknown by spouse.
(s) Five years if on ground of insanity and insane spouse is in out-of-state institution.
(t) If on part of the husband, accompanied by wasting of husband's estate to the detriment of the wife and children.
(u) Joining religious sect disbelieving in marriage.
(v) Unchaste behavior on part of wife after marriage.
(w) No statutory requirement for adultery or felony conviction; two years when ground is separation.
(x) Limited divorce may be enlarged into absolute divorce after 1 year for innocent spouse and after 1 year and 60 days for guilty spouse.

(b)

DIVORCE LAWS AS OF JANUARY 1, 1959*

Grounts for absolute divorce

Separation or absence	Felony conviction or imprisonment	Drug addiction	Fraudulent contract	Infamous crime	Relationship within prohibited degrees	Prior decree of limited divorce	Other	Period before parties may remarry after final decree — Plaintiff	Period before parties may remarry after final decree — Defendant	State
	★	★				(b)	(c)	60 days	60 days(d)	Alabama
	★	★					(e)			Alaska
5 yrs.	★						(f)	1 yr.	1 yr.	Arizona
3 yrs.	★			★						Arkansas
	★							(g)	(g)	California
	★	★						(i)	(i)	Colorado
7 yrs.	★		★	★						Connecticut
3 yrs.	★						(j)	3 mos.(k)	3 mos.(k)	Delaware
	★					★	(l,m)			Florida
	★		★		★		(n)		(k)	Georgia
	★	★								Hawaii
5 yrs.	★	★								Idaho
	★						(o)			Illinois
	★			★			(q)			Indiana
	★							1 yr.(k)	1 yr.	Iowa
	★		★					6 mos.	6 mos.	Kansas
5 yrs.	★		★				(o,u,v)			Kentucky
2 yrs.	★						(x)	wife, 10 mos.	wife 10 mos.(y)	Louisiana
		★								Maine
3 yrs.	★						(aa)			Maryland
	★	★						6 months	2½ yrs.	Massachusetts
	★						(m)		(ab)	Michigan
2 yrs.(ac)	★						(ad)	6 mos.	6 mos.	Minnesota
	★			★			(n)		(ae)	Mississippi
	★		★		★		(f,af)			Missouri
	★									Montana
	★							6 mos.	6 mos.	Nebraska
3 yrs.	★			★						Nevada
2 yrs.	★						(u,ag)			New Hampshire
								3 mos.(k)	3 mos.(k)	New Jersey
	★						(e)			New Mexico
									(ai)	New York
2 yrs.	★						(c)			North Carolina
	★	★						(k)	(k)	North Dakota
1 yr.	★		★				(m)		(aj)	Ohio
	★		★				(e,m)	6 mos.	6 mos.	Oklahoma
	★							6 mos.	6 mos.	Oregon
	★		★		★		(ak)		(y)	Pennsylvania
10 yrs.		★			★		(am,an)	6 mos.	6 mos.	Rhode Island
		★								South Carolina
	★								(ao)	South Dakota
2 yrs.	★			★			(ak)		(y)	Tennessee
7 yrs.	★							(ap)	(ap)	Texas
3 yrs.(ac)	★							3 mos.(k)	3 mos.(k)	Utah
3 yrs.	★						(aq)	6 mos.(k)	2 yrs.(k)	Vermont
	★			★			(c,ar)	4 mos.	4 mos.(as)	Virginia
5 yrs.	★		★				(at)	(i)	(i)	Washington
	★	★						60 days	60 days(au)	West Virginia
5 yrs.	★							1 yr.	1 yr.	Wisconsin
2 yrs.	★			★			(f,af)			Wyoming
5 yrs.	★					(av)		6 mos.	6 mos.	Dist. of Columbia

(y) When divorce is granted on ground of adultery, guilty party cannot marry the accomplice in adultery.
(z) Two years if on ground of insanity.
(aa) Any cause which renders marriage null and void *ab initio*.
(ab) Not more than two years in court's discretion.
(ac) Under decree of separate maintenance.
(ad) Limited divorce may be enlarged into absolute divorce after 5 years.
(ae) When divorce is granted on ground of adultery, court may prohibit remarriage. After one year court may remove disability upon satisfactory evidence of reformation.
(af) Husband a vagrant.
(ag) Wife's absence out of state for 10 years without husband's consent.
(ah) No time specified. Parties must be residents when offense committed; or married in state; or plaintiff resident when offense committed and action commenced; or offense committed in state and injured party resident when action commenced.
(ai) Defendant is prohibited from remarrying unless after 3 years court removes disability upon satisfactory evidence of reformation.

(aj) In cases where alimony or child support is granted, the decree is delayed until payment is made.
(ak) Incapable of procreation.
(al) Or a lesser time in court's discretion.
(am) Void or voidable marriage.
(an) Gross misbehavior or wickedness.
(ao) When divorce is granted on ground of adultery, guilty party cannot remarry.
(ap) When divorce is granted on ground of cruelty, neither party may remarry for 12 months.
(aq) Intolerable severity.
(ar) Two years fugitive from justice; wife a prostitute prior to marriage.
(as) When divorce is granted on ground of adultery, the guilty party cannot remarry. After 6 months the court may remove disability for good cause.
(at) Want of legal age or sufficient understanding.
(au) In court's discretion, guilty party may be prohibited from remarrying for a period not to exceed one year.
(av) Limited divorce may be enlarged into absolute divorce after 2 years.

(c)

Marriage
and family
counseling resources

appendix **D**

The resources listed below are only a few of the many responsible agencies from which professional assistance for marital problems may be obtained. Interested persons might also consult the council of social agencies in their local community for additional resources.

American Association of Marriage Counselors, Inc., 27 Woodcliff Drive, Madison, New Jersey.
American Institute of Family Relations, 5287 Sunset Boulevard, Los Angeles 27, Calif.
American Social Health Association, 1790 Broadway, New York, 19, N.Y.
Council of Jewish Federations and Welfare Funds, 729 Seventh Ave., New York 19, N.Y.
Family Life Commission, Lutheran Church, Missouri Synod, 210 N. Broadway, St. Louis, Missouri.
Family Service Association of America, 215 Fourth Ave., New York 3, N.Y.
National Association for Mental Health, Inc., 10 Columbus Circle, New York 19, N.Y.
National Catholic Welfare Conference, Family Life Bureau, 1312 Massachusetts Ave. N.W., Washington 5, D.C.
National Council of Churches of Christ in the U.S.A., Department of Family Life, 475 Riverside Drive, New York 17, N.Y.

Planned Parenthood Federation of America, Inc., 501 Madison Ave., New York 22, N.Y.

Rabbinical Assembly of America, 3080 Broadway, New York 27, N.Y.

Name index

Subject index